Gramsci and the history
of dialectical thought

Gramsci and the history of dialectical thought

MAURICE A. FINOCCHIARO
UNIVERSITY OF NEVADA, LAS VEGAS

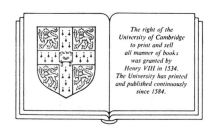

The right of the
University of Cambridge
to print and sell
all manner of books
was granted by
Henry VIII in 1534.
The University has printed
and published continuously
since 1584.

CAMBRIDGE UNIVERSITY PRESS
CAMBRIDGE
NEW YORK   NEW ROCHELLE   MELBOURNE   SYDNEY

Published by the Press Syndicate of the University of Cambridge
The Pitt Building, Trumpington Street, Cambridge CB2 1RP
32 East 57th Street, New York, NY 10022, USA
10 Stamford Road, Oakleigh, Melbourne 3166, Australia

First published 1988

Printed in the United States of America

Library of Congress Cataloging-in-Publication Data
Finocchiaro, Maurice A., 1942–
Gramsci and the history of dialectical thought / Maurice A.
Finocchiaro.
p.   cm.
Bibliography: p.
ISBN 0-521-36096-X
1. Gramsci, Antonio, 1891–1937.   I. Title.
B3630.G674F56   1988   88–3789
195 – dc19

British Library Cataloguing in Publication Data
Finocchiaro, Maurice A.
Gramsci and the history of dialectical
thought.
1. Italian philosophy. Gramsci, Antonio –
Critical studies
I. Title
195

ISBN 0 521 36096 X

Contents

v

Contents

Contents

Preface and acknowledgments

In preparing an earlier work on the epistemology and methodology of the history of science (*History of Science as Explanation*, 1973), I found useful some of Benedetto Croce's ideas on the philosophy of history in general, when I applied them to the situation in the historiography of science. This got me interested in a deeper understanding and criticism of Croce, and in the pursuit of this new interest it was inevitable that I would come across Antonio Gramsci's *Historical Materialism and the Philosophy of Benedetto Croce*. I was so impressed by that volume that I felt the need for a more systematic study of Gramsci.

My concern with this seminal thinker was reinforced via another route. This additional connection was provided by what I had learned while working on a book dealing with logic and scientific method (*Galileo and the Art of Reasoning*, 1980). Because the theoretical lessons in this work of mine were grounded on a critical analysis of Galileo Galilei's *Dialogue on the Two Chief World Systems*, my investigation forced me to face and to overcome a number of crucial issues in the theory and practice of textual interpretation, and it led to a number of conclusions in general scientific methodology. Thus, as I was beginning to discover Gramsci's Prison Notebooks by the other route, I was also beginning to feel that my epistemological and hermeneutical experience with a classic of past physical science would be helpful in the epistemological use and critical interpretation of this modern classic in social and political theory.

Now my hope is that I have been able to actualize this feeling of mine effectively, and thus to achieve with my present effort at least the same degree of success encountered by my earlier works. The moral and material support this effort received from many individuals and institutions renders my hope not unfounded, and they certainly ought to share the credit for any such success, although, needless to say, the responsibility for whatever shortcomings may turn up is entirely mine. Having made this clear, I can now proceed to name at least some of these supporters.

To begin with my own institution, the University of Nevada, Las Vegas: I have been fortunate to enjoy there the freedom of research necessary to pursue these investigations, which, because of their broad interdisciplinary ramifications (not to mention the geopolitical ones), might have encountered difficulties in a different academic environment. In particular, I have benefited from the following specific indications of this university's commitment to scholarship: two summer fellowships in 1978 and 1981; two Barrick Distinguished Scholar awards, for the years 1981–82 and 1986–87; a research leave in the year 1983–84; a sabbatical leave in the fall of 1986; and three-hour reductions in teaching load in the spring of 1987, the fall of 1987, and the spring of 1988.

I also gratefully acknowledge the support of the following institutions: the National Endowment for the Humanities for a fellowship for college teachers in the year 1983–84, during which most of this book was written and a first draft completed; the Istituto Gramsci in Rome for the use of its facilities during the same year, which I spent in Rome; the Library of the Chamber of Deputies of the Republic of Italy for the privilege of using its collections during the same period; and the Hoover Institution at Stanford for the privilege of being a visiting scholar there in the summer of 1984.

For helpful encouragement, support, comments, or criticism at various stages, I am indebted to many individuals, especially Walter Adamson (Emory), Norberto Bobbio (Turin), Joseph Buttigieg (Notre Dame), Joseph Femia (Liverpool), Milton Fisk (Indiana), Elsa Fubini (Istituto Gramsci), Eugenio Garin (Florence), Dante Germino (Virginia), Valentino Gerratana (Istituto Gramsci), Tullio Gregory (Rome), Sidney Hook (Hoover Institution), Edmund Jacobitti (Southern Illinois), Martin Jay (Berkeley), Luciano Pellicani (LUISS, Rome), Marcello Pera (Pisa), Paul Piccone (New York City), Giovanni Somai (Rome), Philip Steedman (Cincinnati), Giuseppe Tamburrano (Rome), Claudio Torneo (Rome), Marx Wartofsky (Baruch College), and my institutional colleagues: Cyrill Pasterk, Rick Tilman, Thomas Tominaga, John Unrue, Craig Walton, and Thomas Wright.

Finally, acknowledgments are also due to the appropriate publishers and editors because some parts of this work have already appeared in print, as follows: the nucleus of Chapter 1 in "Gramsci's

Crocean Marxism," *Telos* 41(Fall 1979): 17–32, and translated into Italian in chapter 1 of my *Gramsci critico e la critica* (Rome: Armando Editore, 1988); the section entitled "Literary Criticism for Logicians" of Chapter 2 in "Croce's Essay on Petrarch's Defective Sonnet: Literary Criticism for Logicians," *Rivista di studi crociani* 10(1973): 43–49; the nucleus of Chapter 3 in "Science and Praxis in Gramsci's Critique of Bukharin," *Philosophy and Social Criticism* 6(1979): 25–56, and translated into Italian in chapter 2 of my *Gramsci critico e la critica*; the nucleus of Chapter 4 in "Philosophical Theory and Scientific Practice in Bukharin's Sociology," *Studies in Soviet Thought* 21(1980): 141–74; the nucleus of Chapter 5 translated into Italian in chapter 3 of my *Gramsci critico e la critica*; and the section entitled "The Dialectic of Philosophy: Metaphilosophy Versus Dialectical Theory" of Chapter 7 in "Dialectic and Argument in Philosophy: A Case Study of Hegel's Phenomenological Preface," *Argumentation* 2(1988): 23–38.

Introduction: An approach to Gramsci

The interpretation of Antonio Gramsci's Prison Notebooks has been compared to the deciphering of a hieroglyphic,[1] and the comparison is particularly apt now that the critical edition of this work is available.[2] A second major interpretative difficulty arises because the work is pervaded by the views of, and by references to, Benedetto Croce, so much so that it is no exaggeration to say, with E. J. Hobsbawm, that "the Notebooks are in one sense a long, half-rebellious, half-admiring dialogue with this intellectual father figure."[3] Since Croce's own views, especially those related to Marxism, are extremely obscure and excessively liable to misinterpretation,[4] the result is a compounding of the problem.

One way out of these difficulties involves adopting certain suggestions made by Gramsci himself: "If you want to study . . . a world view that has never been systematically expounded by its founder . . . it is necessary as a preliminary to do a detailed philological work conducted with the greatest scruple for exactness, scientific honesty, intellectual sincerity, and absence of preconception and apriorism or *partis pris*."[5] This means something like burying oneself in Gramsci's notes, and, as much as one can, collating and grouping them on internal evidence; such activity is now made possible by the critical edition and addresses itself primarily to the first difficulty I mentioned.

Another suggestion deals with the second interpretative difficulty and involves essentially a distinction between method or approach and substantive theses.[6] Continuing the thought just quoted, Gramsci adds that "the search for the leitmotif, the rhythm of thinking as it develops, must be more important than the casual single claims and separate aphorisms."[7] Applying this statement to the Crocean background of Gramsci's views, we find it is of paramount importance to learn and understand the spirit animating

1

Croce's work: Such a leitmotif is the theory and practice of criticism.[8] We would thus expect a critical approach to be the leitmotif underlying Gramsci's thought.

The plausibility and potential fruitfulness of this suggestion are attested by Gramsci's own confession, in a letter dated December 15, 1930, that "all my intellectual development has been of a polemical sort . . . ordinarily it is necessary to place myself from a dialogical or dialectical point of view, otherwise I do not feel any intellectual stimulus."[9] Moreover, he was convinced that such a critical approach is both a theoretical consequence of his historicism and a practical requirement for the effective communication of new doctrines that have not yet become part of popular belief; in fact, we find him arguing that such doctrines "must be expressed and diffused with a 'polemical' attitude; otherwise they would be a 'utopia,' since they would appear as individual 'whim' or good for a conventicle; on the other hand, 'historicism' cannot conceive itself as expressible in an apodictic and sermonlike style, and it must create a new stylistic taste."[10]

Combining an emphasis on Gramsci's critical approach and a scrupulous philological analysis of text, I will concentrate on those notes that contain explicit critiques and whose topics are most frequent. Thus I will begin by collecting and systematizing Gramsci's notes on Croce, on Bukharin, and on Machiavelli.

Besides these hermeneutical and philological reasons for such an approach, the following substantive, theoretical, and historiographical considerations are also relevant. If, as I said, the Notebooks have been labeled a hieroglyphic, the secondary literature on Gramsci is a veritable labyrinth.[11] It contains, nevertheless, three threads that may be used to find one's way.

The area of greatest concern has been, of course, Gramsci's politics, which is examined in order to understand or to criticize his role in the history of Italian communism. His was an undeniably significant role, not only while he was actively engaged in the foundation and leadership of the Italian Communist Party but even after his arrest in 1926 and during a ten-year ordeal in prison, and *especially* after his death in 1937, which was easily and effectively mythologized by the party's postwar leader, Palmiro Togliatti. Gramsci's politics has also interested Marxist activists of various persuasions, either because they see his early career (especially the years 1917–20) as a model of revolutionary purity and zeal or because they see his later thought in prison as laying the theoretical foundations for a democratic model of socialist revolution in Western industrial societies. Now, there is a connection between Gramsci's politics and Machiavelli: Gramsci usually discusses his thoughts on more directly political topics under the explicit label of either "Machiavelli" or "The Modern Prince."

In recent years Gramsci has attracted increasing attention for his approach to the problem of the nature and status of religion. At present this is perhaps the most vigorous field of Gramsci studies.[12] From this point of view he is seen as a religious reformer who tried to set the foundations for a new lay, nontranscendent, nontheological religion, alternative and superior to Catholicism. Hence many authors of these works, though not all, are Catholics who see Gramscism as a threat, and thus as an enemy to be studied and understood in order to be effectively combated. Polemics aside, and despite the fact that Gramsci's concern with religion has been a well-kept secret (the first pioneering book was Hugues Portelli's *Gramsci et la question religieuse* in 1974), one can no longer reasonably doubt the centrality, depth, and persistence of Gramsci's interest in the religious question. The connection between his religious views and his critique of Croce might have been surmised from Gramsci's well-known statement in the August 17, 1931, letter to his sister-in-law. Referring to himself and to many other intellectuals of the time of his formative period, he says: "We belonged in whole or in part to the movement of intellectual and moral reform promoted in Italy by Benedetto Croce, whose first point was this, that modern man can and must live without religion, meaning without revealed or positive or mythological religion."[13] The connection might also have been inferred from Gramsci's well-known thesis about the difference between Marxism and Catholicism:

The position of the philosophy of praxis is the antithesis of the Catholic one. The philosophy of praxis does not tend to leave the "simple" in their primitive philosophy of common sense, but tends rather to lead them to a higher conception of life. If it affirms the need for contact between intellectuals and simple, it is not in order to restrict scientific activity and preserve unity at the low level of the masses, but precisely in order to construct an intellectual-moral bloc that can make politically possible the intellectual progress of the masses and not only of small intellectual groups.[14]

To infer the connection, however, one would have also needed to know that Croce's philosophy was meant as an alternative not only to revealed religion but also to Marxism. At any rate, we are now able to go beyond surmises and suspicions because a detailed ex-

3

amination of Gramsci's explicit notes on Croce shows that the religious problem is their main underlying issue.[15]

The thinnest thread in the labyrinth of secondary literature on Gramsci is what may be called the "lay" or "laicist" approach emphasizing his concern with developing a science of politics, history, and society. In a sense this is the approach in Croce's own first judgment on Gramsci, expressed in 1947 after the publication of the *Letters from Prison*: "As a man of thought he was one of us, one of those who, in the first decades of the century in Italy, were bent upon acquiring a historical and philosophical mind able to cope with present problems."[16] It is a pity that Croce not only did not develop this interpretation, but soon changed his mind, declaring that Gramsci's central aim was to found a new political party and to defend the interests of a social class, and that his thought was merely instrumental to this aim.[17] It seems that after Croce's first impression he had come to accept the Togliattian interpretation of Gramsci, which in the late 1940s was being publicized and elaborated with greater and greater determination. This was the view of Gramsci as the "head of the Italian working class,"[18] and of the *Prison Notebooks* as the "echo of the struggles of preceding years"[19] and the "continuation of these struggles,"[20] a view that soon acquired hegemony and that corresponds to the first approach to Gramsci that I mentioned. It is ironic that whereas Croce moved from the view of Gramsci as a man of thought to a view of him as a party man, Togliatti moved in the opposite direction; in fact, in his last judgment on Gramsci, just before he died in 1964, Togliatti found the occasion to say:

It has been completely right and natural for us to regard Gramsci's life as an integral part of the life of our party, of its political investigations and elaborations, of its struggles, of its sacrifices. I hope that this view has not reduced the personality of our comrade, or given it a wrong emphasis, such as to fail to include and explain all its aspects and its real essence. . . . One thing is sure, that today . . . it seemed to me that the very person of Antonio Gramsci should be placed in a more living light that transcends the historical vicissitudes of our party. . . . Antonio Gramsci is the critical conscience of a century of history in our country.[21]

Ironies and great personalities aside, the view of Gramsci as a man of science has been the one to which social scientists have been naturally attracted, when they have been able to overcome the initial barrier posed by the politicized interpretation.[22] The lay interpretation is also suggested by Gramsci's explicit declaration in a letter

4

from prison that he wanted to undertake a project of study for eternity,[23] and by one of the most characteristic and frequent phrases we find in the Notebooks, namely, "the art and science of politics." This is not the place to mention and criticize the confusions and misunderstandings that abound in regard to the "laicist" and "scientific" interpretation of Gramsci. Suffice it to say that, however tenuously, this hermeneutical tendency exists in the secondary literature, and that the present volume attempts to address some of the same concerns by taking seriously Gramsci's critique of Bukharin, which emphasizes the questions of the meaning of the concept of "science" and of the nature of the scientific method.

It is more important at this juncture to repeat the point mentioned earlier: that the understanding of Gramsci's notes on Croce, Bukharin, and Machiavelli is extremely significant. Philologically, the notes reflect crucial themes of the content of the Notebooks; methodologically, they promise to give us an insight into Gramsci's critical-dialogical manner of thinking; historiographically, they can put us in touch with the enormous amount of secondary literature and thus provide some orientation in that labyrinth; and theoretically, they will acquaint us with Gramsci's views of religion, science, and politics. It is equally important at this point to introduce a distinction and to discuss a feature of the present approach that may be seen either as a limitation or as an indication of its fruitfulness in generating new research problems. The religious, scientific, and political questions that will arise will be primarily conceptual, in the sense that what will be most directly relevant will be the fundamental meaning that these notions have. That is, we will not be concerned, except indirectly and secondarily, to articulate and criticize the content and substance of Gramsci's religious views, his scientific theories, and his political doctrines. Such details are best worked out *after* we know what he means by religion, science, and politics. This order of inquiry is especially important in a "hieroglyphic" work like the Notebooks, since there is a great deal of indeterminacy, if not arbitrariness, in grouping the many notes that were neither labeled nor collected by Gramsci himself. Once we have his conceptual framework, we can use his concepts to help us find more order in the Notebooks and to construct accounts that have a more real basis for claiming to be his own *religious* views, his own social *science*, his own *political* doctrines.

Finally, a word should be said about my concentration on the Prison Notebooks, which may be viewed either as a limitation or as the foundation for a sounder understanding of Gramsci's whole life. First, it should be noted that one underlying problem is the understanding and evaluation of Marxism, and certainly nothing is wrong with examining a particular work to determine what solutions, if any, it provides. The question might arise, if at all, about the propriety of so much emphasis on Gramsci to the exclusion of other authors, say, Karl Popper, Leszek Kolakowski, and Sidney Hook, to mention just a few.[24] Such a query would be the mirror image of the one that could be formulated from Gramsci's side: How can one reconstruct the Notebooks without giving a reconstruction of the rest of his life? That this question could, with equal justice, be reversed provides the key to the answer: Is it proper to give an account of Gramsci's life and ignore completely, or give minimal attention to, the Notebooks, as is done so often in historical works that concentrate on Gramsci's active political life?

I would justify my limitation to the Notebooks as follows: First, given the mountains of historical studies of his political life, and the paucity of analytical textual reconstructions of the Notebooks, my emphasis is a good corrective to the prevailing situation; in a sense it corresponds to the call that was launched, at the time of the publication of the critical edition in 1975, for a theoretical restoration, now that the philological restoration had been supplied. Second, the elaboration of such an analytical-theoretical reconstruction does not presuppose that it would be the end of the story, because obviously there is no reason why it should not be incorporated into a historical account at a later stage. Nor is it committed to the existence of a radical break in Gramsci's life between his preprison and his post-arrest phases, by contrast to an alleged continuity; in accordance with Gramsci's own conception of the dialectic, elaborated in Chapter 6, I would say that the proper thing to do would be to search for those elements that represent breaks *and* for those that represent continuity; this would be part of the full historical account, which should be based on an already given theoretical reconstruction. Fourth, it is true that the historical method, which is unobjectionable per se, would favor an approach where earlier phases are examined and reconstructed before later developments. In the case of Gramsci, however, this aspect of the historical approach has been carried to an extreme, and consequently his mature period is made to recede farther and farther into the distance.[25] This conflicts both with the requirement of balance (mentioned in the first point above) and with another aspect of the historical method, which would favor, other things being equal, that later stages of a person's life, being more mature than

6

earlier ones, should be given more attention. Fifth, it would be both un-Gramscian and incorrect to portray Gramsci as a pure intellectual whose ideas were derived merely from those of previous thinkers, without taking into account the social, political, and economic conditions in which he lived; but there is no reason why a reconstruction of Gramsci's thought should necessarily lead to this distortion, any more than the examination of such conditions must necessarily lead to irrelevance, that is, to leaving them unconnected to thought.[26]

On this last point, three clarifications are useful. One is that, before searching for the origin, be it "material" or "intellectual," for a given thought, we must obviously know and understand *what* the thought *is*. The second is that when we examine Gramsci's critique of Croce, Bukharin, and Machiavelli, our *primary* aim is to determine *what* Gramsci's thought *is* rather than where it originated from, since, as noted, the critical-polemical nature of his thinking renders it necessary to introduce the ideas of those other authors for the mere identification of his thought. The third point to notice is that the intellectualist distortion (or materialist lack of integration, as the case may be) would be a problem at the level of the full historical account, rather than at the level of analytical reconstruction we are dealing with.

Last, concentration on the Notebooks, despite its relative rarity, now corresponds to an emerging tradition or trend,[27] which may be taken to constitute a fourth kind of approach to Gramsci. Although distinctive, this approach does not exclude but overlaps with the three hermeneutical threads mentioned earlier. We are thus in a position to add to argument authority and tradition, in justification of the approach pursued in this volume.

Chapter 1

Gramsci's Crocean critique of Croce's philosophy

It is readily apparent even to the casual reader of Gramsci's Note-books, and it is generally admitted by scholars, that the critique of Croce's philosophy constitutes one of its central topics. It is also universally recognized that Gramsci's attitude toward Croce was not totally negative but partly appreciative and partly critical. The critical edition of the Notebooks now makes possible the detection and elaboration of two seldom discussed aspects of the Gramscian critique. One is that Gramsci is making a serious and partially successful attempt to understand Croce by putting forth an interesting and insightful interpretation of his philosophy; the second is that Gramsci's criticism is largely internal and logical, and hence more or less Crocean in a number of identifiable ways.[1] Gramsci interprets Croce as first and foremost a critic of Marxism, but such that there remain strong Marxist, or at least Marxian, elements in Croce's thought. Gramsci's criticism of Croce is itself Crocean in the sense that it uses some Crocean elements against other Crocean elements. The accepted and used elements are Croce's definition of religion, his notion of the identity of history and philosophy, and his techniques of criticism. The rejected and criticized elements are Croce's liquidation of historical materialism as an old-fashioned theology, his dismissal of Marx as cognitively worthless, and his own philosophy of history and politics.

CROCE AND MARXISM

It would be an exaggeration to claim that Benedetto Croce was obsessed[2] with Marxism throughout the long philosophical career (1893–1952) of his long life (1866–1952). One reason why this claim would go too far is that he showed a no less deep and sustained interest in aesthetics and literary criticism. To make that claim, however, would be merely an exaggeration and not a groundless fabrication. In fact, virtually all of his voluminous writings on topics other than aesthetics and literary criticism may be divided into works (1) dealing explicitly with Marxism or with directly related topics, (2) on the philosophy of history, and (3) on political and moral philosophy. Croce's philosophy of history consists of theoretical and applied works on both historical events and historical inquiry; its connection with Marxism is that he was trying to provide an alternative to historical materialism. His political and moral philosophy consists of theoretical and applied studies of what he calls philosophy of practice ("of the practical"), the latter an idea he derived from his early studies of Marxism.[3]

Croce's explicit interest in Marxism falls into two periods. The first, which may be called his "revisionist" period, is concentrated in the late 1890s and may be extended up to 1911, the date of an interview in which Croce proclaimed "The Death of Socialism."[4] This is the time when he was encouraging Antonio Labriola to write down his thoughts on Marxism and was editing or helping to publish the other's books. It was also the time when Croce was developing Marxist interpretations similar to those of Georges Sorel and Edward Bernstein, who were being inspired and influenced by him and who acknowledged the inspiration and influence; this was to lead to the first "crisis of Marxism" to follow Marx's death. It was during this period, too, that Croce felt honored to be regarded as a socialist, although he would point out that in fact he had never joined the Socialist Party. Characteristic of these years is also his acknowledgement of the Marxian origin of his philosophy of the practical,[5] and his description of the main theses[6] of his interpretation and criticism of Marxism as the "justification of Marxian economics, understood not as general economic science, but as sociological comparative economics that treats of labor conditions in societies,"[7] "as the liberation of historical materialism from every apriorist conception . . . and the construal of the doctrine as indeed fruitful, but simply as a canon of historical interpretation,"[8] and as the internal criticism that the law of the fall of the rate of profit (in the third volume of *Capital*) does not follow from the basic principles of Marxian economics.[9]

The later period of Croce's interest in Marxism germinated in 1911 (with the "Death of Socialism") and matured with World War I, which to him provided tangible evidence that Marx's concept of class struggles had been superseded by that of national struggles.[10] Croce's new attitude could then only be crystallized by the Russian Revolution, which must have appeared to him as a revolt against *Capital* rather than against capital(ism), as the self-styled Crocean Gramsci described it at the time in a classic article.[11] This may be called, following Gramsci,[12] the "liquidationist" period of Croce's involvement with Marxism, because his aim now was to "liquidate" it, to get rid of it once and for all. He fought the battle on at least four fronts. First, cognizant that the human mind abhors a vacuum, he developed an alternative philosophy of history. Second, he denied that Marxism had had any formative influence on his views; using Gramsci's brilliant simile,[13] we may say that Croce tried to claim that Marxism had been like a chemical catalyst for the development of his own thinking, and that just as no trace of the catalyst remains in the product resulting from a catalytic chemical reaction, so there was no trace of Marxism in his own philosophy. Third, Croce tried to deny the philosophical character of Marxism, assigning to it merely a practical, "ideological" status. Fourth, he tried to reduce Marxist doctrines to "vulgar" Marxism and thereby dismiss them.

Thus, although "obsession" is too strong a word, we may say that Croce was continually concerned with Marxism, but for different reasons, in different ways, and with different results at different times of his life. Generally speaking, as far as appearances go, it would seem that Croce's revisionism was largely successful, and his liquidationism, largely unsuccessful: Marxism was indeed revised, but not liquidated. Yet the reasons for the failure may be more instructive than those for the success, because the reasons for that failure, rather than being accidental, may be intrinsic to the nature of Croce's own thought, which may itself be Marxist. In fact, thinkers as diverse as Giovanni Gentile and Gramsci have called attention to the Marxist character of Croce's thought.[14] One might think that this convergence should settle the matter, yet, obviously, even if Croce is a Marxist of sorts, it remains to determine exactly what constitutes his peculiar brand of Marxism. To begin with, one would have to distinguish between Croce's work on the philosophy of history, politics, society, and morals and his equally voluminous work on aesthetics and literary criticism; the Marxist label is applicable only to the former and not to the latter. Next one would have to distinguish between Croce's self-image and his effective thought and note that he never (even during his revisionist period) regarded himself as a "follower" of Marx, although he would admit being a follower of Vico and Hegel. A third distinction should be made between Croce's earlier revisionism and his later liquidationism. The former would be Marxist insofar as it succeeded; the latter, insofar as it failed. One would want to distinguish as well between the sound or acceptable and unsound or unacceptable parts of Croce's thought, and here Gentile would say it is the unsound part that is Marxism, whereas Gramsci would say it is the sound part. In short, whatever Marxism there is in Croce, it is *Crocean* Marxism and the real problem is to understand its character. I believe that an analysis of Gramsci's critique of Croce can reveal both the character of this Crocean Marxism and the nature of Croce's liquidationist critique of Marxism.

MARXISM AND THEOLOGY

Bearing the title "The Philosophy of Benedetto Croce," the tenth of the Prison Notebooks was written in the years 1932–35 and was divided into two parts, the first dealing almost exclusively and directly with Croce (Q1207–38),[15] the second (Q1239–1362) dealing also with such other topics as Gramsci's elaboration of his own philosophy of praxis, his introduction to philosophy, and his economic theory. Altogether we have ninety-eight main sections labeled or numbered as paragraphs by Gramsci himself or by the editor of the critical edition, if we count separately the subsections of paragraphs 29, 31, 37, 38, 41, and 59 of part II and the prefaces to each part (Q1207–11, and Q1239). Of these ninety-eight sections, fifty-nine deal directly and explicitly with Croce.[16]

The Croce sections may be provisionally organized into various interrelated and somewhat overlapping but distinguishable groups. The most frequent topic is Croce's criticism of Marxism and is itself criticized by Gramsci in twenty-seven sections.[17] Next in frequency comes a group of nineteen sections[18] that criticize Croce's own philosophy of history, politics, and religion. Third, we have a series of discussions, consisting of thirteen sections[19] that are primarily interpretative of, and favorable toward, Croce, rather than critical. Finally, four sections (II: 4, 13, 17, 47) are of marginal import or uncertain character.[20]

A central concern in Gramsci's critique of Croce's critique of Marxism is Croce's liquidationist dismissal. This was expressed most eloquently by Croce in 1914–15 in a book on the history of historiography. It deserves quotation at length because it had not been previously translated into English:

In scientific terms, it was not possible to escape the dilemma: Either historical materialism, continuing on the path of the old philosophy of history, was forced resolutely to become a revelation of the meaning of history, that is, of the real history that underlies the apparent one; or else, obeying the better impulse of whatever novelty it contained, it was forced no less resolutely to humanize the economy, treating it as a mental activity or aspect of mental activity, and to conceive history as a unified whole in which one cannot distinguish (as Goethe's saying goes) the grain from the chaff. But, in the second case, it would have negated its principle and ceased to be materialism, that is, it would have nullified itself and would have been displaced by a new and better philosophy.[21]

[Whereas] the first was a very old metaphysical and transcendent idea, and therefore also a naturalistic one and one apt to ally itself with positivistic and evolutionist currents: Matter, or the so-called Economy, conceived as the hidden God of history, as the one who pulls the strings of individuals and their actions, as Reality versus Appearance, as Substance versus Accident, as the new form or new word by which one presents anew the transcendent God or Providence of theologians, or the Absolute, the Idea, or the Unconscious of the no less transcendent and more recent metaphysicians. To call such a transcendent concept God, Providence, the Idea, the Absolute, and the Unconscious, or else Matter and Economy, does not change anything of the essence because, being transcendent, it is as unknowable as it is unreal and is translated only in mythological images; nor are any of the consequences changed, because from the transcendent Matter and Economy, as well as from the analogous principles of theology and of metaphysics, we obtain the same conception of history as moving with a preordained design, with a beginning and an end in time, with an origin of the world and of society and with a terminal state or state of perfection, be it paradise, the beatific vision, or even nirvana, or be it the coming into being of Communism and the transition from the slavery of Necessity to the kingdom of Freedom, which the theologians of historical materialism prophesied. From this feature of historical materialism, just as in the old theological and metaphysical systems of Philosophy of History, derives the methodological tendency to construct history a priori and to turn a deaf ear to or to silence the genuine voices of facts that documents render audible in the mind of those who welcome them with a desire for understanding.[22]

Gramsci seems to agree about the existence of two versions of Marxism because he speaks of a "lower current" of the "philosophy of praxis" (Q1291) and of a presumably higher current that neither crudely separates superstructure and structure nor conceives the latter theologically and transcendently (Q1300). Concerning Croce's criticism of the higher current (second horn of the dilemma), Gramsci suggests that it reduces to a verbal or terminological point (Q1274), for the "new and better philosophy" of which Croce speaks is supposedly Croce's own, and Gramsci thinks that "what there is which is healthy and progressive in Croce's thought is nothing but the philosophy of praxis presented in speculative language" (Q1268); later in this chapter, I discuss Gramsci's criticism of Croce's constructive philosophy and denial of Marxist influence. For the moment, I follow Gramsci in interpreting Croce's dilemma not to be a genuine one since the latter is claiming that the only proper interpretation of Marxism is the "theological" one. In fact, Croce speaks only of the lower current when repeating this type of criticism in 1924[23] and again in 1930.[24] Gramsci replies to it in Notebook 10's longest and best-organized section (Q1291–1301),[25] to which many others connect as well.[26] He argues that Croce's dismissal of the theological version of Marxism (the lower current) is inconsistent with Croce's own (1) earlier revisionism,[27] (2) intellectual objectivity,[28] (3) anti-Masonic attitude toward religion,[29] (4) realistic, anti-intellectualistic historical interpretations,[30] (5) analysis of the nature of religions,[31] (6) appreciation of Luther vis-à-vis Erasmus,[32] (7) metaphilosophy,[33] (8) theory of error,[34] (9) dialectic of distincts,[35] (10) attitude during World War I,[36] and (11) opposition to Catholic modernism.[37]

Croce's "theological" interpretation of Marxism is inconsistent with his earlier revisionist claim that historical materialism is a valuable canon of suggestive though not universal validity for explaining historical events on the basis of economic factors (Q1275).[38] It is also inconsistent with Croce's earlier critical rejection of Stammler's construal of Marxism, which was precisely the "theological" interpretation that Croce later adopted (Q1280).[39] The problem Gramsci emphasizes here is that Croce at no time subjected his own earlier revisionist work to a critical analysis exposing its earlier errors and justifying the need for the theological interpretation (Q1301, 1254). This makes Gramsci suspect that Croce's change of mind has no rational motivation but, rather, a practical political one, the second of his charges that I cited.

Gramsci's second objection is strengthened by other evidence of a practical motivation. For example, referring to Croce, he points out that "before 1900 he felt honored to pass even politically as a follower of the philosophy of praxis, because at that time the historical situation made this movement an ally of liberalism, whereas nowadays [1932–35] things have changed greatly and certain games would be dangerous" (Q1301). Moreover, there was then (at the time of Gramsci's writing) some concern about the imminent cultural and intellectual strengthening of Marxism, and Gramsci thinks Croce is reacting against this trend (Q1249). One other problem noted by Gramsci is that Croce's liquidationist critique aims to strengthen his own camp rather than to convert opponents, since he does not polemicize with Marxists, does not seem too well informed or up-to-date, does not expose the errors of his earlier revisionism, but merely equates Marxism with historical economism (Q1254). Finally, Gramsci notes that Croce praises Henri De Man's book against Marxism, even though it is intellectually mediocre and artificially oriented toward psychoanalysis, of which, at any rate, Croce has a very low opinion (Q1264–65).

In his third objection, Gramsci compares Croce's liquidationist critique of Marxism to the criticism of confessional religion by anticlerical Masons and vulgar rationalists (Q1292); whereas "Croce's anticlericalism is an aristocratic atheism that abhors the plebeian rudeness and crudity of vulgar anticlerical critics" (Q1303).

Gramsci's fourth objection is that Croce falls into the intellectualistic position "of judging a historical movement from its propaganda literature and of failing to understand that even a banal booklet can be the expression of very important and vital movements" (Q1292). This contrasts with the typical Crocean attitude, exemplified by Croce's recognition "that the moralists of the seventeenth century, though of small stature compared to Machiavelli, 'represented an ulterior and superior stage in political philosophy' " (Q1301).[40]

Next, Gramsci argues that "precisely the analysis of religions that Croce made in the *History of Europe* and the concept of religion that Croce elaborated serve to understand better the historical meaning of the philosophy of praxis and the reasons for its resistance to all attacks and all desertions" (Q1292–93). In fact, Croce's concept of religion is that "the essence and intrinsic character of every religion . . . resides always in a world view and a corresponding ethic,"[41] and he also states that the moral aspects of religions are "forces and capacities worth assimilating and gradually transforming, but not to be destroyed without somehow knowing how to replace them or without actually replacing them."[42] To Gramsci it is obvious that Marxism is a religion in Croce's sense (Q1292), and it is also evident that Croce was unwilling or unable to popularize his philosophy so as to become a norm of conduct (Q1294). It follows that his liquidationist critique is misconceived, or inconvenient, unrefined, inhumane, and politically naive, to use words Croce applied to a Voltaire type of criticism of the Catholic church in the nineteenth century.[43]

A related objection is Gramsci's analogy between Croce's attitude and Erasmus's opposition to the Reformation. Croce's dismissal of Marxism as an outmoded philosophy of history is similar to Erasmus's dictum that "wherever Luther appears, culture dies," and Croce's aristocratic lack of interest in popular enlightenment is similar to the failure of Renaissance culture to filter down to the masses the way Protestantism did (Q1293). The differences are to Croce's disadvantage, for he "relives a position that has been shown historically to be false and reactionary and which he himself has contributed to showing to be false and reactionary" (Q1293), and he forgets that the Reformation and the "regressive" Luther were instrumental in the emergence of classical German philosophy and ultimately of the ideas of Croce himself (Q1293–94).

To show the conflict with Croce's theory of philosophy, Gramsci notes that whereas Croce objects to the Marxist conception of superstructures as appearances, one of his own most famous theses is that of the historicity and nondefinitiveness of philosophical thought, which is merely another way of expressing the same idea (Q1298–99). More generally, Gramsci notes that Croce deserves credit for having articulated a view of philosophy whereby "he has stressed the value of the concept of philosophical problem, by contrast to the concept of system, has denied that thought abstractly produces other thought, and has declared that the problems that philosophers have to solve are not an abstract result of previous philosophical thought but are proposed by the actual historical development" (Q1225). However, Gramsci adds that it is precisely because of this that the concepts of the philosophy of praxis must be conceived immanentistically rather than speculatively; for example, the structure must be conceived not as a "hidden God" but "as the set of social relations in which actual men move and operate, as the set of objective conditions that can and must be studied with the method of 'philology'" (Q1226).

Gramsci's criticism about the theory of error claims that whereas Croce objects to the Marxist thesis that morality, philosophy, art, and other superstructual elements are illusions, one of his most typical doctrines is his theory of the practical origin of intellectual errors. The inconsistency can be seen if we, somewhat implausibly here, follow Gramsci in identifying both what Croce calls errors and what Marxists call illusions with the various historically conditioned mental forms arising from practice (Q1299).

The problem about the dialectic of distincts is that Croce ought to know better than to find objectionable the Marxist distinction between structure and superstructure, since an essential element of his own philosophy is a fourfold distinction, which can be easily misinterpreted by those, such as Gentile and his followers, who want to misconstrue it (Q1300). The four distincts in Croce's system are: expressive cognitive acts (identified with art), ratiocinative cognitive acts (identified with philosophy), general volitional acts (identified with economic practice), and moral volitional acts (identified with moral action). Gramsci's point is that because Croce interprets the interrelations among his four distincts in a dialectical fashion rather than as an abstract separation, there is no good reason why he should not be able to interpret the relationship between structure and superstructure in a similarly dialectical manner.

These nine Gramscian replies to Croce exhaust the range of topics of the all-important paragraph II41.I of this notebook (Q1291–1301). Two additional replies are contained in other paragraphs. In the first one of part I, Gramsci discusses Croce's attitude toward World War I. Although Croce never accepted the idea that the struggle between Italy with the Allies and Germany with Austria was a war of morality versus immorality, and of civilization against barbarism, he did not oppose preaching this idea to the common people so that they would be willing to fight and die. His point was that intellectuals should not lower themselves to the level of the masses but should realize that the latter are unable to lift themselves to the level of the former. Gramsci calls this "great statesmanship by contrast to petty politics" (Q1212). Although he does not explicitly state this, it is obviously a very small step to his saying that Croce did not show the same type of statesmanship toward Marxism. Unable to lift the masses to his allegedly superior philosophy, Croce seemed unwilling to let them have the half truths of the "lower current" of Marxism.

A final inconsistency is exposed by Gramsci in another important and otherwise appreciative paragraph (Q1302–7). It stems from Croce's opposition to the turn-of-the-century movement of Catholic reform that came to be condemned by Pope Pius X as "modernism." One may perhaps hold it against Croce that his opposition strengthened the forces of reaction within the church (Q1213), and his attitude may be taken as a sign of "lack of civic character and courage" (Q1304). Gramsci's main concern, however, is Croce's reason for his opposition, namely, "that between transcendental religion and immanentistic philosophy there cannot exist an uncertain and equivocal *tertium quid*" (Q1304). The criticism implicit here is that because Croce allowed transcendent religion for the Catholic masses, he should also allow it for the working masses, toward whom the lower current of Marxism is aimed.

I think that Gramsci's critique is fundamentally accurate, meaning that the Crocean inconsistencies just mentioned do, indeed, exist and that the underlying interpretations of Croce are basically fair and correct. Such basic justice should not make us forget, however, that the critique is essentially an evaluation of Croce with Croce, that is, of one part of his philosophy with another. I say this not because I think such a feature renders Gramsci's critique invalid but because this feature suggests that Gramsci is essentially a Crocean. The main doctrines of Croce's philosophy that Gramsci seems to accept here are the other's philosophy of religion and his metaphilosophy. Gramsci's main argument seems to be that Croce's liquidationist dismissal of Marxism involves a misapplication of his own theories of religion and philosophy, and that their proper use can reveal the proper place that a vulgar version of Marxism has. Indeed, vulgar Marxism need not be vulgarized.

More will be said about metaphilosophy in the next section. As for Croce's philosophy of religion, the above-mentioned "indirect" evidence (namely, evidence implicit in Gramsci's critical practice) can be strengthened by direct evidence (namely, explicit favorable acknowledgments) that Gramsci accepts the essence of this element of Croce's philosophy. This occurs in a paragraph that specifically discusses "Croce and religion" (Q1217) and considers that his philosophy of religion "is one of the most important points to be analyzed in order to understand the historical meaning of Croceanism" (Q1217). After stating Croce's definition of religion, Gramsci approvingly concludes that "religion is every philosophy, namely, every world view, insofar as it has become 'faith,' that is, insofar as it is considered not as a theoretical activity (creating new thought) but as a stimulus to action (concrete ethico-political activity, creating new history)" (Q1217). In a later paragraph (Q1250–52), Gramsci shows appreciation and admiration of Croce's (critical) response to the Lateran Treaty and argues that it is much wiser than Gentile's.

MARXISM AS A PHILOSOPHY

The second horn of Croce's dilemma quoted in the preceding section may be called his liquidationist *replacement* of Marxism, because it claims that Marxism is incapable of taking a "higher" form and should be replaced by a better philosophy, presumably Croce's own. Croce makes the linguistic point that historical materialism would be a contradiction in terms if its "matter," namely, the economic structure, is given a humanistic, "spiritual," or social-relations interpretation. We may agree with Gramsci that this is a verbal quibble (Q1274). But Croce has another argument, namely, that by its nature Marxism is not a cognitive, philosophical system of thought but, rather, a practical, political expression of ideology.[44] Croce supports this claim with his interpretation of such texts as Marx's allegation that in Hegel philosophy stands on its head, and that one must put it back on its feet; Marx's eleventh thesis on Feuerbach, that philosophers have only interpreted the world in various ways whereas the point is to change it; and Engels's claim that the German proletariat is heir to classical German philosophy. Croce concludes that Marxism is essentially the attempt to replace philosophical theory with sociopolitical action.

Gramsci replies to this in the second-longest paragraph of this notebook (Q1269–75), to which the first two discussions of part II are directly connected (Q1240–42). His counterinterpretation of Marx's allegedly turning Hegel right side up is that whereas Hegel makes theory prior to practice, one must make practice prior to theory (Q1273):

If philosophy is history of philosophy, if philosophy is "history," if philosophy develops because of the development of the general history of the world (that is, the social relations by which men live), and not because a great philosopher is followed by a greater philosopher, and so forth, it is clear that by working practically to make history, one also makes "implicit" philosophy that will be "explicit" insofar as philosophers will elaborate it coherently, and one stimulates cognitive problems that, besides a "practical" type of solution, will sooner or later find a theoretical type of solution by specialists, after having taken the ingenuous form of popular common sense, namely, of the practical agents in historical developments.

This is plausible and interesting, but it is important to note that the premises from which Gramsci argues (the antecedent clauses of his long and complex hypothetical sentence) are central theses of Croce's metaphilosophy.[45]

Gramsci's counterinterpretation of Marx's eleventh thesis on

Feuerbach is that it is an expression of "annoyance toward philosophers and their parrotism and an energetic affirmation of the unity of theory and practice" (Q1270). Similarly, Engels's dictum about the German proletariat "means precisely that the 'heir' continues the predecessor, but continues it 'practically' since from mere contemplation he has deduced an active will, transformer of the world, and in this practical activity is also contained the 'knowledge' that is 'real knowledge' rather than 'scholasticism' only in practical activity" (Q1271). This, too, is acceptable, and here Gramsci himself notes that his interpretations are simply "an affirmation of the historicity of philosophy made in terms of absolute immanence, of 'absolute secularism' " (Q1271). Such an affirmation, in turn, is obviously an adaptation of Croce's metaphilosophy (Q1241).

What we have here, then, is an argument by Gramsci to the effect that Croce's denial of the philosophical character of Marxism is inconsistent with Croce's own historicist view of philosophy because the Marxist theses on which he grounds that denial are essentially equivalent to Croce's own metaphilosophy. To be sure, Gramsci also criticizes him for the excessively speculative (Q1271), abstract (Q1272), bookish and antiquarian (Q1242) approach, for being unable to apply properly his own theory (Q1240–41). For Gramsci, "only the identification of history and politics" (Q1242) could solve this problem, and that would lead to a concept of history as contemporary: "If the politician is a historian (not only in the sense that he makes history but also in the sense that while operating in the present he interprets the past), the historian is a politician, and in this sense (which after all appears even in Croce) history is always contemporary history, namely politics" (Q1242). Since the thesis that all history is contemporary history is one of the most characteristic Crocean principles,[46] Gramsci's point really amounts to saying that the primary difference between Croce and Marxism is verbal: "Croce has retranslated in speculative language the progressive achievements of the philosophy of praxis, and in this retranslation lies the best of his thought" (Q1271).

To conclude, Croce's denial of the philosophical character of Marxism is untenable, but it is his historicist conception of philosophy that provides the best justification of its philosophical character. Here, too, Croce is misapplying his philosophy to the case of Marx. In making such a criticism, Gramsci is accepting the essential part of Croce's metaphilosophy.

If this analysis of Gramsci's critique of Croce's denial that Marxism is a philosophy shows that Gramsci's (critical) practice is in one sense Crocean, it does not as such constitute evidence that he *explicitly* accepts Croce's historicist conception of philosophy, namely, that Gramsci's *theory* is Crocean. Just as in the case of the philosophy of religion, however, we have direct evidence that Gramsci is aware that in a sense he is accepting Croce's view. In a paragraph on the relative popularity of Croce's thought, Gramsci asserts that "one must say that the most important element of Croce's popularity is intrinsic to his thought and to the method of his thinking and is to be found in the greater correspondence to life by Croce's philosophy than by any other speculative philosophy" (Q1216). He goes on to summarize the view of philosophy presented by Croce in a 1930 essay[47] where he briefly but clearly expounds his historicist conception. Gramsci concludes by explaining approvingly how Croce's scholarly practice conformed to that view of philosophy.

Thus for both Croce's "religious" and "philosophical" criticisms of Marxism, Gramsci removes the sting by using and adapting Crocean principles. In that sense he is Crocean. But at the same time, because Gramsci's aim is to defend Marxism, which is thus made to emerge triumphant, he is both being Marxist himself and identifying the Marxist elements in Croce's thought. The two points may be combined by saying that Gramsci is developing his own Crocean Marxism. Explicit evidence for this is Gramsci's statement of his general program (Q1233):

One must redo for Croce's philosophical conception the same reduction that the first theorists of the philosophy of praxis did for the Hegelian conception. This is the only historically fruitful manner of determining an adequate reform of the philosophy of praxis, of elevating this conception which because of the necessity of immediate practical life has been "vulgarized," to the height that it must reach for the solution of the most complex tasks proposed by the present development of our struggle; that is, to the creation of a new integral culture that would have the popular character of the Protestant Reformation and of the French Enlightenment and the classic features of Greek civilization and of the Italian Renaissance. This would be a culture that (to use Carducci's words) would synthesize Maximilien Robespierre and Immanuel Kant, politics and philosophy, in a dialectical unity inherent not only in a French or German society, but in a European and worldwide one.

HISTORY AND POLITICS

Let us now examine Gramsci's critique of Croce's philosophy of history and philosophy of politics, whose articulation would have provided one with a constructive substitute for Marxism and thus supplemented Croce's negative criticism. Three important elements of Croce's philosophy of history are discussed by Gramsci: Croce's histories of Europe and of Italy[48] (which we may call his historiographical practice), his theory of history as the story of liberty[49] (which we may call his liberalism), and his concept of ethico-political history.[50]

Gramsci objects to Croce's historiography partly "because its fundamental preoccupation is a panic fear of Jacobin movements, of every active intervention by the great popular masses as a factor of historical progress" (Q1220).[51] The problem here is not that in historical development Jacobinism is always proper but, rather, that it is not always improper; or, to use Gramsci's own language, Croce "presupposes 'mechanically' that the thesis must be 'conserved' by the antithesis" (Q1220–21), and he "elevate[s] to methodological status what is mere immediacy, thus elevating ideology to philosophy" (Q1221).

In another objection, Gramsci points out that Croce's *History of Europe in the Nineteenth Century* begins with the year 1815 and thus neglects the upheaval of the French Revolution and the Napoleonic Wars, and his *History of Italy* begins with the year 1871 and thus neglects the struggles and unrest of the Risorgimento. This neglect is tendentiously in favor of the cultural, legal, reformistic, and relatively passive aspect of historical development (Q1227). Gramsci also charges it with being, in effect, a Fascist apology, since it suggests that the national socialism following the Italian unrest of 1917–21 is the "civilized" manner of achieving a planned economy, that is, the means for a greater production of wealth and a more equitable distribution of it without upsetting the foundation of society; this is somewhat ironic, in view of Croce's anti-Fascism, but the irony does not make it any less real (Q1228).[52]

Third, Gramsci objects that Croce's historiography is "nothing but a form of political moderatism, which proposes as the only method of political action the one in which historical development and progress result from the dialectic of conservation and innovation" (Q1325). This is nationalistic, in the tradition of Gioberti's concept of Italian classicism, which consists precisely of the interplay of conservation and innovation (Q1324–25). Moreover, such moderatism is the result of a practical-political ideology, rather than of objective scholarship, since there is no objective reason why the conservation that is to accompany innovation should consist of the particular items chosen by Croce (Q1325).

The second target of Gramsci's criticism of Croce's philosophy of history is his liberalism. Gramsci argues that either it is philosophical but empty or it has content but is a political ideology. For "if history is the story of liberty – according to Hegel's contention [adapted by Croce] – the formula is valid for the history of mankind of every time and of every place, and even the history of oriental despotism is liberty. Thus liberty means only 'movement,' development, dialectic" (Q1229). Moreover, such a concept "lends itself to being employed even by the Jesuits, against liberals, who become libertines, by contrast to the 'true' partisans of just liberty" (Q1230), whereas it cannot explain "why in 1848 Croatian peasants fought against Milanese liberals, and the peasants of Lombardy and Veneto fought against Viennese liberals" (Q1236). On the other hand, liberalism may be made concrete by identifying it with the "history of liberty conscious of being such" (Q1229) of nineteenth-century Europe; in this case it becomes "a means of conserving the particular political and economic institutions founded in the course of the French Revolution and of the repercussion it had in Europe" (Q1230). Or one could equate liberalism with nationalism and the ideal of liberty with the well-being of the Fatherland (Q1230, 1237), but the problem is that just as plausibly such patriotism "was synonymous with the State, that is with authority and not with 'liberty,' and it was also an element of 'conservation' and a source of persecutions and of a new Inquisition" (Q1230–31). Perhaps the least objectionable interpretation of liberalism is the liberal form of government, "namely, the form that guarantees freedom of movement and of competition to every political force" (Q1327); but Gramsci does not accept even this, since it would amount to "conceiving historical development as a game of sport with its umpire and its preestablished norms to be loyally respected" (Q1328), to "a form of prefabricated history where the ideology stems not from a political content but from a form and method of struggle" (Q1328). To summarize, Croce's philosophy of liberty is either not philosophy or not liberty.

Gramsci's critique of Croce's philosophy of history is not wholly negative, however. In connection with the Crocean concept of ethico-political history some appreciation is shown. This concept underlies both Croce's historiography and his liberalism. Gramsci's main point is that "whatever there is which is healthy and progressive in the thought of Croce is nothing but the philosophy of praxis presented in speculative language" (Q1268). For example, one ought not to neglect the double aspect (ethical and political) of the concept (Q1302):

Ethics refers to the activity of civil society, to hegemony; *politics* refers to state and governmental initiative and coercion. When there is contrast between ethics and politics, between requirements of liberty and requirements of force, between the civil society and the government or state, we have a crisis. Croce goes so far as to say that the true "state," that is, the directing force of historical development, must sometimes be sought not where one would think (in the state legally understood), but in "private" forces and even in so-called revolutionaries.[53]

Nor should we forget that Croce himself theorizes about an economico-political history, distinct from the ethico-political one, which is after all required by his own "dialectic of distincts" (Q1316); moreover, since his two histories (of Europe and of Italy) start at the conclusion of previous revolutionary periods, we may say that "Croce implicitly recognizes the priority of economic facts, namely, of the structure, as a point of reference and of dialectical impulse for the superstructures" (Q1316). In other words, the problem with ethico-political history is not that it has no place in a sound philosophy of history, but rather that in Croce's hands it becomes "a mechanical and arbitrary hypostatization of the aspect of hegemony, of political administration, of consensus, in the life and the development of the activities of the State and of civil society" (Q1222). To prevent such hypostatization, ethico-political history "may be taken as an 'empirical canon' of historical research, always to keep in mind in the examination and understanding of historical development" (Q1235). According to Gramsci, Marxism is far from excluding ethico-political history, "rather the most recent phase of its development consists precisely in the vindication of the moment of hegemony as essential to its concept of the State, and in the appreciation of cultural facts and activities and of a cultural front as necessary besides the merely economic and merely political ones" (Q1224). What Gramsci seems to have in mind here is Lenin's opposition to economism and his cultural interpretation of the idea of "permanent revolution" (Q1235).

Gramsci's critique may be accepted here, but it must be noted that he follows a typical Crocean *method*, even as he argues against Croce's *particular theses*. Gramsci is himself aware of this when he says that "even in the evaluation of Croce's thought must we use the criterion that a philosophical position should be criticized and evaluated not for what it pretends to be but for what it really is and how it manifests itself in concrete historical works" (Q1235). This was one of the most fundamental principles preached and practiced by Croce on innumerable occasions, for example, in his criticism of Hegel, Vico, philosophies of history, literary works, and current political events.[54] Another Crocean feature of Gramsci's approach is his reduction of Croce's ethico-political history to *a* canon of historical interpretation, which is exactly analogous to Croce's revisionist reduction of historical materialism (in the sense of economism) to one such canon.[55] Third, Gramsci's charge that Croce's anti-Jacobinism is "mechanist" is a typically Crocean objection, while Gramsci's attempt to balance his negative criticism with positive interpretations is an effort to emulate the Olympian serenity that was Croce's usual trait and that Gramsci frequently recognizes; this yields a fourth methodological similarity. Thus, what we have here is the use of an essentially Crocean method of criticism to criticize Croce's philosophy of history, in order to extract from it some acceptable Marxist content. This reinforces my earlier conclusion that Gramsci is a Crocean Marxist, whereas Croce is a Marxist of sorts.

Besides his philosophy of history, the other element of Croce's constructive substitute for Marxism is his philosophy of politics. Gramsci's criticism of the latter[56] does not exhibit as strong a Crocean character as the critiques so far examined, but it, too, contains traces of Croceanism; so let us look at the details.

One area Gramsci discusses is Croce's lack of practical political involvement. This is not indifference (Q1261, 1349) but rather a sign of the level and nature of that involvement. For example, although Croce was not a member of any political organization,[57] he did associate himself with the "conservative" newspaper *Giornale d'Italia* and performed the function of chief of cultural propaganda for several "progressive" political groups (Q1352–53). Even after the advent of Fascism, Croce's "noninvolvement" was aimed at the education of the ruling classes (Q1259) and was thus a "reformistic activity from above" (Q1261). Gramsci is not explicit about how this is objectionable, but I suppose what he has in mind is something analogous to his charge of reformism and moderatism, made in connection with Croce's historiography; that is, Croce's reformism from above may be occasionally appropriate but cannot be regarded as universally valid, on pain of mechanistically hypostatizing a particular ideological interest. This makes sense, but let us note that again we have a typical Crocean objection, applied to Croce himself.

Another target of Gramsci's criticism is Croce's alleged conception of political science. According to it, presumably, although politics is the expression of passion and interest, political science dissolves them as it gives them a theoretical explanation; Gramsci objects that this is intellectualistic and illuministic and turns political science into a "medicine" of passions (Q1307–8). Moreover, party leaders are living proof that the theoretical articulation of political interests does not destroy those interests (Q1309).

Regarding Croce's identification of politics with passion, Gramsci shows appreciation for what he thinks is Croce's underlying motivation. That is, Croce did take an interest in the improvement of the conditions of disadvantaged classes, and he thus theorized that political action stems from the need to remove an injustice. Gramsci objects that this explains only what might be called "defensive" political action, but that there is such a thing as "offensive" political activity. Hence, Croce's analysis is one-sided and should be regarded as a special case of the Marxist theory of permanent struggle (Q1349). This criticism may be sound, but it certainly conforms to the typically Crocean technique of criticizing a view by arguing that it is merely an aspect of a more comprehensive one.

Finally, one of the most important points concerns Croce's doctrine of political ideology. This is an example not so much of error as of implicit Marxism. Political ideologies, for Croce, are practical constructs, instruments of political control; they are deceptions suffered by the governed and perpetrated by the rulers; this is very much like the superstructural analysis by Marxism (Q1319).

Thus, here, too, Gramsci argues plausibly that Croce's political philosophy is right insofar as it is Marxist, which it is to some extent, and wrong otherwise; and his argument is an application of Croce's own method of criticism.

CRITICISM AND DIALECTIC

We may conclude by saying that Croce's liquidationist criticism of Marxism is one of his influential ones. He dismisses Marxism for its theological character, rejects it for its ideological involvement, and attempts to replace it with his own philosophy of history and politics. Gramsci argues cogently that the theological character of Marxism can be explained and justified by Croce's own philosophy of religion, and its ideological character by Croce's own metaphilosophy, while his philosophy of history and politics is Marxist in its sound parts and unsound otherwise. This makes Gramsci's intellectual practice Crocean insofar as he accepts Croce's philosophy of religion, metaphilosophy, and style and method of criticism. It also makes Croce Marxist as regards his theory of "religion" (or popular culture), his theory of philosophy, and the sounder parts of his philosophy of history and politics. All of this helps to establish a Marx-Croce-Gramsci link and helps to define a tradition of Crocean Marxism,[58] as well as to clarify the problem of evaluating Marxism as a religion and a philosophy.

At a deeper level of analysis, it might be said that Gramsci's critique of the Crocean philosophy of history and politics amounts to charging Croce with being undialectial, although I might add that this undialectical procedure is also un-Crocean in the sense of going against the dialectical approach Croce normally followed in his criticism. But to say this is to anticipate discussions and results of later chapters. In fact, such an analysis presupposes a definition of what it is to be "dialectical" in one's manner of thinking (Chapters 6 and 7), and a demonstration that Croce's voluminous critical practice exhibits features that may be conceptualized as "dialectical" (Chapter 2). For the moment, let us note simply that Gramsci, in objecting to Croce's histories of Italy and of Europe, is obviously saying that they are one-sided in focusing on the top-directed, peaceful, and moderate phase rather than the mass-based, violent, and revolutionary phase in the development of those regions. As we will see in later chapters, dialectical thinking is essentially connected with the avoidance of one-sidedness. Moreover, we have already seen Gramsci use the notion of dialectic in his objection to Croce's liberalism, and we may now more pointedly rephrase this objection as the charge that the Crocean philosophy of liberty is either dialectical in form but empty of content or content-specific but undialectical. This is a real difficulty, so much so that, as we will see, Gramsci himself does not escape it when he tries to articulate a dialectical concept of politics (Chapter 5). When he says that Croce's concept of ethico-political history, if properly understood, is part of a conceptual framework that recognizes the other aspects of historical reality, in particular economic-practical history, Gramsci's point is that if we as critics of Croce are not ourselves one-sidedly undialectical, then we would admit that his concept of ethico-political history is properly dialectical. For Gramsci the difficulty is not with the concept but with the way Croce puts it into practice. Similarly, Gramsci's point about Croce's "lack" of political involvement is that it is really a *type* of involvement, and the criticism here would concern only the lack of awareness or its undialectical hypostatization. Finally, Croce's identification of politics with passion is explicitly analyzed by Gramsci as one-sided, and hence the dialectical concern of his criticism is easily seen from the viewpoint of the concept of dialectic I suggested, which will be elaborated on in later chapters.

Chapter 2

Croce and the theory and practice
of criticism

I have reconstructed Gramsci's explicit reflections on Croce as a defense of the religious and philosophical dimension of Marxism from Croce's liquidationist criticism. I also suggested a favorable evaluation of Gramsci's critique, insofar as I reconstructed this critique as an argument to the effect that Croce's negative conclusions about Marxism do not follow from his own principles and methods, which, on the contrary, can serve as the basis for a positive evaluation of Marxism along the same dimension. Although my reconstruction was sufficiently grounded on Gramscian texts to leave no doubt about its accuracy, the same cannot be said of my evaluation, concerning which I may say that it was primarily stated, rather than justified for its accuracy. Such a justification would need to be grounded on a more extensive account of Crocean ideas and texts than was proper to introduce in the context of the discussion in Chapter 1. It is the purpose of this chapter to undertake such a desirable task.

Moreover, such an account is more than merely desirable. It is desirable from the point of view of my evaluation of Gramsci's critique, which was positive and favorable. However, from the point of view of my evaluation of Croce's liquidationist criticism, more Crocean evidence is *necessary*, since my evaluation more or less coincided with Gramsci's, and was thus negative and unfavorable. Such a difference in the kind of justification to be provided stems from a fundamental principle that guides these investigations, namely, that higher standards of hermeneutical evidence apply for the documentation of a negative evaluation than for the documentation of a positive one. This is easy to see, since the claim in question may be formulated by saying that Croce's liquidationist criticism of Marxism is un-Crocean. This thesis is obviously another way of expressing the main Gramscian conclusion reconstructed in the preceding chapter, but it is equally obvious that more needs to be said about what a Crocean critical approach is.

Third, it should be noted that Gramsci's critique of Croce is not entirely negative, in the sense that besides its critical objections, it also contains an interpretative reconstruction. Gramsci's interpretation is that Croce's philosophy consists of two parts: One deals with aesthetics and literary criticism; the other is a critique of Marxism. In other words, Gramsci sees Croce as being in large measure a *critic of Marxism*. This is an important historical thesis and an original one as well. It is also partially correct, but only partially; in fact, it may be generalized into the thesis that Croce was first and foremost a critic: a philosophical critic, a political critic, a historical critic, and an aesthetic critic. Moreover, in addition to being a practioner of criticism, Croce was a *theorist of criticism*, although, as we shall see, the relationship between these two is somewhat problematic.

Finally, since the ultimate intention of our analysis of Croce's critical methodology is, as just stated, unfavorable, this analysis will be more judicious and persuasive if it is conducted in a generally favorable tone. To this we now turn.

CROCE, CRITIC PAR EXCELLENCE

If the greatness of a critic consists in the quality, variety, and quantity of his criticism, then perhaps no critic has ever been greater than Benedetto Croce: neither Voltaire nor Erasmus, neither Taine nor Coleridge nor Ruskin, neither Nietzsche nor Marx, neither Hegel nor Kant nor Hume nor Descartes, neither Jesus nor Socrates, who nevertheless can be said to constitute the criticism Hall of Fame in the history of man.

In one respect, that of *quality*, Croce probably exceeds them all without possibility of comparison: His criticism was fully conscious of itself; the systematic articulation of this reflective awareness constitutes his theoretical philosophy, which provides both an understanding of the nature of criticism and criteria for its adequacy. In other words, Croce was a philosopher not merely in addition to being a critic but *because* he was a critic; his philosophy may be the first methodology of criticism in the history of thought. All the other critics I mentioned were either not philosophers or not systematic philosophers or not philosophers *of* criticism. The last point applies to the philosophers in the list; for though they may incidentally have been critics, criticism as such does not constitute the heart and soul of their philosophy, as it does for Croce's. Thus, Croce's philosophically conscious criticism is superior to theirs, although his philosophy, *qua philosophy*, may not be. Croce may thus be regarded as *the* philosopher-critic in the same sense in which Marx is *the* philosopher-activist, Hegel *the* philosopher-historian of philosophy, Descartes *the* philosopher-scientist, Aquinas *the* philosopher-theologian, Socrates *the* philosopher-moralist – if we agree that Marx's philosophy is aimed at changing society and Hegel's at understanding the history of philosophy, Descartes's is a methodology of science and Aquinas's *ancilla theologiae*, and Socrates' philosophical reflection seeks the good life. In other words, between Croce's criticism and that of his predecessors, say a Voltaire, there is the same distance as between Marx's and Plato's sociopolitical activism, or between Hegel's and Kant's history of philosophy, or between Descartes's and Leonardo's science, or between Aquinas's and Augustine's theology, or between Socrates' and Pythagoras's moral consciousness.

The *variety* of Croce's criticism might also be sufficient to make him the greatest critic that history has ever known, although it alone perhaps might not make his position on that pedestal as secure as does the philosophically self-conscious character of his criticism. His reputation as a literary critic is, of course, pretty universal. But no less real was his activity as a historical critic, that is to say, a critic of historians, historical writings, *and* historical events;[1] so pervasive is this aspect of his work that when he decided to call his system "historicism," the name became generally adopted.

Croce's activity as a political critic was no less significant, although there is a tendency to depreciate it for all sorts of wrong reasons. Some people, for example, would have liked him to be another apostle of revolution or violence like Marx; others would have liked another martyr like Socrates; instead, Croce disappointed them by being himself. Still others blame him for his initial support of Fascism and forget that he became opposed to it in 1925, at which time he wrote and circulated the "Manifesto of Anti-Fascist Intellectuals"; they also forget the critical and yet wise things he had to say during Mussolini's allegedly glorious moments, in 1929 when he was being hailed as the conciliator of church and state or in 1938 when he was being generally acclaimed as a political genius and savior of the peace in Europe. Many of those who would not discern Croce's political criticism are the same people who would ignore, or are ignorant of, his opposition to the 1948 peace treaty between Italy and the Allies.[2] But need I say more? The extent of his political criticism is deemphasized by those who do not like his kind of political criticism.

Finally, like most philosophers, Croce was also a critic of other philosophers and philosophies; but he was a philosophical critic with a difference. The difference is manifold. One, and a superficial one to be sure, though an indicative one, is that he wrote major monographs on three major philosophers: Vico, Hegel, and Marx. I believe this has no counterpart in the activity of other major philosophers, who when explicitly interested in the history of philosophy, confine themselves to rather general remarks but do not become scholarly experts on any one philosopher, let alone three. A second difference is what might be called the *divide et impera* attitude. Croce always divided the doctrines of the philosophers he was criticizing into a sound part, to be accepted, and an inadequate part, to be rejected. Although this displeased the total acceptors and the total rejectors, he could then serenely argue that both groups were wrong. A third difference is that systematic and theoretical philosophy for Croce was a specialty, so that, being primarily interested in criticism, he could not in good conscience, and did not in fact, limit himself to criticism of philosophies. This superior critical awareness shows itself in his criticism of philosophies no less than in his other varieties of criticism.

The *quantity* or *extent* of Croce's criticism is impressive enough even to the naked eye. That is to say, from the mere titles of the various volumes of his collected works, which number seventy-four, one could count *twenty-five* books of criticism: two on Hegel;[3] one each on Vico and Marx;[4] two on seventeenth-century Italian literature;[5] six on modern and contemporary Italian literature;[6] five entitled *Critical Conversations;*[7] one on Goethe;[8] one on Ariosto, Shakespeare, and Corneille;[9] one on Dante;[10] one on ancient and modern poetry;[11] three on late Renaissance poets and writers;[12] and one on eighteenth-century Italian literature.[13]

If the eye sought the aid of the various tables of contents, it might quite possibly be overwhelmed. For one would discover the following additional works of criticism: a critical history of aesthetic ideas from antiquity to the twentieth century in the second half of the *Aesthetic*; the criticism of various concepts of history in the first half of *Theory and History of Historiography*; critical essays on Ranke and Burckhardt in part 3 of *History as the Story of Liberty*; a critical examination of historiographical trends and practices in nineteenth-century Italy, comprising the two volumes of *History of Italian Historiography in the Nineteenth Century;*[14] literary criticism of twenty-six major nineteenth-century European writers in a book whose Italian title means literally "Poetry and Non-Poetry" (*Poesia e non poesia*), and which thus would probably have escaped the naked eye, although it has been translated as *European Literature in the Nineteenth Century;* a critical history of Italian thought and literature in the baroque age constituting the *History of the Baroque Age in Italy;*[15] critical essays on Italian literature from the fourteenth century to the sixteenth century making up *Folk Poetry and Art Poetry;*[16] critical essays on major European poets and writers in part 1 of *Readings of Poets and Reflections on the Theory and Criticism of Poetry;*[17] and critical-political essays in *Italy from 1914 to 1918*[18] and in two volumes of *Political Writings and Speeches* (from 1943 to 1947).[19] The aided eye would thus see about a dozen books of criticism more than the twenty-five seen by the naked eye.

Besides aiding the eye one could easily *train* it according to the following principle: What is ordinarily called history, that is, social and/or political history, can be regarded – and was so regarded by Croce – as criticism of past human actions, that is, as the critical examination of their effectiveness (and morality). Then his history books, his works on history proper, can be seen as more instances of criticism. Thus the list would be augmented by *The Neapolitan Revolution of 1799, Spain in the Italian Life of the Renaissance, Neapolitan Stories and Legends, A Family of Patriots and Other Historical and Critical Essays, History of the Kingdom of Naples, Men and Things of Old Italy* in two volumes, *History of Italy from 1871 to 1915, History of Europe in the Nineteenth Century,* two volumes of *Miscellaneous Writings on Literary and Civil History, Lives of Adventure, of Faith, and of Passion,* and four volumes of *Anecdotes.*[20] This brings the list of books of criticism to about fifty-three.

There remain primarily, in the corpus of Croce's works, the treatises in aesthetics, logic, and philosophy of practice,[21] the systematic books on history, poetry, and modern philosophy,[22] and the collections of philosophical essays.[23] Most, though not all, of the collected essays can be easily identified as criticism of philosophical ideas and doctrines. The treatises and systematic books, too, could be seen, by the mind's eye, to be criticism of alternative philosophical theories and systems. At any rate, I intend here not to show that every one of Croce's seventy-four books is a work of criticism but to give an idea and document the extent of his criticism. Indeed, I do not wish to interpret Croce's systematic philosophy as criticism of some other philosophy, except perhaps incidentally and indirectly. Rather, I wish to interpret it as providing a logic of criticism, in other words, as being a methodology of criticism, an attempt to solve the problem of criticism.

The reasons for this are: First, the methodological interpretation makes Croce's philosophy much more relevant than does the other interpretation, inasmuch as the problem of criticism is much more relevant than the question of the truth in the abstract of the philosophical doctrines Croce was criticizing. Second, the methodological interpretation is much more in the spirit of Croce, for his conception of systematic theoretical philosophy as methodology dethroned it to one of the special "sciences" (i.e., cognitive activities), with the consequence that a philosophy that is primarily the criticism of other philosophies would be too limited, a philosopher's philosophy likely to be impotent in dealing with the criticism of other things; at best it could be a methodology of the history of philosophy, which is the form it did take in its highest expression (Hegel). Third, even if Croce's philosophy were interpreted as criticism of other philosophers, it still would have to be interpreted as a solution to the problem of criticism, if one wanted to provide an adequate justification of that criticism. For his criticism of those philosophies essentially reduces to arguing that they are alive insofar as they contribute to the solution of that problem and dead insofar as they do not.

Thus all of the above-mentioned critical works, those of philosophical criticism no less than those of historical, literary, and political criticism, will be regarded as applications or actualizations or concretizations of Croce's theory (his general logic and methodology) of criticism. It should not be thought, however, that this theory is independent of the actual criticism, whereas the latter is dependent on it. The relation between the actual criticism and the theory is somewhat reciprocal ("dialectical," Croce would say); so the theory should be regarded as the instrument for the criticism. Because we are interested in further using that instrument, it is on the instrument that we shall focus our attention.

Finally, it should be mentioned that Croce was the editor, prime contributor, and at one time sole contributor to the bimonthly journal *La Critica*, which was published without interruption for forty-two years, from 1902 to 1944.

THE GENERAL PROBLEM OF CRITICISM

Criticism is an activity practiced from time immemorial and one that nowadays has become nauseatingly fashionable, at least in its unfavorable form. These facts alone suffice, or should, to make criticism of special interest to the philosopher. Other, more "philosophical" considerations are that the historically earliest practitioners of criticism, the pre-Socratics, are generally regarded as philosophers, that philosophical education usually consists of the criticism of philosophical classics, and that much so-called philosophical practice consists of the criticism of other philosophical works.

The most fundamental fact about criticism is that its objects are things that human beings think, believe, say, feel, want, or do. For it makes no sense to criticize other things, such as natural events and phenomena. Because thinking, speaking, feeling, wanting, and the like are types of doing, one may say that the proper objects of criticism are things that human beings do, in short, *human activities,* or, more simply, activities. This fact about criticism Croce calls its characteristic of "spirituality" (*spiritualità*).

A second fundamental fact about criticism is what Croce calls its characteristic of "concreteness" (*concretezza*). This means that criticism is always aimed at something concrete, definite, real, actual, or existing. For criticism is always criticism of something that has been done, and it makes no sense to criticize something that does not exist, that is, something that has not been done.

A third obvious fact about criticism is that it can be of two opposite kinds: positive, approving, or favorable, and negative, disapproving, or unfavorable. Favorable criticism can be expressed by saying that the thing being criticized is good, true, valid, right, moral, beautiful, successful, efficient, effective; unfavorable, by saying that it is bad, false, invalid, wrong, ugly, unsuccessful, inefficient, ineffective, immoral.

Fourth, it should be noted about criticism that it can be of *several distinct* kinds. For example, the judgment that H. Rap Brown's utterance "Violence is as American as cherry pie" is a brilliant piece of rhetoric is distinct from the judgment that it is a highly poetical expression, although both judgments are favorable; also distinct from each other, though both *unfavorable,* are the judgments that it is an irresponsible statement and that it is a bad argument. The four judgments are concerned either with a different question about the utterance or with a different aspect of it. On the contrary, the judgments that Rap Brown's utterance is a bad argument and that it is a good argument are *opposite but not distinct* kinds of criticism. For although one is unfavorable and the other favorable, the question of whether a particular utterance is a good argument is not conceptually distinct from the question of whether it is a bad one. Fifth, it is obvious that the opposition and the distinction are themselves distinct and not opposed to each other. In other words, the opposition between favorable and unfavorable criticism is different from but not incompatible with the *distinction* among various kinds of criticism. That is, there are pairs of critical judgments that represent *both* opposite and distinct kinds of criticism. For example: This action is decisive but immoral.

The preceding consideration brings to an end the obvious facts about criticism and initiates the list of problems. First, what is the exact connection between favorable and unfavorable criticism? Is the difference between the two a difference in kind or in degree? Isn't it too simplistic to express critical judgments by merely attributing a favorable or an unfavorable characteristic to the thing being criticized? Wouldn't it be better to follow a more comparative approach and speak, for example, of one particular thing being *better* or *more* beautiful, or *more* valid than another? Isn't it arbitrary to draw a sharp line between favorable unfavorable criticism?

Second, how many *distinct* kinds of criticism are there? What makes possible distinct criticisms? Is it the distinct mental attitude that one may adopt toward the same thing? Or do the distinct kinds of criticism derive from the criticism of distinct aspects of the same things? Or from the criticism of distinct objects?

Third, what is the exact connection between opposite kinds of criticism and its distinct kinds? What value do the opposite kinds of criticism have in the light of the fact that distinct kinds are possible? That is, what sense does it make to express an unfavorable (or favorable) judgment when it is perhaps equally possible to express a *favorable* (or unfavorable) but distinct one? For example, what is the point of approving an utterance as being effective when it may have to be disapproved as being logically invalid, or approving an action as decisive when it may have to be disapproved as immoral? Isn't it altogether too easy to express criticism, in view of its indefinitely many distinct kinds?

Precisely, it is altogether too easy *to express* criticism (whether favorable or unfavorable). This fact, which might make one despair of finding one's way out of the problems just mentioned, can be used, and was genially used by Croce, to shift the problem in a more promising direction (one that allows a unified solution of the three problems). If the *expression* of criticism is so easy, let us see if its *justification* is equally easy. The question, once asked, obviously answers itself.

This shift to the justification of criticism provides the basis for the partial answer to the first two problems. First, there is nothing simplistic about expressing critical judgments by attributing a favorable or unfavorable characteristic to the thing being criticized, as long as a justification is also given. For in saying "*a* is bad because *p*," one is relativizing the criticism of *a* to *p*. In other words, simplicism can be avoided and comparisons implicitly introduced if one understands "*a* is bad because *p*" to mean "*a* is bad to the extent that *p*."

As for the second problem, although I will leave unanswered for now the question of the number of the distinct kinds of criticism, it can be noted that what makes distinct criticism possible is the distinct justifications or reasons that may be given for the approval or the disapproval.

Having shifted the problem to that of the justification of criticism, one has to have the insight, which Croce had, to detect the primary obstacle in the way of adequate criticism. It derives from the possibility of *not understanding* the thing being criticized. Obviously, if a critic cannot answer the challenge that he has not understood what he is criticizing, then his criticism loses its force. Understanding is clearly, then, a necessary condition for criticism. But is it also a sufficient condition? And if not, what else is required? That is, what exactly is the role of understanding in criticism, given that it is a necessary element in the justification of criticism? Moreover, if one has understood something, how could one in addition disapprove it or approve it? Isn't that what one is doing in unfavorable and favorable criticism, respectively? That is, doesn't it seem that *lack* of understanding, too, is a necessary condition for criticism? What then is the nature of the understanding required for properly justifying criticism? These questions may be said to constitute *the problem of critical understanding*. They may be reformulated as follows: Is critical understanding possible? If so, what is it and how is it possible? What is the exact connection between understanding and criticism?

TOWARD A GENERAL THEORY OF CRITICAL UNDERSTANDING

For Croce,[24] to understand something critically is to distinguish it from the rest and to relate it to the rest. Obviously it would be possible to distinguish something from the rest without relating it.

To do that may be called descriptive understanding, or more simply, description. It is not possible, however, to relate something to the rest without having distinguished (or without distinguishing) it from the rest. Hence, critical understanding depends on descriptive understanding in a way in which the latter does not depend on the former. Descriptive understanding is in that sense prior and more basic.

In critical understanding, the thing under consideration must be distinguished but *not* separated or abstracted from the rest, and it must be related but *not* confused or compared with the rest. To distinguish *and* to separate or abstract something from the rest is abstract understanding or, more simply, abstraction. To relate *and* to compare something with the rest is empirical understanding or, more simply, classification.

"The rest" of which I speak is in a sense "everything else." But obviously, in any given context it may not be necessary to bring in or worry about *everything* else. It may be sufficient to consider explicitly only part of that everything else, if all else is implicit. In other words, "the rest" means "the *relevant* rest." Hence, it will vary from context to context.

The question arises, then, How does one distinguish something from the rest, and how does one relate it to the rest? The first part is relatively easy to answer. To distinguish something from the rest is simply to individualize it. Hence, descriptive understanding is also individualization. Sometimes this may be accomplished by merely pointing to the thing, sometimes by using its proper name. Sometimes a painting has to be made, as in the case of an artist trying to individualize his image. Or the poet may write a poem in order to individualize his feeling or impression. The novelist may write a book in order to individualize a certain character. Finally, the scientist may have to write an article in order to describe *his solution* of a certain physical problem, or the philosopher may write a book to describe *his conception* of the world.

This leads us to emphasize that in the course of individualization, such things as abstraction and classification may be used, as long as these are instrumental to distinguishing the thing being individualized from the rest. That is, in order to distinguish something from the rest, one may have to distinguish *and separate or abstract other things from the rest* and/or may have to distinguish *and compare other things* with the rest. But this abstraction and this comparison are not operating on the thing being individualized. Those operations not only may be used in the course of individualization but *normally* must be used. No problem results, however, as long as they are kept distinct. An example is the novelist, who in individualizing a certain character makes all sorts of comparisons and abstractions of feelings, emotions, problems, times, and places. Moreover, even critical understanding may have to be used in the course of individualization. To be more exact, even what abstractly considered has to be regarded as critical understanding, may have to be used in individualization. For unless that so-called critical understanding is separated or abstracted from the context, one would see it only as an element in distinguishing an individual thing from the rest. As Croce states, "Philosophical maxims put in the mouth of characters of plays serve as attributes of the characters and not as conceptual claims."[25] One may add that philosophical maxims in the mouth or mind of a philosopher are characteristics of his. Or, more exactly, they are characteristic of his mind and thought. But this is to say that even a philosopher in philosophizing is engaged in individualization, that is, in the individualization of his philosophical ideas, in distinguishing his ideas from others. This clarifies my reference to the scientist and the philosopher.

To summarize, distinguishing something from the rest, which has been defined to be an element of critical understanding, is simply concerned with the individualization of that something. The methods for individualizing are indefinitely varied, since they partly depend on the thing being individualized. This may even be the critical understanding of something. That is, to distinguish something from and to relate it to the rest itself requires the distinction of this distinction-relation from the rest, primarily other distinctions-relations. This is another sense in which individualization is all-pervasive and prior to critical understanding.

The latter is our primary concern here. Having already examined the first element in it, which is autonomous, we can now examine the other element, which is the relating of something to the rest. Abstractly considered, it may be called "universalization." What, then, is this second element? It should be noted that in "examining" the process of distinguishing something from the rest, in my discussion above, I distinguished *but did not separate* individualization from critical understanding. In discussing universalization now, I should distinguish but not separate it from the rest. The rest is here individualization, abstraction, and classification.

What, then, is universalization? It cannot be empirical classification based on family resemblances of the thing being universalized with other things. For universalization is an element of critical understanding, or a step in the justification of criticism, and it makes no sense to approve or disapprove something because it resembles or does not resemble certain other things in certain respects and not in others. Nor can universalization be theoretical interpretation or "rational reconstruction," for this at best would justify the criticism of the abstract entity of the theoretical interpretation or criticism of the reconstructed entity and not of the original real thing.

For Croce, to relate something to the rest is to show how it arises or originates in the mind, in other words, to give the mental genesis of the thing. This universalizes it in the sense that every object of criticism has a mental genesis and thus can be related to every other such object by way of the mind.

The plausibility of this doctrine is most obvious in the case of the criticism of conclusions. The understanding required for the adequate criticism of a conclusion must be clearly such as to include knowledge of the purported rationale of the conclusion. And this rationale is a special case of the mental genesis of the thing under criticism.

Now, Croce points out, to relate something to the rest cannot be done in indefinitely many ways, as was the case with distinguishing it; otherwise universalization would not be distinct from individualization. The relating must be done in a small number of ways, so as to be easily retained in one's mind. So far, we may agree with Croce. But then he tries to argue that to universalize involves to categorize into one of four mutually exclusive, jointly exhaustive, and conceptually interdependent or mutually interdefinable categories: expressive cognitive acts, ratiocinative cognitive acts, volitional acts as such, and moral volitional acts. The argument reduces to an attempt to show that these are the only four conceivable kinds of mental acts. Thus its plausibility is doubtful. But such is the general theory of critical understanding that can be extracted from Croce's *Logic*, when the term *concetto puro* in the latter is philosophically translated as "critical understanding." It should be mentioned that another Crocean theory of critical understanding can be extracted from his *Theory and History of Historiography*, when the term *storiografia* in the latter is philosophically translated as "critical understanding." The basic idea of this latter theory is that critical understanding is the understanding of something for the purpose of properly criticizing it. What is involved (1) to distinguish what the thing being criticized really is, or what it is in practice or in fact, from what it pretends or claims to be; (2) to determine the correspondence between the two. What the thing pretends or claims to be is what the author theorizes that it really is. The first step gives understanding; the second, criticism – unfavorable if there is a discrepancy, favorable if there is correspondence. (This leads to two questions: What is required to determine what a thing really is? and What is required to determine what a thing claims to be? But I shall not pursue these questions here.)

Ultimately it might be better for us to formulate a theory of critical understanding by using as evidence Croce's critical *practice*, rather than by adopting one of his theories of criticism, especially since such theories would have to be grounded on critical practice, either Croce's or someone else's.

THE CRITICISM OF PHILOSOPHICAL THEORIES

"Can he . . . who lives the life of moral, psychological, and historical studies fail to come to grips with the intellectual movement originating from Marx?"[26] Can he who has not struggled with his doctrines call himself a modern man? To Croce in the 1890s these were rhetorical questions. And so we find him struggling with Marxism and coming to grips with it. The direct and immediate results of his study of Marx are recorded in *Historical Materialism and the Economics of Karl Marx*.

As well as being interested in humanistic studies and thinking of himself as "modern," Croce happened to be involved in antiquarian and erudite studies concerning the city of Naples, and he regarded himself very much as a "Neapolitan." Is it likely that such a person would fail to study the writings of an obscure eighteenth-century professor of rhetoric at the University of Naples, author of various ambitious books on scholarly-historical subjects, including one entitled *Principles of a New Science Concerning the Common Nature of Nations?* For us, this question ought to be a rhetorical one. The obscure writer was Giambattista Vico, and Croce's first study of him is recorded in the first five chapters of the historical part of *Aesthetic;* a fuller study can be found in *The Philosophy of Giambattista Vico.*

Finally, a serious and responsible philosophical thinker is bound sooner or later to have to deal with the last great philosophical genius to appear up till then in the history of philosophy. And so, though relatively late, the "leaven of Hegelianism"[27] came to Croce. When it did, he had a new confirmation that books are critically understood only if the reader has already undertaken labors that converge toward the content of those books, and that such works become effective only when they start a dialogue with us and help us clarify our already sketched thoughts, change into concepts our intuitions of concepts, reassure us concerning the road we have already taken on our own; in fact, when in 1905 Croce buried himself in Hegel's books, without recourse to that philosopher's followers and commentators, it was as if he was plunging inward and struggling with his own self.[28] The immediate and direct results of this struggle are embodied in *What Is Living and What Is Dead of the Philosophy of Hegel* of 1906.

Croce valued Marx as the "Machiavelli of the proletariat,"[29] Vico as the first discoverer of aesthetics,[30] and Hegel as the greatest theorist and practitioner of "dialectic."[31] That is, Marx teaches us how to understand critically the effective reality of society,[32] Vico provides us with a critical understanding of the nature of art and poetry,[33] and Hegel has as his primary goal the critical understanding of philosophy itself.[34] Croce thus sees Marx as the philosopher of action par excellence; Vico, as the philosopher of art par excellence; and Hegel, as the philosopher of philosophy par excellence.

This view defines the greatness of each of these philosophers, but it also allows us to see their limitations. For although Hegel understood the nature of philosophy better than anyone before him had, he also tried to reduce everything else to philosophy; he misunderstood other things when he looked at them through his "philosophy of philosophy" spectacles. Marx similarly misapplied the concept of action that he so well understood. Vico did not exactly make an analogous error concerning art; his was primarily one of conceptual confusion. Basically, then, the deficiency of each lies in the merits of the other two, and the merit of each, in the deficiencies of the others.

Between 1895 and 1912, which may be called Croce's "first period," his contributions to the advancement of learning included, in addition to his works on Marx, Hegel, and Vico, treatises on aesthetics, philosophy of the practical or of action, and logic. The temporal contiguity of these books is, however, less important than their logical interrelatedness.

Of course, no one will deny the logical unity of the books on aesthetics, logic, and action, if for no other reason than the *wrong one* that Croce himself believed it, said so, and unified them verbally by referring to them as "philosophy of mind."[35] I am however, no more concerned with this verbal unity (an "aesthetic" unity, as Croce himself might say) than I am with that of the books' expositions; for the expository unity is merely an apparent logical unity (a "pseudological" unity, to use Croce's word). Finally, the most misleading unity of the three books is their theoretical-conceptual one: the fact that a number of concepts are defined and systematically interrelated into a theory. This is unity of an empty and abstract kind, and therefore one may call it formal-logical or abstract-logical. To grasp such a unity would allow one to *manipulate* those concepts but not *genuinely to use* them, that is, to use them to understand critically things beyond themselves. Of course, the temporal, verbal, expository, and abstract unity of Croce's books on aesthetics, logic, and the practical can and should be used as a *clue* to their real logical unity.

The logical unity of the books cannot be found within themselves, and that is why they are being here considered not in the abstract but together with Croce's other important works of what I call his first period. When this is done, however, one striking difference imposes itself between the "philosophy of mind" series of works – on aesthetics, logic, and action – and the works on Marx, Hegel, and Vico. The latter, though not easy by any means, are highly readable, intelligible, and well argued and reasoned, much more so than the former. The philosophical critiques are concrete, whereas the systematic treatises are abstract. To be more exact, they are abstract when taken as abstract, for they can also be regarded as *abstractions*. Abstractions from what? It is difficult to resist formulating the hypothesis that they are abstractions from the philosophical critiques, which could then be regarded as applications of the conceptual system in the treatises. That is to say, Croce's philosophy of mind is a methodology of philosophical criticism, in the sense of the criticism of philosophies.

Now, as Croce himself never tired of reiterating, there is no such thing as philosophy in general, and this is especially true in the case of his own philosophy. Merely to begin to understand it, one must not ignore that it has – indeed, it is – four elements: aesthetics or theory of expression or general linguistics, logic or theory of conceptualization, economics or theory of the useful, and ethics or moral philosophy. Actually, Croce only paid lip service to his economics-ethics distinction. In effect he merged the two into a philosophy of the practical or of practice or of action. Thus, if Croce's philosophy of mind is to be methodology for the criticism of philosophies, then it is his aesthetics, logic, and philosophy of practice that must each be methodologies.

But a methodology is always a methodology of or for something. So the question immediately arises: What are Croce's aesthetics, logic, and philosophy of practice methodologies of? A tempting answer is that aesthetics is methodology of art, that logic is methodology of philosophical conceptualization, and that philosophy of the practical is methodology of action. A second tempting answer is that aesthetics is methodology of art criticism, that logic is methodology of philosophical criticism, and that philosophy of action is methodology of practical criticism. A third tempting answer is that Croce's aesthetics is methodology of criticism of philosophies of art, that his logic is methodology of criticism of logical theories, and that his philosophy of the practical is methodology of criticism of philosophies of action.

The correct answer is that each branch of Croce's philosophy of mind is methodology of philosophical criticism, namely, criticism of what are ordinarily called philosophies, such as the doctrines of Marx, Hegel, and Vico. Thus, any philosophy is inadequate insofar as it does not lift itself to the conception of art extracted by Croce from Vico,[36] to the conception of philosophy extracted from Hegel,[37] and to the conception of action extracted from Marx. As already noted, this criticism would apply to these authors themselves, and the philosophy of each is inadequate to the extent that it does not embody the insights of the other two.

This kind of philosophical criticism may seem shallow and unfair, but closer reflection reveals that this objection would be a case where appearances are deceiving. In fact, Croce's philosophical criticism is the only possible kind, given the widely accepted incommensurability of different philosophical systems, in other words, given Croce's methodological conception of philosophy. In this view, philosophical systems are systematizations of the conceptual instruments for the solution of the problem one faces. Philosophical knowledge is thus both absolute and relative: absolute from the point of view of the problems it solves, insofar as it solves them; relative from the point of view of other existing problems that it was not designed to solve. It follows that a completely fair analysis, an analysis that examines a philosophy in its own terms, could not detect any faults in it; and a completely fair philosophical criticism would only result in the discovery of the incommensurability of philosophies. On the other hand, there is no reason why we cannot say that a certain philosopher solved a certain problem, another philosopher another problem, a third philosopher a third problem, and so forth, and why we cannot appropriate those solutions ourselves insofar as those problems are our own problems. Then, from the point of view of the larger set of problems, each of these philosophies can be criticized insofar as it does not enlighten some of them.

We may summarize by saying that Croce's philosophy of mind is a methodology of philosophical criticism in the sense that: (1) It emerges from his criticism of Vico, Marx, and Hegel; (2) it provides a justification of the broad outline of his criticism of those philosophers; and (3) it provides the means for the criticism of any philosophical system. These facts allow us to speak of the unity of Croce's thought from about 1895 to 1912, which may be called his period of philosophical criticism.

THE METHODOLOGICAL CONCEPTION OF PHILOSOPHY

Wishful thinking, in the sense of expressing unrealistic desires, is *not* a mood in which Benedetto Croce often found himself; he was far too hardheaded a personality for that. All the more reason to attach great significance to his rare moments of wishful thinking. In fact, nothing less than the essential character of his conception of philosophy can be detected in one such pronouncement, in which he expresses his fond wish that the term "philosophy" be replaced by that of "methodology": " 'Philosophy,' " he once said, is "a name which I would willingly do away with but for which I have no hope that it will be substituted by the other, more proper, name of 'methodology.' "[38]

The extent to which Croce, in his own philosophical practice, was faithful to his wish – or to be more exact, the extent to which, in his practice, he replaced what was traditionally called "philosophy" with methodology – can be glimpsed from the fact that in educated but nonphilosophical Italian circles he is regarded as more of a critic than a philosopher. For a critic is an applied methodologist, a methodologist in action.

Croce himself was fully *aware* of the central importance of his methodological conception of philosophy. This thesis is, in fact, a recurring theme in his philosophical essays. It is also the final conclusion of the abstract systematic statement of his philosophy, which he gives in a four-volume series of works. We find that in the fourth volume of this series, entitled *Theory and History of Historiography*, the last theoretical discussion centers on the methodological character of philosophy.[39]

Moreover, Croce was fully convinced of the central importance of this methodological conception of philosophy, so much so that he was willing to stake on it nothing less than the success of his

44

intellectual life. In fact, in a 1930 essay he refers to his theory of the methodological nature of philosophy as the "most general result of my scholarly life"[40] and goes on to add that only by undoing or destroying that theory could someone show that his life had been misdirected or fundamentally misdirected. And by "undoing or destroying" his theory he does not mean "improving" it, which improvement he regards as a distinct possibility as well as quite compatible with his main philosophical tenet, since an improvement obviously presupposes an acceptance of essentials.

Philosophy is, then, methodology. This thesis constitutes Croce's *definition* of philosophy, and the definition is a *formal* one in that it does not, by itself, determine the content or substance that philosophy will have. In other words, not only does such a definition not determine the philosophical answers, it does not determine what the philosophical questions are. It does not even determine Croce's own theory of mental activity.

What, then, is the content of such a conception of philosophy? Its content derives from the fact that it makes a distinction and contrast between philosophy and metaphysics.

The problem of distinguishing the two is one that philosophers, much to their own loss, have somewhat neglected. Lip service is normally paid to the idea that metaphysics is a *branch* of philosophy, namely, the branch that studies "being as such," or a group of concepts or problems such as God, substance, essence, freedom and determinism, mind and body, and matter. I say "lip service" because in practice – that is, in the practice of those who more or less seriously ask, What is philosophy? – we find that philosophy and metaphysics are either confused or equated. For example, the so-called metaphilosophers of the linguistic-analysis school attempt to construct a theory of philosophy; but their work is open to the objection that they support their metaphilosophical claims with inadequate or inappropriate evidence, because this evidence is taken by and large from metaphysical, not philosophical, writings.[41]

A second example is provided by Popper and his followers, who have attempted to solve the so-called problem of demarcation between science and metaphysics.[42] Because it is a distinction that they are trying to make, their work is open to *two* possible objections: that the real distinction they have made is between science and *philosophy* (not metaphysics) or that it is between *philosophy* (not science) and metaphysics.

Thus, the failure to distinguish philosophy and metaphysics does create problems for certain philosophers. More generally, of course, this failure leads them to practice metaphysics, when the need is to practice philosophy-methodology.

But how does Croce's definition of philosophy as methodology make the distinction? The main positive content of the term "methodology" is for him that of an instrument for science and for life,[43] a way or means for getting to know the things or events among which man lives and has to act,[44] an attempt to clarify and better determine the methods and concepts useful for the solution of the problems, whatever these problems may be.[45] Methodology is, then, an activity that does not have a determinate aim or subject matter of its own.

It is this deliberately instrumental, aim-less, and content-free character of methodology that generates the contrast with metaphysics. For Croce takes seriously the time-honored notion of metaphysics as "first philosophy" and the popular idea of metaphysics as a discipline that studies a more or less well-defined number of allegedly fundamental, or general, or eternal, problems, such as those of universals, substance, free will, God, mind and body. Metaphysics, then, does have a determinate aim and specific subject matter.

A second problem that Croce tried to solve was that of the peculiar nature of philosophy. It is generally felt that philosophy is a discipline that is somehow more general, fundamental, comprehensive; in particular, that it is not merely another one of the special sciences. Yet the sense in which philosophy has these characteristics can only be a trivial one if philosophy is equated with anything other than methodology.

A third problem that Croce tried to solve by his definition of philosophy is a historical problem – more specifically, a problem in the history of thought. The problem stems from the fact that the history of philosophy at its best is the history of the thoughts of such men as Socrates, Plato, Aristotle, Augustine, Thomas Aquinas, Descartes, Kant, Hegel, and Marx. Of course, many would delete some of these names and include others. However, few other lists could rival this one for comprehensiveness and fairness. The problem is what makes these individuals philosophers, that is, what makes these thinkers' systems philosophical.

The solution is that their philosophies are all methodologies. For example, Socrates' philosophy was a reflection on the methods for an individual's attainment of a good and fulfilling life. Aquinas's philosophy was a theory of the means for "saving souls" and the attainment of heaven. Descartes's philosophy was a methodology of science, providing means to investigate the natural phenomena of interest to his age. Marx's philosophy was methodology of social action, providing methods for improving the life of the proletariat.

One important thing to notice about the philosophies of the great philosophers is that they have no common subject matter or problems that they would all regard as important or nontrivial. This accords very well with Croce's definition of philosophy, since the reflection on methods has no subject matter of its own (except, trivially and uninterestingly, methods themselves). In fact, a method is always a method *of* or *for* something and cannot be reflected upon separately from that something, which is really the content or subject matter of the reflection, the method being merely the form of the reflection.

Thus, insofar as the methodological conception of philosophy is intended to solve some problems, it is an instrument of understanding. It is also, however, an instrument for criticism. For the distinction between philosophy and metaphysics allows one to criticize writings that are in fact metaphysical but pretend to be philosophical. The error in these writings reduces to the implicit, if not explicit, assertion that to study now the "eternal" problems is to investigate the same things studied by the great classical philosophers. But the "eternal" problems were studied by the classical philosophers *not* when they were "eternal" but when they were clearly relevant problems, that is, when the problems were part of their methodological reflection about *other* problems that concerned them.

HISTORICISM

If a single word was to be chosen to characterize Croce's thought, attitude, and work, what would most readily come to mind would be "historical." Certainly this term came to Croce's own mind, in his mature years, when he once decided that "historicism" was the best name to give to his system of thought; this term is also the one his Italian followers not unwillingly use. If, then, by analyzing Croce's specifically historical work and his notion of historicity, it can be shown that the essential element of his historicism is critical understanding, our conception of the spirit of Croce would acquire additional explanatory power.

What has just been called Croce's specifically historical work can be analyzed into four parts. First, we have a theory of historical understanding; this is the so-called theory of historiography of *Theory and History of Historiography*. Second, we find various histories of historiography.[46] Third, there is a series of ethico-political histories – of Naples, Italy, and Europe. Fourth, we have a theory of history, found primarily in *History as the Story of Liberty*. The theory of historical understanding is a methodology for the critical understanding of historiography; and the histories of historiography are concrete critiques of historical works; both thus become elements of a critical understanding of historical thought and may be said to constitute Croce's historiographical criticism. His ethico-political histories can be understood as case studies aimed at a critical understanding of certain historical facts; and his theory of history as methodology for the critical understanding of the historical process, where the propriety of the critical attitude is guaranteed by understanding the historical process as the result of human actions; both are thus elements of a critical understanding of historical events and may be said to constitute the bulk of Croce's historical criticism, in a restricted sense of "historical," the sense in which it is contrasted to "historiographical."

The best and, surprisingly, the clearest elucidation of Croce's notion of historicity occurs in a passage that may be called the heart of his *Logic*. It is chapter 1 of section 3 of part 1 and bears the title "Identity of the Definitional Judgment, i.e., The Pure Concept, and the Individual Judgment."[47] The importance of the passage was recognized by Croce himself, who included it (as the only selection from the *Logic*) in his intellectual testament, the anthology *Philosophy, Poetry, History*, which he compiled in 1951.[48] Moreover, the passage is the crucial step in Croce's identification of philosophy and history, which is probably the doctrine for which he is best known. Croce argues elsewhere that the definitional judgment, or pure concept, is philosophy; that the individual judgment is the historical judgment, or history; and that history presupposes philosophy in the sense that historical propositions use philosophical concepts, that is, attribute a philosophical concept to an individual thing, fact, or situation. In the present passage Croce argues that, in turn, philosophy presupposes history. By studying this passage we can learn how philosophical or definitional judgments are historical. That is, we can understand what the historicity of philosophy consists of for Croce. What we have, then, is a concrete elucidation of his concept of historicity, and for us, following Croce, a concrete elucidation is the best.

48

Croce's own words are worth quoting:

Every definition is the answer to a question, the solution of a problem. It would not be worth uttering it if one didn't ask questions or pose problems. Why would one bother? What need would force us? Like every mental act, a definition emerges from a contrast, from some labor, from a war that seeks peace, from an obscurity that seeks light. In other words, as we have said, it is a question that asks for an answer. Not only does an answer presuppose a question, but a particular answer presupposes a particular question. The answer must be in tune with the question, otherwise it would not be an answer but the evasion of an answer. This reiterates the fact that the nature of a question colors the answer and that a definition, considered in its concreteness, appears determined by the problem that makes it emerge. As the problem varies, so does the definitional act.[49]

The *mentalistic* character of Croce's philosophy ought to be visible to the perceptive eye from the initial and final words of this passage. "Definition" and "definitional act" denote the same thing for Croce. Thus it is every *definitional act* that is the answer to a question.

Second, Croce's contextualism should be apparent where he tells us that he is speaking of a definition *considered in its concreteness*. To consider something in its concreteness is for him to consider it in its context. Hence what is the solution to a problem is each *concrete* definitional *act*. All of this becomes clear in the next passage:

But, an answer, a problem, a doubt is always individually conditioned. The doubt of a child is not that of an adult, the doubt of an uneducated man is not that of an educated one, the doubt of a beginner is not that of a learned person, the doubt of an Italian is not that of a German, and the doubt of a German of the year 1800 is not that of a German of the year 1900. Indeed the doubt formulated by an individual at a given moment is not the one which the same individual formulates a moment afterward. For the sake of simplicity it is customary to say that in some cases the same question has been asked by many men in various places and at various times. But, in saying this, one is making precisely a simplification, i.e., an abstraction. In reality every question is different from any other. No matter how constant and how bound to certain fixed words it sounds, every definition is in reality different from any other because words, even when they seem materially the same, are effectively different depending on the mental difference of those who use them, who are individuals and thus always in individual and new circumstances. Consider the sentence "Virtue is the habit of performing moral actions." It must have been uttered thousands of times. But, if each time it has been seriously uttered in order to define virtue, then it has been a response to just as many more or less different psychological situations. Therefore it is in reality not one, but thousands of definitions.[50]

In this passage we see what Croce is contrasting concrete definitional acts to: abstract definitional sentences. He obviously doesn't deny the existence of the latter; just as obviously, he is talking about the former in talking of definitions or definitional judgments.

It might be said that, through all these definitions, the conceptualization or conceptual act always remains the same, like the man who wears different clothes from time to time but remains nevertheless the same man. But (leaving aside the fact that not even such a man remains completely the same as he dresses and redresses) the fact is that the relation between conceptualization and definition is not that between man and his clothes. Conceptualizations do not exist except insofar as they are in the mind and verbalized, i.e., insofar as they are defined. As definitions vary, so do conceptualizations. To be sure, all actual conceptualizations are variations or instances of the act of conceptualization in the sense that they are the life of conceptualization and not of representation. But conceptualization does not exist outside of its instances and each conceptual thought is an aspect of conceptualization and is not conceptualization per se. To use some analogies, no matter how far they go, fish cannot swim outside the water, nor birds fly outside the air.

Having accepted the individual and historical conditioning of every conceptual thought, i.e., of every definition (conditions that generate the doubt, problem, or question which a definition answers), one must also admit that, in containing the answer and expressing the conceptualization, a definition at the same time clarifies those individual and historical conditions or that group of facts for what it is, understands it as subject with a predicate, judges it. Since a fact is always an individual thing, an individual judgment is being formed. This is, every definition is also an individual judgment. This is just what had to be proved.[51]

In a concrete definitional act, then, the abstract definitional sentence is the "predicate" of an individual judgment having as subject the facts that the definition is hoping to understand critically. Hence, insofar as historicity involves this kind of individual judgment, it involves critical understanding.

LITERARY CRITICISM FOR LOGICIANS

"Petrarch and the sonnet of the little old man" is the title of a short essay included in Benedetto Croce's *Conversazioni critiche*, third volume.[52] Despite its brevity, it is, from a logical and methodological point of view, one of his richest essays. It is also one of his clearest. And it is one of those essays in which Croce manages to arouse the interest even of an outsider, such as a logician, in the topics he touches upon, which here range all the way from aesthetics, through literary criticism, to Petrarch. The essay is, in short, a gem.

This judgment may generate two initial qualms, which ought to be laid to rest. First, the essay has not been much discussed, if at all, and wouldn't Croce's commentators and interpreters have discussed it if it were that valuable? The answer here is that those commentators must not have understood the central tenets of Croce's philosophy: that philosophy is methodology, that philosophy and history are "identical," that so are history and criticism, and that "identical" are also criticism and criticism of criticism. If these commentators had, they would have been able to draw the consequence that philosophy of art is methodology of art criticism, which means that aesthetic concepts are instruments for the critical understanding of actual and individual works of art, and thus, like all instruments, are most meaningful when they are being used for that purpose. If they had carefully read the essay, they would have recognized it for what it is: an attempt to gain and provide a critical understanding of Petrarch's sonnet, which attempt clarifies and is in turn clarified by certain aesthetic concepts.

Second, the essay was not included in Croce's intellectual testament, *Philosophy, Poetry, History,* his own collection of 1951. And, it might be rhetorically asked, wouldn't he have included it, if he had attached so much importance to it? The answer is that the methodological worth of the essay will be proved in the paragraphs that follow, and if Croce himself was unaware of it, that is a psychological-biographical fact about him, which may invite reflection and explanation and have other interesting biographical consequences, but which is logically and methodologically inconsequential.

The discerning reader will recognize this answer to be a variation of Croce's own remarks about the irrelevance of Shakespeare's intended meaning, when Macduff says, about Macbeth, "He has no children":[53]

Were Shakespeare himself to come forward and declare that he meant what those insipid, moralizing professors declare that he meant, Shakespeare would be wrong, and whoever said that he was wrong would be in better accordance with his genius than he himself, for he was a genius, only upon condition of remaining true to the logic of poetry.[54]

The sonnet in question is the following one by Petrarch, as translated by Macgregor:

> As parts the aged pilgrim, worn and gray,
> From the dear spot his life where he had spent,

From his poor family by sorrow rent,
Whose love still fears him fainting in decay:
Thence dragging heavily, in life's last day,
His suffering frame, on pious journey bent,
Pricking with earnest prayers his good intent,
Though bow'd with years, and weary with the way,
He reaches Rome, still following his desire
The likeness of his Lord on earth to see,
Whom yet he hopes in heaven above to meet;
So I, too, seek, nor in the fond guest tire,
Lady, in other fair if aught there be
That faintly may recall thy beauties sweet.[55]

Croce, in conformity with the idea that art criticism is really criticism of criticism, begins by examining the following attempt to interpret the sonnet as a description of a conflict between wordly love and sacred love:

[Petrarch] has only wanted to say that even in Rome, in the holy city, where all pilgrims devoutly convene to see the Holy Icon, he thinks more of Laura than of Christ; more than with the creator, he is concerned with a wordly creature. As the old and tired pilgrim, kindled by his faith, seeks the image of the One he hopes to be able to see in heaven, so burned by his flame, in the holy city itself, he wretched, sometimes seeks in other faces the desired image of his woman, to whom he longs to go back. The wordly love prevents him from seeing the face of Christ. And "lasso," though aware of this guilt, he does not know how to contain and suppress the feeling that carries him away.[56]

This interpretation Croce finds unacceptable on methodological grounds as well as for substantive reasons, which he admits one could dispute by hairsplitting and which need not concern us here. The methodological objection is that such an interpretation is "allegorical and not poetical, is constructed on externals and not born from within, is an image of the interpretation reflected in the poem and not a light emanating from the latter."[57] This means that such an interpretation is an attempt to find the hidden meaning of the sonnet, the meaning concealed behind what is actually expressed, behind the descriptions given, behind the images actually contained in the sonnet. To do that is both logically distinct from and methodologically posterior to identifying and understanding what is actually expressed. In other words, allegorical speculation is not critical explanation and comes after it, if at all, that is, if affordable; allegorical speculation presupposes art criticism.

Another interpretation Croce considers, attributed to the Italian poet Ugo Foscolo, is as follows: In comparing the eagerness with which he finds Laura's looks in the faces of beautiful women to the devotion of a pilgrim who has in mind the image of the Savior, Petrarch intended to dissipate her jealousy. Not that Petrarch is presenting a kind invention to excuse, conceal, and have forgiven an escapade of infidelity. Not that he is trying to reassure her with hyperbolic praise. Rather, having thought of a comparison flattering to Laura because it put her on a level with the most sacred things, Petrarch is lingering on such things, as if to distract her, and then he comes to the point at the end and precipitously, in order to avoid the embarrassment.

About this interpretation Croce notes three things. First, its accuracy has to be justified with evidence external to the sonnet. And although he thinks the interpretation is likely to be true, from the point of view of the sonnet it is conjectural. It is, in other words, a conjectural interpretation and not an explanation *of the sonnet,* although it may well be a nonconjectural explanation of the sonnet *together with other facts of Petrarch's life.*

Second, the interpretation does not contain and cannot be used by itself to justify a critical judgment; hence it is not a *critical* explanation. For the sonnet is actually being construed as basically a non-poem, more specifically a piece of rhetoric, that is, an act of persuasion and not an act of description and expression of images. This being so, the success and value of the act (of persuasion) must be determined by reference to the character of the actual woman to whom it was directed.

Third, if one is interested in aesthetic or poetical criticism, as Croce is, then one is interested in determining whether there is a poem in the sonnet and what it is. And even if the sonnet is basically a nonpoetical act of persuasion, parts of it could be poetical. A poem might very well have come into being in the midst of an attempt to persuade.

In summary, this interpretation, though perhaps useful and acceptable, is neither a critical explanation *of the sonnet,* nor a *critical* explanation of the sonnet, nor a critical explanation of *a poem.*

To attain a critical explanation of the sonnet-poem, one has to examine the sonnet itself. If one does this, what does one find? There are two images: that of the little old pilgrim journeying to Rome and that of the author's own vicarious peregrinations over women's faces. One also finds an attempted combination of the two. The description of the pilgrim is smooth and pleasant; the second description is rather cryptic and strikes one as a kind of afterthought or, to be more exact, a kind of afterimage; and for this reason the comparison does not go very well and is rather artificial. Hence, the whole fourteen lines do not constitute a very good poem. But the first eleven lines by themselves do.

That just about exhausts Croce's critical explanation of the poetry in the sonnet. And no facts about the psychological meaning for Petrarch or about symbolic meanings can affect those aesthetic facts. On the other hand, those aesthetic facts can affect the psychobiographical ones as follows. One may ask, of what psychological condition are those aesthetic facts an indication? Two main possibilities arise here. Petrarch intended either to write a poem, work of art, or work of beauty or else to perform an act of persuasion, to put forth a piece of rhetoric. If the former, then on this particular occasion he was not a very good poet, his poetic talent failed him, and his poetic genius is to that extent diminished. If the latter, then his poetic genius could not help but express itself even in a practical context, and it is thereby enhanced. Biographical evidence would help one to decide which alternative is true. In either case, however, the aesthetic facts of the sonnet would be needed to reach the conclusion concerning the extent of Petrarch's poetic genius.

This little essay is a microcosm of Croce's literary criticism. For in it we find the same kind of opposition to allegorical interpretations that one finds in Croce's book on Dante, the same kind of insistence on the distinction between poetry and nonpoetry (e.g., rhetoric, or philosophy) that one finds in that book as well as in his *Poesia non poesia* (translated as *European Literature in the Nineteenth Century*), the same kind of criticism of criticism that one finds in his essay on Shakespeare.

This essay is also a classic illustration of Croce's aesthetics, his philosophy of art. In fact, for him aesthetics is simultaneously theory of art and methodology of art criticism; in other words, it is the theory of the conceptual instruments needed for the critical understanding of art. And art criticism, of which literary criticism is a branch, is in turn applied aesthetics, or aesthetics in action, or concrete aesthetics. Illustrated is also the sense in which philosophy and history are identical. For philosophy in this context is aesthetics; and history, which is the making of individual judgments, that is, judgment about individual things, in this context coincides with literary criticism.

To be completely objective, however, one should not conceal the following problem. In the course of his discussion, Croce introduces an element that at first strikes one as logically extraneous or worse. That element is two references to poems of Francesco Gaeta. The first reference is introduced by Croce with the alleged purposes of "varying this rather gray critical discussion" and of "being spiteful toward those who have been made spiteful for my praise to my friend Francesco Gaeta."[58] The second reference to this poet is alleged by Croce himself as a second case of spitefulness toward the same group of people.[59]

Now, distractions and spite are not, or at least should not be, part of aesthetic criticism. Thus, if Croce is right about the stated function of his two references to Gaeta, then the logical reader of Croce's essay would regard them as unforgivable sins, and the logical value and purity of the essay would be flawed. The present reader, however, accepts fully Croce's principle that a man is to be judged by his actual achievement rather than by his intentions. I take this principle so seriously that I am not afraid of applying it to Croce himself. The possibility thus arises that a logical function is fulfilled by the references to Gaeta, in spite of what Croce himself declares.

This possibility emerges all the more forcefully in this context because one can hardly avoid comparing the situation in which Croce finds himself to that in which Petrarch finds himself. Just as the poetic reader of Petrarch's sonnet considers whether a poem was created, even if Petrarch had intended to apologize or persuade, so the logical reader of Croce's essay has to consider whether he made valid critical points, even if he intended to be and believed he was being distracting and spiteful.

The question is, then, Do the references to Gaeta have a genuine critical function? The first involves a poem in which some beautiful religious images are expressed by Gaeta, for example, the viaticum being carried on foot to a dying person. These images are certainly logically relevant to the claim Croce has just made that poetical religious images are often present in nonreligious poets, and that profane ones are often present in religious poets. This is, in turn, relevant to Croce's claim that poetry is areligious, which concerns the question of how Petrarch's somewhat irreverent comparison between the Holy Icon and Laura's face affects the quality of the poetry in the sonnet. And the answer is that it doesn't.

Thus Croce's first reference to Gaeta is not irrelevant. However, it must be admitted that the amount of work it does, as compared to the amount of space devoted to it and distraction introduced, is rather insignificant. Logically speaking, then, this first reference is an extraneous element that diminishes the logical smoothness of the essay.

Does the second reference have a more significant logical function? Here Croce quotes one of Gaeta's poems in which is represented the feeling of seeking elsewhere for one's beloved woman, in the sense of seeking for remembrances of her in the women that used to be close to her. The reference illustrates one kind of feeling Croce is claiming *not* to be represented in the last three lines of Petrarch's sonnet.

It might seem, and it did seem to me at first, that this illustration is not only relevant *but required* as part of the explanation of Croce's remark that "the last three lines of the sonnet remain opaque for the poetical reader";[60] for this remark seems to be itself opaque. This initial impression disappears, however, when, on further examination, one discovers that just before introducing his second reference to Gaeta, Croce has already sufficiently explained this remark. This he has done by giving a positive characterization of the feeling expressed in those last three lines, at which characterization he arrives after a first negative characterization of that feeling, to the effect that it is not to be identified with various kinds of other images to be found, for example, in Rodenbach, Ciconi, and D'Annunzio. The positive characterization of Petrarch's feeling at which Croce arrives is that the poet was excusing as best he could his having to procure a substitute for Laura, when away from her.

If, then, Croce has already thusly explained his own opaque remark, and if he has done so without the help of lengthy quotations of poems, his subsequent reference to one of Gaeta's images is largely irrelevant – though admittedly not completely so.

Thus, from the logical point of view, Croce's references to Gaeta are as extraneous as, from the aesthetic point of view, Petrarch's second image is extraneous to the image of the little old pilgrim. That is to say, the attempt to gain a critical understanding of Croce's essay encounters a problem formally analogous to the problem encountered in trying to gain a critical understanding of Petrarch's sonnet. I am somewhat sorry to have to conclude that the formal analogy extends to include the insolubility of the respective difficulties, the logical one and the aesthetic one. However, it is a delight to point out the analogy, which should make it easier for logicians to understand the aesthetic difficulty and for aestheticians to understand the logical one.

TOWARD AN AESTHETICS OF LOGIC

" 'This Round Table Is Square' " is the title of a short essay included in Croce's *Problemi di estetica.* [61] People who are not already acquainted with, interested in, or appreciative of his thought will find that it provides a memorable introduction into what can otherwise be a forbidding system. Students of Croce, on the other hand, ought to find in it a gold mine for the interpretation and continuation of his work.

Croce's discussion is occasioned by certain remarks made by the German linguist H. Steinthal to illustrate the distinction between logic and grammar. The essay provides, in effect, a critical understanding of those remarks; that is, Steinthal's thought is first explained and then critically evaluated in the light of Croce's own doctrines, which are thereby concretely articulated. My own investigation here seeks to be doubly Crocean – in subject matter and in approach. That is why I have chosen a concrete piece of Croce's work and will provide a critical understanding of it; I will thereby concretely articulate my own ideas about Croce and other matters. In short, I will here try to do to Croce's remarks what he thereby did to Steinthal's. This I do not only because I find it natural but also in order to illustrate concretely the notion of critical understanding, which I believe to be the idea that animates Croce's work and is capable of animating its extension and continuation.

The essay begins by referring to the following example used by Steinthal to clarify the difference between logic and grammar: "Someone approaches a round table and says: This round table is square. The grammarian remains silent, perfectly satisfied; but the logician shouts: Absurd!"[62] Croce then explains that the logician's judgment is evidently right because it is self-contradictory to attribute the geometrical property of being a square to something that is round. He adds that the grammarian's judgment seems also right because the utterance in question obeys all the relevant grammatical rules for the construction of a sentence.

It should be noted that Croce says that the grammarian's judgment *seems,* not that it *is,* right.[63] In fact, he objects that this judgment is neither right nor wrong but inappropriate, as a judgment in the same sense as the logician's, namely, as a normative judgment. For, according to Croce, grammar, unlike logic and aesthetics, is not a normative discipline. He asserts that he has arrived at this result in other ways, but in this essay he wants to give in support

57

of the same conclusion a simple and clear argument using Stein-thal's example. The argument may be reconstructed as follows:

1. The utterance "this round table is square" is illogical. This is so because it is self-contradictory.
2. It is unaesthetic. This is so, in this case, because it is illogical.
3. Therefore, it has no meaning as an act of either intuitive or conceptual understanding. That is, it has no meaning as an act of cognition (in the broad sense of "cognition"). That is, it has no cognitive meaning (in the broad sense).
4. But it is grammatical. (This is so because it obeys all relevant grammatical rules.) That is, grammar finds "grammatical meaning" in the utterance.
5. Therefore, grammar tries to understand it as something other than an act of cognition.
6. Now, in addition to acts of cognition, acts of will are the only things toward which it makes sense to express approval or disapproval. This is so because approval or disapproval is meant to bring about a change, because human acts are the only things susceptible to change as a result of approval or disapproval, and because acts of cognition (in the broad sense) and acts of will exhaust the field of human acts.
7. But grammar obviously does not treat utterances like "this round table is square" as acts of will, although in other contexts it would be possible to do so and thus to express moral evaluation, for example, if the sentence was uttered to mislead someone.
8. Therefore, the understanding that grammar gives is not aimed at approval or disapproval. That is, it is not critical understanding. It may be called naturalistic understanding.
9. This is what Croce means when he says that grammar is not "science," or "philosophy," or "criticism" but a system of abstractions and useful practical conventions.

The plausibility I find in this argument should be obvious from my being able to elaborate such a reconstruction. Although step 2 requires more comment, let us pause and reflect on the final conclusion of the argument. Grammar is not a normative discipline in the sense that the understanding it provides is not critical understanding. Its objects of study are mere things, not mental or "spiritual" activities; in other words, it takes the naturalistic point of view of explaining its subject matter as if it were mere things. From this point of view there is no difference between "this round table is square" and "this wooden table is square," if they can both be generated from the same set of rules, as they can.

Croce realizes, of course, that it is possible to pervert the nature of grammar and engage in "grammatical criticism." Whatever validity this activity has is due to the elements of aesthetic, logical, moral, or practical criticism present in it. If an expression is aesthetically, logically, morally, and practically proper, the fact that it violates some grammatical rules would be critically inconsequential.

Croce's reasoning in step 2 is very interesting but also liable to misinterpretation. Moreover, it embodies some of his views about the connection between the logical and the aesthetic, and hence it deserves careful examination.

Croce is saying that it is because the given utterance is illogical that it is unaesthetic. But he is not presupposing that whatever is illogical is unaesthetic, for he qualifies his argument with the phrase "in this case." What he means is: "This round table is square" is illogical in a special way, namely by being self-contradictory. That is, something is done in the subject of the sentence and then undone in the predicate. Because of this, the sentence leaves our imagination blank. And since it is empty from the point of view of our imagination, in that sense it is unaesthetic.

Moreover, Croce explicitly mentions that if the utterance in question were merely factually false, that, too, would make it illogical in the sense of logically unacceptable; but it would not thereby be unaesthetic. For example, there is no problem with putting to aesthetic use statements about nonexisting beings like Zeus and Venus, since we can imagine that they exist.

Finally, Croce discusses another point, both more subtle and more important. Suppose the utterance in question were the name of a logically absurd sentence, instead of being the absurd sentence itself. That is, he supposes the utterance in question were " 'This round table is square' " instead of being "This round table is square." In that case there would be no problem either. For expressions like the following present no problems to the aesthetic imagination: (1) "This round table is square" is a correct English sentence; or (2) John said, "This round table is square." To use the distinction between "use and mention" common among contemporary logicians,[64] one might express Croce's point by saying that there is no aesthetic problem with *mentioning* a logically absurd utterance, but it is impossible to *use* it aesthetically. It is also possible to illustrate Croce's point with a literary example, where logical absurdities are mentioned (though not used) with considerable aesthetic effect. It is the passage in Strindberg's *A Dream Play* where the schoolmaster asks the officer what twice two is:

OFFICER, *clasping his head.* Yes, that's so, one must mature . . . Twice two
– is two, and this I will demonstrate by analogy, the highest form of proof.

Listen! Once one is one, therefore twice two is two. For that which applies to the one must also apply to the other.

S. MASTER. The proof is perfectly in accord with the laws of logic, but the answer is wrong.

OFFICER. What is in accord with the laws of logic cannot be wrong. Let us put it to the test. One into one goes once, therefore two into two goes twice.

S. MASTER. Quite correct according to analogy. But what then is once three?

OFFICER. It is three.

S. MASTER. Consequently twice three is also three.

OFFICER, *pondering*. No, that can't be right . . . It can't be, for if so . . . *Sits down in despair.* No, I am not mature yet . . .

S. MASTER. No, you are not mature by a long way.

OFFICER. Then how long shall I have to stay here?

S. MASTER. How long? Here? You believe that time and space exist? Assuming time does exist, you ought to be able to say what time is. What is time?

OFFICER. Time . . . *Considers.* I can't say, although I know what it is. Ergo, I may know what twice two is without being able to say it. Can you yourself say what time is?

S. MASTER. Certainly I can.

ALL THE BOYS. Tell us then!

S. MASTER. Time? . . . Let me see. *Stands motionless with his finger to his nose.* While we speak, time flies. Consequently time is something which flies while I am speaking.

BOY, *rising*. You're speaking now, sir, and while you're speaking, I fly. Consequently I am time. *Flies.*

S. MASTER. That is quite correct according to the laws of logic.

OFFICER. Then the laws of logic are absurd, for Nils, though he did fly, can't be time.

S. MASTER. That is also quite correct according to the laws of logic, although it is absurd.

OFFICER. Then logic is absurd.

S. MASTER. It really looks like it. But if logic is absurd, then the whole world is absurd . . . and I'll be damned if I stay here and teach you absurdities! If anyone will stand us a drink, we'll go and bathe.[65]

The worth of this essay is primarily *methodological*, and it is considerable. In fact, having reflected on the crucial step in Croce's argument – where the unaesthetic is grounded on the illogical – one is led to ask, Can the aesthetic be grounded on the logical? Can aesthetic value sometimes result from the presence of logical merit? And these questions lead one to discover what I shall call the "poetry of logic."

Before elaborating on and applying this concept, let us note one respect in which such an extension of the ideas contained in Croce's essay follows his approach. In fact, such an extension exhibits the fruitfulness of those ideas and, as Croce himself once asserted (and in so doing he was theorizing what he had always practiced), "for a philosophical idea its very fruitfulness is its proof, since one cannot give any other demonstration of it, as far as I know."[66]

Moreover, such an extension of Croce's ideas constitutes the "critical" part of my critical explanation of his essay, which, as I indicated at the beginning of the present section, is my aim. For the fundamental idea of critical understanding is that of an attempt *intelligently to change* reality. When the reality under consideration consists of philosophical ideas, after an explanation has been provided, the continuation and extension of them constitutes the change in them and also the best form of approval or positive evaluation.

After Croce, a term like "the logic of poetry" should be easily comprehensible to everyone. His work in literary criticism and aesthetics is, in fact, the theoretical articulation and concrete application of such a logic of poetry. Of course, in this concept the term "logic" has a broad meaning. In other words, the Crocean logic of poetry is grounded on the clear distinction between logical thought and poetical activity and thus is not a reductionistic attempt to interpret poetical images, impressions, and expressions as if they were thoughts or concepts.

To the relative popularity of the notion of the logic of poetry, there does not correspond, however, an analogous familiarity with its inverted twin: the poetry of logic. This idea is definitely Crocean in its conception, though not in its concrete application. The idea is that conceptual thinking, the proper subject matter of logical theory, has an aesthetic dimension insofar as it consists of linguistic expressions. In fact, it cannot help but have this "intuitive" aspect; this is another way of stating the Crocean priority of the aesthetic over the logical, of language over thought, of expressions over concepts. All thought is simultaneously language, and all concepts are simultaneously expressions, but not all language is thought, not all expressions are concepts.

While admitting this aesthetic aspect of logical thought, Croce also noted (and rightly so) that *normally* the imagery and expressive value to be found in logical activity are insignificant, that is, insignificant as compared to works of poetry as such. And at any rate the *main* value of logical thinking is essentially and definitionally its conceptual content. All this can be admitted, as long as one underscores the terms "normally" and "main." This is another way of leaving open the possibility that there may be logical works where the expressive and aesthetic element has considerable value. I think there exist such works, which have genuine aesthetic value, in addition to their logical value, so much so that it would be proper to speak of the presence of poetry in them, poetry in the sense of a high concentration of aesthetic value. I believe the works of Galileo Galilei, especially *Dialogue Concerning the Two Chief World Systems*, provide the single best concrete instance of this idea of the poetry of logic.

One of the most touching images in this work is the experiment of agitating with a towel the air of a room, then stopping the motion, then bringing a lighted candle into the room, and then observing the flame to see how soon the air stops moving. This is part of a discussion designed to show that the cause of the motion of projectiles is not the motion of the ambient air but some kind of "impressed force" passed on from the thrower to the projectile:

SALVIATI. Well, if the pendulums have just shown us that the less a moving body partakes of weight, the less apt it is to conserve motion, how can it be that the air, which has no weight at all in air, is the only thing that does conserve the motion acquired? I believe, and I know that you also believe at this moment, that no sooner does the arm stop than the air around it stops. Let us go into that room and agitate the air as much as possible with a towel; then, stopping the cloth, have a little candle flame brought immediately into the room, or set flying a bit of gold leaf in it, and you will see from the quiet wandering of either one that the air has been instantly restored to tranquillity. I could give you many experiments, but if one of these is not enough, the case is quite hopeless.[67]

One of the most expressive passages in the *Dialogue* depicts feelings that people can have toward logical matters and the diversity of their reactions. Galileo, through his spokesman Salviati, has just stated some arguments against the motion of the earth based on the ballistics of cannon shots, involving things unknown at the time of Aristotle or Ptolemy. Salviati shows pride for their novelty, Aristotle's spokesman Simplicio shows self-confidence for their cogency, and the neutral Sagredo shows sarcasm:

SIMPLICIO. Oh, these are excellent arguments, to which it will be impossible to find a valid answer.
SALVIATI. Perhaps they are new to you?
SIMPLICIO. Yes, indeed, and now I see with how many elegant experiments nature graciously wishes to aid us in coming to the recognition of

the truth. Oh, how well one truth accords with another, and how all co-operate to make themselves indomitable!

SAGREDO. What a shame there were no cannons in Aristotle's time! With them he would indeed have battered down ignorance, and spoken without the least hesitation concerning the universe.

SALVIATI. It suits me very well that these arguments are new to you, for now you will not remain of the same opinion as most Peripatetics, who believe that anyone who departs from Aristotle's doctrine must therefore have failed to understand his proofs.[68]

The imagery that pervades the statement of certain arguments is so appropriate that it leaves the reader breathless. For example, toward the beginning of the *Dialogue* the Galilean Salviati argues that the Aristotelian dichotomy between celestial and terrestrial bodies is based on a dichotomy between their natural motion, circular for the former and straight for the latter; consequently, if one shows that all movable bodies have the same kind of natural motion, the celestial-terrestrial dichotomy would be destroyed. After Galileo has so argued, the following exchange occurs:

SIMPLICIO. This way of philosophizing tends to subvert all natural philosophy, and to disorder and set in confusion heaven and earth and the whole universe. However, I believe the fundamental principles of the Peripatetics to be such that there is no danger of new sciences being erected upon their ruins.

SALVIATI. Do not worry yourself about heaven and earth, nor fear either their subversion or the ruin of philosophy. As to heaven, it is in vain that you fear for that which you yourself hold to be inalterable and invariant. As for the earth, we seek rather to ennoble and perfect it when we strike to make it like the celestial bodies, and, as it were, place it in heaven, from which your philosophers have banished it. Philosophy itself cannot but benefit from our disputes, for if our conceptions prove true, new achievements will be made; if false, their rebuttal will further confirm the original doctrines. No, save your concern for certain philosophers; come to their aid and defend them. As to science itself, it can only improve.[69]

The wit of certain passages is quite simply overwhelming, and yet it is usually not mere wit but constitutes an integral part of Galileo's reasoning. What we often have is arguments expressed with wit and deriving strength from that wit, and this is what gives such passages their *poetical* character and assures that the wit is not merely a literary artifice. An example:

SIMPLICIO. . . . . I concur in judging the body of the moon to be very solid and hard like the earth's. Even more so, for if from Aristotle we take it that the heavens are of impenetrable hardness and the stars are the denser parts of the heavens, then it must be that they are extremely solid and most impenetrable.

SAGREDO. What excellent stuff, the sky, for anyone who could get hold of it for building a palace! So hard, and yet so transparent!

SALVIATI. Rather, what terrible stuff, being completely invisible because of its extreme transparency. One could not move about the rooms without grave danger of running into the doorposts and breaking one's head.

SAGREDO. There would be no such danger if, as some of the Peripatetics say, it is intangible; it cannot even be touched, let alone bumped into.

SALVIATI. That would be no comfort, inasmuch as celestial material, though indeed it cannot be touched (on account of lacking the tangible quality), may very well touch elemental bodies; and by striking upon us it would injure us as much, and more, as it would if we had run against it.

But let us forsake these palaces, or more appropriately these castles in the air, and not hinder Simplicio.[70]

THEORY VERSUS PRACTICE IN CRITICISM

As mentioned, the primary purpose of this discussion of Croce's critical methodology is to substantiate Gramsci's claim (from the preceding chapter) that Croce's liquidationist criticism of Marxism is un-Crocean; hence, it is sufficient to expound my interpretation and support it with evidence from Croce's work, but unnecessary to present lengthy discussions of the views of other interpreters of Croce.[71] However, a brief comparison with other interpretations will be useful, especially since this will help us to appreciate another dimension of my interpretation, which connects it with another central theme in this book, namely, the interaction of theory and practice. In short, I have attempted to distinguish and to relate, within Croce's thought, his theory of criticism and his practice of criticism.

First, the idea that Croce was primarily an intellectual generalist or cultural synthesizer rather than a philosopher is given a new twist whose net effect should be to make it more palatable to its former opponents than to its former proponents; for, although Croce was first and foremost a critic, it is *because* he was the kind of critic he was, that he was a philosopher; that is, he was one of the greatest critics who ever lived *and* one of the few philosophers of criticism in the history of thought, but qua philosopher only a typical one.

Second, the usual classification of Croce's writings under the headings of philosophy, history, and literary criticism is being rejected as empirical and abstract; instead, his writings are critically understood in terms of four developmental lines that are distinct, though partly overlapping and partly interacting, each involving the theory and practice of criticism in a particular field. They may be labeled, respectively, philosophy-criticism, history-criticism, literary criticism, and political criticism. It follows that a work like *Poetry and Literature* is to be understood primarily in terms of its relationships to the literary-criticism line, and only secondarily, if at all, in terms of its relationship to the philosophy-criticism line.[72] Similarly, works like *Theory and History of Historiography* and *History as the Story of Liberty* may be understood primarily in terms of their relationship to the history-criticism line and, only secondarily, if at all, to the philosophy-criticism line. The latter, consisting primarily of the *Aesthetic, Logic, Philosophy of the Practical,* and the books on Marx, Hegel, and Vico, involves primarily the criticism of philosophical theories. Hence, there is a vast difference between the *Aesthetic* and *Poetry and Literature:* The former is a methodology for the criticism of philosophical theories; the latter, a methodology for the criticism of poetry.

The next point to note is that I am devaluating the so-called philosophy of mind, that is, the abstract doctrine of the *Aesthetic, Logic,* and *Philosophy of the Practical;* I do so not only because of the second point just mentioned but also because that doctrine has a rather metaphysical character, somewhat unrelated to critical practice. Consider, for example, the general theory of critical understanding that I discussed. It involves the apparently crucial Crocean distinction between the individual and the universal and can be extracted from the "philosophy of mind" works; but I believe it to be a failure, even when one takes into account that it can be interpreted as an attempt to solve a genuine problem, the problem of criticism formulated in an earlier section. Perhaps its value ought to be placed here, as a proof of Croce's awareness of the problem of criticism. I would thus regard his theory of critical understanding as an unsuccesful attempt to construct a metaphysical theory of criticism. Whether it is an altogether bad thing that such a metaphysical theory fails I will not say. When the "philosophy of mind" is taken together with the works on Marx, Hegel, and Vico, there emerges a rather workable methodology for the criticism of philosophical theories, as I showed. But a trace remains of excessive theoreticism, what Croce himself might call a metaphysical criticism of philosophies, or a metaphysics of philosophical criticism. Croce's methodological conception of philosophy is, then, his true methodology of philosophy-criticism, in other words, methodology for the critical understanding of philosophy. Or, more exactly it is a (relatively abstract) theory of the critical understanding of philosophy, since Croce did not make a sufficiently extensive application of his discovery to concrete cases in the history of philosophy. Thus we have the progression from a metaphysics of criticism, through a metaphysics of philosophical criticism, to a methodology of philosophical criticism. Those three sections of this chapter may then be regarded as a unit, and if we use the term "philosophy" in a restricted un-Crocean sense, then this unit interprets Croce's philosophy as critical understanding and contains three parts: Croce's philosophy as theory of critical understanding, as criticism of philosophical theories, and as theory for the critical understanding of philosophies.

Similarly, the first section of this chapter provides an interpretation of Croce's work in general as critical understanding; the section on historicism construes his historical work as critical understanding of historiographical works and of historical actions and events; and the two sections on literary criticism and aesthetics interpret Croce's literary criticism as critical understanding of poetry and of the poetical aspect of literature. And this brings us to Croce's attitude toward science.

His philosophy is usually interpreted as being antiscientific in both theory and practice; in theory because his *Logic* defends an instrumentalist view that deprives science of cognitive-theoretical value, and gives it merely practical import; and, in fact, Croce's voluminous writings contain a lacuna when it comes to analysis of actual scientific works. But I believe the situation is more complicated.

The true Crocean philosophy of science is not the theory of science contained in the *Logic,* according to which science is not a form of understanding but a kind of practical activity. Instead, a Crocean philosophy of science would attempt to do in the field of science what Croce did in the fields of philosophy, history, and literature.[73] Such a philosophy of science would first have to be critical understanding – in order to be philosophy; this, in turn, means it would have to be methodologically confident – in order to be critical, and meticulously nonreductionist – in order to be understanding. In other words, it would have to be science-criticism, properly analogous to the whole range of Croce's literary criticism, which constitutes his true "philosophy of art," and to the whole range of historical criticism, which constitutes his true "philosophy of history."

This science-criticism would have to be critical understanding of the work of such men as Galileo, Newton, and Einstein, just as Croce's literary criticism is critical understanding of the work of such men as Dante, Shakespeare, and Goethe. In other words, the science of a Crocean science-criticism would have to be an enterprise defined empirically and only approximately, not a conceptually and exactly defined one, as would be the activity called "science" in Croce's official theory of science; for such a "science" is not something it is proper to understand critically, rather it is only to be theorized about. To be more exact, only if one wanted a critical understanding of Croce's theory of science, as distinct from actual, historical science, only then would it make sense to engage in criticism of Croce's "science"; but then this enterprise would be Crocean-science criticism, whereas the proper one is Crocean science-criticism.

Finally, to the extent that Croce's official theory of science is true of actual, historical science – that is, insofar as actual, historical science is not a form of understanding but a kind of practical activity – the Crocean philosopher of science will distinguish those elements that constitute understanding from those that do not. In other words, he will examine seriously the possibility that scientific works are, in the domain of conceptual understanding, what prose works are in the domain of poetry or artistic expression; actual, historical science can no more be neglected by him than actual, historical prose was by Croce.

To conclude, Croce's own theory and practice of criticism did not always correspond to each other. Although this may be held against him by all who value a proper synthesis of the two in whatever domain one is dealing, the failure to recognize this may lead to a misunderstanding of his thought. For example, it may lead one to overemphasize Croce's "antiscientific" attitude as much as Gramsci's "anti-Crocean" one, and thus to neglect deeper levels of analysis. But to do this is to fail in *one's own* synthesis of theory and practice.

Chapter 3

Gramsci's methodological criticism of Bukharin's sociology

My interpretative program for Gramsci's Prison Notebooks calls for an elucidatory systematization and a critical evaluation of those notes containing explicit critiques of Croce, Bukharin, and Machiavelli, and implicit discussions of the questions of the status of Marxism as a religion, a science, and politics, respectively. I first systematized the Crocean notes by reconstructing them as defending the religious and philosophical dimensions of Marxism from Croce's liquidationist dismissal. In the preceding chapter I documented my evaluation of Gramsci's argument as soundly rooted in Crocean principles and critical methodology. Continuing with Gramsci's felt need to place himself from a dialogical, polemical point of view, and with my own theme of the foundations of Marxist criticism, I now turn to Gramsci's critique of Bukharin and the problem of the status of Marxism as a science.

Gramsci's critique of Bukharin's sociology has usually been studied from a historical point of view. It has often been seen as an important document for understanding the relationship between Gramsci's Marxism and the Third International.[1] For example, some have argued that the critique is symptomatic of the emerging contrast between the older Bolshevism and the increasingly official Marxism-Leninism,[2] while others have attributed to it a formative function in the development of Gramsci's own philosophy of praxis.[3] More recently, it has been taken by some as evidence that Gramsci belongs to the tradition of Western Marxism,[4] while others have suggested that his philosophical critique is compatible with a deeper similarity of political outlook with Bukharin.[5] By contrast, a few have followed a more analytical approach in striving to elaborate the details of the intellectual content of Gramsci's criticism; here one can emphasize the substantive aspect, consisting of Gramsci's theories of history and of politics,[6] or, as I shall do, the methodological aspect corresponding to his theory of inquiry.

BUKHARIN AND MARXISM

The 1920s have been called by Stephen C. Cohen "the most vital period in the history of Bolshevik thought and among the most interesting in the history of Marxism"[7] because of such developments as the introduction of the New Economic Policy, the death of Lenin, the expulsion of Trotsky, and the triumph of Stalin. Full of ferment and political and economic controversy, the period has contemporary relevance in view of recent developments in the Soviet Union, for in the words of Moshe Lewin, "The literature pertinent to the economic debates of the 1960's and later, the evaluations of the performance of the economic model in the past and present, and the criticisms and proposals for change, show an amazing parallelism, even similarity, to the debate of the 1920's in theme, wording, and phraseology."[8] The most interesting and important personality during that period is perhaps Nikolai I. Bukharin. On the one hand, we find him at various times and over a variety of issues clashing with all three of the top Soviet leaders: with Lenin in 1920–21 about the trade-union debate; with Trotsky in 1923–27; and with Stalin in 1928–29. Yet Lenin, in his "Testament," stated that Bukharin was "not only the most valuable and biggest theoretician of the Party, but also may legitimately be considered the favorite of the whole Party."[9] In the 1920s, Bukharin was generally considered the main spokesman of the period's New Economic Policy, and he held important offices as member of the Central Committee, the Politburo, and the executive committee of the Communist International, as editor of *Pravda* and of *Bolshevik*, and as co-editor of Lenin's works and the *Great Soviet Encyclopedia*.

Moreover, one cannot neglect the works he wrote before this period, which either influenced Lenin's thinking or anticipated the main tenets of Leninism. Bukharin's *Economic Theory of the Leisure Class*, completed in 1914[10] and first published in 1919,[11] was a critique of the Austrian school of economics founded on the concept of a marginal utility and was accepted in Russia as "the definitive statement on the Austrian school, a basic textbook in educational institutions where it was said that no one could treat the subject 'without repeating the arguments of Comrade Bukharin.' "[12] His *Imperialism and World Economy*, completed in 1915[13] and first published in 1918,[14] "preceded and influenced Lenin's own book on imperialism. Lenin openly acknowledged his debt."[15] This is also true of the relationship between Lenin's *State and Revolution* and Bukharin's monograph "Toward a Theory of the Imperialist State," written in 1916 and first published in 1925[16] In 1919 Bukharin co-authored *The ABC of Communism*, a popularization of the party program that became the "best known and most widely circulated of all pre-Stalinist expositions of Bolshevism."[17] His *Economics of the Transition Period* of 1920 was highly controversial; although Lenin expressed some reservations, these "paled against his ecstatic praise for the most 'war communist' sections"[18] of the book; Lenin's evaluation was "generally favorable,"[19] but it was subsequently distorted by political circumstances.[20]

Finally, even after his political defeat by Stalin and the loss of most of his power and positions in 1929, Bukharin managed to retain a surprising vitality: He became a member of the Academy of Sciences, occasionally held such offices as president of the Association of Research Institutes and editor of *Izvestia*, and was the chief architect of the Soviet constitution of 1936. Even his tragic end, at the climax of Stalin's Great Purge, is interesting and significant. His trial and execution, which inspired Arthur Koestler's novel *Darkness at Noon* and Merleau-Ponty's *Humanism and Terror*, may yet prove to have been his finest hour, if we accept Robert C. Tucker's interpretation that Bukharin's words and deeds amounted to an anti-trial, a successful indictment of Stalin's betrayal of the Bolshevik Revolution.[21]

Bukharin's best-known book is perhaps *Historical Materialism: A System of Sociology*. Originally published in 1921, it was translated into German in 1922, into English in 1925, and into French in 1927.[22] It became the subject of a famous review by Georg Lukács in 1923,[23] and of an extended critique by Antonio Gramsci in his Prison Notebooks.[24] More recently, as interest in Bukharin grew, the book was reprinted in the series "Ann Arbor Paperbacks for the Study of Communism and Marxism"[25] and was criticized anew in a journal of radical thought.[26] Moreover, it was singled out by Bukharin's most recent biographer, Stephen Cohen, as especially significant for understanding the relationship between Marxist theory and Bolshevik policy.[27] Sociologists in particular have expressed very favorable judgments: Seymour Martin Lipset asserted that "this book deserves much more attention than it now receives. It represents the one sophisticated effort by a major Marxist to come to terms with the emerging body of sociological theory and research."[28]

Alfred G. Meyer called it "an important landmark between the earlier attempt of this kind made by Engels in his *Anti-Düring* and the present-day ideological handbook of Soviet communism, *Fundamentals of Marxism-Leninism*. Of these three, Bukharin's *Historical Materialism* may well be the most urbane and sophisticated statement of orthodox communism. . . . Bukharin achieves the rare feat of presenting revolutionary Marxism as a coherent and impressive, and also rather modern, sociological system."[29] Although these judgments were not accompanied by corresponding sociological analyses, they cannot be dismissed because they are an indication of sociologists' intuition.

In some ways Gramsci, too, could appreciate Bukharin's *Historical Materialism*, since he used it as a textbook at a party school, though with significant emendations.[30] On the other hand, in the Notebooks this book became the target of Gramsci's criticism as a typical example of Marxism contaminated with positivism and scientism. Thus we may say that this target is not to be regarded as a straw man. In fact, Gramsci's critique is found in one of the longest, most polished, and most important of the Notebooks (no. 11), which also contains an introduction to the study of philosophy and a discussion of the philosophy of praxis.

It is useful to group Gramsci's objections around the four topics that recur most often, namely, popular belief, metaphysics, science, and Marxism. By the last I mean objections involving such notions as revolutionary consciousness, orthodoxy, and ideology, and I shall speak of them as constituting Gramsci's *Marxist-rhetorical criticism* of Bukharin. The objections centered around popular belief refer to what Gramsci terms "common sense" and will be called his *pedagogical criticism*. Analogously, those involving metaphysics will be called his *philosophical criticism*, and those involving the concept of science, his *methodological criticism*.[31] Although they are distinct in terms of direct topic under discussion and critical point of view taken, it will be seen that these criticisms are interrelated, insofar as they are all elements of Gramsci's philosophy-of-praxis conception of Marxism. For the moment we may note that they constitute an elegant way of finding fault with a book whose full title means "The Theory of Historical Materialism: A Popular Textbook of Marxist Sociology." Gramsci's critique reduces to arguing that the book is misconceived as a popular textbook (pedagogical criticism), as a Marxist work (rhetorical and philosophy-of-praxis criticism), as a scientific sociology (methodological criticism), and as a materialistic philosophy of history (philosophical criticism).

71

PEDAGOGICAL CRITICISM

Gramsci begins what he calls his "Observation and Critical Notes on an Attempt at a *Popular Essay in Sociology*"[32] with a pedagogical point: Because Bukharin's book is aimed at a reader who is not a professional intellectual, he should have begun with a critical analysis of the world view uncritically accepted by the average person, which Gramsci calls the philosophy of "common sense" or the "philosophy of nonphilosophers," and whose main elements are provided by religion (Q1396–97).[33] Indeed, Bukharin begins with a critique of systematic philosophy and of theological religion, which are unknown to the common man; Gramsci adds that philosophical and theological systems have only an indirect relation to the masses, by limiting their thinking negatively without influencing it positively, for popular thought is intrinsically incoherent and uncritical.

This interesting critique seems sound, and it is relevant in the sense that Bukharin's first three chapters do criticize theology, teleologism, indeterminism, and idealism. However, in a later discussion of what Gramsci calls "General Questions" (Q1424), we find the apparently contradictory view that "a popular manual cannot be conceived except as a formally dogmatic, stylistically balanced, and scientifically serene exposition of a particular topic"; thus, since Marxism is still embroiled in polemics and controversies and has not reached a classic phase of development, a popularization of it is misconceived; hence, Bukharin's book can only be an illusory and mechanical juxtaposition of elements that have no real connection.

This tension between what seems to be two conflicting pedagogical principles, can also be seen in the two particular examples of pedagogical improprieties charged by Gramsci. In a discussion entitled "The So-Called 'Reality' of the External World" (Q1411–16), he makes certain specific criticisms of Bukharin's formulation and handling of the problem but objects primarily to his including the problem in the book: "The whole treatment is a response more to an itching of intellectual pedantry than to a logical necessity. The popular public does not even think that such a question could be asked, if the external world exists objectively. To state the problem in this way is enough to elicit an uncontrollable and gargantuan explosion of laughter" (Q1141). By contrast, in the paragraph following his statement of the second pedagogical principle (Q1424–25), Gramsci gives the topic of the dialectic as an example of Bukharin's failure to include a topic he should have included.[34] Al-

72

though he does mention in favor of Bukharin the mitigating fact that the dialectic is a very difficult topic, which runs counter to common sense, Gramsci regards this as an instance of capitulation to common belief and vulgar thought, where "the uneducated and crude environment has dominated the educator, vulgar common sense has prevailed over science rather than vice versa; whereas if the environment is the educator, it must in turn be educated" (Q1426). Thus, the reality of the external world was included but should not have been, whereas the dialectic was not included but should have been.

The contradiction between these two examples may be more apparent than real, because Gramsci may be saying that both are subject to the first pedagogical principle, that a popular book ought to begin by criticizing popular rather than technical philosophy. The inclusion of the problem of the reality of the external is a violation because the question exists only within technical philosophy, and hence Bukharin's criticism of the "idealistic" position is a criticism of technical rather than popular philosophy. On the other hand, the exclusion of the dialectic is *also* a violation because the dialectic runs counter to popular philosophy, and hence a presentation of it would be a criticism of popular and not of technical philosophy, as it should be.

This application of the first pedagogical principle eliminates the contradiction of examples, but let us see what happens when the second principle is applied. There are indications that Gramsci may want to apply the latter, since the topic of the dialectic is presented immediately after the statement of the second principle, and since in giving the difficulty of the topic as a reason for excluding it, he comes close to justifying that exclusion. At one point Gramsci compares the pedagogical relationship between "formal logic" and the dialectic to that between classical physics and relativity or quantum theory. If one taught the latter in an introductory course, "children would understand nothing at all and the clash between the school lessons and familiar and daily life would be such that the school would become the object of mockery and caricaturing skepticism" (Q1426). When *this* principle is applied, the result is that the dialectic has no place in a popular book, and hence Bukharin's exclusion is appropriate. The same principle would, of course, dictate the exclusion of the problem of the reality of the external world and hence might be the ground for such a pedagogical impropriety. The problem would then be that the other pedagogical principle would be merely stated and elaborated by Gramsci but not *really* applied to

Bukharin, and thus would be objectionable by reason of abstractness.

In summary, although each of Gramsci's principles is plausible by itself, the two conflict with each other. Although each can be consistently applied to yield the two specific charges he makes, if this is done, then the critical relevance of the other principle becomes questionable. How is this problem to be resolved? Let us see whether the abstract contradiction between the two principles can be removed. I believe this may be possible if the first is regarded as a principle of *philosophical* pedagogy and the second as a principle of *scientific* pedagogy. That is, Gramsci would have two different critiques in mind here, one to the book considered as a popular book of philosophy, the second to the book as an elementary scientific textbook. In fact, in the concluding paragraph of his discussion of the first principle, Gramsci summarizes his point by asserting that it has to do with the "teaching of philosophy," philosophy in the sense of "the critical elaboration of our own thinking in order to participate in an ideological and cultural community" (Q1401). On the other hand, when he stipulates the necessity of "formally dogmatic, stylistically balanced" exposition (Q1424), he is talking about an "introduction to scientific study" *(ibid.)*, scientific in the sense of systematized knowledge. This is, however, a sense of "scientific" as "serious," and in that sense it is as scientific to be (concretely) critical in philosophy as to be (serenely) systematic in teaching a well-established doctrine or to be monographic in expounding an original contribution to knowledge. Similarly, it is "unscientific" to attempt a systematic exposition of an unsettled, controversial doctrine, as Bukharin does. I shall have more to say about science, when and after I examine Gramsci's methodological criticism. For the moment it suffices to say that Gramsci's two-sided pedagogical criticism seems appropriate in the light of Bukharin's own ambiguity of purpose and practice: Bukharin does seem to want to give both a popular exposition of philosophy and an elementary introduction to scientific sociology. Gramsci's principle of philosophical pedagogy applies to the first aspect of the book; the principle of "scientific" pedagogy, to the latter. Bukharin would have been right to exclude the dialectic in elementary "sociology," but not in a book on popular Marxism; and he would have been wrong in either case to include his discussion of the reality of the external world. In short, given Bukharin's inconsistent aims, two formally inconsistent principles are required. Hence, although Gramsci is not completely clear about this, his criticisms in this area are, in effect, that Bukharin's aim wavers inconsistently between philosophy for the masses and "science" for beginners, that he is uncritical toward Marxism for attempting to present systematically such a controversial doctrine, and that he is uncritical toward popular belief in championing it rather than reforming it.

PHILOSOPHICAL CRITICISM

If Bukharin's popular manual aims at the wrong target (systematic rather than popular philosophy), that is not to say he conducts properly his misdirected criticism. In fact, Gramsci begins (Q1401–2) his second series of objections by charging that Bukharin's procedure is dogmatic rather than historical: He is completely incapable of the "somewhat arduous and difficult mental operation" of "thinking a philosophical claim as true in a determinate historical period, that is as a necessary and inseparable expression of a determinate historical action, of a determinate praxis, but as superseded and 'invalidated' in a later period, without however falling into skepticism and into ideological and moral relativism" (Q1402). Gramsci takes this to indicate a naive form of metaphysics.

To this *practice* of naive metaphysics, there corresponds an equally naive *conception* of metaphysics: Apparently Bukharin equates metaphysics with speculative idealism (Q1402) rather than with "any systematic formulation that is taken as an extrahistorical truth, as an abstract universal outside of time and space" *(ibid.)*. From Gramsci's point of view, Bukharin's materialism is no better than speculative idealism or theistic metaphysics: It is "an upside down idealism, in the sense that empirical concepts and classifications replace speculative categories" (Q1403); and it "divinizes an hypostatized matter" (Q1447; cf. 1445).

Finally, Bukharin's conception of *philosophy* is metaphysical in the sense that by "philosophy" he means an extrahistorical, universal, and abstract doctrine. This is clear from "the fact that historical materialism is not conceived as a philosophy [per se], whose theory of knowledge is the dialectic, but as a 'sociology,' whose philosophy is mechanical or metaphysical or philosophical materialism" (Q877; cf. 1425). For Gramsci, this represents a failure to understand and appreciate "the great achievement in the history of modern thought, . . . namely, the concrete historicization of philosophy and its identification with history" (Q1426).

The upshot of these objections is that, from a philosophical point of view, the book is seriously faulty, insofar as it is uncritical of metaphysics: Its dogmatism and materialism are unwittingly metaphysical, its concept of metaphysics is outdated, and the concept of a philosophy free of metaphysics is foreign to it. Since Bukharin does pretend to be critical of metaphysics and philosophy, Gramsci's charges constitute an effective and fair criticism.

METHODOLOGICAL CRITICISM

Gramsci's most comprehensive criticism is methological and is aimed at Bukharin's theory and practice of science. Although it begins in the third section of this part of the Prison Notebooks (Q1403–6), this criticism is the most comprehensive, most later sections being rather direct exemplifications of its general points. It is also the most complex, involving a number of subtle but crucial distinctions.

Gramsci realizes that the term "science" has several meanings and accordingly distinguishes three different concepts of science: the "empiricist" concept, or the search for general laws, constancies, regularities, and uniformities (Q1403, 1429, 1431–32); the "positivist" concept, the approach prevalent in the physical sciences (Q1404); and the "philosophical" concept, or the use of a serious method (Q1404, 1405, 1424). He, of course, favors the last, not that he sees anything wrong with empirical generalizations and with physical inquiry by themselves; the proper procedure is to understand their nature and realize their limitations. In fact, the two most fundamental principles of "scientific" method, in the sense of "serious approach" advocated by Gramsci, involve a statement of the proper relation between serious method and physics on the one hand, and serious method and empirical generalization on the other.

The first principle is formulated by Gramsci as follows:

> One must establish that every inquiry has its own determinate method and constructs its own determinate science, and that the method has developed and has been elaborated together with the development and the elaboration of that determinate inquiry and science, and that it forms a whole with them. To think of making a scientific inquiry progress by applying to it a model of method, selected because it has given good results in another inquiry in which it was appropriate, is a strange deception that has little to do with science. (Q1404)[35]

This comprises simultaneously a criticism of the positivist conception of science, since positivism uncritically adapts the method of the physical sciences, and a critique of Bukharin, since his work is generally uncritical in this way. A good example is the problem of prediction (Q1403–4).

Gramsci accepts Croce's argument[36] that a prediction is not a cognitive act because a prediction is about the future, which by definition does not yet exist, whereas knowledge is always knowledge of something real. Instead, a prediction is really a volitional act because it essentially involves the extrapolation of the past into the future with respect to a uniformity chosen by the predictor. In the natural sciences it "seems" that one can predict natural phenomena because of the decision, grounded on practical usefulness, to ignore certain dissimilarities and certain discrepancies. When dissimilarities and minor discrepancies become important and when the making of the prediction disturbs the situation (Q1429–30), as is the norm in history, politics, and social affairs, the practical aspect of a prediction and its lack of success become clearer. If the plausibility of this argument is not obvious, one could make it so by translating it into the terminology of the so-called problem of induction. At any rate, Gramsci seems right in objecting that it is unscientific – or, simply, wrong – to think that the concept of prediction ought to play the same role in social science that it does in natural science, and that the former is successful to the extent that it can predict the way the latter can.

Regarding empirical generalization, the important principle for Gramsci is to admit its individual legitimacy but to keep it distinct from science in the sense of physics and of methodological seriousness: "Naturally this does not mean that the search for 'laws' of uniformity is not a useful and interesting thing and that a treatise of immediate observations on the art of politics does not have its raison d'être. But one must call a spade a spade and present treatises . . . for what they are" (Q1432–33). Moreover, one should not equate empirical generalizations about natural phenomena with those about social events (Q1429). "Nor should one confuse with a general theory, namely philosophy, the particular internal 'logic' of the various sociological studies whereby they acquire mechanical coherence" (Q1432).

Bukharin seems to engage in these confusions both from the general tenor of his book – which is uncritical about the concept of "sociology" – and from the way he answers a specific objection at the beginning of his work. The objection is that "the theory of historical materialism should under no circumstances be considered a Marxian sociology, and that it should not be expounded systematically; . . . it is only a living *method* of historical knowledge . . . its truths may only be applied in the case of concrete and historical events."[37] This objection, stemming from Croce,[38] denies that the generalizations of historical materialism should be regarded as exact in the sense of the physical sciences; it does not deny that they are correct empirical approximations. Moreover, Gramsci develops Croce's objection in a Crocean manner, though not one explicitly found in Croce: Although historical materialism was indeed born as empirical generalizations, this is a mere accident, and its concepts can be developed philosophically in such a way that they are universally applicable (Q1432–33). In Gramsci, the interpretation of Marxism as a philosophical science is implicitly contained in the second part of this objection, referring to "method." Thus he thinks that although the objection denies the scientific status of Marxism in the positivist sense, it admits such a status explicitly in the philosophical sense, and implicitly in the empirical sense. On the other hand, Bukharin replies merely that "the fact that the theory of historical materialism is a method of history, by no means destroys its significance as a sociological theory. Very often a more abstract science may furnish a point of view (method) for the less abstract."[39]

Having admitted the theoretical legitimacy of science in the sense of empirical generalization, Gramsci goes on to discuss two qualifications about sociological laws that Bukharin ignores but that would be required by the "critical conscience of every scientist" (Q1404), thus indicating how sociological inquiry can be a special case of applying serious method under special conditions. First, sociological generalizations are "laws of tendency" or statistical regularities; they are correct only so long as the masses remain passive. Because the aim of enlightened social action is the development of the critical consciousness of the people, this means that social progress tends to destroy the correctness of sociological laws. This is especially true under modern conditions, where leadership occurs primarily by means of parties rather than single individuals (Q1429–30). Second, sociological laws have no use in causal explanation but are merely a different verbal expression of sociological facts, an abstract duplication of the facts themselves. These qualifications appear sound, and the recent literature in scientific methodology may be taken to confirm them.[40]

A third fundamental principle of scientific method, in Gramsci's sense of "serious" inquiry, is formal logic, although its very generality might make one hesitate to call it a method (Q1404). Nevertheless, it deserves mention because Bukharin's book is allegedly full of sophism, fallacies, and invalid inferences (Q1406); although this fault occurs probably because the book originates from oral discussions, it renders the book "unscientific" in the present sense. Since Gramsci refers to Bukharin's discussion of Rudolf Stammler as a typical example of this problem, let us look at this section.

Bukharin's first chapter discusses cause and purpose in the social sciences, and toward the end examines some of Stammler's relevant views, as found in his *Wirtschaft und Recht nach der materialistischen Geschichtsanffassung*. Bukharin reports Stammler's view as consisting of the following argument:

Social phenomena are distinguished by certain pecularities which are not present in phenomena of any other kind . . . the earmark of a social phenomenon is in the fact that it is regulated from an external standpoint, or more definitely, by the norms of law (laws, decrees, ordinances, regulations, etc.). . . . Who "regulates," and what is the meaning of "regulation"? Men regulate, by creating definite norms (rules of conduct) for the attainment of *purposes*, which are also consciously formulated by *men*. It follows, according to Stammler, that there is a tremendous difference between . . . the natural sciences (*Naturwissenschaften*) and the sciences concerned with society. The social *sciences are sciences with a purpose (Zweckwissenschaften);* the natural sciences consider all things from the standpoint of *cause and effect.*[41]

Bukharin objects that even if it were true that the distinguishing feature of social phenomena is purposeful regulation, it is obvious that one can still ask for a "causal explanation" of whatever purposes and regulations are found to characterize a given social phenomenon. This is indeed correct, but Bukharin infers fallaciously that "for this reason there is no difference *at all* in this regard between the social sciences and the sciences concerned with nature."[42] The main problem is, of course, with the denial of any difference "at all"; that there is no difference between two things from one point of view does not mean there is no difference from another. But suppose we ignore the "at all"; does Bukharin's conclusion follow? I do not think it does, because the only thing that follows is that "in this regard," in other words, from the standpoint of cause and effect, there is no difference between social and natural *phenomena;* it is meaningful to ask for "causal explanations" in both cases. But if the special nature of the social *sciences* is to study those special features of *social phenomena* that are lacking in the natural phenomena studied by the natural sciences – and this is Stammler's view, and an intrinsically defensible one – then the difference between the two types of sciences remains. Although a natural science of society is possible, it is likely to be as fruitful as a social science of nature, assuming the latter were possible.

Bukharin attempts to strengthen his criticism with the irrelevant argument that "if man and human society are portions of nature as a whole, it would really be very remarkable to find that this portion is in complete contradiction with the rest of nature."[43] This way of arguing is seductive indeed, but the history of natural science itself provides us with its *reductio ad absurdum*. Consider how the discovery of electromagnetic interaction (the "Lorentz force law") refuted the widespread belief that if electricity and magnetism are portions of nature as a whole, it would really be very remarkable to find this portion not to behave in accordance with a central force law, which has been found to operate in the rest of nature.

A second objection by Bukharin against Stammler is that, at any rate, it is not true that the distinguishing characteristic of social phenomena is purposeful regulation. The reason he gives is: "Almost all the societies that have existed, to the present day (particularly capitalistic society) have been distinguished precisely by the absence of any regulation, by their anarchy. In the great mass of social phenomena, any regulation that positively regulates in the manner desired by the law givers, has never played a very decisive part."[44] This is true but irrelevant to Stammler's premise. He is talking about regulations external to the individual person as the essential origin of social relations, whereas Bukharin talks about regulation external to (imposed upon) society as a whole. As for the unintended effects of laws and regulations, they are certainly important, but there is no reason why they should be ignored in Stammler's approach, which merely says that society derives from external regulations; the extent to which these fulfill their purpose would certainly be part of the study of social phenomena so defined.

Thus Gramsci seems to have a case when he says that insofar as to be scientific is to be logical, and since Bukharin is often illogical (perhaps owing to his book's oral origin), he may be characterized as unscientific.

The three principles of scientific methodology in terms of which Bukharin's work has so far been criticized are more fundamental but less explicit in Gramsci's critique than the next set, which are stated by him in so many words and labeled explicitly "general criteria which may be said to constitute the critical conscience of every scientist, regardless of his 'specialization,' and which must always be spontaneously kept on guard in his work" (Q1404). By contrast, the connection of these latter principles with later criticism is less explicit, for Gramsci states these principles in the section entitled "The Concept of 'Science'" (Q1403–6), adding that "every one of these points can be developed with the appropriate exemplifications" (Q1405). Nevertheless, the connection is obvious, as will emerge in the discussion that follows. But first let us see how Gramsci formulates these principles. I will begin numbering them with the numeral "4" to acknowledge the three already examined:

We can say that he is not a scientist [4] who shows little assurance about his particular criteria, [5] who does not have full understanding of the concepts used, [6] who has little information and understanding about the preceding state of the problems treated, [7] who is not very cautious in his claims, [8] who does not proceed in a necessary but in an arbitrary way without interconnection, [9] who does not know how to take into account the lacunae which exist in the cognitions arrived at, but is silent about them and is satisfied with purely verbal solutions or connections, instead of declaring that they are provisional positions which may be re-examined and developed, etc. . . . [10] It is not very "scientific," or more simply very "serious," to choose one's opponents among the most stupid or mediocre ones, or to choose the least essential and the most incidental ones among the opinions of one's opponents, and to presume to have "destroyed" the opponent "entirely" because one has destroyed one of his secondary and incidental opinions, or to have destroyed an ideology or doctrine because one has proved the theoretical inadequacy of its third- and fourth-class specimens. Moreover, [11] "you should be fair with your opponents," in the sense that you should make an effort to understand what they really meant and not stop maliciously at the immediate and superficial meanings of their expressions. (Q1404–5)

Before seeing how these principles are applied to Bukharin, some comments are in order. It is rather unclear what Gramsci means by [4]. The problem is with the word "criteria" (*criteri*). If he meant "concepts," then [5] would be basically repeating [4]; if he meant "claims," then [4] would contradict [7]. I believe it is best (most "scientific," by Gramsci's own principles [10] and [11]) to understand the word "criteria" in the same sense operative in the rest of the section on the concept of science, namely, as methodological principles. This means that in [4], Gramsci is advocating a certain amount of methodological self-confidence. In other words, although one should be cautious about particular conclusions reached ([7] and [9]), one should be confident about one's methodological approach.

81

The difference between [10] and [11] may not be apparent at first sight. Gramsci's rationale for them here is helpful and intrinsically interesting. He justifies the principle of fairness, as we might call [11], in terms of the desirability of raising the intellectual level of one's followers so that they will be able to hold their own in discussions with intelligent opponents (Q1405). And he justifies the straw-man principle, as we might call [10], in terms of strengthening one's critical spirit and laying the groundwork for one's own original positive contributions. These political-pedagogical grounds may not be acceptable, but the principles themselves certainly are.

Now we are ready to examine their application. In a section entitled "Judgment on Past Philosophers" (Q1416–17), Gramsci charges that in his book Bukharin judges "all the philosophical past as a delirium and a folly . . . as irrational and monstrous, and the history of philosophy becomes a historical treatise of teratology" (Q1416–17). Such methodological antihistoricism is declared by Gramsci to be partly pedagogicaly misconceived, since it reduces to a pretension of being right merely because of the time of one's birth and forgets that every past age has had *its* past. He finds it also philosophically naive since it is a sign of uncritical metaphysics, and un-Marxian since the *Communist Manifesto* contains the highest praise for the bourgeois world about to disappear. We may also say that Bukharin's antihistoricism is implicitly being declared unscientific since it is an obvious violation of Gramsci's [11], the principle of fairness.

In the next section (Q1418–19), entitled "On Art," Gramsci refers to Bukharin's discussion of the aesthetic concept of the identity of form and content[45] and to his remark on Goethe's poem "Prometheus."[46] It is clear that Gramsci finds here a violation of principles [5] and [6], because he gives this objection as an example of Bukharin's "critical inability in establishing the history of concepts and in identifying their real meaning depending on the doctrine involved" (Q1418). In fact, the content-form identity is a doctrine in idealistic aesthetics (Croce being the best exponent), and in it the concepts of "content" and of "form" have their special meaning: Content does not mean the abstract subject matter, such as the story, and form does not mean the technique, as Bukharin seems to think. As for the "Prometheus," he "apparently knows neither the exact history of this ode by Goethe, nor the history of the Prometheus myth in world literature before Goethe and especially in the period preceding and contemporary with Goethe's literary activity" (Q1418). It would be interesting to study, of course, whether here Gramsci is abiding by his own straw-man and fairness principles [10] and [11], although the prison context of his notebooks would be likely to exonerate him.

In a section on science and scientific instruments (Q1420–21), we find an attempt to fault Bukharin's doctrine of scientific progress. Such criticism may easily be categorized as a charge of violation of principle [4], since we can interpret "assurance" as command, and "methodological criterion" as generally any reflection on science. Thus, Gramsci's charge here reduces to the objection that Bukharin does not seem to have an adequate command of the theory of scientific progress. To what extent this charge is successful will be seen presently.

Gramsci attributes to Bukharin the view that "progress in the sciences is dependent, as the effect from the cause, on the development of scientific instruments" (Q1420). The logical form of Gramsci's objection is as follows: First, he notes that this is a perversion of Marx by the substitution of the instruments of production and labor for the network of social relations of production. Second, he argues that Bukharin's thesis is not true on several grounds: that geology made great progress even while its only instrument was the hammer; that the main instruments of scientific progress are intellectual-methodological, for example, the expulsion of the authority of Aristotle and of the Bible from scientific inquiry; that the thesis confuses the concepts of science and of technology, which the possibility of a *science of instruments* shows ought to be kept distinct; and that the history of mathematics exhibits progress without material instruments and a case of a *science* becoming the *instrument* of others.

These arguments are insightful and could be elaborated and strengthened, and they do disconfirm Bukharin's thesis as stated, and as interpreted by Gramsci. Unfortunately, here Gramsci seems to be violating his own straw-man and fairness principles. In fact, his "material instrument" construal is unfair because the rest of Bukharin's discussion[47] refers to social structure as well, and the selection of this particular thesis sets up a straw man because it is only one element of Bukharin's view, which is much more complex. Even this element is prejudicially reported, since Gramsci omits Bukharin's qualification "among other things." Bukharin's mere summary, which, of course, is not his whole story, makes this clear:

It is easy to conclude from the above: 1. that the content of science is given by the content of technology and economy; 2. that its development was determined among other things by the tools of scientific knowledge; 3.

that the various social conditions now encouraged, now retarded progress; 4. that the method of scientific thought was determined by the economic structure of society; . . . 5. that the class structure of society impressed its class stamp on mathematics. . . . In modern times we find the same causal relations, but they are more complicated and, of course, different in form.[48]

As previously mentioned, one should keep in mind the prison situation in which Gramsci wrote his critique.

Gramsci's next methodological criticism is more impressionistic but also more valid: "Reading the *Manual* we have the impression of someone who cannot sleep because of moonlight and who makes an effort to kill as many fireflies as he can, convinced that the light will diminish or disappear" (Q1423–24). In other words, we have a violation of the straw-man principle [10], insofar as in his criticism Bukharin tends to concentrate not on great intellectuals but on secondary ones, "the ones who chew again ready-made phrases" (Q1423). It is true that in a military battle it is best to hit the enemy at its weakest point, but to do this at the intellectual level is rather insignificant; and though it is true that a given historical period or society is represented by the average intellectual, one must distinguish popular culture from scientific work. This is so because "a new science proves its efficacy and fruitful vitality when it shows how to confront the great specimen of opposing tendencies, when it resolves by its own means the vital questions that they posed or else shows decisively that these questions are false problems" (Q1423).

The section entitled " 'Matter' " (Q1442–45) criticizes Bukharin for misunderstanding (1) the Marxist concept of matter and (2) the role of natural entities and natural science in historical development and in historiographical explanation. The first criticism can be construed as a charge of violation of principles [5] and [6]; the second, as contravening [4]. Bukharin presumably never makes clear that by "matter" historical materialism means neither the physical entity of natural science nor the metaphysical entity of abstract philosophy, but rather the "productive economic element . . . socially and historically organized for production" (Q1443). A particular material thing, such as a machine, is an aspect of the forces of production (Q1443). Matter is thus the sum total of the forces of production, which "is the least variable element in historical development, is the one that from time to time can be ascertained and measured with mathematical exactitude" (*ibid.*), whose variability "is itself measurable and can be established with a certain precision when its development changes from quantitative to qualitative" (*ibid.*), and which "is also a crystallization of all past history and the basis of present and future history" *(ibid.)*.

Gramsci also objects that Bukharin has a wrong conception of how physical entities and scientific theories affect human society, an example being Bukharin's claim that the new theories of the structure of matter (according to which elementary particles are interrelated rather than isolated entities) refute political and sociological individualism (Q1444).[49] According to Gramsci, though physical entities (e.g., steam power and electricity) exist independently of human knowledge, they have no significant effect on human history and society until and unless we know about them (Q1443–44); their effect is thus indirect. On the other hand, scientific theories are the (superstructural) result of the underlying "material" base, and the new atomic theories are the effect, not the cause, of the refutation of individualism.

A distinction should be made here between social and sociological individualism, that is, between individualism in social practice and individualism in the social sciences. Since what presumably leads to the new atomic theory is *social* individualism, it follows that *sociological* individualism could still be the effect of atomic theory, by a process of social scientists imitating physicists. In Bukharin's positivist approach this is what would be happening, and hence his present claim would not be touched by Gramsci's criticism. Thus, both Gramsci and Bukharin may be partly right and partly wrong here.

The last criticism subsumable under the question of what is required to be scientific is Gramsci's brief reference to Bukharin's antiteleologism at the end of this part of the Notebooks (Q1450). The versions of teleology criticized by Bukharin are the crudest ones, so that in his chapter on equilibrium between nature and society, he unwittingly adopts a more refined version close to Kant's teleologism. Bukharin's discussion of teleology is also one of the most visible examples of his fault of presenting previous doctrines as being equally trivial and stupid, thus giving the impression that all past culture was "a phantasmagoria of bacchants in delirium" (Q1450). Such procedures would be unscientific according to Gramsci's principles [6], [10], and [11].

In conclusion, Gramsci's methodological criticism consists of a highly negative appraisal of Bukharin's book in the light of a number of principles of scientific methodology. The concept of science implicit in them is a broad one, according to which scientific inquiry is simply serious inquiry. These principles advocate judiciousness in transposing a method successful in one inquiry into another (especially the method of the physical sciences into other fields), modesty in making use of empirical generalization, soundness of inference, confidence in one's procedures, understanding of one's concepts, awareness of previous contributions, caution in drawing conclusions, depth and fairness in one's criticism. The plausibility of these principles is thus hardly open to doubt. Gramsci's application of them to Bukharin's book is not always acceptable but is accurate often enough so that his overall criticism cannot be dismissed, and it may motivate a systematic firsthand analysis of the "Textbook," undertaken in Chapter 4.

MARXIST-RHETORICAL CRITICISM

What remains in Gramsci's critique is mostly a series of criticisms that, for lack of a better term, I have called "Marxist-rhetorical" because they reduce to the charges that Bukharin's book is reactionary, nonorthodox, and ideological (in the bad sense).

This type of criticism begins with the fourth section of Gramsci's "Critical Observations" (Q1406–11), immediately after he has begun his pedagogical, philosophical, and methodological objections, and, like them, is continued intermittently in subsequent sections. This fourth section may be read as a charge of reactionary conservativism, a charge, of course, that may at first sound strange, directed as it is to Bukharin's book, which prides itself as an attempt to work out a sociology in the interests of the working class that in Russia had recently acquired political power.[50] Let us look at Gramsci's argument.

In words obviously reminiscent of Marx, Gramsci believes that "every dominant social group elaborates its own category of intellectuals" (Q1406–7), and that "every new historical organism, or type of society, creates a new superstructure whose specialized and flag-carrying representatives – the intellectuals – cannot not be conceived as themselves 'new' intellectuals, emerged from the new situation and not a continuation of the preceding intellectuality" (Q1407). In short, "the function of intellectuals is to determine and organize moral and intellectual reform, that is, to make culture and practical life correspond" (*ibid.*). Now, "if the 'new' intellectuals make themselves into a direct continuation of the preceding intelligentsia, they are not at all 'new,' that is, they are not tied to the new social group that organically represents the new historical situation; but they are the conservative and fossilized remains of the social group that has been superseded historically" *(ibid.).* Gramsci calls this latter type "crystallized" intellectuals and adds that they conceive themselves as historically uninterrupted and continuous, and independent of class struggles (Q1406).

If Gramsci had stopped here, we would have a position inconsistent with his historicism. But he goes on to make two essential qualifications. First, "one must however take into account that no new historical situation, even if due to the most radical change, completely transforms language, at least in its external and formal aspect" (Q1407). Second, "on the other hand it is not proper that all the heritage of the past should be rejected: there are certain 'instrumental values' that cannot not be generally accepted in order to continue to elaborate and refine theory" (Q1408). The important thing is to learn to distinguish the conceptual content behind the same linguistic terminology, and the dead from the living within the heritage of the past.

For Gramsci, the grafting of traditional metaphysical materialism onto Marxism is one of the best examples of intellectual "crystallization," which is to say insufficiently revolutionary attitude. Since metaphysical materialism is an outstanding feature of Bukharin's book, in that regard he is somewhat reactionary or insufficiently revolutionary.[51]

I think this is a brilliant criticism, as long as one keeps in mind the qualifications I have emphasized. In Gramsci's sophisticated revolutionism, the problem of the criticism of the past is not an "all-or-none" question, but one of judicious selection. Those who, like Bukharin, think that the philosophy behind Marxism is metaphysical materialism would be guilty of an error of judgment. And this leads to the related question of "orthodoxy."

In a section on "The Concept of 'Orthodoxy'" (Q1434–38), Gramsci states that true Marxist orthodoxy is expressed in the attitude that Marxism "is sufficient unto itself, contains within itself all the fundamental elements for building a total and unified world view, not only a whole philosophy and a theory of the natural sciences, but also to vivify a unified practical organization of society, that is, to become a total and unified civilization" (Q1434). This conception of orthodoxy is taken to be an important consequence of the revolutionary consciousness, for to think otherwise "means really not to have cut your ties with the old world, or even to have succumbed" *(ibid.).* Thus, people like Bukharin, who call themselves orthodox Marxists, are not really so, since they conceive their world view as being subordinated to a general materialistic theory (Q1435).

This error is probably due to confusion between Marx's personal philosophical culture and the essentials or conceptually constituent parts of his world view (Q1435–36). Marx's central point was "the absolute bringing down to earth of thought, an absolute historical humanism" (Q1437).

Finally, Gramsci thinks that *Historical Materialism* falls into ideology, in the pejorative sense (Q1489, 1491), by which he understands a "dogmatic system of absolute and eternal truths" (Q1489). This is a fault to which Marxists are especially prone: Because Marxism "affirms theoretically that every 'truth' believed eternal and absolute has had practical origins and has represented a 'provisional' value . . . , it is very difficult to make one understand 'practically' that such an interpretation is valid even for the philosophy of praxis, without shaking those convictions which are necessary for action" (Q1489). Nevertheless, Gramsci maintains, such ideology is a corruption of Marxism because it is implicit from everything about it that it conceives itself historicistically (Q1487), because it obviously prides itself on being conscious of the conditions from which it originates (Q1488), and because it asserts explicitly that history will at some future time make a transition from the kingdom of necessity to the kingdom of freedom (Q1487–90). Of course, one cannot act now (while in the kingdom of necessity) as if freedom were the case, so that Marxism retains its present validity; but one cannot uncritically forget that "in the kingdom of freedom thought and ideas cannot any longer originate from the ground of contradictions and necessities of struggle" (Q1488), and that hence many concepts of speculative idealism, "which are utopian during the kingdom of necessity, could become 'truths' after the transition" (Q1490).

PHILOSOPHY OF PRAXIS

We have seen that Gramsci's apparently disconnected objections to Bukharin's book can be systematized into four distinct types of criticism (pedagogical, philosophical, methodological, and Marxist-rhetorical), and now it is time for a few words about some interconnections among them.

The phrase "philosophy of praxis" has appeared in some of my quotations from Gramsci. For the purpose of the discussions up to now, it has been sufficient to think of this phrase as Gramsci's attempt to conceal his references to Marxism or historical materialism from the prison censors. But Paul Piccone has argued that the phrase was more than a matter of convenience, "that it was an accurate characterization of his theoretical perspective as part of a long-standing tradition opposed to positivist, naturalist and scientific deformations of Marxism,"[52] going back to Spaventa and Labriola. Independently of the accuracy of this thesis, my analysis unquestionably confirms the view that the label "philosophy of praxis" is not just a prison subterfuge but, rather, points to a distinctive theoretical perspective. In fact, all of Gramsci's criticisms of Bukharin can be said to stem from what he calls the philosophy of praxis.

The connection with Gramsci's Marxist-rhetorical criticism is perhaps the easiest. For him, the philosophy of praxis is simply the philosophy founded by Marx, and his references to Marx as the founder of the philosophy of praxis are too numerous to need explicit citation. Second, the main connection with Gramsci's pedagogical criticism is that the philosophy of praxis has the "tendential character of philosophy of the masses" (Q1397). In other words, to criticize Bukharin's book for its shortcomings in claiming to be a popular book is to criticize it from the point of view of a doctrine that tends to be aimed at the popular public. Third, the historicist, antimetaphysical conception of philosophy, and the conception of metaphysics as being essentially dogmatism, underlies Gramsci's philosophical criticism. He explicitly formulates this criticism in terms of the philosophy of praxis, saying that "divorced from the theory of history and of politics, philosophy cannot be but metaphysics, while the great accomplishment in the history of modern thought [which accomplishment is] represented by the philosophy of praxis, is precisely the concrete historicizing of philosophy and its identification with history" (Q1426).

Next, we have the most interesting connection of all, namely the identification of science and the philosophy of praxis, where, of course, science is understood not in a formalist or positivist sense but as the synthesis of intellectual activity and experimentation. This extremely important passage deserves to be quoted in full:

Should science be understood as the theoretical activity or as the practical experimental activity of scientists? Or as a synthesis of the two activities? One could say that in this we would have the typical unitary process of reality, namely, in the experimental activity of a scientist who is the first model of dialectical mediation between man and nature, the elementary historical cell by which man, placing himself in relation to nature by means of technology, knows it and dominates it. There is no doubt that the establishment of the experimental method separates two worlds in history, two epochs, and it begins the process of the dissolution of theology and of metaphysics, and the process of the development of modern thought, whose crowning is the philosophy of praxis. Scientific experience is the first cell of the new method of production, of the new form of active union between man and nature. The scientist-experimenter is also a worker, not a pure thinker, and his thinking is continuously controlled by practice, and vice versa, until a perfect union between theory and practice is formed. (Q1448–49)[53]

Gramsci here seems to be paying as much homage to science as the positivists themselves do, but it would be unfair to object that he is thereby being inconsistent (1) with his antipositivism and (2) with his "revolutionary" and "orthodox" conception of Marxism. The problem with the first objection would be its abstractness; the positivism Gramsci opposed was positivism in the historial form known to him, namely, as the attempt to model all knowledge on the physical sciences *when the latter are conceived in terms of their distinctive features* (stemming from predictiveness, exact laws, and quantification). If one takes these as special features resulting from a deeper characteristic applied to a special situation, and if one interprets this deeper characteristic in terms of the theory-practice synthesis, then we have a new form of positivism. One would nevertheless remain essentially a positivist if he was thereby intending to "scientificize" Marxism. Analogously, one could thereby be Marxianizing science, which is perhaps Gramsci's attitude, and this would provide him with a way out of the second objection above. A third attitude is obviously possible, and this is the interpretation I would advocate, namely, that one would thereby be attempting a dialectical synthesis of science and Marxism. This is possibly what Gramsci has in mind, and his talk of the philosophy of praxis would support such an interpretation. He would then, once again, become exposed to the second objection; it could be answered, I believe, by emphasizing the "rhetorical" aspect and nature of Gramsci's discussion of revolutionary consciousness, orthodoxy, and ideology. That is, in objecting to *Historical Materialism* that Bukharin is perhaps not being sufficiently revolutionary, orthodox, and free of ideology, Gramsci would be making an objection to which Bukharin himself and other committed Marxists would be sensitive. The criticism would be rhetorically effective because a part of the self-image of most Marxists seems to be that one should try to be as revolutionary, orthodox, and unideological as possible. I have already mentioned that in discussing this problem, Gramsci attaches certain qualifications to such a self-image, which amount to requiring judiciousness in what to accept and what to reject from the past. This qualified position would then be clearly consistent with his attempt to synthesize science and Marxism into the so-called philosophy of praxis.[54]

Such an interpretation is further supported by the above-mentioned interconnections between Gramsci's philosophy of praxis and his pedagogical and philosophical criticism, if we can interpret these as involving other traditions or elements that he is trying to synthesize. There can be little question that his philosophical criticism stems from Croce and is thus an attempt to incorporate the latter into the philosophy of praxis. In fact, as noted in Chapter 2,[55] there is no more typically Crocean doctrine than the identification of philosophy and history, presupposed in Gramsci's criticism of Bukharin, and explicitly mentioned in the statement just quoted to the effect that the philosophy of praxis represents the concrete historicizing of history and philosophy (cf. Q1426). Moreover, Gramsci was also completely aware of the importance of Croce's conception of philosophy,[56] as well as of the need to come to terms with him, in the sense of synthesizing the valuable aspects of his doctrine with those of Marx. The explicit and implicit references to Croce, even in the section of the Prison Notebooks dealing with Bukharin, are too numerous and obvious to need citation. The best illustration of Gramsci's attitude is perhaps the following passage, from the notebook dealing directly with Croce:

It is necessary that the heritage of classical German philosophy be not only inventoried, but that it be made to become again operative life; hence it is necessary to come to terms with the philosophy of Croce; that is, for us Italians, to be heirs to classical German philosophy means to be heirs to Crocean philosophy, which represents the contemporary world aspect of classical German philosophy. . . . It is necessary to come to such terms in the most extensive and profound possible manner. It would be worth while for a whole group of men to dedicate ten years of activity to a work of this kind. (Q1234–35)

It is well known, of course, as discussed in Chapter 1, that one of the longest, most developed, and best-organized of his Prison Notebooks is the one entitled "The Philosophy of Benedetto Croce" (Q1207–1362). Thus, we see that besides science and Marxism, Croceanism is a synthetic element of Gramsci's philosophy of praxis, and that the aspect being elaborated is the one most consistent with the elements taken over from science and Marx. Indeed, Croce's "identity of history and philosophy" is his way of expressing the theory-practice synthesis, whose presence Gramsci also detects in science and in Marx, in their special ways.

Finally, how can Gramsci's pedagogical criticism be made into a synthetic part of his philosophy of praxis? I believe that the assertion I mentioned to the effect that the philosophy of praxis tends to be the philosophy of the masses is Gramsci's way of coming to terms with *religion.*[57] It is his attempt to take from religion what is valuable, and to discard the rest. In fact, in a long section just preceding his critique of Bukharin in the same notebook (Q1375–96), Gramsci discusses the connections among religion, philosophy, and popular belief. For Gramsci, the essence of religion *in the secular rather than the confessional sense* is the unity of faith between a world view and a corresponding norm of conduct,[58] and when so conceived there is no reason for not calling such unity either "ideology" (in a nonpejorative sense) or "politics" (Q1378). Every philosophy that has become a cultural movement (and every philosophy must do this, by the Crocean-Gramscian identification of history and philosophy) has to face the problem of conserving the cultural unity of the social group that accepts that philosophy (Q1380). The strength of actual religions has been that "they feel acutely the necessity of the doctrinal union of the whole 'religious' mass and fight in order that the intellectually superior strata should not separate from the inferior ones" (Q1380–81). Gramsci believes that "one of the greatest weaknesses of immanentistic philosophies in general consists precisely of not having been able to create an ideological unity between the high and the low, between the 'simple ones' and the intellectuals" (Q1381). This is one of the main faults that he finds in Crocean philosophy (Q1217–19),[59] and it is obviously one of the main problems that his own philosophy of praxis is meant to solve. Thus, we see not only that Gramsci is concerned with isolating the valuable element of religion but also that he seems to find in it something – the unity of faith between world view and moral norm – that lends itself in a noneclectic manner to being incorporated into his philosophy of praxis. His pedagogical critique of Bukharin is precisely an expression of this concern.

One last problem remains with this interpretation, namely, the propriety of referring to Marx as the founder of the philosophy of praxis, when the latter is really a synthesis of scientific method, Croceanism, religion, and Marxism. I believe Gramsci could say that in this quartet Marxism is at least *primus inter pares*, so that it would be correct to say that he was Marxianizing science, Croce, and religion in a way that would not hold for the three other possibilities. Moreover, such Marxianizing is not a crass eliminative reduction, since essential elements of the three reduced entities are being retained in such a way as to exert an enriching influence on Marxism. Thus, although Gramsci's philosophy of praxis is a synthesis of science, religion, Croce, and Marx, he himself would hold that it is a *Marxian* synthesis of them. Whether he is correct in this belief, this is not the place to decide the question.[60] I believe, however, that such further investigation could change our understanding only of the character and not of the content of Gramsci's synthesis. Although this content might be augmented, the evidence here presented does establish that Marx, Croce, science, and religion are four important synthetic elements of Gramsci's philosophy of praxis, and that its central concept is that of the synthesis of theory and practice.

To summarize, Gramsci's critique of Bukharin was divided into four elements: the pedagogical criticism, that Bukharin is inconsistent in trying to be both philosophically popular and scientifically elementary, and wrong in making his starting point the criticism of technical philosophy rather than of popular belief; the philosophical criticism, that Bukharin presupposes outdated concepts of metaphysics and of philosophy; the Marxist criticism, that he is not sufficiently revolutionary, orthodox, and free of ideology; and the methodological criticism, that Bukharin's work is pseudoscientific insofar as it pretends to be scientific while he preaches and practices an untenable concept of science. Although the latter criticism is the most frequent, all four are shown to involve essential concerns of Gramsci's philosophy of praxis, respectively, secular religion, Croce's metaphilosophy, Marx, and science. Moreover, all four are shown to be synthetically integrated and not merely eclectically juxtaposed into the philosophy of praxis, the central idea being the synthesis of theory and practice.

Chapter 4

Bukharin and the theory and practice of science

Gramsci's critique of Bukharin requires the same kind of evaluation that had to be undertaken for his critique of Croce. The reasons are the same. First, an attempt should be made to balance the negativism of Gramsci's critique. Second, negative evaluations need more rigorous textual testing than positive ones. Third, we should evaluate more fully Gramsci's criticism. In fact, so far this criticism has been reconstructed primarily as an illustration of Gramsci's philosophy of science and philosophy of praxis; on a few occasions, we also saw that these illustrations were accurate descriptions of Bukharin's work. Now we should examine more systematically to what extent this is so, which will lead us to a reassessment of Bukharin's work.

PHILOSOPHICAL AND POLITICAL IMPORT OF BUKHARIN'S SOCIOLOGY

Any reassessment of Bukharin's *Historical Materialism* must be mindful of two problems that stem from viewing the book from above and from below – or, respectively, from the viewpoint of the philosophical controversy between mechanists and Deborinites and from the viewpoint of the political debates over social and economic policies. Moreover, in studying each problem one must be careful to distinguish between logical and historical connections.[1]

The controversy over mechanism concerned the intrinsic validity and Marxist character of a philosophical doctrine, widely held in Russia in the 1920s, containing elements of positivism, ontological materialism, and determinism. This mechanism was criticized by the followers of Abram Deborin, who opposed to it a doctrine containing elements of dialectics, idealism, and voluntarism. The political debates dealt with such questions as the pace of industrialization, the way to deal with farmers, and the pursuit of world revolution. Bukharin favored a generally moderate, organic, evolutionary, piecemeal approach, and he was regarded as the leader of the party's "right wing." Trotsky favored a radical, revolutionary, and voluntaristic approach and was the leader of the "left wing." Stalin first allied himself with Bukharin to defeat Trotsky, and then he proposed Trotskyite policies against Bukharin, until, in 1929, he managed to prevail over Bukharin.

The problem arises because, on the evidence of the philosophical chapters of Bukharin's *Historical Materialism*, he may plausibly be regarded as a mechanist, and because the theory of equilibrium of the book's sociological sections may plausibly be regarded as providing a theoretical foundation of the somewhat right-wing so-called New Economic Policy that prevailed from 1921 to 1929. Moreover, it so happened that the political and the philosophical controversies were both resolved in April 1929, the latter by a formal condemnation of mechanism adopted at the Second All-Union Conference of Marxist-Leninist Scientific Institutions.[2] These two coincidences – the coexistence within Bukharin's book of both mechanism and the theoretical basis of the right-wing policy, and the simultaneous defeat of both the party's right wing and mechanism in 1929 – helped generate what David Joravsky and Cohen call a "legend."[3] In this view, there was an intimate historical connection between philosophical mechanism and political conservatism. The falsity of the historical connection has been convincingly argued by Joravsky;[4] Cohen follows Joravsky and argues plausibly in support of his own thesis that although a connection between Bukharin's own sociological theory and his political program is undeniable, to emphasize this connection "obscures what was truly interesting about his *Historical Materialism*."[5] This for Cohen was Bukharin's openmindedness: "What *Historical Materialism* really illustrates is that Bukharin, like other 'seeking Marxists' of the Soviet twenties, viewed Marxism not only as the ideology of the party-state, but as a system of living ideas competitive with and alert to the accomplishments of contemporary Western thought."[6] Indeed, the epigraph in this chapter of Cohen's book is Bukharin's assertion that "it would be strange if Marxist theory eternally stood still."[7]

Cohen's interpretation is insightful and acceptable, but he does not adequately criticize the alternative view that Bukharin's political program derives from his mechanism. Primarily he discusses it (1) as originating from post-1929 Stalinist critics of Bukharin,[8] (2) as "a simplistic formulation of the relationship between his social theory and his policies,'"[9] and (3) as resting partly on the above-mentioned "legend" refuted by Joravsky.[10] It can be shown, however, that the view rests on more specific evidence, that it is not simplistic, and that it was held by such non-Stalinist thinkers as Lukács in 1923 and by Gramsci while in prison.

The view is not simplistic because it can be formulated as holding that the connection between Bukharin's mechanism and practical policies is not direct and does not merely involve logical deduction, but is instead indirect and involves partly a methodological connection. The link between mechanism and policy would be provided by his sociological theory, and then we would have two connections, the more or less logical one from sociology to policy, which no one including Cohen denies[11] (although his emphasis is elsewhere), and the more arguable methodological connection from mechanism to sociology. The thesis about the latter would state that Bukharin's sociological theory derives methodologically from his mechanism, that it results from his mechanistic methodological commitments. The thesis derives general support from the co-presence of both entities within the covers of the same book; it also derives support from the authority of Lukács, whose famous and influential review of the book contains an explicit formulation of it. Gramsci's critique of Bukharin also hints at the thesis. Thus, we cannot simply dismiss the possibility of such a methodological connection. It is necessary to examine Gramsci's critique and Lukács's review, and if their own argument fails (as I shall try to show), to make a direct examination of the two parts of Bukharin's book.

CRITICISM OF GRAMSCI

I shall begin with Gramsci's critique, since its central problem will lead directly to an appreciation of Lukács's. It was shown in Chapter 3 that although Gramsci's criticism includes objections involving pedagogical questions,[12] others involving the theory of philosophy and of metaphysics,[13] and others involving Marxist-rhetorical moves,[14] his primary criticism is methodological in that he argues that Bukharin's book is unscientific because it presupposes an untenable concept of science – the mechanist, positivist one.[15] Now, if this is to be a *relevant* objection, Gramsci must be assuming that Bukharin's erroneous concept of science invalidates his specific sociological theories, and for this invalidation to occur these theories must be the result of the erroneous concept. In other words, Gramsci's critique presupposes that the erroneous mechanist concept of science inheres in Bukharin's sociological theorizing. But Gramsci concentrates almost exclusively on the book's philosophical chapters, and on the few occasions when he discusses a specific thesis from Bukharin's sociological theory, he questions its adequacy either on substantive, evidentiary grounds,[16] or on Marxist grounds,[17] rather than on methodological grounds. This means that Gramsci is criticizing primarily the philosophy of science explicitly articulated in the philosophical sections of Bukharin's book, so that if otherwise correct, his critique invalidates Bukharin's theory of science, not his scientific practice, which is his sociological theorizing. In summary, although a methodological connection between Bukharin's mechanism and his sociology is presupposed by Gramsci, it is not demonstrated by him.

This criticism of Gramsci's critique accords, I feel, with the spirit of Gramsci's own Marxism, for one of the main concepts of his philosophy of praxis,[18] and a concept that can serve to unify all of his criticisms of Bukharin, is the synthesis of theory and practice. Moreover, for Gramsci, his philosophy-of-praxis Marxism is to be the basis for a complete world view, culture, and civilization.[19] It follows that the synthesis of theory and practice ought to apply in that particular domain of human praxis that is *criticism*. Or at least the Gramscian critic ought to apply it to his own critical practice. But how is this to be done?

To begin with, the synthesis of theory and practice cannot mean a conceptual identification of theory and practice, for such an identification would involve the failure to distinguish them, and there can be no synthesis unless there is a distinction. To be sure, the distinction ought not to be an abstract separation, but the synthesis cannot be a conceptual confusion either. Nor can the distinction by an empirical one in that certain activities such as eating, factory work, and political involvement can be classified as constituting practice once and for all, while certain others, such as thinking and philosophizing, are classified as being always theory. One could say that the distinction must be conceived as a "dialectical" one, were it not that the term is already so abused; moreover, the description could be easily criticized as mere name-dropping by a sympathetic audience, and as adding further confusion and obscurity to the problem by an unsympathetic one. I believe it is helpful to compare the theory-practice distinction to the conclusion-premise distinction in logic: Just as a proposition cannot be a conclusion except relative to some premise(s), and vice versa, so theory and practice are mutually interdefinable and simultaneously coexisting; and just as the conclusion of one argument can become a premise in another argument, and a premise in one the conclusion of another, so what is theory with respect to one activity, may become practice with respect to another. For example, thinking about social phenomena is obviously theory relative to a social action, but it may acquire the character of practice relative to a piece of philosophizing.

Applying these ideas to critical practice, we get that when we criticize a given work we ought to distinguish the theory from the practice within that work; to check the extent to which they are synthesized and not assume uncritically that they necessarily correspond; to be clear which of our criticisms refers to the theory, which to the practice, and which to the synthesis; to be careful not to ground our criticism of the theory (per se) on evidence from the practice, and criticism of the practice (per se) on evidence from the theory.

Gramsci's pedagogical critique of Bukharin's book refers partly to his philosophizing considered as practice relative to the "theoretical" effort at a philosophical popularization; it is then sound criticism of the synthesis of these two aspects of Bukharin's work. Gramsci also criticizes Bukharin's sociological practice relative to the "theoretical" aim of writing an elementary scientific textbook; the fault here stems from the impropriety of giving a serene exposition of a controversial doctrine, and this would also be a fault in the synthesis of theory and practice.

What about Gramsci's philosophical criticism? Here some elements of Bukharin's practice are his dogmatic, simplistic approach and his materialism; thus his practice is infected with what Gramsci considers metaphysics. But, in theory, Bukharin is opposed to metaphysics because he equates it with speculative idealism. Thus we have a lack of correspondence.

Since Bukharin is utterly ignorant of Gramsci's Crocean, historicist theory of philosophy (the "identity" of history and philosophy), the question cannot even arise as to whether Bukharin's "philosophical" theory and practice correspond. But the question the Gramscian critic should ask is, Does Bukharin's "philosophical" practice in fact correspond to Crocean theory; that is, do those aspects of Bukharin's work that are practice relative to the historicist conception of philosophy correspond to it? If we do not ask this question we run the risk of grounding our criticism of practice on evidence from theory, which in this case amounts to concluding that Bukharin could not, in fact, have accomplished something possessing the formal characteristics of concrete (historical) philosophy, merely because he was not consciously aware of this concept. Here I do not think it can be denied that Bukharin's attempt to combine metaphysical materialism with a sociological theory is an attempt at philosophy-history synthesis in the Crocean sense. It follows that Bukharin's practice is Crocean!

One should not be misled by this conclusion. To say that Bukharin's practice in the book as a whole possesses the formal features of concrete philosophy is not to say that the philosophy he is trying to concretize is the one that Gramsci would want to concretize, any more than Gramsci's would be the same as Croce's speculative idealism. But just as Gramsci could recognize the formal character of Croce's efforts, there is no sound reason for his not formally recognizing Bukharin's efforts in this direction. It would also be a mistake to think that a recognition of effort is an attribution of success. As a matter of fact, I think it is Gramsci himself who somewhat uncritically makes this equation when he acts as if Bukharin's sociological theorizing has been successfully criticized once his philosophical, metaphysical, and abstract methodological views have been refuted. I shall say more about this when I comment on Gramsci's methodological criticism, but first let us turn to his Marxist-rhetorical criticism, which is easier to deal with.

Gramsci's Marxist-rhetorical criticism argues that there is not as much correspondence as there could be between Bukharin's theoretical consciousness of being a Marxist, and his practical acceptance of a conservative traditional element from the past, namely, metaphysical materialism. Moreover, his practical denial of the self-sufficiency of Marxism makes him fall short of his theoretical aim; and so does his failure to take seriously the central Marxian dictum about the transition from the kingdom of necessity of that of freedom.

We now come to Gramsci's all-important methodological criticism. The situation is complicated. It looks as if Gramsci is criticizing Bukharin's scientific practice, in the sense of finding fault with certain things that Bukharin does, in the light of a number of methodological principles. For example, it is *part* of what Bukharin presumably does, to model his approach uncritically on the physical sciences, to engage in fallacious reasoning, to misunderstand several concepts he uses, to ignore previous contributions, to set up straw men, and to be unfair to his opponents.[20] These seem to be "deeds," by contrast, for example, to Bukharin's having allegedly claimed that scientific progress is causally determined by scientific instruments, which Gramsci attempts to refute, though somewhat irrelevantly and unfairly.[21] If we look at the context in which Bukharin does those methodologically objectionable things, however, this very context as considered by Gramsci himself is usually not one where Bukharin is engaged in sociological analysis (his scientific practice, as it were). In fact, the example of fallacious reasoning comes from Bukharin's critique of Stammler's alleged teleologism;[22] examples of misunderstandings are the idealistic concept of identity of content and form, the Kantian concept of teleology, and the *general* concept of "matter";[23] the violations of the straw-man and fairness principles are illustrated primarily with Bukharin's general attitude toward past philosophers.[24] We have to conclude that in his methodological criticism, Gramsci is referring not really to Bukharin's scientific practice but primarily to his theory of science. According to the principle of critical methodology stipulated above, one cannot thereby conclude that Bukharin's scientific practice is as inadequate as his philosophy of science is. It *may* be, but its inadequacy is not demonstrated by the inadequacy of the theory, unless we presuppose a synthesis of theory and practice, which is one of the very things we are trying to determine. Moreover, the evidence so far available from other aspects of Bukharin's theory and practice (pedagogical, "metaphysical," and Marxist) indicates that the synthesis is unlikely to have occurred. This means that the criticism of Bukharin's scientific practice (his sociological theory) remains to be done. Before turning to this task, I shall examine Lukács's review of the book, because he was acutely aware of this problem of concretizing one's methodological criticism, although as we shall see he failed to solve it.

CRITICISM OF LUKÁCS

Lukács's critique of Bukharin's book originally appeared in a German journal a few years after the book itself and was published in English by the *New Left Review* in 1966.[25] Since it is basically a review (eight pages long), and since it explicitly asserts that its scope prevents it from considering many of the book's details,[26] I shall concentrate on its main point, "demonstration of the methodological source of the [book's] error,"[27] but I shall briefly summarize the rest for the sake of perspective.

Lukács holds that "the book admirably fulfills its purpose as a textbook,"[28] judging that it brings together "into a unified, systematic summary that is more or less Marxist all the significant problems of Marxism, and further, that the presentation is generally clear and easily understood."[29] We shall see, however, that Lukács's emphasis is on the book's being rather "less" than "more" Marxist.

As a popularization, Lukács faults the book for containing too many misleading oversimplifications, which he finds to be especially objectionable since Bukharin falls short of the standard "reached by Plekhanov and Mehring,"[30] whose works show how popular presentations are compatible with basic accuracy.[31]

From the point of view of Marxism, Lukács finds the book to be basically un-Marxist because of its materialism and because of its determinism. The former "is suspiciously close to what Marx aptly called bourgeois materialism,"[32] and the book "therefore frequently obscures the specific feature of Marxism: that *all economic or 'sociological' phenomena derive from the social relations of men to one another.*"[33] Against Bukharin's determinism, Lukács gives quotations from Marx, Engels, and Lenin that contradict it, and adds that they are quoted not so much as a refuting argument from authority as because "our purpose is to point out that Bukharin's theoretical aim is different from that of the great tradition of historical materialism."[34]

Lukács's central criticism is directed at Bukharin's substantive thesis that technological developments causally determine social ones and at his sociological methodology.[35] It is not clear exactly what Lukács means by the latter (and accordingly I shall soon try to clarify it), but it is clear that he regards it as the method responsible for Bukharin's technological determinism. Since Lukács holds that this technologism is completely wrong (and this is perhaps the review's most interesting argument), he concludes that Bukharin's methodology must be wrong.

The general form of Lukács's methodological criticism is both interesting and valid. I have discussed this type of argument in other works and I have underscored its importance both for the history of science[36] and for the philosophy of science.[37] What is involved is, first, a distinction between substantive results and methodological procedure; second, a demonstration of the serious factual inaccuracy of a substantive thesis conducted by a consideration of the relevant evidence; third, the identification or description of a method actually used in the work under criticism; fourth, a claim that this method led to the erroneous substantive thesis; fifth, a conclusion that this method is objectionable.

Unfortunately, Lukács's argument fails, primarily at the fourth step, but the third step is also problematic; that fourth step is not only unsupported and merely asserted but contradicts other methodological remarks he makes.

Lukács's refutation of technological determinism (second step) may be accepted here for the sake of the present discussion. He argues that it inverts the true causal connection, which is that socioeconomic relations among men tend to determine technological developments. He is careful to point out that he is denying neither the great importance of technology nor the causal interdependence of it and socioeconomic structure, but merely the historical and methodological primacy of technology. Lukács's argument proceeds first by pointing out that Bukharin's objection to Cunow's naturalism applies to his own technologism.[38] Cunow had held that natural conditions, such as the presence of certain raw materials, causally determine technological development, and Bukharin objected that in order to become raw materials, the natural resources must become the subject of labor, and for the latter to happen there must be a corresponding technology available, so that the influence of nature is itself the result of technological developments. Second, Lukács argues that the transition from antiquity to the Middle Ages cannot be explained by technological determinism, because ancient society was superior in technology but inferior in the organization of labor as compared to medieval society, because "one of the essential co-determinate causes of the breakdown of classical society was, of course, its inability to support the social basis of its productive organization, the wasteful exploitation of inexhaustible slave material,"[39] and because "medieval social organization arose in quite opposite circumstances (shortage of labor, etc.)."[40] Lukács's third argument is that technological determinism could not even explain the transition from feudalism to modern society, since as Marx himself stresses, the change from guild production to manufacture involved no change in technology but mainly one in the division of labor, which is the primary precondition for the creation of a mass market and the invention of new machines.

For Lukács, Bukharin's false substantive thesis is due to his false methodology. A minor problem is that it is not too clear exactly what constitutes such methodology. Lukács describes it variously as fetishism, undissolved quiddity, false objectivity,[41] false naturalism,[42] "attempt to make a 'science' out of the dialectic,"[43] search for a general sociology, natural-scientific approach, preoccupation with the natural sciences,[44] bias toward the natural sciences.[45] Perhaps a clarification can be obtained from Lukács's assertions of his methodological explanation of Bukharin's error. Because I shall argue that Lukács does not support his explanation, it is important to establish that *he does assert it:*

The discussion of the role of technique in social development highlights these remnants of undissolved quiddity [*unaufgelöster Dinghaftlichkeit*] and false objectivity.[46]

Bukharin's solution is typical of his false methodology. . . . The basically incorrect theory of the primacy of technique which we have analyzed is merely the substantive result of Bukharin's attempt to create a general sociology. It is not an accidental oversight, but the necessary consequence of superficially examined premises.[47]

We could hardly ask for a more explicit assertion of the fourth step in the scheme sketched above. But I am able to find no *argument* that Bukharin erred *because* of this methodology. What I find instead is an *independent* argument that one aspect of this methodology is itself erroneous, and a series of assertions that Bukharin's scientific practice and theory of science *do not* correspond. It is incredible to have on one and the same page[48] such mutually inconsistent sets of claims, the method-explanation just quoted, and the following disclaimers:

His leanings towards the natural sciences and his frequently acute dialectical instinct are here inevitably in contradiction . . . his applications of his theory are often much better than the theory itself. . . . It is fortunate that he usually forgets his theoretical presuppositions in his concrete analyses . . . he fortunately forgets his theory in concrete analyses, with the result that the conclusions are frequently very interesting in defiance of his starting point.[49]

In view of these admissions that Bukharin's substantive results are frequently valuable in spite of his methodological presuppositions, and in view of the lack of recognizable argument that his erroneous technologism was due to his methodology, the proper conclusion to draw would be the exact denial of the method-explanation Lukács's argument needs.

As mentioned, we do have independent or "abstract" arguments for the untenability of various methodological views held by Bukharin. But this means that we have substantive criticism of a substantive thesis (technologism) and separate criticism of various methodological views. In other words, in spite of his suggestiveness, Lukács does not give us concrete methodological criticism, does not criticize Bukharin's scientific practice in the light of methodological principles, but rather gives scientific criticism of scientific practice, and theoretical (or abstract) criticism of Bukharin's theory of science. This is fine, except we are not then entitled to believe that we have thereby given a general criticism of his practice, that we have refuted his sociology in general. Accepting Lukács's substantive argument, we have merely the refutation of *one* of Bukarin's sociological theses.

The best example of Lukács's abstract criticism of Bukharin's methodology concerns the latter's assertion that "prediction is possible in the social sciences *just as it is in the natural sciences*,"[50] although "at the moment we are unable to predict the point in time when this or that phenomenon will appear . . . because we are still not sufficiently informed of the laws of social development which are statistical in nature. We cannot tell the speed of social processes, but we know their direction."[51] Lukács objects that the impossibility of prediction is intrinsic, because "*of the objective, qualitative difference in the object itself.*"[52] Even if Lukács is right, this shows only that the quoted assertion in Bukharin's theory of science is wrong, not that any of his substantive theses are. It follows that there is a need to examine Bukharin's sociology in a more concrete way, and to this I now turn.

MECHANISM AND SOCIOLOGY IN BUKHARIN

If one looks in Bukharin's *Historical Materialism: A System of Sociology* for evidence of anything that might be labeled "mechanism," one will find the following: In the first chapter is a rejection of teleological explanation and an interpretation of causal explanation as the only scientific one. Bukharin claims that "the conception of purpose, of planfulness, etc., is absolutely inapplicable to the world as a whole, and that the natural law of phenomena is not a teleological natural law" (p. 22);[53] he is afraid that "Teleology (the doctrine of purpose) leads straight into Theology (the doctrine of God)" (p. 25). For him "both in nature and in society there exists objectively (i.e., regardless of whether we wish it or not, whether we are conscious of it or not) a law of nature that is causal in character . . . this mode of explanation is the sole explanation that is scientific" (pp. 30–31).

In the second chapter is a rejection of free will and a plea for determinism. Bukharin thinks that "at bottom, people completely contradict in their actions the theory of the freedom of the will" (p. 35); that "strictly speaking . . . there are no 'accidental,' i.e., causeless phenomena" (p. 44); and that "prediction is possible in the domain of the social sciences as well as in that of the natural sciences" (p. 48).

In the third chapter is a rejection of idealism in favor of materialism. First, ontologically speaking, "mind cannot exist without matter, while matter may very well exist without mind; matter existed before mind; mind is a special property of matter organized in a special manner" (p. 55). Moreover, epistemologically speaking, "materialism is . . . in a position to explain the phenomena of 'mental life' in society, which idealism cannot" (p. 62).

In the same chapter there is also an attempt "to transcribe the 'mystical' (as Marx put it) language of the Hegelian dialectics into the language of modern mechanics" (p. 75). Bukharin holds that, generally speaking, "in the first place . . . the dialectic method of interpretation demands that all phenomena be considered in their indissoluble relations; in the second place, that they be considered in their state of motion" (p. 67). He notes that "Hegel said: 'Contradiction is the power that moves things' " (p. 73) and comments that "there is no doubt of the correctness of this law" (*ibid.*), but he interprets it in terms of the concept of equilibrium: Motion becomes a loss of equilibrium, contradiction becomes a "disturbance of equilibrium" (*ibid.*), social development becomes "equilibrium in *flux*" (p. 74), and dialectical development becomes a process whose form is: "in the first place, the condition of equilibrium; in the second place, a disturbance of this equilibrium; in the third place, the reestablishment of equilibrium of a *new* basis" (p. 74). The last process is supposedly a demystified version of Hegel's movement from a thesis to an antithesis and then to a synthesis (pp. 74–75). Analogously, the dialectical law about "quantity becoming quality" is reinterpreted in terms of the "theory of sudden changes" (p. 79) in physics: "The transformation of quantity into quality is one of the fundamental laws in the motion of matter; it may be traced literally at every step both in nature and society" (p. 80). In fact, "revolutions in society are of the same character as the violent changes in nature. They do not suddenly 'fall from the sky.' They are prepared by the entire preceding course of development, as the boiling of water is prepared by the preceding process of heating or as the explosion of a steam-boiler is prepared by the increasing pressure of the steam against its walls" (p. 82).

Thus, there is no doubt that the philosophical chapters of Bukharin's book contain elements of antiteleologism, determinism, materialism, and mechanized dialectic. To see whether these are inherent in his sociological theorizing, let us examine his main sociological doctrines.

The central thesis of the fourth chapter is one that might be labeled "sociologism"; it stresses the primacy of society over the individual and the irreducibility of social phenomena to psychological ones. Bukharin is explicit "that society is not a mere aggregate of persons, that it is more than their sum, that their grouping and definite 'disposition' (Marx calls it their 'distribution') in the labor process amounts to something new, something greater than their 'sum' or 'aggregate'" (pp. 94–95). For example, "the price is a social phenomena, a social 'resultant,' and product of the mutual interactions of persons. The price is not an average of the guesses, nor does it in every case approximate the individual guesses, for the individual guesses are a personal matter, concerning one man only, existing only in his mind, while the actual price is something that influences all; it is an independent fact which all must count on; an objective fact though it be immaterial . . . the price, in other words is something new, something that leads its own social life, is independent more or less of individual persons, although it is created by them" (p. 95). Indeed, "individual men are inconceivable outside of society, without society. Nor can we imagine society's having been established by the various persons, living, as it were, in their 'natural state,' coming together and uniting in order to form a society" *(ibid.)*; rather, "the individual draws his motives from the generality, the social environment; the conditions under which the social environment develops provide the limits for the individual's activity; the individual's rôle is determined by social conditions" (p. 101). Even in cases of exceptionally situated individuals like generals and kings, or exceptionally influential great leaders, "it is self-evident that in all these cases society has a certain influence, and that it is impossible to 'develop' except on the basis of this influence within which the social (class, group, general) demand is felt" (p. 99).

These ideas are perhaps not surprising for a work attempting to outline a system of sociology. There is no textual evidence, however, that Bukharin is trying to derive them from his "philosophical mechanism," and there is no logical way of accomplishing the derivation. Indeed, their general content and tenor point in a direction incompatible with what "mechanist" thinkers usually believe. For example, given Bukharin's determinism, there is no more reason to stress the causal determination of the individual by the social, as Bukharin does, than to stress the converse influence, which could be formulated in equally deterministic terms. If anything, from his ontological materialism, the ontological primacy of the individual over society would seem a more likely inference than Bukharin's primacy of society. Moreover, it does not sound very materialistic to say that the price is "an objective fact though it be immaterial" (p. 95), that it exerts a causal influence, and that it has a life of its own. Finally, there seems to be no connection at all between Bukharin's antiteleologism and mechanized dialectic and the sociologism of his fourth chapter.

In the chapter on the equilibrium between society and nature, as Lukács recognized, Bukharin advocates a view that may be called "technologism." The argument is as follows: First, "we already know that in any system the cause of alterations in the system must be sought in its relations with its environment; also, that the fundamental direction of growth (progress, rest, or destruction of the system), depends precisely on what the relation is between the given system and its environment" (p. 107). These two points are obviously derived from Bukharin's general interpretation of the dialectical method, which, as noted, contained two elements: the interrelatedness of all phenomena, and the dynamic point of view. Here, he seeks the cause outside the system because of his commitment to interrelatedness, and he focuses on *alterations* as the phenomena to be explained because of his dynamicism. So far, then, we have a connection with his "philosophical mechanism." Note, however, that the domain of actual sociological theorizing has barely been entered. This is done in the next step of Bukharin's argument.

The important point in this step is that "one part of nature, *external* nature, the part that we are calling the 'environment,' is opposed to another part, which is human society. And the form of contact between these two parts of a single whole is the process of human labor" (p. 108). For Bukharin, "the 'first cause' of social evolution is to be found precisely here" (p. 110). In particular, "the growth of society is determined by the yield or *productivity of social labor* . . . the productivity of labor is a precise measure of the 'balance' between society and nature; it is a measure of the mutual interaction between the environment and the system by which the position of the system within the environment is determined, and an alteration of which will indicate inevitable changes throughout the internal life of society" (p. 113). Next, it is important to note that "the expenditure of labor consists of two components: the labor that is crystallized and included in the instruments of production, and the 'living' labor, i.e., the direct expenditure of working energy. . . . Taken together, these two quantities constitute what we call the *material productive forces of society"* (p. 115). Finally, "we may also glance a little deeper; we may go so far as to say that the instruments of production determine even the nature of the worker. . . . We may therefore definitely state that the system of social instruments of labor, i.e., the technology of a certain society, is a precise material indicator of the relation between the society and nature" (pp. 115–16). This argument from external cause to labor, to productivity, to material productive forces, to technology or instruments of labor, may ultimately be accepted or may be rejected, although I have endeavored to reconstruct it in such a way that it has some plausibility and there is nothing very obviously wrong with it. However, it is clear that the crucial step, from the existence of two productive forces – instruments and workers – to the primacy of instruments (technology) is not grounded by Bukharin on any elements of his "philosophical mechanism," nor would it be sanctioned by them. For example, from the point of determinism, it is obviously undetermined whether instruments or workers are primary as long as there are no exceptions to the principle of causality; one may even say that to decide the question of primacy is a way of adopting a methodologically indeterminist position, since it is tantamount to a decision not to worry about the explanation of the primary phenomenon. Similarly, from a materialist viewpoint it is immaterial whether instruments ultimately determine workers or vice versa, since for materialism they are equally material entities. On the other hand, Bukharin's antiteleologism and his interpretation of the laws of dialectical evolution (contradiction and quantity-quality) do not seem to have anything to do with the present argument. In summary, though Bukharin's technologism may "sound" mechanist because it holds that machines are more important than people for social evolution, it is not mechanist in the more precise sense of deriving from that set of doctrines constituting his "philosophical mechanism."

The next chapter, on the equilibrium between the elements of society, is the longest and most complex one. Here we find his celebrated theory of equilibrium proper. Here we have an account of the interconnections and interactions among technology, economy, politics, law, science, religion, philosophy, and art. The central thesis is that "there is no doubt of the general connection between social phenomena, of the 'adaptation' of certain social phenomena to others, in other words, of the existence of a certain equilibrium within society between its elements, its component parts, between the various forms of social phenomena" (p. 132).

Bukharin begins with a discussion of the relation between technology and economy. We have seen that by technology he means the system of instruments of production. Now it emerges that by economy he understands the system of production relations among men (pp. 143, 146, 148). These relations are of two types: work relations and class relations (pp. 136, 143). Both are determined by the available instruments. In short, "the combinations of the instruments of labor (the social technology) are the deciding factor in the combinations and relations of men, i.e., in social economy" (p. 14). In other words, they determine "the *type of worker*, the degree of his skill, and also the working relation, the productive conditions . . . the division of labor" (p. 137); moreover, "this principle also holds good in such production relations as are simultaneously class relations" (p. 147).

Bukharin's supporting argument is based primarily on comparison and contrast between ancient society and modern society, and its details need not concern us here. The important point for our analysis is to realize that, although the economic structure is based on the technological system, it does not thereby become for Bukharin part of the superstructure but remains an element of the base. This is shown when, in analyzing the various aspects of the superstructure (pp. 150–208), Bukharin traces them to the "productive forces" in general or somewhat indifferently to technology or economy. Moreover, he explicitly makes the point at the end of his discussion of the technology-economy connection when he asserts that "the totality of the production relations, therefore, is the *economic structure of society*, or *its mode of production*. This is the human labor apparatus of society, its 'real basis' " (p. 148). This fact is important because it is a refinement in his equilibrium theory that cannot be derived from any doctrines of his "philosophical mechanism."

Other refinements in his theory of the superstructure are similarly unconnected with mechanism. For example, "political superstructure is a complicated thing, consisting of different elements, which are inter-related. On the whole this structure is determined by the class outline of society, a structure which in turn depends on the productive forces, i.e., on the social technology" (p. 155). But whereas "certain of these elements are directly dependent on technology ('the art of war'), others depend on the class character of society (its economy), as well as on the technology of the super-structure itself ('army management')" *(ibid.)*. Whether this is true or false, justifiable or not, it is clear that mechanism is unhelpful in arriving at it. Or consider Bukharin's view of science, where he first cautions us that "the connection between the state of science and the productive forces of society is of manifold nature. This connection must be studied from a number of angles, for it is not as simple as may first appear. We shall therefore have to turn our attention, in our consideration of science, to its technique, its special organization of work, its content, its method (or alleged method), for all these components interact mutually and produce the level of the given science at a given time" (p. 164). Later, when he sum-marizes his conclusion, he does so with no fewer than five prop-ositions (p. 169). The pattern is clear: Not only does the super-structure consist of a multiplicity of elements, interacting with the two distinct elements of the base, but each main superstructural element consists of a multiplicity of analogously interacting sub-elements. This may strike one as interesting or "baroque," as ju-dicious or as inappropriate for a "popular textbook," but there is little trace of "mechanism," which, if anything, tends to be sim-plistic. Bukharin's most articulate view is perhaps his account of art, where he distinguishes six different aspects of that phenomenon (pp. 189–203), discusses eight different causal relations in which it is involved (pp. 190–95), and then adds that "they do not at all exhaust the subject" (p. 195).

Another series of complications derives from the mutual inter-actions of some of the main superstructural elements. For example, although "in the last analysis" religion results from the productive forces, "its nucleus is the reflection of the socio-political order of society" (p. 179), and hence it is presumably a superstructure of second degree, a superstructural element of another superstructural element. A similar relationship holds between philosophy and sci-ence, according to Bukharin. For him philosophy is something like the science of science (pp. 180–81), so that "philosophy might therefore be said to occupy the highest place in the human spirit and it is more difficult to trace its earthly and material origin than in the case of other subjects. . . . Inevitably we here encounter a complicated form of such dependence, for philosophy does not issue forth directly from technology, being separated from the latter by a number of links" (p. 181).

Finally, Bukharin's account of law and morality is worse than unconnected with "mechanism"; it is likely to conflict with it, specifically with his anti-teleologism and his determinist denial of free will. Speaking of legal and moral rules, he says that "in general, these rules indicate the line of conduct conducive to a preservation of the society, class, or group in question, and requiring the subordination of the individual to the interests of the group. These norms are therefore *conditions of equilibrium* for holding together the internal contradictions of human social systems" (pp. 157–58).

The most significant complication, and the least "mechanist" one, occurs in Bukharin's section on "The Significance of the Superstructure." Here he emphasizes that "the superstructure, growing out of the economic conditions and the productive forces determining these conditions, in its turn, exerts an influence on the latter, favoring or retarding their growth. But, in either case, there is no doubt of this reverse process. In other words: *a constant process of mutual cause and effect is in operation between the various categories of social phenomena.* Cause and effect change place" (p. 228). In short, what Bukharin is outlining is really a "synthetic conception of social life" (p. 227), a unified view of social evolution (p.229). I have not tried here to evaluate its intrinsic soundness, although it appears rather sophisticated and cannot be summarily dismissed as "vulgar Marxism." Instead I have studied this view's relation to the mechanism identifiable in some of the book's philosophical chapters. The best that can be said about this relation is that it is one of logical and methodological *independence;* the worst, that it is one of incompatibility from the point of view of teleologism.

In the next chapter, entitled "Disturbance and Readjustment of Social Equilibrium," Bukharin presents his theory of revolution, change, and progress. Social change in general is for him transition from one state of equilibrium to another. This can happen in two ways: "that of a gradual adaptation of the various elements in the social whole (evolution), and that of violent upheaval (revolution)" (p. 243). Generally speaking, revolution results from a collision between the two elements of the base, the technology or productive forces, and the economy or production relations (p. 244). But since, for example, the small artisan disappeared without revolution, "it therefore obviously follows that *not every conflict between the productive forces and the production relations results in revolution*" (p. 245). The problem is to determine the relevant kinds of conflicts and of production relations by analyzing "how revolutions have actually operated" (p. 245). When this is done, it emerges that "revolution therefore occurs when there is an outright conflict between the increased productive forces, which can no longer be housed within the envelope of the production relations, and [that] which constitutes the fundamental web of these production relations, i.e., property relations, ownership in the instruments of production" (p. 248). If the productive forces *can* develop without a change in property relations, then we have evolution; if they cannot so develop, and the production relations nevertheless cannot be changed, then we have stagnation or decay (p. 249).

So much for the *cause* of revolution. Next, Bukharin discusses its *phases*. First, "the necessary condition for revolution is . . . a revolutionizing of the consciousness of the new class, an ideological revolution in the class that is to serve as the grave-digger of the old society" (p. 255). Then, "the second phase of revolution is *political revolution*, i.e., the seizing of power by the new class. The revolutionary psychology of the new class becomes action" (p. 257). After this, "the third stage of revolution is the *economic revolution.* The new class, now in power, makes use of its power as a lever for economic upheaval, breaks up the production relations of the old type and begins to erect new relations which have been maturing in the womb of the old order, and *in contradiction* with that order" (p. 259). Finally, "the fourth (last) phase of revolution is the *technical revolution.* A new social equilibrium having been attained, i.e., a new and durable envelope of production relations having been created, capable of serving as an evolutionary form of the productive forces, an accelerated evolution of these forces now sets in. . . . New tools are introduced, a new technical foundation is created. . . . Now a 'normal,' 'organic' period in the evolution of the new social form sets in" (pp. 261–62).

All this is well and good, in the sense that it is clear and obviously reminiscent of the *Communist Manifesto*. But as Bukharin himself goes on to stress, what this means is that the revolutionary process "passes through a number of phases, *beginning* with ideology, *ending* in technique, a sort of reverse order, as it were" (p. 262). He repeats this several times. On the next page he states that "we are . . . dealing with things in the reverse order. The analysis is not proceeding from economy to politics, but from politics to economy" (p. 263). And on the page after that, after reviewing how a revolution begins and how it ends, he says that "between this begining and this ending lies the reverse order in *the influence of the superstructures*" (p. 264). Bukharin also stresses that "this is the *peculiarity of the transition period*" (*ibid.*), and he is right that this feature is not present in his theory of equilibrium. However, the unmistakable conclusion for *us* to draw in the present context is that we have here a contradiction of his materialism. Of course, all that this means is that the doctrine of reducing "mind" to "matter," though present in the third chapter, does not inhere in his discussions of the structure of revolution (sixth chapter). That is, his philosophical theory and his scientific practice are in conflict in this regard.

Another instance of the same conflict is Bukharin's theory of progress, in the sense of social *growth*. He distinguishes two kinds: material progress and mental progress. The essential characteristic of material progress is that "as the productive forces grow, more and more labor is applied in the production of instruments of production. With the aid of these constantly increasing instruments of production, which are a part of the social *technique*, a much smaller part of the work than formerly will produce a much greater quantity of useful products of all kinds" (p. 269). Then Bukharin pursues an interesting analogy between this and mental progress. He asserts that past "paintings, for the painter, are an instrument of production" (p. 271), that a "book is a congealed ideology, an instrument of ideological production" *(ibid.)*, and that the same is true of such things as laboratories, museums, libraries, and botanical and zoological gardens. His conclusion is that "the accumulation of mental culture is therefore not only an accumulation of psychological and ideological elements in the minds of men, but also an accumulation of things" (p. 272).

Now, in a sense this is a "materialist" theory of *mental* progress, and so it might be taken to exhibit Bukharin's "mechanism." But this materialism is at the level of the *definition* of a social phenomenon, rather than the explanation of its occurrence. In other words, Bukharin is saying that mental or cultural progress can be conceived as being essentially an accumulation of (material) instruments of mental production, or perhaps, less strongly, that mental progress can be so "measured" or correlated. In any case, once attention has been called to such a phenomenon of accumulation, it is obvious that the first step in its explanation will be in "mental" terms: laboratories and libraries are (normally) built for "ideological" reasons. Of course, for Bukharin "in the last analysis" these ideological reasons are themselves the result of the technical-economic base. But this further explanation would not undo the first, nor would the first (tracing the accumulation to mental elements) be inadequate in the absence of the second. It follows that this phenomenon of accumulation is causally determined by "mind," hence, as far as it is concerned, "idealism" is right and "materialism" wrong. Bukharin himself seems to recognize this when, in the title of this section, he speaks of "the materialization of social phenomena" (p. 269), since materialization is a process whereby "matter" is created out of mind, spirit, or other nonmaterial entity. In short, Bukharin seems here an "idealist."

The last chapter deals with classes and class struggles. Given the topic, it is perhaps not surprising that we find an emphasis on nonmechanist elements. Three aspects in particular seem to be a little hard to reconcile with determinism or materialism; they involve, respectively, humanistic, social, and mentalistic themes.

Bukharin begins by stating that "we have already seen the important function of the classes in the evolution of human society" (p. 276). This was seen when, in his discussion of the basic contradiction causing revolution, he argued that "since *men* make history, the conflict between the productive forces and the production relations will not find its expression in an attack made by dead machines, *things*, on men, which would be a monstrous and ridiculous assumption. Obviously, the evolution of the productive forces places *men* in a position of outright opposed situations, and the conflict . . . will find its expression in a conflict *between men*, between *classes*" (p. 254) The same point is repeated at the end of the chapter, in a discussion of classes as an instrument of social transformation, when he notes that "the structure of society changes *through* men and not outside of men; the production relations are as much a product of human struggle and of human activity as are flax or linen" (p. 308).

The emphasis on the social as opposed to the material is found in his analysis of the differences among class, caste, and vocation, and of the relation between class struggle and state power. In the former, Bukharin first points out that the difference in the vocation of a metal turner and a mason involves a difference in their relations to things, the one toward metal, the other toward stone. "Yet the essence of the matter is not in the *thing*, for vocation is simultaneously a social relation. . . . However different these relations [to things] may be, they are all subsidiary to the differences that prevail in the principal phase: *the differences between the work of those who command and those who obey*" (pp. 281–82). In his account of the nature of the state, Bukharin objects to the anarchist argument that even a communist society would be a state since the characteristic feature of the latter is a centralized administration. He clarifies that "the 'essence' of the state is not in the *thing* but in the *social* relation; not in the centralized administration as such, but in the *class envelope* of the centralized administration . . . so centralization *per se* by no means necessarily signifies a state organization" (p. 303).

Finally, Bukharin's stress on consciousness partly derives from Marx's distinction between a "class in itself" and a "class for itself" (pp. 292–93). The account begins with the claim that "the most primitive and general expression of class interest is the *effort of the classes to increase their share in the distribution of the total mass of products*" (p. 285). This is then distinguished from class struggle: "*A class interest arises when it places one class in opposition to another. The class struggle arises when it throws one class into active conflict with the other*" (p. 297). He concludes that "class struggle, therefore, in the true sense, develops only at a specific stage in the evolution of class society" (p. 297), namely when the class has acquired consciousness of its class interest. Nevertheless, it remains true for him that the history of all hitherto existing society is the history of class struggles, primarily because "the ruling classes . . . are waging the class struggle *unceasingly*. For the existence of the state organization proves that the ruling class has 'constituted' itself as a class *for itself* . . . this implies a complete consciousness of the fundamental interests of this class" (pp. 301–2). Secondarily, the class struggle of the oppressed classes, even when not explicitly present, may be said to be developing, for "let us not forget that dialectics conceives of everything as in course of *motion,* evolution" (p. 301).

In summary, it is possible to find in Bukharin's *Historical Materialism* a group of philosophical theses of a mechanistic character. They occur in the first three chapters and may be described as antiteleologism, determinism, metaphysical determinism, and a version of dialectic inspired by modern physical theory. This philosophical mechanism is somewhat naive and implausible, and may be regarded as having been effectively criticized by Gramsci and Lukács. On the other hand, the main elements of Bukharin's system of sociology are a socially oriented theory of human nature, a technology-oriented theory of interaction between nature and society, an equilibrium-oriented theory of social structure, an activist-oriented theory of revolution, and a subjectivist-oriented theory of class struggle. These sociological doctrines are usually sophisticated, plausible, and almost completely independent of, or incompatible with, his philosophical mechanism. The only traces of mechanism involve his version of dialectic, which, though inspired from mechanical physical theories, is the least mechanist element of his philosophic theory; in fact, its mechanism is merely a manner of speaking. What follows from this divergence between philosophical theory and sociological practice is that Bukharin's sociology does not derive from his mechanism and hence is unaffected by the inadequacy of the latter. It also follows that the favorable intuitive judgments of contemporary sociologists about Bukharin's sociological theories are thereby vindicated.[54]

DIALECTIC IN BUKHARIN

A new problem now arises. If Bukharin's philosophical theory and his sociological practice do not correspond, is there a philosophy that may be inherent in his practice, of which he was not conscious? For my results so far may seem primarily negative, and it would be desirable to put forth a more constructive interpretation. Moreover, to do so is suggested, or perhaps even demanded, by the earlier discussion of the synthesis of theory and practice. There I noted that this synthesis is explicitly regarded by Gramsci as an essential element of Marxism and argued that he failed to put to use this idea in his own critical practice. It was in the context of that failure that I embarked on the foregoing analysis of Bukharin's work, noting that to accept the idea of such a synthesis does not mean to assume uncritically that the synthesis is necessarily actualized on a given occasion. This is especially true in a situation, as here, where it is natural to understand "theory" as the explicit reflections on scientific knowledge and method in general, and "practice" as the study of social phenomena. My analysis required the abandonment of a naive, absolutist (mechanist?) conception of theory and practice, and the adoption of a contextual, relativist (dialectical?) concept, so as to realize that in this inquiry theory and practice did not refer to the same things as they did in, for example, Cohen's investigations,[55] where theory denoted sociology, and practice denoted social and political action. My account so far, however, must be regarded as at best a first approximation. "Theory" must now be conceived as the philosophy *implicit* in scientific practice, as the general, mostly unconscious pattern that characterizes it. We cannot *now* uncritically assume that there is no underlying pattern, no "theory" giving a structure to Bukharin's sociological system. If we can identify and characterize such a structure, we will have detected a "theory" that is synthesized with his practice.

Before we identify this, let us add a complication that will ultimately make it easier to detect the pattern. Given that we are now searching for the theory inherent in practice, there is no reason to limit ourselves to Bukharin's sociological theorizing. His philosophical theorizing may now be regarded as a part of his total intellectual practice (in his book). In other words, we now think of the whole book as a series of discussions on topics more or less related to social phenomena. If it has a pattern (this is the "theory" we are looking for), it may be present in the philosophical as well as the sociological chapters. If so, it will be easier to recognize. I believe there is such a pattern. It is the following.

Each chapter (even the introduction) may be regarded as a discussion of a pair of opposites, or distinction between two things, that are important to understand for building a system of sociology. Bukharin's discussion usually tries to reach a judicious (equilibrated) position, a synthesis between the two extremes.

The introduction may be regarded as a discussion of history versus theory (esp. pp. 13–15); the opposites of the other chapters are, respectively, the following: cause versus purpose; necessity versus free will; matter versus mind, and static versus dynamic approaches; the individual versus society; society versus nature; structure versus superstructure; evolution versus revolution; and oppressed versus ruling classes.

These topics are rather obvious, at least after a little reflection; the opposite nature of the members of each pair is also obvious, though the opposition is not always of the same type. In fact, the exact nature of the opposition is part of what needs to be established in a system of sociology. What is not so obvious is Bukharin's judiciousness in his resolution of the opposition. So let us examine the various cases.

The discussions of structure versus superstructure and of evolution versus revolution are clearly the most judicious. We have seen that, for Bukharin, the structure and the superstructure are in reality a *mutually* interacting system; each exerts a causal influence on the other. We have also seen that for him social change is *both* evolutionary and revolutionary, sometimes one, other times the other. What of his technological determinism in the discussion of society versus nature? Since he conceives of technology as the primary aspect of labor and regards the latter as the process of interaction between nature and society, his technologism clearly is a judicious attempt to take both into account and give each its due.

The discussion of classes may at first appear as an instance where Bukharin favors one (the oppressed classes) to the exclusion of the other (the ruling classes). But where this favoritism, this intolerance, is relevant and has a point – namely, for the present and future – it takes the form of advocating that the oppressed class (proletariat) become the ruling class. To be sure, after the *political* revolution the formerly oppressed class needs to become oppressive (dictatorship of the proletariat), but Bukharin's ideal, hope, and prediction is that as the economic and technological revolutions develop, the oppression will gradually cease, and the ruling class will actually disappear as a class. In a general way, these speculations may be regarded as a determined effort to come to terms with both sides of this opposition.

Bukharin's introductory account of history versus theory, which I have not yet discussed, admits the legitimacy of both the historical study of social phenomena and their general, systematic study. He conceives of sociology as theoretical history, dealing with "general questions, such as: what is society? On what does its growth and decay depend? What is the relation of the various groups of social phenomena (economic, legal, scientific, etc.), with each other; how is their evolution to be explained?" (p. 14). The relation of history and sociology is one of mutual interaction and benefit. In formulating general laws of social development, sociology provides history with principles for explanation: "If, for example, sociology establishes the general doctrine that the forms of government depend on the forms of economy, the historian must seek and find, in any given epoch, precisely what are the relations, and must show what is their concrete, specific expression" (*ibid.*). On the other hand, history provides sociology with a data base: "History furnishes the material for drawing sociological conclusions and making sociological generalizations, for these conclusions are not made up of whole cloth, but are derived from the actual facts of history" (*ibid.*). Incidentally, it is clear that Bukharin's own sociological theorizing conforms to *this* (explicit) epistemological view, since his generalizations are usually supported with historical evidence.

Bukharin's remaining discussions are prima facie all one-sided: He seems to stress the social and not the individual, and to opt for causal to the exclusion of teleological explanation, for necessity to the exclusion of free will, for matter to the exclusion of mind, and for motion to the exclusion of rest. With our new perspective, let us reexamine those discussions to see whether they are as one-sided as they appeared when we were checking whether the book's philosophical chapters could plausibly be regarded as mechanist. I believe it remains true that the previously detected "mechanism" and sociologism predominate, although some refinements will become apparent.

To clarify the problem, it will be useful to distinguish two ways in which a given position can be held: (1) methodologically or heuristically and (2) metaphysically or ontologically. Bukharin's emphasis on the social rather than individual aspects of phenomena is a methodological necessity, given that one wants to construct a sociology; however, it is equally obvious that at the ontological level, society is for him an aggregate of individuals. This aggregate is a "real aggregate" or system (p. 85) because the interaction among its parts is constant and long-lasting, but I do not think he is hypostatizing societies and social phenomena. This may become clear from his assertion that although "society as a whole, is greater than the sum of its parts [and] it cannot in any way be reduced to these parts" (p. 93), the same "is also true of many systems of various kinds, both living organisms and dead mechanisms" (*ibid.*), such as a watch. I would conclude that although there is no question of Bukharin's methodological sociologism, neither is there any of his metaphysical individualism.[56] This is a compromise of sorts between the two present extremes.

I think that Bukharin's "equilibrium" in other problematic cases is of a similar type. Methodologically he is antiteleological since he believes that only causal explanation is scientific, but metaphysically he admits the existence of human purposes (although, of course, he vehemently rejects divine ones). He quotes with approval the passage from the *Capital* where Marx explains that "what distinguishes the worst architect from the best of bees is this, that the architect raises his structure in imagination before he erects it in reality" (p. 27). Bukharin comments that "Marx here draws a sharp line between man and the rest of nature, and he is right in doing this, for no one can deny the thesis that man sets himself goals" (*ibid.*). But he rejects "the inferences drawn from this fact by the adherents of the 'teleological method' in social science" (*ibid.*).

On the question of necessity and free will, Bukharin's determinism amounts to a categorical denial that any events, including human actions, are uncaused, but he argues plausibly that this is a middle ground between indeterminism and fatalism, both of which he criticizes. On the one hand, "if the human will were entirely independent of everything it would be impossible to act at all" (p. 35). On the other hand, "*social determinism* . . . must not be confused with *fatalism*. . . . This teaching denies the human will as a factor

119

in evolution, which determinism does not" (p. 51). Determinism recognizes that social phenomena "are accomplished *through* the will of man. Social phenomena *without* humans, without society, would be something like a round square or burning ice. . . . Marxism does not *deny the will, but explains it*" (*ibid.*).

In the discussion of mind and matter, I think it is clear that Bukharin is a metaphysical materialist because for him "psychical phenomena are a property of matter organized in a certain manner" (p. 55). However, methodologically he is a dualist, working with both mind and matter, giving mind some role to play in his system, and defining materialism's greatest contribution as the materialistic explanation of *mental* phenomena. Speaking of the materialistic point of view in sociology, he says that "this point of view . . . by no means denies that 'ideas' have their effects. Marx even said distinctly, in discussing the highest stage of consciousness which is scientific *theory:* 'Every theory becomes a force when it secures control over masses.' But materialists cannot be satisfied with a mere reference to the fact that 'people thought so.' They ask: why did people in a certain place, at a certain time, 'think' so, and 'think' otherwise under other conditions?" (pp. 61–62).

Finally, Bukharin's discussion of a static versus a dynamic approach in his interpretation of dialectic is basically a more generalized account of his theory of "equilibrium in flux" that is concretely developed in his analysis of revolution and evolution. Whatever one may say about his interpretation of the dialectic, there is no doubt that he makes a plausible attempt to give both motion and rest their due importance. There is also no doubt that what could be regarded as philosophical "theory" in these sections of the third chapter, corresponds to the sociological practice of the chapter on revolution. In fact, we have seen that this element of his "philosophical mechanism" is the one generally in conformity with various features of his sociological practice.

Thus, the most striking feature of Bukharin's whole work is the synthesis of opposites. "Synthesis" here means judicious arbitration. The most obvious comment on this is that, since many thinkers[57] regard the synthesis of opposites as an essential element of the dialectic, Bukharin's *Historical Materialism* is a dialectical work through and through. As for Lenin's judgment that Bukharin "never has learned, and I think never fully understood the dialectic,"[58] we would have to say that this correctly applies to Bukharin's *theory* of the dialectic, not to his practice. I might further comment that my analysis may be regarded as a confirmation, deepening, and elaboration of Cohen's judgment that Bukharin's book had a "maverick, contentious quality [and] contained something to please and displease almost everyone."[59]

The conclusions I should like to stress relate to what might be called the hermeneutics of negative evaluation. A common idea in critical circles is that it is easy to make negative, destructive criticism and hard to be positive and constructive. I accept this as a psychological truism, but it is false from a logical and methodological point of view. What is easier about negative criticism is the *expression* of it, but if we move to the level of *justification*, the situation is just the reverse. *Sound* negative criticism is harder than *sound* positive criticism because the supporting arguments for negative criticism are subject to stricter standards than those supporting positive criticism. The reason is that a positive criticism is the identification of some *value* in the work being criticized. Whether this value is really present or not, if it is to be a value at all, then it possesses its own intrinsic worth. Perhaps the (positive) critic has read too much into his subject matter, perhaps his criticism tells us more about him than about the subject matter; then we may regard his "interpretation" as an original contribution, for which the subject matter merely acted as a stimulus. The relative inaccuracy of his interpretation does not affect too much the intrinsic worth of the ideas put forth. An alteration of the original subject matter may have been accomplished, but then it makes sense to consider the alteration by itself.

The same is not true for a negative evaluation. Here the critic is saying that the subject matter *lacks* some (or any) merit. If the interpretation is inaccurate, what lacks merit is merely the critic's alteration. But if this lacks merit, it does not merit consideration or serious discussion by itself as criticism; it self-destructs, so to speak. Hence, the negative critic has to be more careful about the evidence he gives in support of his interpretation, for he runs a much greater risk than does the positive critic, of accomplishing nothing with his negative criticism. In short, negative criticism is pointless if grounded on an inaccurate interpretation, whereas positive criticism is valuable even if inaccurate.

On the other hand, negative criticism is potentially more instructive,[60] for if it succeeds, it provides a contrast between the negatively evaluated subject matter and the principles on which the criticism is grounded, which must possess a positive quality if the criticism was successful. This may partially explain the greater frequency of negative criticism. It may also be the basis of the highly fruitful critical method of "criticism of criticism."

Hence I was quite well justified earlier in damning Gramsci's and Lukács's criticism for failing to prove the alleged methodological connection between Bukharin's "mechanism" and his sociology. In Gramsci's case, I also used one of his own principles against him, namely, the idea of the synthesis of theory and practice. Since this idea is regarded by him (and many others) as an essential element of Marxism, the present study may also be regarded as a contribution toward a Marxist critical methodology, as an extension of Marxism into the field of intellectual criticism. Indeed, "it would be strange if Marxist theory eternally stood still."[61]

To summarize, Bukharin's *System of Sociology* has been examined from the point of view of the distinction between what a scientist says about scientific method and knowledge in general, and what he actually does in his concrete scientific investigations. The need for such a reexamination stemmed partly from recent sociologists' intuitive judgments about the work and partly from the negativism of Gramsci's criticism, both of which are expounded in the preceding chapter and tested in this one. Bukharin's sociology has been defended from Gramsci's and from Lukács's philosophical critiques. In the central portion of the investigation, the relation between Bukharin's philosophical mechanism and his sociological practice has been analyzed, and it has been argued that there is little correspondence between the two and that hence his sociological theories are not invalidated by the inadequacy of his mechanism. Finally, the pattern implicit in his practice has been analyzed, with the argument that it consists of the judicious synthesis of such opposites as individual and society, society and nature, structure and superstructure, and evolution and revolution.

Chapter 5

Gramsci's dialectical interpretation of Machiavelli's politics

Besides Croce and Bukharin, a third main source of intellectual stimulus[1] for Gramsci in his Prison Notebooks is Machiavelli. The underlying theoretical problem now is no longer that of the religious and the scientific dimensions of Marxism, but rather that of its status as politics; to be more exact, the problem concerns the articulation of a Marxian or Marxist concept of politics. The connection between these two apparently disparate items will be seen in due course; for the moment, we may simply note that it should not be at all surprising if, in the process, Gramsci will have to construct his own reinterpretation of Machiavelli's politics, Marxian politics, and whatever intermediate concepts will be needed to bridge the gap.[2]

A preliminary glimpse at the magnitude of the task may be had by examining a single note where Gramsci raises many of these issues before we proceed to a systematic analysis. This examination is especially important also because the note happens to be one of the best illustrations of how the new critical edition of the Prison Notebooks[3] tends to superannuate previous interpretations and to move Gramsci scholarship onto a new plane. The note is the one on "politics as an autonomous science," printed in the previous edition[4] from Notebook 13, paragraph 10 (Q1568–70), and it begins as follows:

The first question that must be raised and resolved in a study of Machiavelli is the question of politics as an autonomous science, of the place that political science occupies or should occupy in a systematic (coherent and logical) conception of the world, in a philosophy of praxis.

The progress brought about by Croce in this respect in the study of Machiavelli and in political science consists mainly (as in other fields of Croce's critical activity) in the dissolution of a series of false, nonexistent, or wrongly formulated problems. Croce based himself on his distinction of the moments of the Spirit, and on his affirmation of a moment of practice, of a practical spirit, autonomous and independent though linked in a circle to all reality by the dialectic of distincts. In a philosophy of praxis, the distinction will certainly not be between the moments of the absolute Spirit, but between the levels of the superstructure. The problem will therefore be that of establishing the dialectical position of political activity (and of the corresponding science) as a particular level of the superstructure. One might say, as a first schematic approximation, that political activity is precisely the first moment or first level; the moment in which the superstructure is still in the unmediated phase of mere wishful affirmation, confused and still at an elementary stage.[5]

This passage is puzzling, and the following questions have been raised: First, why should a study of Machiavelli have to begin by dealing with the problem of the autonomy of political science? One can easily see why the elaboration of a political philosophy, and of a philosophy of praxis, might have to begin in that manner, but not why the study of Machiavelli has to do that.[6] Second, Gramsci seems to be confusing political science and political activity, for the passage begins by referring to the former and ends by giving a definition of the latter. Third, this passage seems un-Marxist insofar as it ignores the distinction between structure and superstructure when it suggests that Croce's "philosophy of the Spirit" ought to be replaced by a theory of the superstructure; in other words, it seems to be equating the philosophy of praxis with the philosophy of the superstructure.[7]

It turns out that this passage is one of those that appear in the Notebooks in two versions, an earlier and a later one. Moreover, it so happens that this note is *an exception* to the rule that later versions are improved elaborations of the earlier ones. In fact, the quoted passage, which is the one used in the first Italian edition and in the latest English translation, is the later text of a note whose first version does not contain any of the three problems just stated. As seen in the quotation below, the structure of the first sentence and its last clause answer the first question; Gramsci's point seems to be that if you want to approach Machiavelli's politics as a philosopher, then you should have a clear concept of politics to begin with. The second problem does not even arise because here Gramsci does not claim to be putting forth a view of political science, but only of political activity (as being, essentially, undifferentiated volition). Third, we do find an explicit mention of the distinction between structure and superstructure, and a claim that Croce's philosophy of the (theoretical and practical) Spirit is to be replaced by a philosophy of the (structural and superstructural) praxis. The earlier note appears in Notebook 8 and may be translated as follows:

The question: what is politics? namely what place political activity must have in a systematic (coherent and consequential) world view, in a philosophy of praxis, is the first question to resolve in a treatment of Machiavelli, because it is the question of philosophy as a science. [Worthy of note is] the progress in Machiavelli studies and in political science made by Croce in this regard, progress that consists essentially in the elimination of a series of false and nonexistent problems. Croce presupposes a distinction among moments of the Spirit, and the existence of a moment of practice or practical Spirit, autonomous and independent though circularly tied to all reality by means of the dialectic of distincts. Where everything is practice, in a philosophy of praxis, the distinction will not be be made among moments of absolute Spirit, but between structure and superstructures; one will have to fix the dialectical position of political activity as a distinction within the superstructures, and one will be able to say that political activity is precisely the first moment or first level of the superstructures, the moment in which all superstructures are still in the unmediated phase of mere volitional affirmation, indistinct and elementary. (Q977)[x]

Let us then proceed to a systematic analysis based on the critical edition.

MACHIAVELLI'S POLITICS

Machiavelli is unquestionably one of the most frequent topics of reflection in the Prison Notebooks. Not only are two "special" notebooks (nos. 13 and 18) devoted to him, but Gramsci frequently thinks that many other topics can be related to him, since his name is put by Gramsci in the titles of many notes, or "paragraphs," sixty-five, to be exact,[9] whose discussions have no direct connection to Machiavelli. Perhaps all these topics can be integrated in a discussion of him, but before doing this one should try to make sense of those paragraphs dealing more directly with Machiavelli. Of these, five are mere bibliographical notes.[10] Sixty-five other notes remain for us to examine,[11] the most important ones being in Notebook 13.

The analysis of these remaining notes reveals that they may be arranged into three groups.[12] First, we have a series of historical interpretations in the course of which Gramsci puts forth his view of Machiavelli indirectly by criticizing or qualifying a number of common interpretations.[13] Second, we have a series of conceptual elucidations in which Gramsci makes several distinctions between politics and other activities, as well as between various elements within political activity.[14] The rest of these notes deal with miscellaneous topics[15] that raise no new important points.

I have already referred to the important note where Gramsci discusses the need to determine the dialectical position of politics among human activities (Q977–78, 1568–70). In it he states that such a conceptual clarification is "the initial question to resolve in a treatment of Machiavelli" (Q977, 1568). Nevertheless, Gramsci himself does *not*, in fact, begin with this question: The first of the two "special" notebooks on Machiavelli (no. 13), which is an attempt at a systematic exposition and elabortion, begins with the question of the fundamental character of *The Prince* (Q1555); and this shows that for Gramsci, the question of the "autonomy of politics" is not *really* the first in a logical sense. Neither is it the first chronologically, because one of the first notes of the earliest notebook (no. 1) discusses the problem of interpreting Machiavelli historically (Q8–9). Thus it is best to begin by analyzing the historical series of notes.

A common view interprets Machiavelli as a model for general politics good for all times, as the scientific theorist of politics par excellence, as an exponent of pure politics; accordingly, the main lesson to be learned from him would concern the nature and value of volitional coherence in the art of government, that is, the steadfast and ruthless pursuit of chosen ends. Gramsci criticizes this interpretation as having led, in fact, and as being liable to lead, to excesses and exaggerations (Q8, 1572); I suppose that here Gramsci has in mind the reduction of Machiavellianism to the maxim that the end justifies the means. For Gramsci, this is unhistorical because it ignores that Machiavelli's end was both specific and progressive, namely, the creation of a strong, unified, national Italian state, free of exploitation by the papacy and able to resist interferences by the already centralized states of France and Spain (Q9, 1572). Moreover, the ruthlessness and absolute power of the prince – the proposed means – was to be directed against external enemies and internal anarchy and remnants of feudalism.

Ironically, the attribution to Machiavelli of the "pure politics" kind of universal relevance tends to dilute his relevance and can lead to a failure to appreciate other aspects of his thought. For example, Jean Bodin is often regarded as an anti-Machiavellian because he opposed the absolutism of the French monarchy and supported the interests of the people of the Third Estate, and because of his polemic against Machiavelli. This polemic, however, is "a mere literary accident" (Q1573), whereas the former stance occurred in a more advanced sociopolitical situation than the one faced by the Florentine thinker, namely, in a France that had already acquired territorial unity and in which the power of the king needed to be balanced with more consent by the people (Q1574). One should not forget that "in Machiavelli one can discover *in nuce* the separation of powers, and parliamentarianism or representative government" (Q1572), primarily in the *Discourses* but also in *The Prince* (Q1564); moreover, the choice between dictatorship and republic cannot be based on principle, for that would involve the hypostatization of the concepts of individual authority and general liberty (Q1564).

A more significant example would be the present-day relevance of Machiavelli. Nowadays, when the analogue of his prince is the modern political party (Q1558), one can adapt his lessons if one discards both the excessively specific maxims and the excessively general "pure politics," neither of which is useful. One thing that can be copied is what might be termed the literary-rhetorical structure of *The Prince*, whose fundamental character is that of "a 'living' book, where political ideology and political science are fused together . . . [and] the rational and doctrinal element is impersonated in a 'leader,' who represents plastically and anthropomorphically the symbol of the collective will" (Q1555). Another lesson would be the emphasis on the development, organization, and expression of the collective will, which Gramsci calls the *Jacobin* element in Machiavelli (Q1559). Finally, "an important part of the 'Modern Prince' will have to be devoted to the question of a moral and intellectual reform, namely, to the religious question or question of a world view" (Q1560); this would correspond to Machiavelli's fundamental revolutionary motivation of wanting to found a new state.

Gramsci's first interpretative thesis is, then, a criticism of the view of Machiavelli as the theorist of ruthlessness, on the grounds that this view is excessively abstract, that is, insufficiently historical, in being insensitive to the concrete situation faced by Machiavelli and to present-day political problems.[16]

Another current of anti-Machiavellian criticism[17] charges him with malicious duplicity, or contemplative ingenuousness (Q1617), or inconsistency (Q1600). The criticism would be grounded on a "democratic" interpretation of *The Prince*, which can be found in

Rousseau's *Social Contract,* Foscolo's *Sepolcri,* and Mazzini's essay on Machiavelli, and according to which Machiavelli feigns to give lessons to rulers in order to give them to the people, by revealing to the latter all the subterfuges of the former (Q1617, 1689–90) and thus leading them to hate tyranny. Although this interpretation would be proposed as a favorable one by certain democrats, and thus Machiavelli would be redeemed in their eyes, it can also be used against him by his critics. The moralist criticism would be that Machiavelli is being duplistic insofar as he deceives those to whom he is giving advice, by using fraud even while he advises the practice of fraud (Q1617). The authoritarians would attribute to him the ingenuous violation of a fundamental principle of politics, namely, that certain things are to be done but not to be said (Q1600, 1617), and for this transgression he would be charged with undermining the prestige of authority and rendering more difficult the art of governing (Q1690). In addition, his logical or "political" inconsistency would be that he is not being "Machiavellian" toward the people, insofar as he presumably is one of those who know the rules of the game of governing, but he goes against one of his own alleged rules that recommends deception (Q1600).

Against all this, Gramsci maintains the following: First, although the "democratic" interpretation needs enrichment, it is correct insofar as Machiavelli's *Prince* is directed primarily at the people; in fact, although it is abstractly true that the work can be useful to both tyrants and democrats, the work is not essentially a dispassionate, scientific, objective analysis, because this would be an anachronism (Q1617), because Machiavelli's "is a style of a man of action" (Q1599), and because the invocation in the book's last chapter is highly dramatic (Q1556, 1600); nor is the work really aimed at princes since "Machiavelli himself notes that the things he writes about are applied and have always been applied by the greatest men of history" (Q1600), and since a prince is brought up by his family in such a way that he "acquires almost automatically the characteristics of a political realist" (Q1600); thus, there is only one obvious alternative left.

To Gramsci, however, "it seems that Machiavelli's intentions in writing *The Prince* were more complex and also 'more democratic' than they would be according to the 'democratic' interpretation" (Q1690). They would be more democratic insofar as he is trying to accomplish something better that a mere exposé of tyrants' practices, namely, the political education of the people, and something more difficult than instilling a hate of tyranny, namely, a recognition of the instrumental necessity of an absolute monarchy: "He intends to bring about the political education of 'those who do not know,' not the negative political education of haters of tyrants, as Foscolo would seem to think, but the positive one of those who must recognize certain determinate means, even if characteristic of tyrants, because they have willed determinate ends" (Q1600). Machiavelli wants "to persuade" (Q1601), to make the people "convinced and aware" (Q1691) of a realistic politics. The conventional democratic view is an oversimplication partly because it forgets that "popular masses . . . in reality forget the means employed to reach an end if this end is historically progressive, namely, solves the essential problems of the time and establishes an order in which it is possible to move and to work in peace" (Q1618); moreover, it tends to ignore that "Machiavelli's 'democracy' is of a type suitable to his time, namely, it is the active consent by the popular masses to an absolute monarchy, insofar as it limits and destroys feudal and aristocratic anarchy and the power of the clergy, and it founds a great national territorial state" (Q1691).

This deeper and more historically sensitive democratic interpretation obviously invalidates the moralistic and logical-practical criticisms by undermining their foundation, but it is not clear how it affects the authoritarian criticism. To answer it fully, Gramsci makes a number of interesting political considerations, involving a comparison between Machiavelli's politics and Marxism. Today one must develop "a theory and a technique of politics that can serve both sides of the struggle, although they will ultimately serve especially the side that did not know, because it is the progressive force of history" (Q1601). To those who would object that this plays into the hands of the ruling class by helping it to avoid mistakes, Gramsci's answer is that the objection is tied to "the puerile theory of 'the worse it gets, the better it is' . . . to the silly idea of always regarding one's opponents as stupid . . . and to not understanding the historico-political necessity that 'certain errors have to be committed' and that to criticize them is useful for the education of your side" (Q1690).

Gramsci's second interpretative thesis is, then, a criticism of the conventional democratic interpretation, for being excessively superficial, and of various inconsistency charges based thereupon, for being historically unfounded or politically naive.

A third type of criticism of Machiavelli[18] claims that he was not a "true politician," by contrast, for example, to Francesco Guicciardini, because Machiavelli did not limit himself to operating within effectual reality, whereas a statesman must deal with the "is" and not with the "ought." For Gramsci, this judgment, too, is an error of excess, now in the domain of political realism, and he adds that such excessive realism is a sign of superficiality and mechanism (Q1577, 990). Conceptually speaking, there are two important distinctions that the criticism ignores; we have the reality of the diplomat and the reality of the politician, and we have the abstract or utopian "ought" of people like Savonarola or Dante and the realistic "ought" of the "scientific" politician. This, in turn, generates several levels of "effectual reality," depending on how far one looks "beyond the length of one's nose" (Q1577). Whereas Guicciardini is a mere diplomat, and Savonarola a utopian dreamer, Machiavelli is both a political scientist and a realistic revolutionary politician.

One difference between politics and diplomacy is that "in politics the volitional element has a much greater importance than in diplomacy" (Q760–61). Another is that one is essentially conservative, the other essentially innovative and creative: "Diplomacy sanctions and tends to conserve situations created by the clash of the politics of states; it is creative only metaphorically or by the philosophical convention that all human activity is creative" (Q761). These differences in turn lead to a third, namely, that the diplomat is more skeptical and pessimistic than the politician (Q761). Fourth, diplomacy is, but politics is not, a specialized profession or technical field (Q762, 781). Since Machiavelli wants to establish a new national Italian state, it would be a mistake to judge him by the criteria that can be used for the diplomat Guicciardini.

But was Machiavelli's wish well founded? His ability to look beyond the available Italian experience, to the examples of the unified monarchies of France, Spain, and England put him on the plane of a European effectual reality; it is the possibility suggested by this evidence that prevents his proposal from being utopian (Q760). Moreover, he realizes that reality is not static, but rather a system of forces in continual development; so his prescription is "scientific," realistic, and concrete since "to apply one's will to the creation of a new equilibrium of really existing and operating forces, basing oneself on that particular force that one considers progressive, and strengthening it to make it triumph, is always to move in the realm of effectual reality, but to dominate it and to go beyond it, or to contribute to so doing" (Q1578).

Finally, one should not misinterpret the fact that Machiavelli did not succeed, that he was not able to bring about what he thought should happen, for after all he was only a private individual not a head of state; he did not have at his disposal an army of men, but only one of words. However, it would also be wrong to regard him as a "disarmed prophet" since "Machiavelli never says that he is thinking or planning to change reality himself, but only concretely to show how historical forces should have operated in order to be effective" (Q1578). But again, this does not mean that the prince is merely a figment of his personal biography; this can be clearly seen by contrasting Machiavelli with Dante, whose "emperor" was supposed to put an end to factional struggles within medieval Italian city-states by imposing a stronger external power and law (Q758–60). The crucial difference is that whereas Machiavelli theorizes the progressive tendencies of his time, Dante dreams of going back to the past Roman Empire, either the ancient one of Rome, or the "holy" Germanic one of the earlier Middle Ages. This is so in spite of the fact that Machiavelli, too, was motivated in part by the memory of Roman history (Q968, 1563), for this motivation is not his primary one; moreover, such an appeal to ancient Rome is much more concrete and less utopian at his time than at the time of Dante, for Machiavelli had the experience of the humanistic movement and of the Renaissance behind him and could therefore presume that there was no reason why the same Italy that had revived the arts of poetry, painting, and sculpture, could not revive the "art of war" (Q968, 1563).

Thus, in his third thesis Gramsci is arguing against two extremes: that Machiavelli was not really or not sufficiently realistic, as Guicciardini was, and that he was not really or not sufficiently prescriptive, as Dante and Savonarola in their different ways were; in fact, Machiavelli was both descriptive and prescriptive: descriptive of the deeper reality of the progressive historical development of nation-states, and prescriptive of the nonmoralistic, nonutopian goal of a unified Italy.

Next, someone might object (Q1038)[19] to Machiavelli's economic deficiency, for there is an almost total absence of economic considerations in his work, and, insofar as he has any explicit views, Gramsci himself admits that "they could not go outside the mercantilist framework" (Q985). Gramsci's approach here is to move the discussion to the implicit level, namely, to consider what kind of economics is implicit in Machiavelli's noneconomic views and programs. Here the most significant matter is his proposal in *The Art of War* for a nonmercenary national militia to be recruited primarily from the peasants. Although Gramsci realizes that Machiavelli's explicit intention is political (Q1573), nevertheless the proposal may also be taken as evidence that "Machiavelli tended to establish ties between city and country and to expand the function of urban classes by asking them to give up certain feudal-corporative privileges in regard to the country, so as to incorporate rural classes into the state" (Q1039). What this means, in turn, is that we have the germ of physiocratic economics (Q1039, 1575),[20] which then paves the way for classical political economy. Thus Machiavelli is de facto economically progressive.

This economic appreciation, should not, however, blind one to a genuine limitation of Machiavelli's military views that Gramsci is willing to endorse. The weakness is Machiavelli's failure to recognize the importance of artillery, a military error that stems from an excess of political involvement in the unified Italy project (Q9, 1573); thus, from a purely military point of view, he fails to be progressive.

Elaborating further, we may say that Gramsci's fourth thesis is about *The Art of War:* This work has military, political, and economic aspects; the military one is obvious but somewhat unprogressive in its neglect of artillery; the political aspect corresponds to Machiavelli's fundamental motivation and progressively theorizes the development of a nation-state; the economic aspect anticipates the physiocratic approach and is also progressive. It would be an excess of literalness the *emphasize* the military viewpoint, and an excess of profundity or pedantry to *emphasize* the economic aspect, which leaves us with the alternative that "even in *The Art of War* Machiavelli must be considered as a politician who has to get involved in military art" (Q1573).

To summarize, the group of Gramsci's notes on Machiavelli involving historical interpretations may be understood and analyzed as discussing four issues: ruthlessness, democracy, realism, and military strategy. The anti-Machiavellian criticisms would be, respectively, that Machiavelli is a ruthless advocate of the end's justifying the means, that his words are inconsistent with his deeds (because he preaches authoritarianism and deception but acts democratically and openly in publishing his *Prince*), that he is unrealistically out of touch with what is feasible in his time, and that his military proposal is unprogressively flawed. In each case the essence of Gramsci's efforts seems to be a plea for avoiding excesses, exaggerations, one-sidedness, and superficiality. The ruthlessness criticism carries too far the basically sound feeling that Machiavelli is politically relevant; the inconsistency criticism does not go far enough in developing the insight that he is a democrat; the lack-of-realism criticism goes too far with the basically sound concern for working within effectual reality; and the military criticism is too literalistic in evaluating Machiavelli's interest in the art of war.

A CONCEPT OF POLITICS

As stated in the preceding section, another group of Gramsci's notes on Machiavelli consists of a series of conceptual distinctions around and within the notion of politics. Gramsci is here concerned with distinguishing political and aesthetic art, private and political morality, politics and economics, great and petty politics, politics and philosophy, morality and politics, the political and the apolitical, sociology and political science, the politics of force and the politics of consent, and politics and diplomacy (which we have already encountered).

The first question to be considered under this heading[21] is that of what politics is. This abstract-sounding question is immediately reformulated by Gramsci as "what place political activity must have in a systematic (coherent and consequential) world view" (Q977). A fundamental thesis, which Gramsci accepts from Croce and which he is never tired of reiterating, is what he calls "the autonomy of politics," that is, "the claim implicit in his [Machiavelli's] writings that politics is an autonomous activity which [has] its principles and laws different from those of morality and religion" (Q1599). A second Crocean principle that Gramsci accepts, with qualifications that are not relevant here,[22] is that of the so-called dialectic of distincts; this means that the distinction between politics and other things, such as morality and religion, must not be a separation, and therefore in addition to distinguishing them one must also relate them to one another. This immediately leads to the question of "what kind of dialectical relation between it and the other historical manifestations" (Q503; cf. Q1316). Next, departing from Croce, for whom these were relations within the "Spirit," and adopting Marx's practical orientation, Gramsci goes on to say that in a philosophy of praxis, "where everything is practice" (Q977), the basic framework will be that of structure and superstructure (Q977). Gramsci's fourth step, perhaps one of his own original contributions, is emphasis on the superstructure, and thus the problem becomes that of "establishing the dialectical position of political activity (and of the corresponding science) as a determinate superstructural level" (Q1569); here a first approximation is to say, as pointed out earlier, that politics is "the first moment or first level of the superstructures, the moment in which all superstructures are still in the immediate phase of mere volitional affirmation, indistinct and elementary" (Q977, 1569). Fifth, Gramsci asserts a thesis about the primacy of politics: that in a certain sense all historical manifestations and human activities reduce to politics or, more simply, "that all life is politics" (Q977; cf. Q1569). One meaning of this is that "art, morality, philosophy 'serve' politics, that is, are implicated in politics, may be reduced to a moment of it, but not vice versa" (Q503). In this fifth step, one must not forget the second step, about dialectic, for Gramsci is certainly sensitive to the possibility that "politics destroys art, philosophy, morality" (Q503); this happens when political activity is "exterior, imposed by force, in accordance to a preestablished plan" (Q1316). Finally, regarding the other "things" from which politics should be distinguished and to which it should be related, we cannot adopt an a priori, absolute scheme, like that of Hegel or Croce, but must follow a more realistic, historicist approach as suggested by Marx (Q1317); this, I believe, is the justification for the series of distinctions Gramsci discusses, which may at first seem random, namely, the distinctions already mentioned between politics and aesthetics, the private sphere, economics, morality, apoliticism, sociology, and diplomacy, between great and petty politics, and between force and consent. Let us turn to these.

One of Gramsci's most frequent phrases in his notes on Machiavelli and politics is "the science and art of politics." When used in the context of this expression, the notion of the art of politics is probably less likely to lead to confusion; however, when one speaks of the art of politics without the contrast to political science, one may confuse it with art in the sense of aesthetics. The occasion for Gramsci's distinction was the confusion he found in a 1929 article by a certain Azzalini (Q656–62). Gramsci agrees to discuss the question in terms of the concepts of intuition and expression. Thus, one problem is to clarify the "distinction of political intuition from aesthetic, lyrical, or artistic intuition" (Q661):

Political intuition does not occur in the artist, but in the "leader"; and by "intuition" one must understand not "cognition pertaining to individuals," but the rapidity of connecting among themselves apparently extraneous facts, of conceiving the means appropriate to the end in order to find the interests at stake, and of arousing human feelings and channeling them toward a determinate action. (Q661)

As regards expression, whereas that of the artist is essentially linguistic (with words, colors, or sounds), "the 'expression' of the
'leader' is 'action,' in a positive or negative sense, that is, to bring
about a deed or to prevent the occurrence of a determinate action,
depending on whether or not there is correspondence with the end
that we want to reach" (Q661).

The complementary distinction to this one involves the clarification of the relationship between the science of politics and other
disciplines with which it may be confused. Gramsci is anxious to
distinguish political science from what he calls "sociology," as he
understands the latter term (Q1765–66). Although the conceptual
issue is clear and important, in my opinion Gramsci's point turns
out to be primarily a terminological one. By "sociology" Gramsci
means the study of society with the method of the natural sciences,
when this method is specifically (and "superficially") interpreted
as the search for the immutable and eternal laws of nature, rather
than more deeply as mere "seriousness" of research[23] or as simply
"the proper logic of the proper object."[24] He claims that the sociopolitical reason why this "sociology" arose in the nineteenth century
was the belief that the establishment of constitutional and parliamentary goverment had begun "an epoch of natural evolution"
(Q1765) for society; at the same time, the term "politics" presumably
acquired the bad connotation of parliamentary maneuvering and
cliquish intrigue. Gramsci, however, accepts what he regards as a
fundamental Marxist insight, namely, "that there does not exist an
abstract, fixed, and immutable 'human nature' . . . but that human
nature is the ensemble of historically determinate social relations"
(Q1599), from which he concludes that "political science must be
conceived in its concrete content (and also in its logical formulation)
as a developing organism" (Q1599). Moreover, Gramsci contends
that "there really exist ruled and rulers, managers and managed.
All of political art and science is based on this primordial fact"
(Q1572), and so he argues:

If political science means science of the State, and the State is the whole
complex of practical and theoretical activities by which the ruling class not
only justifies and maintains its power, but succeeds in obtaining the active
consent of the ruled, it is evident that all essential questions of sociology
are nothing but questions of political science. (Q1765)

This anti-"sociological" attitude can be misunderstood as antiscientific,[25] especially since Gramsci adds that "if there is any res-

idue, this cannot be but false problems, namely uninteresting problems" (Q1765). Such an interpretation would be incorrect, however, partly because Gramsci explicitly says that the residual problems are false in the sense of uninteresting; so he is aware that there is an element of choice. This cannot be ignored, because in the same context Gramsci also says that because "all is 'political'" (Q1766) in a certain sense, science "is itself 'political activity'" (Q1766), although, of course, one must then distinguish the political activity of the politician from the political activity of the scientist, and so forth. An essential feature of the latter kind of political activity is what Gramsci calls "the method of philology and criticism" (Q1599), which, in the context of the historicist argument above, he admits is applicable within certain limits for the factual determination of the ensemble of social relations (Q1599). Clearly, if one defines "sociology" as the critical, "philological," serious, and "objective" study of a given stage of society, then Gramsci, far from having anything against it, would regard it as a foundation for the science of politics. His opposition is to a sociology embedded in a nonhistoricist, apolitical philosophy of sociology.

One of the most important relevant distinctions is that between politics and morality. For Gramsci, this is the distinction between private or particular ethical rules and public or universal ones (Q749–50). He explains that every association requires its members to abide by certain norms, for the sake of cohesion and in order to accomplish its ends; although there are exceptions, such as criminal organizations, which have only selfish aims, an association normally has a universalistic tendency, that is, it "conceives itself as an aristocracy, an elite, a vanguard, namely . . . as tending to extend itself to a whole social group, which is itself conceived as tending to unify all humanity" (Q750). The difference and the relationship between the two are, then, that "politics is conceived as a process that will lead to morality, namely, as tending to lead to a form of coexistence in which politics and therefore morality will both be superseded" (Q750). But unless and until the unification of humanity has actually occurred, politics is unavoidable and on some occasions it would be wrong to take the moral point of view. For example, suppose there is a conflict between two groups, which do not recognize and submit to any higher authority and which are making actual and practical sacrifices in order to carry out the struggle (Q1709–10); typically in such a conflict, who is right depends on conditions that are subject to change as a result of the struggle itself; then a judgment that equity or justice favors one side is clearly itself an element of the conflict, and so "the only possible judgment is the 'political' one, namely, that of conformity of means and end" (Q1710).

The question of the distinction between politics and economics would seem to be one of the most crucial ones for a Marxist, and so Gramsci's relevant notes deserve careful scrutiny. One claim, which was implicitly made in the first conceptual note discussed, is a distinction in terms of structure and superstructure, with political activity being the first superstructural moment, and with the structure being the network of such elements as technology, science, labor, and class (Q977–78, 1568–70). Another difference involves the concepts of political passion and economic interest; the former relates to the latter insofar as a long-standing passion can arise only from an economic condition; but, Gramsci adds:

. . . it is also distinguished from the latter, and so one can speak separately of economy and of politics; one can speak of "political passion" as an immediate impulse to action, which springs from the "permanent and organic" soil of economic life but supersedes it, by bringing into play sentiments and aspirations in whose incandescent atmosphere even the calculations of individual human life obey laws different from those of individual accounting, etc. (Q1022)

One wishes that Gramsci had elaborated the elliptical "etc." Although he does discuss on other occasions the general topic of "the identity of politics and economics" (Q465, 472–73, 1448, 1492–93), and that of the role of passion in politics (Q888–89, 1307–10, 1567–68), no significant elaboration is given. A more useful aspect of the present note (Q1022) is the explicitness with which Gramsci explains that the "identity" of which he speaks involves a relation *and* a distinction between the two.

A third difference between economics and politics involves Gramsci's concepts of economic versus political versus military forces (Q1582–86). Economic forces are those strictly tied to the structure of the material forces of production, independent of human will, measurable with the methods of the exact or physical sciences, generative of social groupings, and indicative of the possibility of social transformations, that is, indicative of the degree of realism and feasibility of the various ideologies resulting from those forces. Political forces are those involving the "degree of homogeneity, self-awareness, and organization reached by various social groups" (Q1583). From the point of view of awareness, four species are definable under this genus: Certain economic-corporative forces pertain to the interests of single homogeneous professional groups, such as the solidarity of merchants with one another but not with building contractors; other economic-corporative forces stem from the interests of a whole socioeconomic group, aim at political and legal equality with the dominant groups, and operate within the existing state framework; third, national political forces stem from the awareness that the interests of one's groups can and must become concretely coordinated with those of other groups, discuss questions on a universal rather than corporative level, and tend to establish a state characterized by a "continual forming and surpassing of unstable equilibriums (within the context of the law) among the interests of the fundamental groups and those of subordinate groups" (Q1584); this third type involves genuine politics and "marks the clear transition from the structure to the domain of complex superstructures" (Q1584); finally, international political forces, such as religions, the Masons, the Rotary Club, the Jews, and career diplomats, "may be inserted into the social category of 'intellectuals,' whose function at the international level is that of mediating extremes, 'socializing' the technical findings that allow the functioning of all directorial activities, and devising compromises and escape routes among extreme solutions" (Q1585). Regarding military forces, there exists a type that might be called "political-military," in addition to the technical-military; for example, when one country is militarily occupying another one comparably extended and populated, "the relationship is not purely military, but political-military; in fact, such an oppression would be inexplicable without the state of social disintegration of the oppressed country and the passivity of the majority of its people; thus its independence cannot be reached with purely military forces, but with military and political-military ones" (Q1586).

Within politics, two basic types[26] distinguished by Gramsci are what he labels variously great, high, or creative politics, and what is labeled petty, small, or daily politics. His explanation is:

Great politics covers questions connected with the foundation of new states, with the struggle for the destruction, defense, or conservation of particular organic socioeconomic structures. Small politics covers the partial and daily questions that arise within an already established structure in the struggles for preeminence among various factions of the same political class. Thus it is great politics to try excluding great politics from the internal processes of the life of a state and reducing all to small politics. . . . Instead it is characteristic of dilettantes to pose questions in such a way that every element of small politics must necessarily become a question of great politics, of the radical reorganization of the state. (Q1563–64)

In international politics, questions involving the balance of power relate to great politics, whereas diplomacy deals with small politics. As examples of great politics, besides Machiavelli and Giolitti (Q1564), Gramsci gives that of Croce's attitude toward Germany and toward popular Italian anti-German feeling during World War I (Q1212). Another example he gives is the cosmopolitanism of Italians during a phase of the Renaissance, which contrasted with the poverty of vision of the internal politics of the Italian states of the period (Q1832).

Another important distinction within politics is between, on the one hand, the aspect pertaining to such things as force, authority, violence, agitation, and tactics and, on the other hand, the aspect involving consent, hegemony, civilization, propaganda, and strategy (Q1576). Although the relation between these two aspects can be misinterpreted as the mechanical one of temporal succession, the connection is a dialectical one; for example, in taking the first perspective by defending one's own physical existence, an individual may simultaneously be taking the second perspective and acting according to the best and most refined human and civil values.

Finally, we have the distinction between party politics and individualistic apoliticism. Gramsci is very scornful of the latter: " 'Parties' can present themselves under the most diverse names, even that of 'anti-party' or 'negation of parties'; in reality, even so-called individualists are party men, only that they would like to be 'party chiefs' by the grace of God or of the stupidity of those who follow them" (Q1753–54); individualism is "a whimsical satisfaction of momentary impulses" (Q1754), as well as "animalistic apoliticism" in the sense of being an element "admired by foreigners like the acts of the inhabitants of a zoological garden" (Q1755). On the other hand, party politics, in a sense to be clarified in the next paragraph, is for Gramsci a necessary consequence of the most fundamental fact of the science and art of politics, namely, that "there really exist governed and governors, leaders and led" (Q1572). To be sure, the origin of this fact is a problem that needs separate study, and, moreover, one should always remember to consider whether to act in such a way that this division will always remain so, or in such a way as to encourage its disappearance.

Nevertheless, the division exists, even within the same social class; "in a certain sense one can say that this division is an expression of the division of labor, is a technical fact" (Q1752).

The most essential principles of this Gramscian party politics are the following: First, one should expect obedience not to be automatic but to be based on argument and to be subject to discussion. Gramsci does not state this principle positively, as I have, but negatively by objecting to its opposite; that is, he says it is a "serious" and even "criminal" error to expect that "obedience should be automatic, should not only occur without the need of a demonstration of necessity and rationality, but also be unquestionable . . . that obedience 'will come' without being asked, without indicating the road to follow . . . that something will be done because the leader believes it is right and rational that it be done" (Q1753). A second serious and criminal error is "to neglect to avoid useless sacrifices" (Q1753) imposed on the masses being led. Third, "the party spirit is the fundamental element of the state spirit" (Q1755), understanding by the latter concept the sense of "continuity toward the past, namely, toward tradition, as well as toward the future, that is . . . that every act be the moment of a complex process, which has already begun and which will continue" (Q1754); Gramsci adds that "it is evident this consciousness of 'duration' must be concrete and not abstract, namely, in a sense, must not go beyond certain limits" (Q1754) and that "the 'cult' of tradition has a tendentious value, implies a particular choice and aim, namely, is the basis of an ideology" (Q1754); the judicious sense of tradition must be dialectical or, as he says, must operate "organically, in a historical sense" (Q1754), so that, for example, if we stipulate that what needs to be considered is one past and one future generation, then we could not mechanically set a generation to equal, say, thirty years. All this should make it clear that by party spirit Gramsci does *not* mean sectarianism, which for him is a form of apoliticism.

In summary, we may say that in the conceptual series of his notes on "Machiavelli," Gramsci makes a number of distinctions between aspects of politics and between it and other activities. He is conceiving politics as being superstructural or volitional (by contrast to the economic sphere); as being one of several "distinct" activities that are the subject matter of systematic philosophy; one of the practical rather than "fine" arts; a historical process to be properly studied only within a historicist framework; potentially but not yet identical with morality; and subject to taking the form of great or small, force or consent, and social persuasion or individual arbitrariness.

If the analysis in the two preceding sections solves the historical-scholarly problem of making internal sense out of Gramsci's notes on Machiavelli, it also generates several questions of a more theoretical sort.

First, what is the relation between what I have called the historical and the conceptual notes? From the point of view of Machiavelli, we might say that the notion of politics elaborated by Gramsci in the second group of notes is for him the concept found *in nuce* in Machiavelli. That is, the various theses about politics in the conceptual notes are for Gramsci the theoretical-political lessons that one may derive from Machiavelli. Given the positive appreciative character of these lessons, as well as of Gramsci's historical interpretations, we need not discuss at great length the question of the extent to which these Gramscian theses are "really" derivable from Machiavelli. Suffice it to say that, although a negative, unfavorable criticism has to be grounded on evidence of a rigorous and high order,[27] the same does not apply to positive interpretations, for the content of the latter can always be considered on its own merits, independently of the source. I believe Gramsci's evidence is sufficient to show that the ideas in the notes we have considered have *some* relation to Machiavelli; for the rest, we may take them to be Gramsci's own ideas.

A second question raised by the above analysis is Gramsci's relationship to Croce. This is partly a problem for the history of ideas, but more importantly it pertains to the nature of Gramsci's thought and of his fundamental perspective and presuppositions. It is worth mentioning that Croce put forth *two* main theses about Machiavelli: the claims that inherent in his work one can find a concept of politics that "represents the true and proper foundation for a philosophy of politics"[28] and that Machiavelli did for the unification of Italy into a nation-state what Marx did for the emancipation of the proletariat as a class.[29] With this in mind, it seems obvious that Gramsci is elaborating on these two Crocean theses, the second one in the historical notes, and the first in the conceptual notes. This adds further support, both quantitatively and qualitatively, to the idea of a Crocean character of Gramsci's work; the evidence represented by the analysis in the two preceding sections is qualitatively novel in the sense that our evidence in Chapter 1 showed that in the *Prison Notebooks*, Gramsci was accepting Croce's concepts of religion and philosophy, as well as his style and method of criticism, in his own critique of Croce. This, in turn, meant that there Gramsci was being Crocean in a context where perhaps it was more difficult to escape Croce's influence, because the subject matter of the discussion was Croce's philosophy. In the present context, however, we find Gramsci working within a Crocean framework by refining two of Croce's specific theses, even though the subject matter is different;[30] this is more analogous to his influence in Gramsci's critique of Bukharin.

From the point of view of politics, the analysis in the two preceding sections helps to correct the widespread interpretation of Gramsci as being first and foremost the theoretician (and organizer) of the political (or, more restrictedly, the revolutionary) party. Political theorists continue to hold this view, or at least to practice it in their research, even if they pay lip service to the assertion that the concept of the party is not the central theme of the Prison Notebooks.[31] The overemphasis on the party derives partly from the literary brilliance of the image embodied in the phrase "The Modern Prince," used by Gramsci to describe the needed present-day analogue of Machiavelli's *Prince*. Moreover, the theory of the party unquestionably has a basis in the text: For example, the first note (in the historical series) discussed in the foregoing analysis contains explicit references to the "Modern Prince" and implicit ones to the party, while the last (conceptual) note discussed explicitly mentions the notion of party. Nevertheless, it is equally clear that in these notes on Machiavelli and the concept of politics, the focus lies elsewhere.

This leads us to the most important question: What is that central focus? It is easy to say where it is *not* to be found. Gramsci makes no one overarching point either about Machiavelli or about politics at the substantive level. If we want to find a unifying theme, we have to look for it at the level of method, structure, or approach. What, then, is in the structure of the notes analyzed in the foregoing account?

We saw earlier that in his historical notes Gramsci's essential point was that Machiavelli was indeed ruthless, but judiciously rather than mindlessly so, in the sense that his ruthlessness was historically specific and specifically aimed; that he was indeed a democrat, but again judiciously rather than dogmatically so, insofar as he sought to educate the masses about the necessity of an absolute ruler; that he was indeed realistic, but in the sense that a realist is a judicious advocate of change, rather than a utopian dreamer or a diplomatic operator within the status quo; and that his military views were more judicious than commonly believed, if regarded as an expression of the politics and economics of town-country relations, rather than from a purely military point of view. The analysis of the historical notes has also given us a picture of the critical practice of Gramsci as interpreter of Machiavelli; the essential feature of that practice is implicit in Gramsci's arguments against critics of Machiavelli, and explicit in his frequent statements to that effect; it is the judicious avoidance of excesses, exaggerations, superficialities, and one-sidedness.[32] If we equate judiciousness with the exercise of the art of judgment,[33] we get a Machiavellian practitioner of the art of political judgment, and a Gramscian practitioner of the art of critical or hermeneutical judgment.

In such a "judgmental" interpretation, the term "judgment" is meant to be synonymous with "judiciousness," which is taken in its more or less intuitive and commonsense meaning. To proceed further, we first have to establish a connection with the notion of "dialectic." Without going into the controversies about the nature of dialectic (discussed in Chapters 6 and 7), we can agree that *one* of its meanings is that of a process antithetical to a mechanist approach.[34] But judiciousness, in the sense of avoiding one-sided extremes, is also the antithesis of mechanism. This is explicitly recognized by Gramsci when, in discussing the realism problem in Machiavelli, he says that the source of the erroneous interpretation is "excessive (and hence superficial and mechanical) political realism" (Q1577); in fact, Gramsci's inference from "excessive" to "mechanical" amounts to an equation of "injudicious" and "undialectical." From this, the step to equating "judicious" to "dialectical" is a small one indeed. Thus we may also say that Gramsci's interpretation is "dialectical," in the double sense that Machiavelli is being portrayed as a dialectical politician and that Gramsci is thereby acting as a dialectical critic.

This dialectical interpretation can be given more direct confirmation, as follows: Whatever else the dialectic may be, one of its essential elements is the synthesis of opposites. Gramsci's first historical thesis (on ruthlessness) gives us a Machiavelli who synthesizes the opposition between means and ends, the perception of which synthesis requires Gramsci's own (hermeneutical) synthesis between the two extremities within the dimension of relevance. In his second thesis, Gramsci presents Machiavelli's synthesis between dictatorship (or authority) and democracy (or consent) as well as between theory and practice, while constructing his own synthesis between superficiality and profundity, and between extreme charitableness and extreme negativity of interpretation. In Gramsci's third thesis (on the realism problem), we obviously have a Machiavelli who synthetically combines description and prescription, and a Gramsci working essentially along the same dimension by reaching a balance between descriptivism and prescriptivism. Finally, Gramsci's fourth thesis has Machiavelli come to grips with the dichotomy of politics and economics, while trying itself to overcome the twin extremes of literalness and pedantry in interpreting *The Art of War*.

The notion of dialectic is, in turn, helpful for dealing with the conceptual notes. The "dialectical" intention of the concept of politics there elaborated by Gramsci is explicit enough. For, in the fundamental note in which he sketches his program for this part of the Notebooks, he says he wants to examine the "dialectical position of political activity" (Q977, 1569); and in one of his most explicit notes on the concept of dialectic, in the notebook on Croce, Gramsci immediately introduces the concept of politics as an example to which the dialectic is to be applied (Q1316). From this we may conclude that he is trying to elaborate a dialectical concept of politics, that is, a concept of dialectical politics. To see concretely the dialectic involved here, however, we need to add to the synthesis of opposites just mentioned, a synthesis of differences. This accords with Gramsci's explicit endorsement of a Crocean type of "dialectic of distincts," which, as stated in the preceding section, involves recognizing that although there are distinct (or different) activities besides opposite ones, these distinctions (or differences) lead not to separations but to interrelations; the synthesis is here provided by such interrelated distinctions.[35] Let us, then, examine Gramsci's main theses in his conceptual notes from this point of view.

Gramsci's first conceptual thesis is that philosophy and politics are distinct in that politics (along with such other activities as morality, religion, economics, etc.) is one of the things studied by philosophy, and that the two are related insofar as philosophy is a form of politics. His second thesis is that politics is related to aesthetic activity insofar as it is itself an art, and that the two are distinct because politics is the art of leadership grounded on the ability to connect means and ends, whereas aesthetic art is the skill of linguistic expression involving the connecting of form and content. The third thesis is that the science of politics and "sociology" are distinct inasmuch as the former has to be historical whereas the latter tends to be ahistorical, and they are related insofar as sociology can be turned into a branch of political science by being embedded in a historicist framework. In his fourth thesis, Gramsci is saying that politics and morality are distinct insofar as politics consists of rules of restricted validity and morality consists of rules of universal validity; they are related in that morality is the future politics of all humanity and politics is the past and present necessity and predicament of all mankind. The fifth thesis on economics and politics distinguishes the two as structure and superstructure, and relates them insofar as sustained political will normally can arise only from economic interests, and insofar as aspects of politics (e.g., organization) can become material, military, or economic forces. Gramsci's last three theses involve the oppositions of great versus small politics, force versus consent, and party spirit versus individualism, and the dialectic inherent therein was rather explicit in our earlier analysis; here it will suffice to note that this is (1) a dialectic of opposites rather than differences and (2) an internal dialectic within politics, rather than external in the sense of involving its relations and differences with other activities.

I have argued, then, that the deep structure of Gramsci's notes on Machiavelli is a dialectical one in the sense specified, that Machiavelli is portrayed by Gramsci as a dialectical politician, and that the concept of politics that he is motivated to elaborate at a general level is dialectical in the same sense. These results are sufficient for present purposes, but they would be somewhat undialectical if at least a few comments were not made about questions raised, and other lines of inquiry suggested, by the present investigation, for said comments pertain to the relationship between this investigation and others.

Two interesting problems involve viewing Gramsci's concept of dialectical politics sketched here from above and from below, as it were. The view from below involves how this concept relates to the political practice of Gramsci or of his political followers (e.g., among the Italian left); in other words, did Gramsci or his followers practice this aspect of his theory of politics? Viewed from above, this concept of dialectical politics would have to be related to Gramsci's general theory or concept of dialectic, if he has one; in other words, his notes on Machiavelli that contain the concept of dialectical politics would now be viewed as (theoretical) practice, whose relation to the higher level or more abstract philosophical remarks on dialectic in general would constitute an open question. A third problem, which, to continue the spatial metaphor, might be regarded as stemming from viewing Gramsci's concept from the side, would be to ask for its practical-political relevance, that is, to ask whether we can today put the concept into practice and, if so, how.

The outlook for this last project may seem rather unpromising. The objection, anticipated by Gramsci himself, would be:

In reality, historical forces clash among themselves for their "extreme" programs. That one of these forces assumes the function of "synthesis" which overcomes opposite extremes, is *a dialectical necessity, not an apriorist method*. To be able to find for each particular issue the point of progressive equilibrium (in the sense of one's own program) is the art of the politician, not the art of the golden mean, but precisely of the politician who has a very definite line of great potential for the future. [This is the problem] of "Proudhonism" and of the antidialectic of empirical and shortsighted opportunism. (Q1825, my italics)[36]

One could question whether it is a drawback that a concept such as dialectical politics is merely an instrument for understanding political history and current events, and not one for creating new history and changing the world. One could perhaps argue that this feature could be turned to advantage, for it provides a scientifically objective "method of philology," as Gramsci himself might put it. Another approach, however, is to ask whether Gramsci's theory of dialectic just quoted is correct. This is not the only place where he discusses the topic, and we would first have to articulate his theory, as is done in Chapter 6. Such a problem is closely tied to the one stemming from the second of the three problems formulated in the preceding paragraph, the one "from above." Thus we have a motivation for a systematic analysis of Gramsci's notes on the dialectic. These are the ones in which he discusses such topics the concepts of passive revolution, revolution-restoration, reformism, transformism, political moderation, classicism (as inhering in the thought and action of such people as Gioberti, Cavour, and Croce), "domesticated" dialectic, and "Proudhonism."

Chapter 6

Gramsci's political translation of Hegelian-Marxian dialectic

The interpretation of the notes on Croce, Bukharin, and Machiavelli was motivated by Gramsci's confession about the polemical-dialogical character of his intellectual life,[1] by the philological fact that they play a crucial function in the composition and structure of the Notebooks, and by the theoretical importance and thematic interrelatedness of the problems they deal with. It is different with his thoughts on the topic of the dialectic. The need to examine them stems directly out of our previous discussions, most obviously the one in Chapter 5. It systematized Gramsci's notes on Machiavelli as an attribution to the Florentine of a concept of dialectical politics along with an exemplification (by Gramsci's own critical practice) of dialectical interpretation, and such Machiavellian politics seemed to involve a kind of moderation that Gramsci elsewhere wants to reject as undialectical. My analyses in preceding chapters have also led to the question of the nature of dialectic.

Up to now I have shown that Gramsci's critique of Bukharin's sociology is right insofar as it is grounded on a valid concept of what it means to be scientific, but wrong insofar as it fails to perceive the dialectic inherent in Bukharin's sociological practice and sees only the positivism of his philosophical theory. This raises the question of whether Gramsci failed to see Bukharin's dialectic-in-practice because he did not pay sufficient or sufficiently direct attention to Bukharin's concrete sociology or because he had a different conception of the dialectic. To test the second possibility we have to articulate Gramsci's theory of the dialectic. I have also shown that Gramsci's critique of Croce is best understood as a sound justification of the religious dimension of Marxism, grounded on Croce's own concept of religion, metaphilosophy, and style and method of criticism. Because this defines a sense in which Gramsci is Crocean, we also have a problem due to Gramsci's well-known

147

explicit objection to Croce regarding things dialectical: the "dialectic of distincts," the alleged confusion between the process and the concept of dialectic, and the corruption of the dialectic through the attempt to "domesticate" it. To understand more fully the character of Gramsci's Croceanism, we need to determine exactly what Gramsci meant and whether he was right. This will tell us whether he was more Crocean than not, whether he was a Crocean in spite of himself, whether he merely intended to be anti-Crocean, and so forth.

In short, the dialectic constitutes a central theme of what may be called the deep structure of the Prison Notebooks, by contrast with the others so far examined, which pertain more to the surface structure. That is one reason why it is as true today as it was in 1958, when the judgment was expressed by Norberto Bobbio, that "it does not seem to me that the theme of the dialectic in Gramsci has yet received the attention that the importance of the concept requires."[2] Moreover, Bobbio suggests that the dialectic is perhaps also a unifying theme (besides being a central one), when he adds, "Yet, to understand the philosophy of a Marxist writer, it is useful to begin with the conception he has of the dialectic and with the function he assigns to it."[3] In fact, as our analysis proceeds we will see how the question of the dialectic will shed new light on some of the topics already dealt with.

Unlike Gramsci's critiques of Croce, Bukharin, and Machiavelli, which are scattered in the prison writings and also concentrated in special notebooks, his notes on the dialectic were not the subject of any such concentration. Thus the first problem is to identify and locate them, before they can be systematized, analyzed, and evaluated. Since in the present undertaking the primary interest is the meaning Gramsci attached to the dialectic, the initial guide will be occurrence of the terms itself. In view of the terminological pervasiveness, however, we need to distinguish between places where the term is being casually used from those where the discussion deals relatively explicitly with the nature of the concept. These explicit discussions are the object of our search.

There are several mutually complementary ways to proceed. One is to collect Gramscian passages mentioned in the secondary literature[4] on Gramsci's dialectic. Another is to examine passages referred to by the entry *dialettica* in the critical edition of the Prison Notebooks. Third, one may pursue all the leads that originate from Gramsci's explicit discussions of Croce's views and uses of the dialectic, of Bukharin's attitude toward the dialectic, and of the problem of connection between dialectic and politics in the notes on Machiavelli. When this is done, we have about one hundred notes dispersed throughout almost all the notebooks. They consist of various subgroups dealing with particular themes.

Thirty-one notes[5] deal in whole or in part with such interrelated and overlapping questions as Proudhon and the domestication of the dialectic, the Italian tradition of passive revolution (of which Croce is a special case), the problem of political moderation, the mediation of opposite extremes, and the connection between dialectic and politics. Nineteen passages discuss Bukharin and the pedagogy of dialectic,[6] or the dialectic of nature,[7] or the dialectic of quantity and quality.[8] Eleven notes are concerned with how the dialectic relates to bureaucratic, organic, and democratic centralism.[9] Eleven others tackle questions pertaining to the science of dialectic.[10] Ten concentrate on Trotsky and how the dialectic relates to permanent revolution;[11] nine are on Croce and the so-called dialectic of distincts;[12] five give important examples of dialectic relationships or processes;[13] three discuss Hegel and the inversion of the dialectic;[14] and eight deal with important miscellaneous topics.[15]

This preliminary classification is, of course, only tentative, its main use being to provide something like a working hypothesis. Additions and deletions will be made in the course of a more analytical examination. Nevertheless, the notes just listed constitute a relatively neutral data base, with which any interpretation of Gramsci's concept of the dialectic will have to deal.

DIALECTIC AND CLASSICAL EUROPEAN CULTURE

Almost all students of Marxism acknowledge the view that its cultural origin lies in German classical philosophy, British classical economics, and the politics of the French Revolution. Without denying the fundamental correctness of this thesis, Gramsci asks the crucial question of which of two alternative interpretations is more valid: Did each of the three sources contribute, respectively, to the articulation of the philosophy, economics, and politics of Marxism, or did Marx synthesize the three sources in such a way that each is somehow present in every aspect of his doctrines? Gramsci thinks that the second is the superior interpretation, and this leads him to the problem of formulating the "unifying synthetic aspect" (Q1247)[16] that can be extracted from each of those three sources and that characterizes Marxism.

The unifying theme cannot be any of the things usually mentioned under the other interpretation, namely, Hegel's theory of historical development by a process of thesis-antithesis-synthesis, Ricardo's labor theory of value, and the revolutionary ideal of equality-fraternity-liberty. All these need not be rejected, but they are specific acquisitions, and Gramsci suggests trying to determine what single way of thinking, point of view, approach, or method they reflect. To do this one must go to a deeper level of analysis, define and then compare the essential characteristic of the three sources. This applies even to the theory of thesis-antithesis-synthesis, which is reminiscent of the dialectic, and which in fact is one of the standard meanings of the term. Thus we come to an important terminological point, since Gramsci also wants to use "dialectic" to refer to the methodological heritage Marx took from Germany, Britain, and France.

The clearest indication that in this context Gramsci is discussing the dialectic may be easily missed, both because the crucial passage occurs in a letter from prison rather than in a notebook as such, and because the point is made indirectly by means of the term "immanence." Nevertheless, the evidence is unambiguous. For, on several occasions, including the main note where he is most clear about his synthetic interpretation of the three sources of Marxism, Gramsci tells us that "the unifying synthetic aspect, it seems to me, should be identified with the new concept of immanence, which, with the help of French politics and English classical economics, has been translated from its speculative form offered by classical German philosophy into a historicist form" (Q1247). Then, in a letter dated May 30, 1932, while elaborating an interpretation of English classical economics, he states that with the help of Ricardo's contributions "one has found reasons to reduce the 'immanentistic' conception of history (expressed in idealist and speculative language by German classical philosophy) into a realistic and immediately historical 'immanence' . . . and one has synthetically identified it with the dialectical reasoning of Hegelianism."[17] Thus, in the present context, we may understand the "immanentistic" approach that Marx learned from his three sources as the "dialectical" approach, which is the subject of our present analysis.

To this textual evidence one may add a more general reason why the dialectic is the topic of discussion in those notes where Gramsci defines the essential cultural heritage available to Marx. The crucial consideration here is that Gramsci accepts the widely held thesis that the dialectic constitutes Hegel's greatest contribution. Hence, the essence of this contribution, as viewed by Gramsci, helps to define his concept of the dialectic. If, then, this essence corresponds to, or is an aspect of, the British economic and the French political contributions, we may say that for Gramsci the dialectic is the unifying theme of all these contributions.

Let us begin with Hegel, who, for Gramsci, has a unique place in the history of philosophy insofar as with him "one has, in a single system and in a single philosopher, that awareness of contradictions that previously resulted from the whole ensemble of systems and of philosophers, in polemic and in contradiction with one another" (Q1487).[18] Unfortunately, in Hegel himself this approach allegedly took the form of "philosophical fiction," and so it was made more concrete and historical by Marxism, according to which "the philosopher himself, whether as an individual or as a whole social group, not only understands the contradictions but also places himself as an element of the contradiction" (Q1487). The essential point is to (try to) free oneself "from every one-sided and fanatical ideological element" (Q1487), to avoid and destroy "all dogmatically one-sided concepts" (Q1487).

The dialectical heritage from British classical economics is best appreciated by studying Gramsci's notes on the methodological and epistemological status of Ricardo's concepts of *Homo oeconomicus,* the market, and law of tendency.[19] The specific details of these concepts and laws are for Gramsci all subject to the historical proviso that Marx's "critique" of political economy added to the classical version of political economy.[20] But this greater appreciation of historical contingency represents their difference. If we want to understand their similarity, we have to define the essential trait of those concepts.

For Gramsci, *Homo oeconomicus* is indeed an abstraction from empirical reality, but one that inheres in history,[21] namely, a "determined abstraction" (Q1276). By using such puzzling and almost self-contradictory language, Gramsci is trying to say, I think, that the *Homo oeconomicus* of a given social formation or historical period is a resultant or synthesis of the economic needs and operations of a given society. It corresponds to the "*ensemble* of the hypotheses made by economists in their scientific elaborations" (Q1265, my italics), which in turn corresponds to the "*ensemble* of the premises that are at the basis of a particular form of society" (Q1265, my italics). Similarly, the market is "the *ensemble* of concrete economic activities in a given social formation, assumed to obey uniform (that is, abstract) laws, but without the abstraction ceasing to be historically determined" (Q1276–77, my italics). Gramsci here seems to be making an analogy with Hegel's ensemble of philosophical systems.

The dialectical import (in the sense of synthesis of a multiplicity of elements) is even clearer in connection with the concept of law of tendency. Gramsci's point emerges in his criticism of Croce's interpretation of the Marxian law of the tendential fall of the profit rate.[22] The law says that in a capitalistic system there is a tendency for labor to become more and more capital-intensive; and as this happens, the amount of profit relative to invested capital (which is to say, the *rate* of profit) tends to fall, since profit derives only from labor (specifically "surplus" labor).[23] Croce was one of the first to object that this law was invalid because it ignored the increased productivity of capital-intensive labor.[24] Gramsci replies that the oversight is Croce's own and not Marx's, because before formulating the law about the profit rate in the third volume of *Capital*, Marx had formulated another law about increased productivity (or relative surplus value) in the first volume of *Capital*.[25] So Marx's point is that there are (at least) two results of technical progress and capital accumulation: One is higher productivity; the other is lower *rate* of profit. This kind of criticism by Croce is a good example of violation of the dialectic, namely, "the error of having examined the law of the fall of the profit rate by isolating it from the process in which it was conceived, not for the scientific purpose of a better exposition, but as if it were valid absolutely; rather it is valid as a dialectical term of a larger organic process" (Q1283). The implicit point about the concept of law of tendency is that "in political economy every law cannot not be tendential insofar as it is obtained by isolating a certain number of elements and thus neglecting opposing forces" (Q1279). The concept of dialectic extracted by Marxism from British classical economics is then that of the individual identification and proper interrelation of economic tendencies, or, in other words, the analysis *and* the synthesis of aspects of the economy.

From French politics it is the Jacobinism of the Great Revolution that Marxism appreciates, according to Gramsci. A specific example of this appreciation[26] he frequently points to is Marx's talk of permanent revolution in 1848–50. What Gramsci has in mind is Jacobinism in the original, proper, historical, or "classical sense of the word" (Q1834), as referring to a particular party of the first several years of the Revolution of 1789. The essence of this classical Jacobinism may be summarized as follows. To begin with, it pursued its program with a style of political action and of government "characterized by extreme energy, decisiveness, and resoluteness, deriving from the fanatic belief in the goodness of that program and that style"(Q2017). The general character of the program of the Jacobins was realism, that is, it went "in the direction of actual historical development" (Q2029), since they created not only a bourgeois government but a bourgeois state and the modern French nation. Gramsci insists it is the combination of this historical realism and this volitional energy that is significant: "They were convinced of the absolute truth of the formulas of equality, fraternity, and liberty, and, what's more important, of such truth were convinced the great popular masses that the Jacobins instigated and brought into the struggle" (Q2028). The specific content of their program was the integration of the many factions and special interests that made up the Third Estate, the main divisions being those between city dwellers (mainly Paris) and peasants (the provinces) and those between the intellectual elite and the economically active strata. Gramsci is explicit about the synthetic nature of this achievement:

The Jacobins were thus the only party of the revolution-in-action, insofar as not only did they represent the immediate needs and aspirations of the actual physical persons who happened to constitute the French bourgeoisie, but they represented the revolutionary movement in its entirety, as an integral historical movement; for they represented even future needs, and again, not only of those particular physical persons, but of all national groups that had to be assimilated by the fundamental existing group. (Q2028)

Thus, the central lesson from classical French Jacobin politics seems to be the recognition of the many different existing and "progressive" political interests and forces, their harmonization into a coherent direction, and the resolute pursuit of this goal.

Gramsci not only credits the successes of the Jacobins to this attitude but blames their eventual downfall on a betrayal of this approach: "They were unwilling to grant workers the right of coalition . . . and as a consequence . . . they thus broke up the Parisian urban bloc: their assault forces, which were concentrated in the city, were dispersed and disillusioned, and the Thermidor prevailed" (Q2029–30). Besides the failure to recognize or integrate an important historical force, another thing that can go wrong is to follow the style of the classical Jacobins without having the appropriate (realistic) program. This dissociation has frequently happened and has given the term "Jacobinism" a second, more common connotation, but this is a corrupted meaning.[27]

The connection with the dialectic is not only implicit in the methodological similarity between Jacobinism so conceived and Hegelianism as described above, but also can be seen as follows. First, on several occasions,[28] Gramsci refers with approval to Marx's statement in *The Holy Family*[29] about a correspondence between Jacobin politics and German classical philosophy. Second, at one point Gramsci explicitly says that the dialectic is involved in the Jacobin combination of intellectual and peasant forces.[30] And in a note critical of French culture, he gives the failure of classical Jacobinism as a typical example of what happens when one "does not have a dialectic mentality" (Q1257).

One might ask at this point, to what extent Gramsci's interpretation of these Marxist sources is accurate, that is, whether it is true that the "unifying synthetic aspect" he discusses is present in Hegel, in Ricardo, and in Jacobinism, whether it was really appreciated by Marx himself or by Marxism. The most important of these questions, the one relating to Hegel's own conception of the dialectic, is examined in Chapter 7. For the moment our interest is Gramsci's concept of the dialectic; so far I have argued that for him the dialectic is first and foremost the methodological heritage of classical European culture, and that this heritage consists of avoiding all one-sidedness, be it with respect to philosophical system, economic tendency, or political interest.[31] One question we need to examine now is how commitment to, or choice of, one side fits into this scheme. For after all, Gramsci tells us, as we have seen, that the Hegelian philosopher "not only understands the contradictions but also places himself as an element of the contradiction" (Q1487), and that the Jacobin politician is a resolute leader of a particular class (the Third Estate). And in his discussion of the tendential fall of the profit rate, Gramsci asserts that when all is said and done (when the other opposing tendency has been taken into account), the Marxist holds that *this* tendency will prevail over the other.[32]

I believe this is a difficulty in Gramsci's view of the dialectic, and I am not sure he has a satisfactory solution. It is a difficulty related to the problem of dialectical politics that emerged in the analysis of his notes on Machiavelli, and to the problem of distinguishing philosophy from ideology that will emerge in the context of Gramsci's critique of the domestication of the dialectic. I would suggest that his point is that the dialectician makes his choice with the awareness of all sides; his commitment is presumably *his* synthesis of the many aspects of the situation. This would locate the difference between a dialectical and an undialectical approach in the comprehensiveness and depth of the analysis of the situation; the dialectic would then have that much content, although it would not determine a choice. This is perhaps as it should be, for one of Gramsci's most frequent themes is the contrast between a dialectical and a "mechanist" approach.

LOGIC AND DIALECTIC

The most numerous and influential group of opponents of the dialectic are the (formal) logicians, whereas the so-called dialectical materialists are its most numerous and influential proponents. This was as true half a century ago when Gramsci wrote his prison notes as it is today. Hence it will be instructive to analyze a set of notes[33] wherein he argues against the two corresponding misinterpretations of the dialectic.

Let us begin with a terminological clarification. When Gramsci speaks of formal logic, he is *not* contrasting it to whatever might be called material logic, or to informal logic. Moreover, when he speaks of logic without qualification, he usually means the same thing as formal logic. In both cases he is referring to the science and art of reasoning, which is the special kind or aspect of thinking exemplified by the classic syllogism "All men are mortal; Socrates is a man; therefore Socrates is mortal" or by Babbitt's "simplistic" argument quoted by Gramsci from Sinclair Lewis's *Babbitt:*

A good labor association is a good thing because it hinders the revolutionary unions which would destroy property. But no one should be forced to join an association. All labor agitators who try to force everyone to join an association should be hanged. In short, speaking between us, no association should be allowed; and since this is the best manner of fighting them, every businessman should belong to an association of entrepreneurs and to the Chamber of Commerce. To unite is to be stronger. Therefore every solitary egoist who is not a member of the Chamber of Commerce should be forced to join it. (Q1466)

When logic is understood in this manner, Gramsci thinks it is a practical and useful skill, and a legitimate technical discipline.[34] Moreover, he argues against Croce's criticism of formal logic and refers with approval to Engels's remarks in the *Anti-Dühring* that it is not innate but has undergone a long historical development and that it is to be retained even after the innovations of Marxism.[35] Gramsci's emphasis is on pedagogy: The need "is the more acute the more reference is made, not to intellectuals and the so-called educated classes, but to the uneducated popular masses for whom it is necessary even today to learn formal logic and the most elementary grammar of thought and of language" (Q1464). This is a crucial point to remember "for the construction of didactic programs" (Q1464). We should not expect too much from logic, but the benefits will be real: "It certainly will not create great philosophers, but it will provide criteria of judgment and of control, and it will correct the malformations of the ways of thinking of common sense" (Q1464).

Thus, for Gramsci, the dialectic is not something *opposed* to logic.[36] There is, nevertheless, a *difference*. But before making this differentiation, is it useful to formulate briefly two more common properties besides the one (already implicitly mentioned) that both logic and the dialectic are *ways of thinking*. The dialectic, too, is a *skill* that needs to be developed from the commonsense outlook.[37] Like logic, the dialectic is a *technical* discipline; for example, although Gramsci would disagree about the details and evaluation, the Crocean analysis of the concept of "speculation"[38] and principle of the "dialectic of distincts"[39] are regarded by him as dialectical technicalities.

Gramsci's formulation of the difference may be difficult to find, because he does not give it in the notes where he discusses logic or in those where he discusses the dialectic explicitly. The clue to its location is given by the pedagogical thesis that seems to be his primary interest in his discussion of logic. In fact, on a different occasion, in the context of a discussion of journalism, he makes a very similar pedagogical point about a different way of thinking (which I believe is the dialectical one): that such a cognitive skill is "acquired and not innate" (Q2267) and needs to be taught to the masses.

The "journalistic" context may give the impression that this identification of Gramsci's definition is strained and artificial, but such an impression would betray a misunderstanding of the kind of journalism he is talking about, as well as of his conception of philosophy. In fact, "the type of journalism that is considered in these notes is the one that could be called 'integral,' . . . that is, the one that not only intends to satisfy all the [intellectual-moral] needs of its public but intends to create and to develop these needs, and thus in a sense to challenge its public and progressively to extend its size" (Q2259). But now recall Gramsci's analysis of the nature and interrelationships of philosophy, religion, and common sense,[40] where he articulates a conception of philosophy essentially identical to this "integral journalism." The most eloquent passage deserves deep reflection:

To create a new culture does not mean only to make individually some "original" discoveries; it means also and especially to communicate critically some truths already discovered, to "socialize" them, so to speak, and thus to make them become the basis of vital actions and an element of coordination and of intellectual and moral order. That a mass of men is led to think coherently and in a unified manner about reality, is a "philosophical" fact of much greater importance and "originality" than the discovery by a philosophical "genius" of a new truth that remains the property of small intellectual groups. (Q1377–78)

This identification of philosophic and journalistic activity, together with Gramsci's general commitment to the "dialectical" nature of the former, constitutes strong evidence that a crucial feature of his "dialectic" is given by his view of the essential feature of journalistic activity. Well, what is that?

In no uncertain terms Gramsci declares that "the most delicate, misunderstood, and yet essential skill of the critic of ideas and historian of developments is *to find the real identity under the apparent differentiation and contradiction and to find the substantial diversity under the apparent identity*" (Q2268, my italics).[41] This skill of the historian-critic is presumably dialectic thinking par excellence, or dialectic in a special restricted sense. For Gramsci goes on to add that the characteristic trait of the professional intellectual in general is (ideally) to combine "deduction and induction, formal logic and the dialectic, identification and distinction, positive demonstration and destruction of what's old" (Q2268). This synthesis of cognitive activities corresponds to the conception of dialectic (as avoidance of all one-sidedness) articulated earlier in connection with the classical European heritage. Moreover, we see logic and the dialectic explicitly distinguished, but not opposed, any more than deduction and induction are; and this corresponds to what we learned just now from Gramsci's discussion of logic. It also emerges that identification and distinction, whose synthesis constitutes dialectic in the special and restricted sense, are formally analogous to induction and deduction whose synthesis presumably constitutes logic; this implies that there is a dialectic within logic and suggests there may be a logic within the dialectic.

Finally, what is the relation between dialectic in the narrow sense of identification-distinction and dialectic in the wider sense of synthetic avoidance of one-sided cognition? Gramsci does not say, and so I offer the following speculation. Avoiding one-sidedness presupposes that one has defined the various "sides," which is simply to distinguish them. The avoidance, if it is to be done through some kind of synthesis, involves identification in the sense of finding what they all have in common, or what they presuppose, or what they imply, or what action they all require. In this way, the apparently wider sense of dialectic would become in reality a particular case of the apparently narrower one.

To summarize, the dialectic and logic for Gramsci are distinct but not opposed ways of thinking. Logic refers to reasoning, whereas the dialectic refers to distinguishing-relating. But they are both valuable skills to be learned and technical disciplines that may be studied. In turn, this new sense of dialectic is distinct but (perhaps) not opposed to its previous conception as synthetic avoidance of one-sidedness, for this avoidance may be seen as an instance of distinguishing-relating.

"DIALECTICAL MATERIALISM"

This analysis of the relationship between the dialectic and logic now allows us to understand relatively easily one of his two major objections to so-called dialectical materialism. For dialectical materialism presumably trivializes their relationship by making the dialectic a simple specific case of formal logic, namely, the case dealing with reasoning about movement and change.[42] Besides this reason for regarding dialectical materialism as undialectical, Gramsci has another, which relates to the undialectical character of its "materialism."

According to Gramsci, in the first half of the nineteenth century this term had two meanings: One was metaphysical materialism; the other was "any philosophical doctrine that excludes transcendence from the domain of thinking" (Q1408), which we may call "immanentism." The dialectical materialists assumed uncritically that Marx's talk of the materialist conception of history referred to the first meaning,[43] and thus they became guilty "of lack of historical sense in perceiving the various aspects of a process of historical development, that is, of undialectical thinking" (Q1408). They should have stayed away from metaphysical materialism because it is no better than metaphysical idealism, whereas dialectic "supersedes both traditional idealism and materialism, and in so doing it includes their vital elements" (Q1425).

In contrast to this combination of formal-logical dialectic and traditional metaphysical materialism, which is what goes under the label of "dialectical materialism," Gramsci proceeds to sketch what might be properly so called, although he uses not this label but, rather, as is well known, that of "philosophy of praxis." We have both epistemological and ontological considerations. For the latter, Gramsci suggests that one might *begin* with the idea of matter as consisting of what physics tells us, that is, the set of its physical properties.[44] This "matter" would be considered not in the abstract but in relation to man, in particular as an element of economic production. This in turn would yield the concept of the "ensemble of the material forces of production" (Q1443). Matter so conceived "is the least variable element of historical development, is what time after time can be ascertained and measured with mathematical exactitude . . . is both a crystallization of all past history and the basis of present and future history" (Q1443). This "materialism" is dialectical in the sense that the matter of physics is first distinguished from the human world, but then related to it through the phenomenon of economic activity and through the historical process.

The immanentist epistemology which Gramsci would require in a dialectic approach would take history as its starting point. Then one would realize that "from history one cannot separate politics and economics, including the specialized phases of political art and science and of theoretical and political economics" (Q1448). Next, in the properly epistemological undertaking, one would formulate a framework "in which the general concepts of history, of politics, and of economics would be tied with each other in an organic unity" (Q1448). Finally, one would study "how history and politics are reflected in economics, how economics and politics are reflected in history, how history and economics are reflected in politics" (Q465).

THE "DIALECTIC OF NATURE"

In this critique of dialectical materialism Gramsci's target was primarily Bukharin. But Gramsci is of the opinion that "any conversion and identification of historical materialism into vulgar [metaphysical] materialism can only determine an opposite error, the conversion of materialism into idealism" (Q469). The exponent of a version of dialectical idealism that he has in mind is this context is not Croce but Lukács. Although Gramsci confesses that he is only vaguely acquainted with Lukács, he knows enough to note that "it seems that Lukács states that one can speak of dialectic only for human history and not for nature" (Q1149).

The criticism is not altogether negative, for we are told that Lukács "may possibly be wrong and may possibly be right" (Q1449). Although Gramsci does not tell us in what sense he thinks Lukács's thesis is right, I would interpret it to be that there is no dialectic *in* nature but only *in* man. This interpretation is supported by the fact that (1) it follows from Gramsci's essential conception of the dialectic as a way of thinking and (2) it makes sense of the misgivings he expresses in this context about Engels's attempt to show the dialectic to be a cosmic law.[45]

The sense in which Gramsci objects to Lukács's statement must be that the dialectic (approach) cannot be applied *to* nature but only *to* man. This, in fact, corresponds to the assertion actually made by Lukács,[46] and it allows us to understand Gramsci's supporting argument. His rationale is basically that such a dichotomy would be undialectical because man and nature would have been distinguished but not significantly related. Or in his own words, Lukács's claim "presupposes a dualism between nature and man . . . which does not really succeed in unifying and interrelating man and nature" (Q1449). For Gramsci, the best way to study the interaction is through the history of science, which is precisely the history of the interaction between man and nature since "the experimental activity of the scientist . . . is the first model of dialectical mediation between man and nature" (Q1449).

Thus, for Gramsci there is no such thing as "the dialectic of nature," when taken literally, as dialectical thinking *in* nature *separate* from man, but there is in the sense of "dialectical thinking *about* nature *and* man." This leads to the quesion of the possibility of dialectical thinking *about* nature *separate* from man. That is, can one think dialectically about natural phenomena as such?

Gramsci's answer is that this is not possible, except metaphorically.[47] In other words, it is certainly possible to study physical phenomena by trying to ascertain the real similarities under their apparent differences, and their differences under their apparent similarities, which, as we have seen, is the essence of dialectic. The problem with this would be that such a "physics" would not be dealing with "nature," since the concept of nature by definition refers to an unchanging entity, and hence the study of nature must be the search for uniformities, regularities, constancies, preferably measurable, quantitative ones.[48] Even when change and variation are being studied, one acts as if "the variability of the ensemble of the material forces . . . is itself measurable and one can establish with a certain precision when its development turns from quantitative to qualitative" (Q1443). In short, about "nature" one tries to ascertain only the real similarities under the apparent differences of "natural phenomena," which is only one side of the dialectical enterprise.

This opposition between the dialectical and the naturalistic approaches[49] should not be confused with that between the dialectical and the scientific methods. Insofar as one connotation of science is that of natural science, of course we would have the same opposition. But there is a more general conception of science as rationality, and then we would have *no* opposition; instead, to be dialectical would be a special case of being "scientific."[50]

One way Gramsci avoids this terminological confusion is by using terms like "mechanical," "mechanist," "mechanistic," "mechanism," and "mechanicism" to refer to the scientific approach in the sense of natural science. I suppose, his reason is that mechanics is the natural science par excellence, the most fundamental branch of the most basic of the natural sciences (physics). This, in turn, allows us to understand a pervasive lexicographical feature of the notebooks, namely, the contrast between "dialectic" and "mechanism"; indeed, Gramsci uses these terms as antonyms. As they are defined above, dialectical equals antimechanist and mechanist equals undialectical, although not in the sense of being strict opposites, for the proper content of "mechanism" is *part* of the full content of "dialectic." The opposition seems, nevertheless, justified in that, starting with mechanism as the search of the uniformities underlying differences, dialectic *adds* a procedure that in some obvious sense is its opposite, namely, the examination of the differences underlying uniformities. Thus, when contrasted to mechanism, "dialectic" refers merely to its added distinguishing element.

To summarize, Gramsci's critique of the "dialectic of nature" gives us not only his view on a standard "dialectical" topic but also a further elaboration (application) of his concept of the dialectic, which we identified earlier in this chapter. The contrast to mechanism also helps us appreciate better the full dialectical import of a number of other discussions where Gramsci argues against various "mechanist" practices, to which we now turn.

DIALECTIC AND CENTRALIZATION

One of the best examples concerns the problem of bureaucracy and centralization.[51] Although interpreters of Gramsci usually discuss this problem only in relation to the organization of a political party,[52] Gramsci himself says explicitly that the question arises also for the life of a state (in the form of union versus federation), for international alliances, for cultural associations, for religions (in the form of Catholicism vs. Protestantism), for labor unions, for business corporations (in the form of the problem of cartels and trusts),[53] and even for military organizations and the art of war.[54] So it is all-pervasive in human affairs.

For Gramsci, centralization per se is neither good nor bad; in other words, there is a good form and a bad form of centralization. The good form he calls "democratic centralism"; the bad, "bureaucratic centralism."[55] Characteristic of bureaucratic centralism is a "precise program of real dominance by a part over the whole" (Q1633), whether the part be a class of intellectuals, or a privileged geographical region, or a single individual "infallible bearer of truth [or] enlightened by reason" (Q1650). Gramsci regards this as a case of upside-down Jacobinism,[56] and hence undialectical in that sense, as seen in the preceding sections. Another defining characteristic is the existence of a "system of doctrines rigidly and rigorously formulated" (Q337), grounded on faith in being able "to build an institution once and for all, already objectively perfect" (Q337); for Gramsci this involves a mechanist conception of ideology, as if it were a dress to put around the body at will, rather than the skin that is organically tied to it. As for command, bureaucratic centralism does not realize that "from one group to another the art of command and its manner of expression change a lot" (Q796), and it conceives discipline "as a passive and quiet acceptance of orders, as a mechanical execution of a task" (Q1706); of course, this view "is tied to a mechanist conception of history and development" (Q796). Fourth, the bureaucratic-centralist relation between leaders and led is "of a purely bureaucratic, formal kind" (Q1505), in that the leaders have knowledge but no feeling, whereas the led feel but do not know; the error here is that the elementary passions of the people are not "being dialectically tied to the laws of history" (Q1505); in other words, we have a failure of the "intellectuals-masses dialectic" (Q1386). Finally, in bureaucratic centralism, the individual member of an institution tends to think of it "as an entity extraneous from himself – a fetish" (Q1770); this involves transcendence, and hence anti-immanence, and hence failure of the dialectic.

The conception of the dialectic inherent in these critiques is the familiar one, as seen from Gramsci's general criticism that bureaucratic centralism is a *one-sided* reaction to disorder and dispersion,[57] and from his contrast between bureaucratic and democratic centralism. The latter is "centralism in motion, so to speak; that is, a continuous adaption by the organization to real developments, a matching of the pushes from below with the command from above" (Q1634). The formula underlying this process is almost identical to Gramsci's definition of the dialectic:

Democratic centralism offers an elastic formula, which lends itself to many incarnations; it lives insofar as it is continuously interpreted and adapted to various necessities: It consists in *the critical search for what is equal in the apparent diversity, and distinct and even opposite in the apparent uniformity,* in order to render organic and to connect closely what is similar, but in such a way that the organic process and the connection appear as a practical and inductive, experimental necessity, and not as the result of a rationalistic, deductivist, and abstractionist process, characteristic of pure intellectuals. (Q1635, my italics)[58]

In conclusion, for Gramsci, bureaucratic centralism is undialectical because it is mechanistic and essentially one-sided; whereas democratic centralism is an instance of diversity within unity and unity within diversity, and hence it is dialectical.

DIALECTIC AND REVOLUTION

Corresponding to these two types of centralized administration, though not distinguished as clearly in Gramsci's text, are two main kinds of revolutions.[59] One, the analogue of bureaucratic centralism,[60] is called "passive revolution" and has as a prototype the Italian Risorgimento; it is discussed in the next section. The prototype of the other is the French Revolution, and although Gramsci uses such locutions as "profoundly popular," "mass-driven," "from below," and "from the base,"[61] he does *not* in fact use the more or less obvious label "democratic revolution." He does frequently refer to this type of revolution as Jacobin (which is not at all surprising, given his dialectical conception of Jacobinism and of democratic centralism analyzed earlier in this chapter); however, he makes no explicit effort to formulate a general concept of Jacobin revolution. On some occasions[62] he uses the misleading phrase "permanent revolution," which usually he finds objectionable because it has so frequently been given a mechanist interpretation, for example, by Trotsky.[63] Hence, Gramsci prefers to speak of "hegemony."[64] An analysis of the latter would, I feel sure, reveal it to be a dialectical phenomenon,[65] but such a revelation would need to be grounded on a view of what the dialectic is, since the relevant texts are not explicit, although they pervade all the Notebooks. In the present context, since we are in the process of elaborating Gramsci's concept of the dialectic, we need explicit textual evidence. This brings us back to the problematic "permanent revolution," because it is in connection with this notion that Gramsic makes an important explicit dialectical remark: "The dialectical mediation between the two methodological principles stated at the beginning of this note may be found in the political-historical formula of permanent revolution" (Q1578). The principles in question were adapted from Marx's 1859 preface to *A Contribution to the Critique of Political Economy* and stated by Gramsci as follows:

(1) that no society makes for itself tasks for whose solution the necessary and sufficient conditions do not already exist or at least are not about to appear and develop; and (2) that no society is dissolved and can be replaced until it has worked out all the forms of life which are implicit in its [structural] relationships. (Q1579)

Our present task is to interpret Gramsci's dialectical remark about permanent revolution and to see what concept of dialectic he has in mind.

Let us begin with the historical development that provides for Gramsci the best example of a permanent revolution. It is the French Revolution, but Gramsci is careful to point out that this must be understood not as the mere seizure of the Bastille on July 14, 1789, or even as the subsequent series of upheavals culminating in the crowning of Napoleon Bonaparte as emperor in 1804, but as the whole period from 1789 to 1871. Gramsci's rationale is that only with the Paris Commune of 1870–71 do the developments begun in 1789 significantly exhaust themselves: One reason is that in 1871 "the new class that struggles for power defeats not only the representatives of the old society (which had not wanted to be regarded as decisively superseded), but also the very new groups (which claim already superseded the new structure emerged from the upheaval begun in 1789)" (Q1581); moreover, only with the Third Republic, created in 1871, "France has sixty years of balanced political life after eighty years of increasingly long waves of upheavals:

1789–1794–1799–1804–1815–1830–1848–1870" (Q1582). Thus, we see an alternation of periods of revolutionary activity in the strict sense and periods of restoration, that is, an alternation of innovation and conservation.

Returning to the two principles Gramsci takes from Marx's 1859 preface, we see that the first one by itself is a principle of innovation, whereas the second by itself is a principle of conservation.[66] The first says, in effect, that if a social problem has emerged, so have the means for its solution: It is up to us to find them or create this solution, which may not be easy, but we can at least demand it. The second principle says, in effect, that we should try as much as possible to work within the framework that already exists in society. How does the general concept of permanent revolution represent a "dialectical mediation" between these two principles? In the sense that it calls attention to the revolutionary continuity underlying the discontinuity of the various particular developmental stages of the whole process,[67] while not denying the reality of this discontinuity, as expressed by the political differences characterizing those stages. But this is precisely what the dialectic is all about, as we have seen.

In speaking of permanent revolution (understood dialectically) as a "political-historical formula" (Q1578), Gramsci means that it is a general concept useful for the *interpretation* of various events in political *history*. He does not mean that the concept is itself a *political* formula, in other words, that it can *now* provide a program or strategy for the politician. On the contrary, Gramsci holds that as a political program, the concept is no longer valid. Its *political* inapplicability is precisely one of the consequences of the French Revolution (broadly understood, as noted above): "Moreover, with 1870–71, there is a loss of effectiveness for the set of principles of political strategy and tactics born in practice in 1789 and developed ideologically around 1848, those which are summarized in the formula 'permanent revolution'" (Q1582). This is so because "the formula is specific to a historical period in which there were no large mass-based political parties and no large labor unions, and in which society was still, so to speak, in a state of fluidity in many ways" (Q1566). In the period beginning 1871, "all those elements change, the internal and international organizational relations of a state become more complex and massive, and the forty-eightish formula of 'permanent revolution' is elaborated and superseded in political science with the formula of 'civil hegemony'" (Q1566). Gramsci's criticism of Trotsky's theory of permanent revolution[68] both supports and is supported by this political analysis. The same is true for Gramsci's subtle qualification concerning "backward countries and colonies, where still prevail forms that elsewhere have been superseded and become anachronistic" (Q1567), and hence where the political inapplicability of the concept may not apply.

In short, for Gramsci, although the concept of permanent revolution originates from the history of the French Revolution, it potentially provides a useful historiographical principle for the interpretation of political history in general. Moreover, as such a historiographical concept it is dialectical in the sense we have been elaborating in this chapter. The concept, however, is not part of Gramsci's own political program and strategy, as it was for the Jacobins after 1789 and for Marx in 1848–50, because the situation Gramsci faces is significantly different. Yet in (much of) nineteenth-century Europe it was a viable political program, and this is one reason why those who were putting it into practice *then* were thereby fashioning a "democratic" revolution and, consequently, were being, in their own way, dialectical.

DIALECTIC AND REFORMISM

The situation is different with "passive revolution." For, instead of the double dialectical nature of permanent revolution (in a potentially general historiographical sense, and in a limited political sense), Gramsci argues that although the historiographical concept of passive revolution is dialectical, its political formula is not; indeed, he almost defines passive revolutions as misconceptions of the dialectic. Whether he is altogether correct in so doing will be seen as our analysis proceeds.

Gramsci's argument is rather complex and the relevant notes[69] constitute the most numerous and intensely dialectical group. Let us begin with his prototypical illustration[70] of the notion "passive revolution." The Risorgimento is the period of nineteenth-century Italian history starting with the collection of numerous statelets sanctioned by the Congress of Vienna in 1815 and ending with the unification of the peninsula with the Savoy dynasty as monarchs in 1870. This monarchy was the result of the fact that they originally ruled the Piedmont region of Italy, and their Piedmontese state had managed to dominate the most crucial revolutionary developments. The "Piedmont factor" is for Gramsci one of the central facts of the Risorgimento. The state of Piedmont capitalized on whatever nationalist and anti-Austrian feelings existed amd managed to organize and lead those sparse elements throughout Italy, which "wanted that a new force, independent of any compromise and condition, should become the arbiter of the nation" (Q1822). Two other features are "the historical fact of the absence of popular initiative in the development of Italian history and the other fact that change has taken place as a reaction by the dominant classes to the elementary, inorganic, and sporadic subversivism of popular masses" (Q1324–25). A fourth important fact concerns the character of the leadership and the asymmetry or imbalance between the two main parties. The self-styled Moderate Party, led by Piedmontese statesman Cavour, tended to favor diplomatic and legal means; whereas the so-called Action Party, led by Mazzini and Garibaldi, tended to favor popular insurrection and a republican constitution. According to Gramsci, the crucial asymmetry that allowed the moderates to prevail over the activists was that Cavour understood Mazzini and hence himself, whereas Mazzini did not understand Cavour and hence not even himself;[71] moreover, "in their propaganda the moderates were without scruples, while the men of the Action Party were full of patriotic and national generosity and respected all who had really suffered for the Risorgimento" (Q2074). Hence, it is not surprising that even on occasions when popular initiatives led by the activists were more successful than those led by the moderates (e.g., the revolts in Rome, Milan, and Venice of 1848–49, and the liberation of southern Italy in 1859–60), the activists did not gain in a way commensurate with their actual contribution, and "thus they were prevented from determining a more advanced result, along a line of greater progress and modernity" (Q1774). Another consequence of the asymmetry in understanding and forcefulness was the phenomenon known as "transformism," which meant the absorption by one side (the Moderate Party) of more and more leaders of the other side (the Action Party).[72] In summary, the Italian Risorgimento was for Gramsci essentially the enlargement of the state[73] of Piedmont, accomplished with little or no mass-based popular participation, accompanied by "temperate and reformistic conservativism" (Q1221), and led by a party that lacked effective competition for leadership.

These generalized characteristics are, in turn, easy to detect in Gramsci's general definition. For example, in his earliest note on the subject, he states, "the concept of passive revolution seems to me to be correct not only for Italy, but also for other countries, which modernized the state through a series of reforms or of national wars, without going through a political revolution of the radical-Jacobin type" (Q503). Here he emphasizes the lack of popular initiative, and we have thereby the previously mentioned contrast with the revolution of the French or "democratic" type. In the light of our analysis of the concept of the dialectic, this contrast may be taken as a hint that Gramsci will find a passive revolution to be an inherently undialectical phenomenon, but this is not the way he happens to elaborate his *explicit* criticism, as we will see presently.

Gramsci also explains that passive revolution is such that

. . . a state is substituted to local social groups in leading a struggle for renewal. It is a case in which these groups have the function of dominating rather than leading: a dictatorship without hegemony. There is hegemony by a part of the social group over the whole group, not by the latter over other forces in order to strengthen the movement, to radicalize it, etc., as in the "Jacobin" model. (Q1823–24)

The beginning of the last sentence in this passage is reminiscent of Gramsci's view of bureaucratic centralism,[74] discussed earlier in this chapter, to the effect that it involves "real dominance of a part over the whole" (Q1633). Of course, hegemony is better than dominance, insofar as it includes consent from below; but in this passage Gramsci's point is one about incomplete or misplaced hegemony, for the state is leading the local groups, and these are merely dominating the rest of society. Thus there may be a democratic-centralist relation between the state and the active local groups, but the relation between these groups and the mass of the population is bureaucratic-centralist, and so the overall relationship is undemocratic and presumably undialectical. This analogy between a passive revolution and bureaucratic centralism is made more explicit by Gramsci when, in summarizing his views about passive revolution, he states that his objection is related to a "revision of certain sectarian concepts about the theory of parties, which represent a form of fatalism of the 'divine right' type" (Q1827). Once again, however, although this fits with Gramsci's criticism of passive revolutions as undialectical, it is not in these terms that he happens to formulate *explicitly* his main objection.

His *explicit* dialectical criticism of the politics of a passive revolution relates to its temperate, reformistic conservativism and its unbalanced leadership. However, before examining this difficult topic, it will be easier to tackle Gramsci's justification of the dialectical character of the *concept* of passive revolution, as a principle of historical interpretation.

For Gramsci, when we think about a passive revolution as a past historical event, we should understand it as a developmental stage that often comes after and may be followed by a period of popular revolutionary activity, and also as merely one of at least two tendencies[75] existing during the period when it predominated.[76] In other words, the process of a passive revolution should be considered not in isolation but in relation to what came before and (perhaps) after and to other coexisting elements. In so doing one is giving a "dynamic judgment" (Q1767) of passive revolutions, which are thus seen as part of the "cunning of Divine Providence, in Vico's sense" (Q1767), that is, as a historical necessity "to determine a more rapid maturation of the internal forces kept tied down by the reformistic practice" (Q1328). Whatever political difficulties passive revolutions may embody, "the conception remains dialectical, in the sense that it presupposes, indeed it postulates as necessary, a vigorous antithesis that would present in an intransigent manner its possibilities of explication" (Q1827).

The concept of dialectic inherent here corresponds to the one analyzed so far, since the historian of revolutions is proceeding as follows: First, in defining a "passive" type of revolution in the first place, he is formulating a difference that underlies the apparent sameness of revolutions; and in investigating the extent of the "antithesis," he is showing that periods of passive revolution are not that passive after all. Second, and more important, by studying the effect of this passive element on the coexisting active one, and by studying how the passive tendency may have been the result of an earlier popular initiative, he is exploring the similarities underlying the differences. It is this second aspect of dialectical thinking that Gramsci is practicing when, while discussing the Risorgimento, he asks the more or less rhetorical question, "in the Cavour-Mazzini struggle, in which Cavour is the exponent of passive revolution/war of position and Mazzini of popular initiative/war of maneuver, are they not both indispensable to the same precise extent?" (Q1767).

If, then, the (historiographical) concept of passive revolution is a dialectical one, how can Gramsci object to the politics of passive revolutionaries? Indeed, how can he say that the (political) program of passive revolution is undialectical? In fact, it should be noted that his opposition to the strategy of passive revolution seems to be stronger and more global than his opposition to the strategy of permanent revolution, for he does not think that passive revolution was right even in the past, even when it prevailed as in the Risorgimento.

If we examine his most articulate discussions on this topic,[77] we find the following objections. In a note on Croce and the Italian moderate tradition, Gramsci charges that in deriving moderate (political) lessons from passive revolutions, "they mechanically presuppose that in the dialectical process the thesis should be conserved by the antithesis" (Q1220–21), whereas "in real history the antithesis tends to destroy the thesis" (Q1221), that is, "every antithesis must necessarily place itself as a radical antagonist of the thesis, up to the point of proposing to destroy it completely and to substitute it completely" (Q1328). Moreover, such political moderation is allegedly intellectualistic because the apologists of passive revolution "conceive themselves as the arbiters and the mediators of real political struggles, as those who impersonate . . . the synthesis of the dialectical process itself, synthesis that they manipulate speculatively in their brain by mixing its aspects 'properly'" (Q1222).

The component of liberal reformism also comes under attack. By "reformism" Gramsci means the view "that proposes as the only method of political action that in which progress and historical development result from . . . the mixing in right proportions of conservation and innovation" (Q1325). By "liberalism" he means the view that "the liberal form of the state is untouchable, that is, the form that guarantees every political force to move and struggle freely" (Q1327). The problem is that this liberal reformism "tends to unnerve the antithesis, to break it up into a long series of elements, that is, to reduce the dialectic to a process of reformistic evolution" (Q1328).

The unbalanced asymmetry in the leadership of passive revolutions is found objectionable because it "consists precisely in this: In the dialectical opposition only the thesis really develops all its possibilities of struggle, up to the point of winning over the self-styled representatives of the antithesis" (Q1768). On the other hand, the dialectic requires that "every member of the dialectical opposition must try to be all that it can and throw into the struggle all its own political and moral resources, and only in this way there is a real overcoming" (Q1768).

The intellectualism of the theorists of the passive revolution can take a subtler form. Some admit the principle that "the dialectical terms must develop in all their power and as contradictory extremes" (Q1791), and so they try to invent an extremism of dialectical mediationism. In so doing, they forget that the dialectical mediation of opposite extremes is to be done by the historical development itself, rather than intellectualistically; the intellectual attempt at dialectical mediation cannot be a genuine dialectical term. Gramsci is not too clear about why this should be so, but he does say that dialectical extremism "is alive only in the brain of a few intellectuals of no great stature" (Q1791). Perhaps he would also say that the intellectual attempt at dialectical mediation cannot by its nature be extremist.

One final fault concerns the attempt to portray practitioners of passive revolution (such as Cavour) as dialectical politicians in the sense of practitioners of the art of reaching the right mean between opposite extremes. Gramsci objects that although political intermediation may correspond (as in the case of Cavour) to their self-image and propaganda, it does not correspond to what they actually did. For example, in relation to popular initiatives and opposing political leaders, someone like Cavour is not a mediator but a conqueror. Moreover, Gramsci thinks that to interpret Cavour as a politician of dialectical mediation is unflattering to him and diminishes his real stature, since the essential element of his politics lies in his greater political awareness and intelligence as compared to other leaders. In short, "in reality, historical forces clash among themselves for their 'extreme' program. That one of these forces acquires the function of a 'synthesis' superseding the opposite extremes is a dialectical necessity, not an apriorist method" (Q1825) of political action.

Underlying all these criticisms of the political content of a passive revolution, there seems to be a dialectical "law" about historical development, namely, that history develops by a process of thesis, antithesis, and synthesis, such that the synthesis results from an actual clash between the opposing forces called thesis and antithesis. The dialectic here seems to be a process going on in the real world, rather than a way of thinking that occurs in human minds. To be undialectical here is to think or act in such a way as to try to interfere with the process. Such a dialectic corresponds to the allegedly Hegelian view, and to the main one of the three meanings analyzed by such interpreters as Bobbio.[78]

What is the relationship between this triadic conception of dialectic and the other one that has emerged thus far, namely, a way of thinking that looks for diversity within unity and for unity within diversity? There seems to be a great difference: Not only is one an historical-political process and the other a mental one, but there seems to be no correspondence or parallelism in the patterns of the two processes. I do not think they are inconsistent; that is, there seems to be no reason why, by following the dialectical "law of thought," one might not come to hold the dialectical "law of development." Nevertheless, I must confess that the lack of unity or coherence makes me uncomfortable. The crucial question is whether Gramsci thinks that by thinking dialectically one could never come to deny the law of development, whether by thinking dialectically one would be allowed to become a convinced practitioner of passive revolution, for example. And is someone who proceeds, however critically, in accordance with the dialectic of development, necessarily proceeding dialectically in the other sense? In other words, although there need not be a conflict, is a conflict possible? If so, which notion would be more important? At any rate, what is the basis for Gramsci's confidence in the law of development?

Because of the weight of the previous evidence, which favors the mentalistic concept of dialectic, we should explore the possibility that this concept underlies Gramsci's present criticisms of the politics of passive revolution, to the effect that it is an "illegitimate" attempt to "domesticate" the dialectic (through moderation and mediation) and to mutilate it (by "transformistic" stratagems). This exploration is all the more important since the present critique of a passive revolution appears to advocate a form of extremism that seems uncharacteristic of Gramsci.[79]

Let us begin with an internal difficulty in Gramsci's critique of passive revolutions. In fact, his concept of dialectical development seems to introduce a dangerous dichotomy between the real and the mental. On the one hand, he states that it is a dialectical necessity that a mediation of opposite extremes should result from the political historical process;[80] on the other hand, he claims that it is wrong for the politician or historical agent to *aim* at such a mediation, but rather that he should aim at actualizing his own particular program to the fullest. This would not only be a failure of the unity of theory and practice, and a violation of historicist principles, but it might lead straight into irrationalism. This may be the self-criticism Gramsci is anticipating when he says that ultimately the dialectic "does not give rise to forms of irrationalism and arbitrariness, like those contained in the Bergsonian conception" (Q1221). Similarly, Gramsci cautions that he is aware of "a danger of historical defeatism, that is, indifferentism, since the general formulation of the problem can make one believe in fatalism" (Q1827). Elsewhere[81] we even find him elaborating on this question of fatalism by arguing against the principled opposition to compromise, which seems to be similar to the principled pursuit of the dialectical clash of the present context. There he argues, first, that the principled opposition to compromise is an expression of fatalism, since it amounts to believing there are natural laws of society that will make certain events happen independently "of any volitional initiative tending to predispose these situations in accordance with a plan" (Q1612); this sounds like a criticism of the "law" of dialectical development as well. Second, whenever "the union of two forces is necessary to prevail over a third one . . . compromise is the only concrete possibility" (Q1612–13); this may be an implicit admission that the Hegelian triadic scheme is also an oversimplification with respect to the number of elements involved, that as it stands it has "the form of a philosophical piece of fiction" (Q1487). Third, because opposition to compromise usually includes a blind faith in the need eventually to use force and violence, it must hold that there can be destruction without compromise, and this involves a mechanist view of destruction, rather than a dialectical conception of it as one side of the destruction-construction pair, which would need compromise for the construction element.[82] This argument is significant because it amounts to an illustration of behavior that is dialectical in the sense of the triadic law but undialectical in the sense of the mentalistic conception.

The key to the solution of our difficulty lies, I believe, in another series of charges, which Gramsci levels against passive revolutionaries and which constitute a deeper and more plausible criticism; more plausible because not dependent on an unsubstantiated "law" of development by thesis, antithesis, and synthesis. Mixed together with his more explicitly "dialectical" criticism of political moderatism, Gramsci avers that "the error is to elevate to methodological principle what is pure immediacy, thus elevating ideology to philosophy" (Q1221). And in the midst of his critique of liberal reformism, he objects that it is "the manifestation of a unilateral practical-political tendency, which cannot be the foundation of a science, but only of an immediate political ideology" (Q1325). Again, while criticizing the unbalanced leadership characteristic of Italian passive revolution, he is more critical of the Action Party than of the moderates; for, on the one hand, Mazzini and his followers can be faulted for having violated the "dialectic" of development by moderating their demands or by allowing themselves to be absorbed by the other side, since this constituted a betrayal of their own "democratic" or "Jacobin" approach; on the other hand, although the nature of the dialectical process was also misunderstood by

Cavour and his followers, "the theoretical incomprehension by these people was the practical expression of the necessity of the 'thesis' to develop all that it can, up to the point of being able to incorporate a part of the antithesis itself, in order not to be overcome" (Q1768). Finally, apropos the impossibility of an extremism of dialectical mediation, which had been advocated by Ugo Spirito, Gramsci concludes that "if the fault of Croce is that of wanting to appear different from what he really is, the same is the fault of Spirito and his group" (Q1791–92); in other words, they are trying to pass as philosophers when they are in fact acting as politicians.

The central question in all these remarks concerns the theoretical awareness of one's own political practice. Cavour's greatness lay precisely in this awareness, whereas the philosophical apologists of passive revolution lack it because they do not realize that the *politics* of passive revolution cannot be given a *philosophical* justification, namely, one that is universally acceptable. This argument cuts both ways, however, and it shows at the same time that Gramsci's own politics of anti-passive-revolution[83] is not *philosophically* justifiable either. If this is so, then it is best not to interpret Gramsci's criticism the way it often appears, namely, as charging that the program of passive revolution violates the law of the dialectic by trying to domesticate and mutilate it. Otherwise, Gramsci would be guilty of the same fallacy of pseudophilosophical justification. This in turn allows us to give secondary importance, or at least to diminish the philosophical significance of, the second meaning of "dialectic," which is embedded in that pseudophilosophical criticism. But does this bring us nearer to the primary concept of dialectic elaborated earlier? Is there a way of construing Gramsci's present critique of passive revolution in terms of the technique of distinguishing and relating?

I believe there is, at least as regards the plausible content of the triadic law. That is, to accept the existence of a thesis and an antithesis may be regarded as part of the enterprise of defining differences amid apparent uniformity, while the dialectical mediation into a synthesis may be regarded as part of the procedure of finding similarities among apparent differences. In other words, the triadic and synthetic aspects of the law may be viewed as a methodological consequence of the primary concept of dialectic. This is how, as we have seen, the historiographical concept of passive revolution is shown to be dialectical in the primary sense.

Regarding the extremist content of the law of development, I do not think it is derivable from Gramsci's primary concept of the dialectic. In fact, in view of its being inconsistent with much else that Gramsci said and did, it is best treated as an erroneous addition and best discarded.

Nevertheless, an important problem remains. For, even without being extremist, Gramsci seems to hold that in politics one is supposed to pursue one's particular interest rather than that of the whole; the latter will result as a dialectical synthesis of the political process. The problem arises because, according to Gramsci, the historian always finds that a dialectical synthesis is what has happened, but one is not supposed to use this historical and political-theoretical knowledge in one's practice as a historical and political agent. To put it another way, Gramsci seems to be saying that the dialectic is useful only in theory but not in practice, or that the dialectical way of thinking (in the primary sense of the concept) can be used only in the context of understanding and interpreting the world, not to criticize it or change it. Again, what seems to be happening is that, in theory, one is supposed "to find the real identity under the apparent differentiation and contradiction and to find the substantial diversity under the apparent identity" (Q2268), but in practice, one is supposed to pursue only the substantial diversity under the apparent identity.

The solution of this problem cannot be pursued here, but a line of inquiry can be sketched. In political action, one's own substantial diversity – one's own particular interest – is not a selfish whim but is related to one's social class; moreover, one's social class is supposed not merely to dominate but to lead other classes, which involves winning their consent. All of this already involves searching for the real identity under the apparent differentiation. The real questions, then, are how much to pursue and how far to go in distinguishing, and how much to pursue and how far to go in relating. It would seem this is a matter to be left to "judgment." Hence, a study of this concept will allow us to appreciate better, and to see the limitations of, Gramsci's dialectic. Moreover, we are also led to study directly and systematically his views on politics, to see to what extent the concept of the dialectic revealed here inheres there, and how he may have concretely resolved this tension between the theory and practice of the dialectic.

To summarize Gramsci's view of passive revolution, we may say it has four elements. His historical illustration of the concept is the Italian Risorgimento. His general definition is that it is a government-led series of reforms accomplished without popular initiative and without balanced top-level representation. His historiographical justification is that such a concept can be seen as a dialectical way of thinking about certain events in political history. His political criticism of the strategy is twofold: (1) a superficially more striking charge that to advocate a passive revolution violates the Hegelian law of dialectical development and (2) a more plausible criticism that the politics of passive revolution cannot be given a *philosophical* justification, and that apologists of passive revolution have failed to realize this or have tried to hide the fact. Although my account of the first three elements was primarily expository, to criticism 1 I objected that the presupposed concept of dialectic conflicted with Gramsci's primary concept, with criticism 2, and was generally un-Gramscian. This led to a new problem about the theory (i.e., theoretical formulation) and practice (i.e., practical use) of the primary concept, whose solution may lie in a study of the judgment concept and of Gramsci's political theory.

THE "DIALECTIC OF DISTINCTS"

Critical rejection of the law of dialectical clash that Gramsci *seems* to be advocating puts us in a better position to deal with another law of dialectic that Gramsci seems to presuppose in his critique of Croce's "dialectic of distincts," for we can now be more suspicious about the propriety of any such laws, and only if we attribute to Gramsci another partial error can we make sense of the relevant notes.[84] The "law" in question is the principle that there is no dialectic of distincts but only one of opposites. The situation is complicated and ironic because in the terms just stated Croce would agree, although his meaning would be different from Gramsci's.

By the "distincts" Croce means[85] a set of four categories in terms of which one could presumably understand all of reality. Three categories correspond to the "transcendental" attributes of the philosophical tradition: the true, the good, and the beautiful; to these Croce added the useful. They also correspond to the mental activities that underlie these categories: ratiocination, universal volition, expression, and volition per se, respectively. Again, these categories can be related to the domains of philosophy, morality, art, and practical economics. Strictly speaking, these are the only distincts, but more loosely Croce also regards as "distincts" such activities as science, politics, religion, and history, which he tries to define in their terms. One of his main motives in conceptualizing the distincts is to uphold their critical integrity, or to ensure that in evaluating each domain, one does so with principles pertaining to it, rather than in terms of principles applying to other domains.

In addition to the distincts, Croce uses another series of concepts, which he calls "opposites" and which come in pairs: the true and the false, the good and the bad, the beautiful and the ugly, and the useful and the useless. His main point in distinguishing the two sets is to underscore the very different relationship that holds between, for example, the beautiful and the ugly, and the beautiful and the true.

Croce himself thinks that the dialectic applies only to opposites; in fact his primary meaning of "dialectic" is precisely "synthesis of opposites." In elaborating this point he thinks he is correcting Hegel, who had allegedly misapplied the dialectic to the distincts as well, thus formulating such absurdities as art-thesis, religion-antithesis, and philosophy-synthesis, which were the sort of triadic game that gave Hegelianism a bad name.[86] Thus, Croce does not speak of the "dialectic of distincts."

Nevertheless, the phrase "dialectic of distincts," which *Gramsci* uses, can plausibly be taken to refer to a view of how the distincts relate to one another. For Croce they form not a hierarchy but rather a circle in the order art-philosophy-utility-morality-art-and so forth; but each is irreducible and autonomous. Some of their relations are: Both art and philosophy are cognitive acts, but morality and utility are volitional; both art and utility involve individualization; both philosophy and morality involve universalization; philosophy presupposes art, and morality presupposes utility, but not vice versa; and theory and practice presuppose each other.

Gramsci's plausible criticism of this (Crocean) "dialectic of distincts" is that it tends to be apriorist, abstract, and mentalistic: "The 'distinctions,' whose methodological principle Croce is proud to have introduced into the 'dialectical' tradition, turn from scientific principle, into a cause of abstractness and antihistoricism, when formalistically applied" (Q1462–63). What Gramsci wants to do is to devise *his own* more practical, political, and historically oriented "dialectic of distincts": "Where everything is practice, in a philosophy of praxis, the distinction will be not among moments of absolute Spirit but between structure and superstructures; one will have to fix the dialectical position of political activity as a distinction within the superstructures" (Q977). Gramsci's reason for wanting to formulate a different "dialectic of distincts" is the same as Croce's: to preserve their critical integrity.

This criticism, so interpreted, wholly accords with Gramsci's own (primary) concept of the dialectic. He has, however, another objection, which does not fit in as readily. While criticizing Croce, Gramsci frequently objects that "the so-called dialectic of distincts . . . is a contradiction in terms since we have dialectic only of opposites" (Q1316).[87] If the crucial terms of this sentence are given their Crocean meaning, it constitutes an invalid criticism of Croce, since it is, in fact, Croce's objection to Hegel. If "dialectic" is understood in Gramsci's (primary) sense, and "distincts" and "opposites" are taken in their Crocean *reference* (e.g., respectively, truth and beauty, and truth and falsehood), then the dialectic of distincts is not self-contradictory, since Gramsci's dialectic is not restricted to "opposites." In fact, as we have just seen, a central aim of Gramsci's philosophy of praxis is to formulate a dialectical theory of politics and other distinct but not opposite superstructures such as philosophy and religion. Moreover, throughout the Notebooks, Gramsci speaks of, and theorizes about, the dialectic of structure and superstructure,[88] and of the masses and the intellectuals,[89] which are distincts rather than opposites in Croce's sense, since both involve the pair theory-practice and for him practice and theory are distincts.

Finally, a third semantical possibility is that Gramsci uses the terms "distincts" and "opposites," as well as "dialectic," with his own special meanings. In some contexts,[90] by "distincts" he seems to mean elements of the ideological superstructure, and by "opposites" he seems to mean elements of the economic structure. Then, although the dialectic of distincts would not be strictly self-contradictory, Gramsci might be simply denying the dialectic for the distincts and allowing it for the opposites. This would amount to restricting the dialectic to processes in the real world (or at least to historical developments), as contrasted to the minds of men; that is, it would be another way, analogous to the previous case of the triadic law, of emphasizing "real" or "materialistic," rather than "ideal" or "mentalistic" dialectic. This third interpretation would seem to fit very well not only with Gramsci's "historical materialism" but also with his self-image that the present critique is doing to Croce what Marx did to Hegel, namely "to put man back on his feet, to make him walk with his feet and not with his head" (Q1240).[91] But one could raise about such a "materialist" law of the dialectic all the questions that arose about the triadic one. The main difficulty is that such a "dialectic of opposites" is not dictated by the dialectical approach of Gramsci's primary concept of the dialectic. Hence, although he may have independent arguments supporting the "materialist" law, they have nothing special to do with the dialectic. Because our interest here is in the dialectic, such arguments are not part of our present task.

We see, then, why Gramsci's critique of the "dialectic of distincts" is confusing:[92] Taken at its face value, his point is simply that Croce's dialectical theory of art, philosophy, politics, and the like is excessively abstract and speculative, and should be replaced by a more concrete and historically oriented dialectical theory of the same things. But he also seems to reject in principle the possibility of a dialectic of distincts; this rejection is either misdirected against Croce, or inconsistent with Gramsci's own prevalent view of the dialectic, or grounded on a principle of dialectic that needs an independent justification.

TWO GRAMSCIAN CONCEPTS OF DIALECTIC

Our examination has revealed that hermeneutically and philologically speaking, Gramsci's notes on the dialectic may be divided into eight subgroups, which explore respectively the relation between the dialectic and classical European culture, logic, first philosophy, nature, administration, revolution, reformism, and Croce. Thus, the dialectic is the methodological, as distinct from substantive, heritage of classical German philosophy, classical British economics, and classical French Jacobin politics. The dialectic is also not opposed to logic but is simply a cognitive activity different from reasoning. Far from being materialist in the conventional metaphysical sense, dialectic is inherently opposed to any first philosophy. The dialectic of nature is, strictly speaking, a contradiction in terms, and hence dialectic is inconsistent with "science" when the latter refers to natural science, that is to say, mechanism; but it is part of "science" if the latter is conceived generally as rationality. The administration of human affairs inevitably involves some centralization: democratic centralism is an application of the dialectic, while bureaucratic centralism is undialectical. Although the historiographical principle of permanent revolution is a dialectical concept, the political program of permanent revolution is not always so, especially when labor unions and mass-based political parties are allowed. And although the historiographical principle of passive revolution is a dialectical concept, the political program of passive revolution is never dialectical since it is an attempt to domesticate and mutilate the dialectic of development. Finally, Croce's philosophy of "distincts" is undialectical because it is unhistorical and intellectualistic (and hence one-sidedly speculative and mentalistic), and because there is no dialectic of distincts but only one of opposites.

Conceptually speaking, these discussions contain three views of the dialectic, two overlapping ones and a third inconsistent with them. The primary concept refers to the combination of two mental activities: One is the search for identity, equality, or uniformity; the other, the search for differentiation, diversity, or distinction. A related concept refers to the avoidance of all one-sidedness or proper combination of all aspects of a situation, whether they be philosophical points of view, economic tendencies, political forces, or cognitive activities. I have suggested that this second concept may be subsumed under the first insofar as the avoidance of all one-sidedness requires that various sides be distinguished and that they be united into a combination. We may add now that the primary concept can also be subsumed under the second one in that the former involves the combination of two cognitive activities. So the two concepts may be largely equivalent. On the other hand, the third view of dialectic refers to recognizing and following one (or perhaps two) law(s) of real dialectic: that historical developments are actual syntheses of the clash between two extremes (a thesis and an antithesis); and that only opposites, not distincts, behave dialectically; this is a formalistic, mechanist concept, inconsistent with the other(s), even if such dialectical laws should happen to be true.[93] Because of this inconsistency and other discrepancies, I have argued that the more typically Gramscian concept of dialectic is the other one, involving distinction within unity.

If my account can be taken to settle the textual-historical problem of Gramsci's concept of the dialectic, it merely opens up the theoretical-evaluative problem of analyzing in more detail the exact nature and meaning of this concept. Such an analysis is undertaken in the next chapter.

Chapter 7

Hegel and the theory and practice of dialectic

I have argued that two concepts of dialectic inhere in the Prison Notebooks, a formalist one pertaining to "real" dialectic and a judgmental one referring to "ideal" dialectic; that there is a tension (though not an outright contradiction) between them; and that the judgmental concept is the more typically Gramscian one. If this settles the matter from the point of view of interpretation and internal evaluation, it also leads to the problem of assessing the two concepts with independent arguments. One way of proceeding is to point out that the two concepts correspond to Gramsci's theory and his practice of the dialectic, respectively. That is, the formalist concept is the meaning Gramsci attaches to the dialectic when he is most explicit in his pronouncements about what the dialectic is and about how it operates, whereas the judgmental concept is what he means when he is using the term in the context of other issues that relate to the dialectic more implicitly and indirectly. In short, Gramsci's official view is that the dialectic is the process of thesis-antithesis-synthesis that exists only at the level of the socioeconomic structure, whereas his implicit view is that it is a way of thinking in which one avoids one-sidedness and searches for unity in diversity and diversity in unity. Thus, Gramsci's dialectical theory and his dialectical practice do not correspond. Assuming the primacy of practice, we would have to conclude that the judgmental notion is what Gramsci really means by dialectic. If we want a more independent evaluation, we have to determine which, if any, of Gramsci's two notions corresponds to what the dialectic really is. The most authoritative source is undoubtedly Hegel, and so the question reduces to one of articulating Hegel's concept. Before examining Hegelian texts directly, however, we will examine various interpretations of Hegel's dialectic. This is needed both because of the magnitude of the problem and because it provides an excellent opportunity for the enrichment, in this particular domain, of one of our central themes – the relationship of theory and practice.

THE DIALECTIC AND ITS INTERPRETERS

Interpretations of Hegel's dialectic tend to group themselves into four[1] types, which I shall term, respectively, triadic, systemic-immanent, onto-phenomenological, and metaphilosophical.

The triadic view is perhaps the most widespread, although the least plausible.[2] The dialectic is taken to be a process whereby a thesis and an antithesis lead to a synthesis. The process is supposed to be at least mental, thus making dialectic so conceived a way of thinking; some view it also as a historical or natural process. In their canonical form, thesis and antithesis are abstractions, or "moments" of the process, whereas only the synthesis is concretely real. The relation between thesis and antithesis is one of mutual contradiction, whereas the relation between them and the synthesis is not an ordinary logical one; in particular, the latter is not deducible from the former; rather, the synthesis overcomes, mediates, supersedes, and reconciles the thesis and antithesis, in such a way as to undo both for whatever they contain that is inadequate, while preserving whatever is valid in each. Typical examples of such Hegelian triads are: being, nothing, and becoming; identity, difference, and ground; art, religion, and philosophy; being, essence, and notion; and logos, nature, and spirit.

This interpretation of Hegel's dialectic has a certain amount of justification in the summaries, outlines, and tables of contents that Hegel compiled for his books. It also has the virtue of simplicity and prima facie intelligibility. Moreoover, it receives added authority from the fact that both Marx and Gramsci pay some lip service to it,[3] and it has been elaborated at great length by such serious scholars as McTaggart. Its deceptive fascination is evident from the fact a recent leading scholar, who is otherwise very critical of this interpretation, nevertheless lapses into describing the triadic tendency of Hegel's works as constituting their dialectical structure.[4]

The exposé of the nullity of the triadic conception of Hegel's dialectic goes back at least as far as Croce's monograph of 1906.[5] His main criticism was based on something that even triadically oriented interpreters like McTaggart did not deny (having, in fact, helped to establish it),[6] namely, that in almost all of Hegel's triads it was impossible to understand how the third term came from the other two. Given such arbitrariness, the question for Croce reduced to that of choosing between two alternatives: declaring Hegel's philosophy nonsensical or declaring the triadic interpretation inadequate. To someone like Croce who, despite his *partial criticism* of Hegel, felt very strongly the depth and power of Hegelian philosophy, the rejection of the triadic interpretation was the obvious choice. Croce's criticism amounts to pointing out that a triadic dialectic cannot be found in Hegel's *actual philosophical practice*. Moreover, as Walter Kaufmann has incisively argued,[7] neither do we find in Hegel any theoretical articulation of the dialectic as synthesis of thesis and antithesis; instead, we find him explicitly warning readers not to take too seriously the triadic structure of his own tables of contents. Thus, one is inclined to accept J. N. Findlay's memorable statement that the triadic procedure has as little to do with the dialectical philosophy of Hegel as the *terza rima* has with the poetry of Dante's *Divine Comedy*.[8] I would add to this only the qualification that it is perhaps undialectical to be totally negative toward the triadic interpretation; and if one wants to avoid such one-sidedness, then one might credit it with having helped to emphasize a genuinely important element of the dialectic, namely, the notion of synthesis.[9]

A more plausible interpretation than the triadic one is what I call the "systemic-immanent view." It holds that the Hegelian dialectic is the process whereby higher forms of consciousness *and* higher logical or ontological categories are derived by Hegel from lower ones. The process is also presumed to be taking place in reality, to which his derivations presumably correspond. The forms of consciousness are such human experiences as sense-certainty, perception, understanding, self-consciousness, reason, spirit, religion, and philosophy, which provide the subject matter of the *Phenomenology of Spirit*; whereas the categories are such forms of being and thought as becoming, identity, difference, existence, causality, subjectivity, objectivity, all the way up to the absolute idea, which are the topics in the *Science of Logic*. If the details of the process were left unspecified, the systemic interpretation would not in principle conflict with the triadic one, which could be taken as a special case of the former. But since, as just argued, the triadic process does not, in fact, characterize Hegel's actual procedure, it is obvious that what gives special interest to the systemic interpretation is the nature of the actual process that one finds upon examining Hegel's works. Although similar accounts were given earlier by Jean Hyppolite[10] and Findlay,[11] the clearest, most comprehensive, and most recent elaboration is Charles Taylor's.[12]

For Taylor the dialectical procedure used by Hegel has a structure identical to that of some Socratic-Platonic discussions attempting to define a concept, such as that of justice in the first book of the *Republic:* "This dialectic thus involves three terms: it starts with (1) a definition of justice, and (2) certain criterial properties of justice, and shows these to conflict when we try (3) to realize the definition in a general practice."[13] Substitute specific forms of consciousness or specific categories, and the same structure yields Hegelian dialectic. For example:

A concept of reality comes into conflict with the criterial properties of such a concept when we try to "realize" it, that is, apply it systematically to the world. Qua concept of reality, it conflicts with its own criterial properties. And hence any reality which meets this concept must be in conflict with itself.

Now the contradiction in Hegel's Logic comes from the fact that certain concepts are both indispensable *and* incoherent.[14]

Similarly, Findlay holds that "the basic characteristic of the dialectic method is that it always involves *higher-order comment* on . . . one's mode of conceiving things . . . in which step 2 is a true and inevitable and sometimes ironic comment on what has been present at step 1, step 3 a true and inevitable comment on what has been present at step 2, and so on."[15] Hyppolite, too, was articulating the same interpretation when he said that the dialectic is a structure of the description of the life of consciousness,[16] which may be characterized as follows:

Experience bears not only on knowledge but also on the object, for this particular knowledge is knowledge of an object. Consciousness tests its knowledge in order to render it adequate to what it holds to be true – a certain world posited as existing in-itself – but, when its knowledge changes, its object also changes. The latter had been the object of a certain knowledge; this knowledge having become other, the object also becomes other. In testing out its knowledge of what it took as the in-itself, what it posited as being the absolutely true, consciousness discovers the latter to have been *in-itself* only for it.[17]

The differences among these interpreters are, I believe, minor as compared with what they have in common, namely, their emphasis on the element of systemic development rooted in internal or immanent critique.

This interpretation is extremely helpful because, at least in Taylor's version, it suggests a way of combining the two main dialectical traditions: (1) the ancient, dialogical one stemming from Socrates and (2) the modern one associated with the name of Hegel. Moreover, it has an advantage over the triadic interpretation insofar as the systemic-immanent procedure is "actually evinced in [Hegel's] philosophical practice," as Findlay puts it.[18] Finally, the interpretation has the additional merit of corresponding to some of Hegel's own self-reflective pronouncements in the introduction to the *Phenomenology*. Unfortunately, although these theoretical reflections do articulate an important feature of the procedure used in the book, they are not presented by Hegel as a theory of dialectic as such or as an analysis of the concept. The only explicit connection is found in a single sentence where he is actually defining his concept of experience by reference to the kind of systemic-immanent process just described: "*Inasmuch as the new true object issues from it,* this *dialectical* movement which consciousness exercises on itself and which affects both its knowledge and its object, is precisely what is termed *experience.*"[19] This contrasts with the rather lengthy explicit theoretical pronouncements one finds in the preface to the same book, in the introduction to the *Science of Logic,* in paragraphs 79–83 of the *Eycyclopedia,* and in the *Lectures on the History of Philosophy.* Therefore, it may be objected that the present interpretation fails to take into account Hegel's own theory of what the dialectic is, although it admittedly corresponds to his philosophical practice when he is engaged in philosophizing about consciousness and the categories. This is a very serious difficulty given Hegel's great stress on self-consciousness and the "identity" of object and subject and of thought and being.

In short, I am denying neither the general importance of the systemic-immanent method in Hegel's philosophy, nor its specific relevance, that is, specific to what might be called his dialectical practice. In fact, I believe this method may be accepted as *an* important element of the Hegelian dialectic, corresponding to what other interpreters call the notion of "totality," as well as to Hegel's own famous slogan that "the True is the whole."[20] But I am saying that a preferable interpretation would be one based both on Hegel's view of what the dialectic is and on his use of it in philosophical practice.

A third important and influential interpretation faces a difficulty that is the reverse of the one just considered. Originating perhaps with Hartmann, and elaborated more or less independently by Kojève, the onto-phenomenological interpretation has the consequence that Hegel did not, in fact, practice the dialectic about which he theorized so much. Indeed, the dialectic of the real is such that he *need not* have engaged in it. Or, more extremely, if his theory of dialectic is correct, then he *could not* have proceeded dialectically in *his own* practice. In calling this interpretation onto-phenomenological, I wish to underscore that it claims Hegel's dialectic is an ontological or metaphysical doctrine about a so-called real-dialectic or dialectic-of-the-real, while also claiming that his methodological practice is phenomenological in the sense that essentially the doctrine descriptively reflects or mirrors the real "dialectical movement."

According to Hartmann, Hegel is better understood in relation to Aristotle than as a representative of post-Kantian developments.[21] To perceive the closeness of their dialectics, however, one must not take as Aristotle's dialectic what he himself called that in the *Organon*, namely, a type of argumentation that is nonapodictic but where the participants in the discussion try to agree on what seems to them true or most plausible;[22] but, rather, one must focus attention on his metaphysical theories of contrariety, substance, form versus matter, and contradictories. In fact, Hartmann's concept of dialectic is such that "dialectical solutions consist in nothing but letting contradictions subsist in real facts."[23] Thus, Hegel's originality lay not so much in dialectic per se, not in having devised a dialectical approach, but in discovering the (real) dialectic of human consciousness: "This new tack is Hegel's discovery, a *novum* in philosophy, a trajectory of the self-conception of consciousness in its transformations on the basis of its conception of its objects in their transformations."[24] Finally, Hartmann is clear that dialectic's real contradictions are "really" oppositions of contrary tendencies rather than logical contradictions:

What we usually designate as contradiction in life and reality is, in fact, not contradiction at all, but conflict. The clashing of forces, powers, and tendencies, even of heterogeneous legalities, occurs in many realms, perhaps we may say, in all realms, surely in all higher levels of reality. Such conflict is a real and actual contentiousness, *Realrepugnanz*; it can have the direct form of conflict, even of open battle. With contradiction, however, it can have no similarity because the conflicting reality never has the relationship of A to non-A, of a positive to a negative; rather it has that of positive against positive.[25]

Nevertheless, since conflicting interests and forces often become expressed in conflicting philosophical systems, insofar as the latter are real entities in the world of the history of philosophy, and insofar as conflicting philosophies involve logical contradictions, then Hegel is entitled to speak of "real logical contradictions."

Kojève is very clear about this secondary character of real logical contradictions, as well as about the consequences of this type of interpretation. He, too, sees the essence of the meaning of Hegelian dialectic in the concept of negativity,[26] and for this reason he argues that Hegel was unjustified in extending his dialectic of the real to a dialectic within nature, since the negating action can only originate from a person.[27] In fact, the "real" dialectic that he attributes to Hegel might be better called "active"[28] since what he is talking about is primarily the world of human action and that of the history of philosophy: "Hegelian discourse is dialectical to the extent that it describes the real Dialectic of Fighting and of Work, as well as the 'ideal' reflection of this Dialectic in thought in general and in philosophical thought in particular."[29] Such an "active" view of dialectic, together with an emphasis on the phenomenological-descriptive aspect of Hegel's procedure, leads Kojève to conclude that "in itself Hegel's discourse is not at all dialectical . . . it is a pure and simple 'phenomenological' description of the real dialectic of the Real and of the verbal discussions which reflected this dialectic in the course of time."[30] In seemingly paradoxical terms, Kojève tells us also that "if you please, the Hegelian method is purely 'empirical' or 'positivist': Hegel looks at the Real and describes what he sees, everything that he sees, and nothing but what he sees."[31] That is why "Hegelian Dialectic is not a *method* of research or of philosophical exposition, but the adequate description of the *structure* of Being"[32] and why "he was the first who could knowingly abandon Dialectic conceived as a philosophical *method*."[33]

An internal criticism of the onto-phenomenological interpretation is that it presupposes that real, active dialectic has come to completion at the end of history, so as to allow a Wise Man like Hegel merely to look.[34] A little exercise of a (perhaps different kind of) empirical method obviously invalidates the assumption.[35] In the present context, however, note that the interpretation violates what may be called the requirement of unity of theory and practice, by portraying a Hegel supreme theorist of the (real) dialectic, but nonpractitioner of the art. It is also in accordance with the present project that I would mention the emphasis on the element(s) of contradiction, opposition, and negation as an important insight that this interpretation makes to the understanding of Hegelian dialectic.

We may summarize this critical review by saying that the triadic kind of dialectic can be found neither in Hegel's practice nor in his theory of dialectic, that the systemic-immanent type of dialectic can be found in his practice but not in his theory, and that the onto-phenomenological one is present in his theory but not in his practice. Although this is a strong reason to search for some other interpretation, we may accept their respective insights according to which synthesis, totality, and contradiction are three important elements of Hegelian dialectic.

In calling the fourth type of interpretation "metaphilosophical," I mean to convey the idea, explicitly, that this view interprets Hegel's dialectic as an essential ingredient of the nature of philosophy. Implicitly, however, since metaphilosophy is necessarily and inevitably self-referential, we can more readily appreciate the desirability of a convergence of Hegel's theory and practice. Such an interpretation is, I believe, much closer to the truth. To see how and why, it will be useful to examine in greater detail the most significant exponents, namely, Croce, Mure, and Gadamer.[36]

For Croce, the central problem with which Hegel grappled was that of the nature of philosophy, and thus the articulation of a logic of philosophy is his most important achievement.[37] The dialectic is then seen as the principal part, though not the entirety, of Hegel's conception of philosophy.[38] It cannot be overemphasized that when Croce refers to philosophy in this interpretation, he means it in a specific sense, that is, he means philosophy as distinct from mathematics, empirical science, historiography, art, moral activity, and economic activity. This thesis is a valuable one and has received wide acceptance.[39] In fact, few have been as eloquent as Croce in formulating it. Moreover, for him the dialectic so understood represents the sound and valid part of Hegel's philosophy, the part which is alive and to which Croce is referring in the first half of his monograph's title.

A second element of Croce's interpretation concerns the conceptual content of Hegel's dialectical approach to philosophy. The only explicit concept Croce discusses is that of the synthesis of opposites; his clarification is similar to and reminiscent of the triadic synthesis of thesis and antithesis. The difference is that the asymmetry of thesis and antithesis is eliminated; moreover, the only genuine opposites Croce recognizes are such pairs as truth and falsehood, good and evil, and beauty and ugliness, and he excludes as being nonopposites such pairs as truth and goodness, goodness and beauty, and ugliness and evil. Such a Crocean theoretical analysis of Hegel's dialectical "synthesis of opposites" gives the wrong impression, for if we look carefully at the Crocean arguments in support of his favorable evaluation, we find that what Croce has actually in mind is the synthesis of *philosophical* opposites such as monism and dualism, pessimism and optimism, and rationalism and realism. After all, only such opposites can make the synthesis of opposites an element of the logic of philosophy, as distinct from mathematics, empirical science, poetry, moral activity, and the like. Thus, we may interpret Croce as having clarified Hegel's concept of dialectic in terms of the synthesis of opposite philosophical systems.

The third and last element of Croce's interpretation that I wish to consider here is the explicit claim that Hegel's philosophical practice actually corresponds to the concept of dialectic he formulated. In Croce's monograph we frequently find such statements as "Hegel was not only the theorist par excellence of that form of thinking, but also the most complete dialectician who has ever appeared in the course of history,"[40] and "in his logical doctrine, and in his actual thinking in conformity with it consists, therefore, the indomitable drive, the inexhaustible fruitfulness, the perpetual youth of Hegelian philosophy."[41] This is a promising thesis, but Croce's supporting argument leaves much to be desired. Part of his argument[42] consists of examining, approvingly, a number of Hegel's philosophical doctrines, to show how his concept of dialectic is inherent therein. These involve the questions of how negativity is the source of development, how the real is rational and the rational real, how the "cunning of reason" is a very important phenomenon, how Hegel's philosophy can justify both conservatism and revolutionism despite the fact that personally he was conservative, and how his dialectic and his historicism are intimately tied. This part of the argument is acceptable as far as it goes. The rest and longer part of Croce's argument shows how Hegel, having made the important philosophical discovery of the dialectic, went on to try to apply it everywhere, with many disastrous results. Hegel's misapplication of the dialectic to historical events and to empirical facts is only the most obvious, well-known, and absurd instance, for, as Croce argues, this is the logical result of Hegel's misconceiving the methodological autonomy of historiography and of empirical science; this misconception in turn is due to his regarding historical and scientific inquiry as semiphilosophical activities, in such a way that history, science, and so forth are to be perfected and superseded by philosophy. This amounts to treating the relations between the concepts of science, history, and philosophy dialectically; but these concepts are distinct from each other and from philosophy, rather than opposite, and so the dialectic (i.e., the "synthesis of opposites") does not apply to their relation.

In short, Hegel misapplied the dialectic not only to historical events and empirical facts but also to such autonomous activities as science, historiography, and art, and thus to philosophical categories related by neither opposition nor synthesis. This critical part of Croce's argument is perhaps the most impressive achievement of his monograph. However, as a justification of the third interpretative thesis being now considered, it really suggests the opposite of what is required. For if Croce is right that Hegel misapplied his own concept of dialectic in so many ways, it would appear that on such occasions he was not really practicing his own theory of dialectic. Thus, if we want to explore further the metaphilosophical interpretation of Hegel's dialectic, we should proceed by examining other, more truly dialectical elements of his philosophical practice, or articulate his theory of the dialectic differently or more fully than Croce's account.

Before proceeding to do this, let us see what else can be learned from other metaphilosophical interpretations. Mure explicitly acknowledges that "Croce, I think, was right in holding that the logic of philosophy was the main goal towards which Hegel's effort was directed,"[43] that the greatest contribution of his logic of philosophy is the dialectic,[44] and that the latter is a conception of philosophical truth, as distinct from mere correctness.[45] From a logical point of view, Hegel was presumably trying to solve the problem represented by the dilemma: "Either inference is a tautologous *petitio principii*, or it is an inconsequent leap to a fresh intuition."[46] His solution was that this is a false dilemma arising from an undialectical separation of two aspects of thinking that are different but united, for "thought is intuitive, but so far *merely* immediate. It is discursive, but this *discursus* is its own activity of self-mediation. Moreover, this mediation is a self-development towards new immediacy which mediation enriches; a progress and yet a return upon itself."[47] In other words, dialectical truth "is the identity of thought in its *own* difference, the identity-in-difference of a thought which is not *in se* unintuitive and empty but concretely universal."[48] From an ontological point of view, according to Mure, dialectic is essentially the clarification of how "thought and Being reveal their unity through difference."[49] Hence, for Hegel as a dialectical metaphysician, "the whole question, then, turns on what kind of identity-in-difference the unity of thought and Being manifests."[50]

For the present inquiry, this means that Mure takes identity-in-difference, or diversity within unity, or the synthesis of identity and difference, to be the main conceptual content of the dialectic.

In fact, he also judges the section of Hegel's logic that discusses the concepts of identity and difference, the so-called Doctrine of Essence, as "his most brilliant achievement in logic."[51] Unfortunately, Mure's analysis of the relevant Hegelian texts about these concepts[52] is too obscure to be of much use, and so we will want to undertake our own examination.

To Croce's talk of a Hegelian "logic of philosophy," and Mure's "conception of philosophical truth," there corresponds Gadamer's interpretation that Hegel's dialectic is a "theory of philosophical demonstration," as distinct from a theory of logical cogency.[53] Such a Hegelian philosophical demonstration seems a kind of conceptual analysis that avoids one-sidedness. In fact, for Gadamer,

Hegel's dialectical method . . . consists in thinking a determination in itself and by itself, so that it displays its onesidedness and thus forces us to think its opposite. The opposed determinations are pushed to contradiction precisely by being thought *in abstracto*, by themselves. Hegel sees the speculative nature of reflection here: what stands in contradiction is reduced to *momenta*, the unity of which is the truth.[54]

The most important "determinations" to which Gadamer refers are the concepts of identity and difference.[55] This concept of dialectic is found by Gadamer in some of Hegel's most self-reflective analyses, namely, when he tries to extract it from ancient Greek philosophy, especially from Plato's theory of philosophizing in the *Parmenides*, and from Aristotle's philosophical practice in the *Metaphysics*. For Gadamer, the fact that Hegel does philosophical violence to the Greek texts is not as important as the fact that at a deeper level there is a genuine convergence of thought.

Gadamer also argues that the procedure actually followed by Hegel in his *Logic* is a dialectical method so conceived.[56] For example, he analyzes Hegel's first "dialectical deduction" of becoming,[57] and he does so not in terms of the usual triadic nonsensicalities about the synthesis of Being and Nothing, but rather in terms of the dialectic of identity and difference:

Becoming is not determined as coming-into-being and passing-away on the basis of a pregiven difference of Being and Nothing, rather, this difference emerges from Becoming in thinking the determination of Becoming as transition. Being and Nothing, respectively, "become" in it. Coming-into-being and passing-away are thus the self-determining truth of Becoming. They balance each other out, as it were, insofar as there is in them no other determination than the directionality implied in "from-to," which in turn is determined only by the difference in direction.[58]

When so interpreted, I believe Gadamer's account is a model of the theory-and-practice type of interpretation I am here exploring.

In summary, it may be said that the most promising ideas put forth by the metaphilosophical interpreters of the Hegelian dialectic are that the dialectic is a method characteristic of philosophical thought, that Hegel both elaborated such a dialectical method in his theory of philosophy and used it in his philosophical practice, and that the main conceptual content of this dialectic is the synthesis of identity and difference and the avoidance of one-sidedness.

DEFINING THE DIALECTIC:
NEGATIVE VERSUS POSITIVE DIALECTIC

What does Hegel mean by dialectic? In the introduction to the *Science of Logic* he states that "the grasping of opposites in their unity or of the positive in the negative . . . is the most important aspect of dialectic."[59] An example of a pair of opposites would be thought and object, which he studied at great length in the *Phenomenology of Spirit*; and to grasp them in their unity would amount to appreciating the main result of the latter work, namely a view of philosophy or "science" as *"thought in so far as this is just as much the object in its own self, or the object in its own self in so far as it is equally pure thought."*[60] By the positivity of the negative, Hegel means that

. . . the recognition of the logical principle that the negative is just as much positive, or that what is self-contradictory does not resolve itself into a nullity, into abstract nothingness, but essentially only into the negation of its *particular* content, in other words, that such a negation is not all and every negation but the negation of a specific subject matter which resolves itself [into something positive].[61]

In speaking of this as "the most important aspect of dialectic," Hegel implicitly suggests the existence of some other secondary aspects of the dialectic. What he calls the "negative aspect of dialectic"[62] consists of realizing "the *necessity of the contradiction* which belongs to the nature of thought-determinations [which] is nothing else but the inner negativity of the determinations as their self-moving soul."[63] Examples of such thought-determinations are things like the beginning of the world, which were the subject of Kant's antinomies, although Hegel believes such "contradictions" are much more pervasive and are not merely mental but have "reference to what is intrinsic or in itself."[64]

This distinction between negative and positive aspects of dialectic, together with the analysis of each, is in some respects clearer in the *Encyclopedia*. The only important exception is that the official definiendum in paragraph 82 is not the dialectic: "The *speculative* or *positively rational* comprehends the unifying unity of the specific-determinations [of the Understanding] in their opposition, the *affirmative* which is contained in their dissolution and transformation."[65] The definiens here, however, is so close to the one I quoted from the introduction to the *Science of Logic* that there can be no doubt that Hegel is talking about the primary sense of dialectic, that is, its positive aspect. Moreover, the first explanatory note to the same paragraph of the *Encyclopedia* is more explicit, and it contains a reformulation of the above-mentioned principle of the positivity of negation:

Dialectic has a *positive* result because it has a *specifically-determined content;* that is, because its result is not truly *empty abstract Nothingness,* but the Negation of *certain specific-determinations,* which are contained in the result precisely because this latter is not an *immediate Nothingness,* but a result.[66]

The negative aspect of the dialectic is defined in paragraph 81, where the official definiendum is simply "the dialectical aspect" of "the logical": "The *dialectical* constituent-element is the act-of-dialectical-self-overcoming of these finite specific-determinations and their transformation into their opposites."[67] Again, the similarity of this definiens with that of the introduction to the *Science of Logic,* together with the explanatory notes to paragraph 81, leaves no doubt. Moreover, paragraph 79 also indicates that part of Hegel's distinction in the *Encyclopedia* is the same as that in the *Science of Logic:* "With regard to its form, *logic* has three aspects: (a) the *abstract* or *understandable* aspect; (b) the *dialectical* or *negatively rational* aspect; (c) the *speculative* or *positively rational* aspect."[68]

The relationship between these two aspects of the dialectic is a little more difficult to ascertain. Of course, it is clear that the distinction is not a separation. In the *Encyclopedia,* however, Hegel makes them seem to be co-equal elements,[69] whereas in the *Science of Logic,* as noted, negative dialectic is a lower and more restricted form. I believe their proper relationship is best understood in terms of the concept of one-sidedness. In fact, in the second explanatory note to the paragraph (no. 81) discussing negative dialectic, Hegel makes the deeper claim that "dialectic . . . is this *immanent* going beyond, in which the one-sidedness and the limitation of the specific-determinations of the Understanding are represented as what they are, namely as their negation."[70] And in the editorial

193

addition *(Zusatz)* to the paragraph defining speculation, we find the remark that "a one-sided proposition therefore can never even give expression to a speculative truth";[71] this is followed by the very clear and significant illustration that "if we say, for example, that the absolute is the unity of subjective and objective, we are undoubtedly in the right, but so far one-sided, as we enunciate the unity only and lay the accent upon it, forgetting that in reality the subjective and the objective are not merely identical but also distinct."[72]

Thus, Hegel's idea seems to be that negative dialectic is the process that exposes or recognizes one-sidedness, while positive dialectic is the process of overcoming one-sidedness. Applying common Hegelian terminology, used by Hegel elsewhere, we can say that the unity of negative and positive dialectic consists in the identity of their common element of one-sidedness, while their diversity consists in the difference in their relations to it. This in turn introduces the very important Hegelian concept of identity-in-difference or diversity-within-unity, whose first function is to enable us to see the sense in which Hegel's own definitions of dialectic are themselves dialectical. He is using dialectic while in the process of theorizing about it.

So far, then, Hegel has distinguished but not separated, and united but not confused, the positive or speculative and negative aspects of the dialectic, and in the process he has formulated two other aspects. Thus, we have dialectic as the process of overcoming contradictions, one-sidedness, and differences. Contradictions are overcome by recognizing their necessity and the intrinsic negativity of reality, and by recognizing the unity of opposites and the positivity of negation. One-sidedness is overcome by recognizing its all-pervasiveness and by finding ways to avoid it. And differences are overcome by appreciating how they presuppose and are presupposed by similarities.

THE HISTORY OF THE DIALECTIC: SUBJECTIVE VERSUS OBJECTIVE DIALECTIC

Some of Hegel's most explicit clarifications of his notion of dialectic are made in the context of discussing the history of dialectic in his *Lectures on the History of Philosophy*. There are five main contributors in his view: Zeno, Heraclitus, Plato, Proclus, and Kant. The historical accuracy of Hegel's interpretations will not be my concern. Instead, I shall concentrate on two questions: whether Hegel's account is dialectical and whether it contains additional theoretical lessons about the meaning he attached to the concept.

The most significant lesson is perhaps the distinction between subjective or external and objective or immanent dialectic.[73] This distinction is neither between two conceptions of the dialectic nor between two aspects of the same concept. Instead it involves a difference in the location of the process: "Subjective dialectic . . . rests in the contemplative subject,"[74] whereas the other inheres in the contemplated object. Given this distinction, Hegel's history may be interpreted as the story of the emergence of his own dialectical understanding of the two.

For Hegel, "what specially characterizes Zeno is the dialectic which, properly speaking, begins with him."[75] Zeno's paradoxes about motion are intended to show not that there is no motion but that we have no comprehension of it: "The fact that there is movement is as sensuously certain as that there are elephants; it is not in this sense that Zeno meant to deny movement. . . . Movement, however, is held to be untrue, because the conception of it involves a contradiction."[76] Hegel feels he can give a theoretical explanation of why dialectic should have begun with the analysis of motion: "The reason that dialectic first fell on movement is that the dialectic is itself this movement, or movement itself the dialectic of all that is. The thing, as self-moving, has its dialectic in itself, and movement is the becoming another, self-abrogation."[77]

Although "Zeno's dialectic has greater objectivity than [Kant's] modern dialectic,"[78] it is essentially subjective, "inasmuch as it rests in the contemplative subject, and the one, without this movement of the dialectic, is abstract identity."[79] Now, "the next step from the existence of the dialectic as movement in the subject, is that it must necessarily itself become objective."[80] Thus enters "Heraclitus [who] understands the absolute as just this process of the dialectic."[81] Hegel's opinion of him is so high that he confesses, "There is no proposition of Heraclitus which I have not adopted in my Logic."[82]

In Plato, Hegel finds his greatest dialectical predecessor, so much so that "the speculative dialectic . . . commences with him."[83] In fact, by way of introduction Hegel states his own definition that "the Notion of true dialectic is to show forth the necessary movement of pure Notions, without thereby resolving these into nothing; for the result, simply expressed, is that they are this movement, and the universal is just the unity of these opposite Notions."[84] Plato did not have as full a theoretical awareness as Hegel, but he was as much of a practitioner: "We certainly do not find in Plato a full consciousness that this is the nature of dialectic, but we find dialectic itself present."[85] What was Plato's dialectical achievement?

Historically speaking, it was a synthesis of the subjective dialectic of Zeno and the objective dialectic of Heraclitus. In fact, Plato

. . . took into the objective dialectic of Heraclitus the Eleatic dialectic, which is the external endeavour of the subject to show forth contradiction, so that in place of an external changing of things, their inward transition in themselves, i.e. in their Ideas, or, as they are here, in their categories, has come to pass out of and through themselves.[86]

And, conceptually speaking, Platonic dialectic means identity in difference. For

. . . we see that Plato, in respect of content, expresses nothing except what is called indifference in difference, the difference of absolute opposites and their unity. To this speculative knowledge he opposes the ordinary way of thinking, which is positive as well as negative; the former, not bringing the thoughts together, allows first one and then the other to have value in their separation; the latter is, indeed, conscious of a unity, though it is . . . superficial.[87]

This dialectic of identity and difference was carried further by Proclus, though the dialectic of object and subject suffered:

What distinguishes [Proclus] is his more profound study of the Platonic dialectic; in this way he occupies himself in his Platonic theology with the most acute and far-reaching dialectic of the One. It is necessary for him to demonstrate the many as one and the one as many, to show forth the forms which the One adopts. But it is a dialectic which to a greater or less extent is externally worked out.[88]

Similarly, Kant, in his transcendental dialectic, discovered the necessity of contradictions but restricted this necessity to the subjective realm. Referring to the antinomies, Hegel says that

. . . the necessity of these contradictions is the interesting fact which Kant has brought to consciousness; in ordinary metaphysics, however, it is imagined that one of these contradictions must hold good, and the other be disproved. . . . transcendental idealism lets the contradiction remain, only it is not Being in itself that is thus contradictory, for the contradiction has its source in our thought alone.[89]

Hegel's criticism of Kant's dialectic gives us some further insight into Hegelian dialectic. For Hegel, Kant did not realize the seriousness of the problem engendered by his one-sided emphasis on subjective dialectic. The problem is that "Kant shows here too much

tenderness for things: it would be a pity, he thinks, if they con-
tradicted themselves. But that mind, which is far higher, should
be a contradiction – that is not a pity at all."[90] However, just as
Hegel's own dialectic requires the avoidance of such one-sidedness,
so it requires the unity of the opposites in question: "The true solution would be found in the statement that the categories have
no truth in themselves, and the Unconditioned of Reason just as
little, but that it lies in the unity of both as concrete, and in that
alone."[91]

We may conclude by saying that Hegel uses in several ways his
own concept of dialectic in his account of its history. This history
is, in one sense, a study of the interaction between subjective and
objective dialectic. These do not constitute two different meanings
of the dialectic, but they refer to two different entities where the
dialectical process may be taking place. Hegel's account is dialectical
with respect to the "opposition" between the objective and the
subjective, and in the senses of the three notions: unity of opposites,
overcoming of one-sidedness, and identity in difference.

THE DIALECTIC OF PHILOSOPHY:
METAPHILOSOPHY VERSUS DIALECTICAL THEORY

Hegel's preface to the *Phenomenology of Spirit* has been widely acclaimed as a philosophical masterpiece in its own right, even independently of the rest of the book.[92] Given the main conclusion
elaborated therein, to wit, that the nature of philosophy is to be
dialectical, it should not be surprising that the preface turns out to
be a dialectical masterpiece as well. Yet, to my knowledge, no one
has provided the dialectical analysis the essay deserves.[93] Since,
moreover, the preface contains some of Hegel's most explicit dialectical texts, it is imperative to examine it to see what can be
learned about the Hegelian dialectic.

From the point of view of content, the subject matter of the preface is the nature of philosophy and its difference from various
forms of pseudophilosophy and from other nonphilosophical disciplines such as mathematics. The essay proceeds in the form of a
"preface" to the *Phenomenology*, which includes a qualification about
the propriety of philosophical prefaces, a statement of the book's
relation to other contemporary works, a formulation of its main
conclusion or result, a description of its content or subject matter,
a summary of the form in which this content is organized or procedure used, and a justification of this procedure. The "method"

in all this prefatory material could be described as that of analysis of similarities and differences between philosophy and other activities, as well as of some of its internal structure. Finally, as was stated, the essay's main result is the conclusion that philosophy is dialectical. Let me add that, for reasons to appear shortly, this claim is meant to convey as much information about dialectic as about philosophy; and, of course, this is the claim that corresponds to the central thesis of what I earlier called the "metaphilosophical" interpretation of the Hegelian dialectic.

The claim appears more than once toward the end of the preface and involves more than one element of philosophy. For example, it is the dialectical nature of philosophical truth that Hegel is referring to when he says that "the true . . . is merely the dialectical movement" (K448).[94] The point is expressed in terms of philosophical demonstration when Hegel asserts that "once the dialectic has been separated from proof, the notion of philosophical demonstration has been lost" (M40);[95] this may be interpreted as meaning that dialectic and philosophical proof must not be separated (but merely distinguished), otherwise there would be no such thing as a philosophical proof, and hence philosophical proof should be dialectical. Hegel is most explicit about philosophical exposition, for he declares that "in keeping with our insight into the nature of speculation, the exposition should preserve the dialectical form" (M41).

These explicit metaphilosophical and dialectic-theoretical views can be connected in two ways with the bulk of the preface, which constitutes the relevant philosophical and dialectical practice. First, we may examine what the preface says about philosophy from the point of view of whatever Hegel claims to mean by "dialectic" in this context. The only relevant such remark here is that "the dialectical movement [is] this course that generates itself, going forth from, and returning to, itself" (M40). This sentence may be interpreted as meaning that the dialectic is the process whereby differences are generated and then overcome, which corresponds to the notion of diversity within unity discussed earlier as central to the dialectic. Hence we need to examine how Hegel's various metaphilosophical theses amount to characterizing philosophy in terms of diversity within unity, and how his practice in the preface amounts to philosophy so conceived.

Second, we begin by taking the proposition that philosophy is dialectical as being another way of saying that dialectic is the essence of philosophy. This metamorphosis of a metaphilosophical thesis into a dialectic-theoretical one is justified because, as Hegel himself argues, metaphilosophical claims are simply special cases of philosophical propositions, and the relation between linguistic subject and predicate is a peculiar one in a philosophical proposition. Using the examples of "God is being" and "the actual is the universal," Hegel argues (M38–39) that philosophical propositions state essential identities even when they have the subject-predicate form, and hence they are convertible in just the way required to yield the above metamorphosis. Once we have the claim that dialectic is the essence of philosophy, then all we need to do is examine what (Hegel tells us) the essence of philosophy is, and these features will be applicable to dialectic. Since our previous analysis revealed that the unity of opposites and the positivity of the negative are central conceptual elements of Hegel's dialectic, then we can examine whether and how those features of philosophy reduce to these concepts. And since we want to analyze Hegel's own practice in the preface, we also need to examine to what extent these concepts inhere therein.

Thus, through both kinds of considerations, we conclude that a dialectical analysis of the preface requires examining in what way the three notions of diversity within unity, unity of opposites, and positivity of the negative inhere in Hegel's metaphilosophical theory and in his actual philosophical practice in that essay.

Hegel's first metaphilosophical thesis occurs in the context of his initial qualifications about the character of prefaces to philosophical books. In discussing the propriety that a preface should include an explanation of the differences vis-à-vis other works on the same topic, Hegel comments on what is perhaps the central datum of philosophy, namely the existence of a multiplicity of philosophical systems. He proposes that one should "comprehend the diversity of philosophical systems as the progressive unfolding of truth" (M2), by contrast to an attitude that "rather sees in it simple disagreements" (M2). What is required when faced with such an opposition is something few people know how to do, namely, "to free it from its one-sidedness, or maintain it in its freedom by recognizing the reciprocally necessary moments that take shape as a conflict and seeming incompatibility" (M2). This is obviously a usage of the notions of unity of opposites and identity in difference. The opposites are the various philosophical systems, and Hegel is advocating eliminating the conflict not by doing away with all but one system but rather by recognizing the necessity of the conflict. When this has been done, then it is no longer one-sided. Note that

Hegel is attributing one-sidedness to the (uncomprehended) conflict or opposition rather than merely to one of its elements. Finally, we may add that the positivity of the negative is present here insofar as the negative is a way of describing the opposition, and it becomes positive in the sense of necessary.

After this plea for philosophical pluralism, by way of an initial qualification, the discussion turns to a clarification of the relation of Hegel's work to others, involving two relevant theses. One is that philosophy is conceptual in nature. Hegel first expresses this thesis in a characteristic way (which strikes me as somewhat pseudorigorous), namely, by saying that philosophical "truth finds the element of its existence only in the Concept" (K374). Then he expresses the same idea negatively (but in a way that strikes me as ironically edifying) by declaring that "philosophy must beware of the wish to be edifying" (M6). At this point Hegel is contrasting concepts to feelings and intuitions, and the crucial fault of the latter is that they operate "by confounding the distinctions of thought, by suppressing the discriminating Concept" (K376). Thus, in holding that philosophy is conceptual Hegel means that it must make distinctions and be discriminating. This claim may be regarded as a clarification of the notions of unity of opposites and identity in difference; it is a reminder that such unity and identity are not a confusion, that the difference of the opposites is not suppressed by philosophical concepts.

Feeling and intuition, however, are not the only sources of unphilosophical confusion. Another is abstract formalism, which, because of its philosophical pretense, generates a type of pseudophilosophical attitude. Hegel's thesis here is that philosophy must avoid formalism, or as we shall put it, is concrete. This is part of what he has in mind when he criticizes philosophies that try to be esoteric rather than "exoteric" (M7), or those that try to "pass off one's absolute as the night in which, as one says, all cows are black" (K386). The content of Hegel's criticism, together with my comments in the preceding paragraph, makes obvious the undialectical character of these pseudophilosophies:

They subject everything to the absolute idea which then appears to be recognized in everything and to have developed into a comprehensive science. But when this comprehensiveness is considered more closely, it becomes manifest that it was not attained insofar as one and the same principle differentiated itself into different forms, but it is rather the formless repetition of one and the same principle which is merely applied externally to different material and thus receives a dull semblance of differentiation. (K384)

Although the effect is similar to that produced by substituting feeling for conceptualizing, namely, confusion and lack of discrimination, this is now produced by superficial and externalistic unification of opposites and identification of differences.

The preface now continues with what looks like a formulation of the book's main result(s) or conclusion(s). I believe there are three principal metaphilosophical theses, about the self-reflective, the self-generating, and the systematic nature of philosophy. Hegel's exposition here often looks like a self-parody of the "night where all cows are black," and it is instructive to elaborate how this is so. He begins by declaring that "everything turns on grasping and expressing the True, not only as *Substance*, but equally as *Subject*" (M10); after a few paragraphs he assures us that "what has just been said can also be expressed by saying that Reason is *purposive activity*" (M12), and that "the need to represent the Absolute as *Subject* has found expression in the propositions: *God* is the eternal, the moral-order, love, and so on" (M12); then he varies this into the idea that "knowledge is only actual, and can only be expounded, as Science or as *system*" (M13), so that he can go on to dazzle us with the triple equivalence: "That the true is actual only as system, or that Substance is essentially Subject, is expressed in the representation of the Absolute as *Spirit*" (M14). This attempted equation of five ideas, each of which is distinct, is, I suppose, the kind of confusion that gives Hegelianism a bad name.

One of the things Hegel seems to be saying is that philosophical knowledge is subjective as well as objective. That is, the opposition between object and subject must not be allowed to become an abstract separation. This presumably means that in philosophizing, one should never completely lose sight of the consciousness (the philosopher) engaged in it. Hegel's best formulation of this thesis is a negative one and does not lack a certain eloquence: "The standpoint of consciousness which knows objects in their antithesis to itself, and itself in antithesis to them, is for Science [i.e., philosophy] the antithesis of its own standpoint" (M15). In prosaic terminology we may rephrase this by saying that philosophy must be self-reflective.

Similarly, *mutatis mutandis*, we may attribute to Hegel the view that philosophy must be self-generating, as an interpretation of his talk about the "spiritual" nature of philosophy. Philosophy is spiritual in the sense that it must recognize that reality (the Absolute) is spiritual and that it is itself the spiritual reflection of this spiritual reality. But what is spirit? It is "that being . . . which is in truth actual only insofar as it is the movement of positing itself, or the mediation between a self and its development into something different" (K388), or "that which has *being in itself* . . . which *relates itself to itself* and . . . in its self-externality, abides within itself" (M14), or again, "self-identity that moves itself . . . or, reduced to its pure abstraction, simple becoming" (K390–92). The idea conveyed is one of change and activity as opposed to rest and stasis, a change that comes about through internal division and integration. Hegel's best formulation is again a negative one: "The situation in which consciousness knows itself to be at home is for Science one marked by the absence of Spirit" (M15). The connection with dialectic is that the spiritual process so defined may be conceived as an instance of identity in difference.

The systematic nature of philosophy is elaborated by Hegel when he says that "the true is the whole" (K390) and that "the true is its own becoming, the circle that presupposes its end as its aim and thus has it for its beginning – that which is actual only through its execution and end" (K388). He means that in philosophical inquiry there is no absolute distinction between beginning and end, which is reminiscent of dialectical unity applied to these two opposites. Moreover, a philosophical principle, no matter how basic, is by itself just a lifeless universal, and thus it needs to be elaborated and applied; this elaboration may be regarded as a removal of "its initially one-sided form of being *immediate*" (M13). This gives us another dialectical aspect of systematicity.

In the section of the preface just discussed, Hegel adapts conclusions reached in the body of his *Phenomenology* and generalizes them by expressing them in metaphilosophical terminology. In the following section he does the same thing concerning the book's procedure so as to formulate the thesis that philosophy is negative in its approach. The basic procedure in the *Phenomenology* is to describe the emergence of philosophical consciousness regarded as the highest, out of lower forms of experience, such as sensation and Understanding. Although the lower forms are superseded, the pathway through these cannot be dispensed with, partly because they exemplify world-historical evolution, partly because they inhere in individual-psychological development, partly because "each is itself a complete individual shape" (M17), that is, has its own autonomous integrity, and partly because some (most notably the Understanding) have "the most astonishing and mightiest of powers" (M18). In other words, it is precisely the nature of philosophical consciousness not to forget its low origins:

The life of the Spirit is not the life that shrinks from death and keeps itself untouched by devastation, but rather the life that endures it and maintains itself in it. It wins its truth only when, in utter dismemberment, it finds itself. It is this power, not as something positive, which closes its eyes to the negative, as when we say of something that it is nothing or is false, and then, having done with it, turn away and pass on to something else; on the contrary, Spirit is this power only by looking the negative in the face, and tarrying with it. (M19).

This, of course, is a good description of that element of dialectic consisting of recognizing the negative as necessary and hence "positive."

In this context (M21) Hegel mentions another aspect of the negativity of philosophy, which deserves separate mention because it can be clearly interpreted as the thesis that philosophy is self-referential. Once philosophical consciousness has emerged, not only does it not forget its dark past, but its starts reflecting upon its ever-dark present:

Spirit becomes object because it is just this movement of becoming an *other to itself*, i.e. becoming an object to itself, and of suspending this otherness. And experience is the name we give to just this movement in which the immediate, the unexperienced, i.e. the abstract, whether it be of sensuous being, or only thought of as simple, becomes alienated from itself and then returns to itself from this alienation, and is only then revealed for the first time in its actuality and truth, just as it then has become a property of consciousness also. (M21)

Thus such self-referentiality is an obvious consequence of the "spiritual" nature of philosophy discussed above. The dialectical character of this self-reference not only derives from the latter but is given explicit recognition by Hegel when he says later (in the introduction) that "*inasmuch as the new true object issues from it*, this *dialectical* movement which consciousness exercises on itself and which affects both its knowledge and its object, is precisely what is called *experience*" (M55).

In this first half of the preface, Hegel has explained how philosophy is pluralistic, conceptual, concrete, self-reflective, spiritual, systematic, negative, and self-referential. Here the metaphilosophical orientation and the dialectical content, although ascertainable, are not as explicit as they are in the second half. In fact, in this latter part, his explicit aim (M22, par. 38) is to discuss the nature of philosophy and its difference from other disciplines, in order to justify the procedure of the *Phenomenology* just described. The discussion involves several specific ways in which philosophy is by its nature negative, and several pairs of opposites that need to be superseded.

He begins with a clear "dialectical" account of the concepts of philosophical truth and falsity. These are typical and important examples of opposites that the philosopher must learn to sublimate. The distinction (which is not to say separation) between these two concepts is that "to know something falsely means that there is a disparity between knowledge and its Substance. But . . . their identity . . . is the truth" (M23). Now, this means that both concepts presuppose the subject-object distinction, and hence they may be regarded as aspects of this distinction, and in that sense as having their unity in it. We should be careful, however, not to misunderstand this (dialectical) unity as a case where one opposite is an aspect of the other, that is, "we cannot therefore say that the false is a moment of the True, let alone a component part of it" (M23). That unity, however, does imply that there is negativity in the notion of truth, the negativity consisting precisely of the subject-object distinction: "Truth . . . is not truth as if the disparity had been thrown away . . . disparity, rather, as the negative, the self, is itself still directly present in the True as such" (M23). Moreover, since the distinction between object and subject needs to be itself sublimated, there are occasions when "the terms 'true' and 'false' must no longer be used" (M23), or as we might put it, when the terms do not rigorously apply. It should be noted that Hegel is explicit about the metaphilosophical aim of this discussion; for he hastens to add that this view applies specifically only to philosophical inquiry and not to other disciplines, such as history, where "to such questions as, When was Caesar born? . . . a clear-cut answer ought to be given" (M23). Finally, Hegel stipulates defining "dogmatism" as the opposite of his view, and so we may express the present claim as the proposition that philosophy is undogmatic.

The next specific feature of philosophy concerns the way in which it differs from mathematics. In what is perhaps one of the most interesting and readable parts of the preface, Hegel explains (M24–25) that whereas in mathematics proof is a method for knowing truth rather than an aspect of it, in philosophy the process of arriving at the truth is an aspect of it; that is, although the process of proving a mathematical truth and the ontological genesis of the corresponding true fact are separate, in philosophy the epistemological process and the ontogenetic one are inseparable (though distinct). Moreover, mathematics is such that: The construction of a proof has no internal necessity but only the external expediency of enabling the deduction of the wanted result, insofar as there is some *arbitrariness* in the choice of the initial step, the particular intermediate consequences to draw, and the auxiliary assumptions and constructions to make (M25, par. 44); the ultimate purpose is quantification, which examines the *superficial* rather than essential aspects of things (M25–26); the subject matter, for example, space and numbers, is *abstract* rather than actual (M26); one proceeds *formalistically*, that is, by searching exclusively for equalities and identities, thus ignoring distinctions and differences (M26); its application to natural phenomena yields no real proofs but presupposes empirical propositions (M26–27); and it allegedly does not deal properly with the concept of time and temporal processes (M27). By contrast, philosophy deals with what is essential and concretely actual; more importantly, it also deals with the evanescent insofar as it is essential, with change that does not itself change, and with necessary forms of thought insofar as they develop from one to another (M27–28).

These differences between mathematics and philosophy seem to center around two things. One is their respective treatment of the distinction between method and result: In mathematics they are treated as separate, in philosophy they are dialectically united insofar as they are aspects of the same process of thought. The other concerns the single-mindedness of their respective aims: Mathematics one-sidedly looks for constancies and uniformities, philosophy takes the other side into account by *also* searching for the changes and irregularities. That is, philosophy looks for what is constant amid changes, and what is changing amid constancies, for as Hegel puts it, "The evanescent itself must, on the contrary, be regarded as essential, not as something fixed, cut off from the True, and left lying who knows where outside it, any more than the True is to be regarded as something on the other side, positive and dead" (M27). Such avoidance of one-sidedness is, of course, an element of the dialectic.

Another distinction superseded by philosophy is that between form and content, and this is argued by Hegel in a discussion of philosophic method proper. The primary contrast here is to the approach of any schematizing formalism which imagines that comprehension can be achieved by externally attaching labels to things, that is, by classifying them in terms of various predicates, even if these are ones like subject, object, substance, and cause (M29–31). For Hegel, philosophic method has two parts (M35). The first is not to separate itself from its content, and it is a requirement of scientific method in general, for "scientific knowledge . . . demands precisely that we surrender to the life of the object or – and this is the same – that we confront and express its inner necessity" (K434); in other words, one should penetrate the inner nature of the object, rather than externally impose upon it formulas developed elsewhere. The second is to determine spontaneously the rhythm of the development of the subject matter, and it is a consequence of a main conclusion of the *Phenomenology* that the absolute is subject as well as substance (M33); for this implies that "knowledge is not an activity that handles its contents as something strange" (K434) and that the nature of things is "to be their Concept in their being" (K436). This process is inherently negative:

> The movement of beings is, first, to become something other and thus to become their own immanent content; secondly, they take back into themselves this unfolding or this existence of theirs, i.e., they make themselves into a mere moment and simplify themselves into determinateness. In the first movement negativity consists in the differentiation and positing of existence; in the return into itself, it is the becoming of determinate simplicity. (K432)

The process corresponds to the so-called spirituality of reality and of philosophy discussed earlier. Here, Hegel uses it to make a strictly methodological point, to the effect that philosophic method has to be phenomenological (in the ordinary meaning of this term). His point could also be expressed by saying that philosophy must be materialistic, in the sense of emphasizing "matter" rather than "form," although such a formulation would be bound to be confusing and misleading. At any rate, the relevance to dialectic, besides the necessity and hence positivity of the negative, involves the union of form and content. This union does not abolish their distinction but stipulates that the form of one's approach must be governed by the content. Plausibly construed, this is another formulation of the concreteness of philosophy.

The next point concerns the linguistic expression of philosophical thought, and in particular the grammatical subject-predicate structure of sentences. On the one hand, philosophy cannot avoid their use, and this leads one to think that the philosophical subject and the philosophical predicate are separate and are being related by the relation of predication. On the other hand, because of their subject matter and their meaning, a predicate in a philosophical sentence is trying to express the essence of the subject, and thus the sentence is really an identity. This creates special problems for philosophical thinking, communication, intelligibility, and expression, the only solution of which is not to deny them but to understand the true nature of philosophical expression. In Hegel's words:

The nature of the judgment or proposition, which involves the distinction between subject and predicate, is destroyed by the speculative proposition; and the identical proposition into which the former turns contains the counterthrust against this relation [but] in the philosophical proposition . . . the identity of subject and predicate is not meant to destroy the difference between both that is expressed by the form of the proposition; rather their unity is meant to emerge as a harmony. (K444)

This seems to mean that a philosophical proposition is the synthesis of the difference between subject and predicate (suggested by the grammatical form) and their identity (underlying this appearance). And the dialectical nature of this claim is obvious, since it involves the elements of unity of opposites, identity and difference, and avoidance of one-sidedness. The positivity of the negative is also present in this discussion insofar as Hegel is saying that philosophical exposition is handicapped by (i.e., negative because of) the subject-predicate grammar, and necessarily (i.e., positively) so.

After these implicitly dialectical accounts of philosophical truth and falsity, method and result, change and permanence, form and content, subject and predicate, Hegel formulates explicitly his thesis of the dialectical nature of philosophy in a number of ways that we discussed at the beginning of our analysis of the preface. To conclude the essay, a discussion of the relationship between philosophy and common sense holds that although there is no royal road to it, philosophy is intrinsically technical. Although these remarks do not have any obvious dialectical content, they have some plausibility if interpreted as a criticism of dilettantism. Indeed, "philosophizing should again be made a serious business" (M41) and its "true thoughts and . . . insight are only to be won through . . . labour" (M43).

So far the analysis of Hegel's essay has attempted to clarify and enrich his concept of the dialectic by examining exactly how its meaning (first ascertained from other texts) inheres in his various claims about the nature of philosophy. More exactly, I have identified a number of nonexplicitly dialectical metaphilosophical theses in order to determine in what sense they entailed that philosophy is dialectical, which is to say, I have reconstructed the details of his *argument* supporting this metaphilosophical conclusion. Assuming the correctness of those metaphilosophical premises, I have argued that the relevant sense of dialectic is the one articulated by Hegel in his more explicit definitions examined earlier; that is, I have also shown the validity of the reconstructed metaphilosophical argument, or, to be more exact, that it is valid if and only if "dialectic" means what he says it means.

The possibility of interpreting the preface as such an argument enriches its dialectical content. One can now say that what Hegel mainly does in this essay is *argue* that philosophy is dialectical, and that in this argument he is *using* the concept of the dialectic. The argument is that philosophy is dialectical because it is pluralistic, conceptual, concrete, self-reflective, spiritual, systematic, negative, self-referential, and *because* it supersedes the oppositions of truth and falsity, method and result, change and permanence, form and content, and subject and predicate. There are, of course, missing premises in this argument: They are the propositons, stating connections between these features and the dialectic, that I have supplied in the course of my analysis. Moreover, what I have tried to establish, that Hegel's metaphilosophical argument is valid, means that his dialectic-theoretical exercise is self-consistent. For I have shown that in every case, the missing premises of Hegel's argument follow from his general (fourfold) definition of dialectic, and so the concept he uses in the preface to the *Phenomenology* is the one that he elaborates in the introduction to the *Logic* and in the *Encyclopedia*, and that which he uses in the *History of Philosophy*.

But if this defines a sense in which Hegel is theorizing about the dialectic in the essay, it says nothing about whether he is practicing the dialectic. His dialectical theorizing consists of applying his concept of the dialectic to the case of philosophy or, alternatively, extracting the concept from an analysis of the nature of philosophy. But the form of this theorizing – in particular, whether it conforms to a dialectical approach – has not yet been examined.

The most evident dialectical aspect of Hegel's procedure concerns the distinction between dialectic and philosophy. My analysis began by indicating that his metaphilosophical conclusion is also a dialectic-theoretical proposition, if we apply his dialectical analysis of grammatical subject and predicate in philosophical sentences to that conclusion. In other words, the interweaving of the metaphilosophical and dialectic-theoretical themes in the essay is Hegel's own way of uniting the two opposites of dialectic and philosophy, or of identifying them in their difference.

Another aspect of dialectical procedure involves the distinction between form and content, also briefly mentioned at the beginning of my analysis. We may say now that the content of Hegel's essay is the metaphilosophical argument reconstructed in the course of my analysis and just now more explicitly defined. The form of the essay, we have seen, is that of a preface to the *Phenomenology*, which begins with some qualifications about the status of philosophical prefaces; it goes on to clarify some differences between the book and other contemporary works, to summarize its main conclusions, and to outline the basic steps of its procedure, and finally it justifies this procedure on the basis of the nature of philosophy. The integration of these two elements represents a union not only between form and content but between the particular and the general. Ironically, it is the essay's content that generates its general relevance, whereas it is its form that gives its particularity. In other words, Hegel's metaphilosophical argument is obviously concrete and therefore dialectical, since it is conducted not at a purely abstract level but with illustrations from the *Phenomenology*; there is also concreteness because of the frequent contrasts between philosophy and other activities, such as edification, formalism, history, and mathematics.

I also stated earlier that the essay's basic method could be described as metaphilosophical analysis, the opposite pole of which is the result about the dialectical nature of philosophy. I believe that the metaphilosophical, dialectical-theoretical argument as I have reconstructed it completely clarifies the integration between these two "opposites": It is the union, or identity-in-difference, or, more simply, the relationship between premises and conclusion of an argument.

As to avoidance of one-sidedness, perhaps the essay's most striking feature is Hegel's attitude toward rigor and precision. On the one hand, he is very critical of the sloppiness, confusions, and superficialities of edifying pseudophilosophies and of uneducated common sense; on the other hand, he is very confident that the niceties of mathematics are not what philosophy should strive for.

The positivity of the negative is more problematic. There is no question, of course, about the prevalence of the topic in the *content* of the essay and its argument; few other topics are equally pervasive. It is not clear, however, that there is any negativity in the approach followed by Hegel's theorizing. In other words, although the negativity of the procedure in the *Phenomenology* is obvious from the discussion in the preface, the negativity of the preface itself is not. I am reluctant to mention the only possibility that comes to mind, and so I present it as a conjecture. Perhaps this is a situation where we should rigorously apply Hegel's concept of the spiritual and of union of subject and object. To do so in this case would amount to saying that as we immerse ourselves in all the talk about the negativity of the procedure of the *Phenomenology* in particular and of philosophy in general, our own minds acquire that characteristic. That is, if we lift ourselves to "pure self-recognition in absolute otherness, this ether as such" (K398), and if, indeed, we have abided by the principle that "science on her part demands of self-consciousness that it should have elevated itself into this ether to be able to live – and to live – with her and in her" (K398), then we are assured that our metaphilosophical theorizing has experienced the negativity of philosophy being theorized about. My reason for hesitating in joining Hegel in this ether is a dialectical one: Such talk, especially if "rigorously" applied, comes close to confusion, that is, to abolishing the distinction between object and subject, which admittedly should not be separated. For just as we should distinguish the concepts of distinction and of separation, so should we distinguish dialectical union from confused union.

So, perhaps the way out of the problem is the following: The absence of negativity from Hegel's precedure (in the preface) may be recognized as a negative feature. It may then be asked whether it was necessary or accidental. How could Hegel have followed a negative approach in discussing the negativity of the *Phenomenology?* I don't see that he had any other alternative but simply to explain and justify it, unless he had wanted to repeat the long and arduous road followed in the book itself, which was precluded by the context of the preface. But this necessity amounts to the positivity of that absence. Thus the essay does exemplify the positivity of the negative, after all, and this is the relevant dialectical element.

In conclusion, it may be said that Hegel's preface to the *Phenomenology* is, as we expected, indeed a dialectical masterpiece. It not only theorizes about the concept of dialectic, by concretizing its content in the course of a lengthy metaphilosophical argument about the dialectical nature of philosophy, it also practices the dialectic about which it theorizes. It does so insofar as it exhibits the positivity of the negative, the avoidance of one-sidedness, and the uniting of such "opposites" as dialectic and philosophy, metaphilosophical content and prefatory form, and its own method and result. Moreover, in both Hegel's dialectical theory and his dialectical practice the concepts of identity and difference play a fundamental role.

THE DIALECTIC OF DIALECTIC: LAWS OF THOUGHT VERSUS DETERMINATIONS OF REFLECTIONS

An analysis of Hegelian dialectic would not be complete without examining that part of *Science of Logic* where Hegel discusses the concepts of identity and difference.[96] One reason is that, as noted, these concepts are perhaps the ones with the most fundamental role in what he means by dialectic. Another reason is that in these passages Hegel gives a critique of formal logic and the so-called laws of thought, a criticism that is widely regarded as[97] what Hegel's concept of dialectic reduces to. In accordance with the metaphilosophical interpretation I have been developing, my program is to try to identify the dialectical practice and the dialectical theorizing within these passages,[98] and see how they correspond.

This section of the *Logic*, which Hegel entitles "Determinations of Reflections," is also particularly instructive because it is a microcosm of the difficulties that alternative interpretations of Hegelian dialectic face. In fact, the triadic view is afflicted by insurmountable problems: whether in the main triad of this section the synthesis of identity (as thesis) and difference (as antithesis) is "contradiction" (as the *Logic* suggests) or "ground" (as in the account of the *Encyclopedia*) or "stable essentiality" (as McTaggart claims that it should properly be);[99] what sense to make of the triad within the category of difference consisting of absolute difference, diversity, and opposition (found in the *Logic*), and of the triad within the category of essential difference consisting of opposition, polarity, and contradiction (found in the *Encyclopedia*, par. 119); and what are the syntheses if any, for each of the pairs – likeness and unlikeness, and positive and negative – that Hegel discusses at some length? Moreover, the systemic-immanent interpretation is dealt a severe blow by the pun with which Hegel generates or derives the category of ground out of lower ones: "Both Positive and Negative are therefore explicit contradiction; both are potentially the same. Both are so actually also; since either is the abrogation of the other and of itself. Thus they fall to the Ground."[100] Finally, the apparent differences in structure and detail between the *Logic*

211

and the *Encyclopedia* make a sham of the onto-phenomenological interpretation, for they are clear proof that much more is required than what Kojève, for example, claims, namely, that "Hegel looks at the Real and describes what he sees, everything that he sees, and nothing but what he sees."[101]

More than ever, to this part of the *Logic* is applicable Hegel's own advice (given in the introduction) not to take too seriously "the subdivisions and titles of the books, sections, and chapters indicated in this work, as well as any [remarks] connected with them."[102] Putting this advice into practice, we find, however, a bewildering mixture of discussions centering around three themes. One is the analysis of such categories as identity, difference, diversity or variety, opposition, contradiction, likeness versus unlikeness, and the positive versus the negative. A second theme is the critique of such laws of thought as those of identity, of noncontradiction, of diversity or variety or identity of indiscernibles, and of the excluded middle. Finally, we have a metaphilosophical theme consisting of a number of principles of philosophic methodology. The connection between these discussions and dialectic is difficult to work out in detail, in fact, as difficult as it is superfically obvious in the light of our previous analysis in terms of unity of opposites, positivity of negativity, identity in difference, and nature of philosophy; moreover, the apparent dialectical connection is strengthened by the readily noticeable fact that a central criticism of the laws of thought is Hegel's claim that they are one-sided.

Let us begin with the metaphilosophical theme, which is the easiest to disentangle. One philosophical procedure is expressed in the principle of identity and difference. One purpose of this principle is to distinguish good from bad philosophy: "It is important to come to a proper understanding on the true meaning of Identity: and for that purpose we must especially guard against taking it as abstract Identity, to the exclusion of all Difference. That is the touchstone for distinguishing all bad philosophy from what alone deserves the name of philosophy."[103] In part, the principle aims to differentiate the activity of philosophic reason from that of abstract or external reflection: The former involves showing how "everything is in its self-sameness different from itself and self-contradictory, and that in its difference, in its contradiction, it is self-identical, and is in its own self this movement of transition of one of these categories into the other" (M412);[104] whereas the latter operates with "that identity which is aloof from difference, and difference that is aloof from identity" (M412). The principle also provides a contrast between philosophy and natural science:

In the case of difference, in short, we like to see identity, and in the case of identity we like to see difference. Within the range of the empirical sciences however, the one of these two categories is often allowed to put the other out of sight and mind. Thus the scientific problem at one time is to reduce existing differences to identity; on another occasion, with equal one-sidedness, to discover new differences.[105]

Another principle of philosophic method may be descriptively named the principle of diversity and opposition. It stipulates that "thinking reason, however, sharpens, so to say, the blunt difference of diverse terms, the mere manifoldness of pictoral thinking, into *essential* difference, into *opposition*" (M442). Or, more explicitly, understanding that "essential difference is therefore Opposition; according to which the different is not confronted by *any* other but by *its* other,"[106] we may say that "the aim of philosophy is to banish indifference, and to ascertain the necessity of things. By that means the other is seen to stand over against *its* other."[107] But this emphasis on opposition is not one-sided, for it is meant to counteract the common tendency to linger in indifference: "Ordinary thinking when it passes over to the moment of the *indifference* of the [opposite] determinations, forgets their negative unity and so retains them merely as 'differents' in general" (M441). In fact a main concern of Hegel's analysis of opposition is to point out that "opposite magnitudes are, first, merely and in general opposite, and, secondly real or indifferent" (JS57),[108] or, more explicitly, that "opposites, therefore, contain contradiction in so far as they are, in the same respect, negatively related to one another or *sublate each other* and are indifferent to one another" (M441). After all, the principle of contradiction and resolution is another essential principle of philosophical methodology for Hegel.

According to this principle, philosophy must also show how everything is self-contradictory, and how this self-contradiction resolves itself into all movement, vitality, and change: "*Speculative thinking* consists solely in the fact that thought holds fast contradiction, and in it, its own self, but does not allow itself to be dominated by it as in ordinary thinking" (M440–41), whereas the latter is such that "in considering contradiction, it stops short at the one-sided *resolution* of it into *nothing*, and fails to recognize the positive side of contradiction where it becomes *absolute activity*" (M442). Besides the reference to one-sidedness, and the notion of self-contradiction causing change, another preliminary clue to what Hegel means by contradiction is his interpretation of Zeno's paradoxes, when we are told that "the ancient dialecticians must be granted the contradictions that they pointed out in motion; but it does not follow that therefore there is no motion, but on the contrary, that motion is *existent* contradiction itself" (M440). This is perhaps enough to show that Hegel is not talking about logical contradiction, about which more needs to be said later in this section.

Finally, there is the principle of relatedness, which prescribes that

> . . . it is of the greatest importance to recognize this quality of the Determinations of Reflections which have been considered here, that their truth consists in their relation to each other, and therefore in the fact that each contains the other in its own concept. This must be understood and remembered, for without this understanding not a step can really be taken in philosophy. (JS65)

The "determinations of reflections" in question are identity and difference, diversity and opposition, and contradiction and resolution. For each member of these pairs to contain the other member, means that philosophical inquiry should overcome the kind of one-sidedness that the metaphilosophical principles just mentioned recommend avoiding. Thus we have here an additional general reference to this element of the dialectic. Moreover, given the identification of philosophy and dialectic in the preface to the *Phenomenology*, the metaphilosophical content of the passages of the *Logic* just analyzed may be viewed as a dialectic-theoretical analysis of the connection between the concepts of the dialectic and one-sidedness.

At any rate, explicit metaphilosophical theorizing is not here, unlike in the preface to the *Phenomenology*, the main topic. I have begun with it because, from the present viewpoint, the theses just presented are the most concrete. Next in order of concreteness comes Hegel's interpretation of the "laws of thought." This critique is obviously an example of philosophical practice, and I shall be examining whether and in what way it constitutes dialectical practice as well. That is, I shall be concerned with how Hegel is using or applying his own concept of the dialectic while philosophizing about the laws of thought.

Hegel's most general criticism of the "laws of thought" is that they are not really laws of thought, or not laws of philosophical thought, but rather laws of abstract understanding, laws of the undialectical mind. This is what he means when he concludes that "the result of this consideration is, first, that the Laws of Identity and Contradiction . . . are not Laws of Thought, but quite the opposite" (JS43); this opposition is not to being a law, but to "thinking" since he says elsewhere that such a law "instead of being a true law of thought, is nothing but the law of abstract understanding."[109] Although Hegel's general tone may be negative, the positivity of his negative criticism should not be missed, for he is not denying the laws' formal correctness from the viewpoint of abstract understanding. Thus, the law of identity is "the expression of an empty *tautology*" (M413); the law of diversity "is a very superfluous proposition" (M422); the law of the excluded middle "is so trivial that it is not worth the trouble of saying it" (M438).

What are the grounds for Hegel's criticism? Let us consider the law of identity, which states that "everything is identical with itself."[110] The central problem is that it is one-sided: "The Law of Identity expresses only a one-sided determinateness" (JS40). This one-sidedness affects its content, its justification, and its application or instantiation.

Its content may be contrasted with that of the law of diversity, which declares that "everything is different from everything else" (M422). It should also be contrasted with what Hegel calls the law of opposition, which states that "everything is an *opposite*" (M438), that is, everything is the opposite of something.

There is no denying that Hegel frequently speaks as if these laws were in conflict. For example, in referring to the law of diversity he claims that "this proposition is, in fact, opposed to the law of identity, for it declares: *A* is distinctive, therefore *A* is also not *A*" (M422). He also asserts that the law of opposition "most expressly controverts the maxim of Identity: the one says that a thing should be only a self-relation, the other says that it must be an opposite, a relation to its other."[111]

In the same discussions, however, we also find such remarks as that the laws of identity and of diversity "are held apart as indifferently different, so that each is valid on its own without respect to the other" (M422). And occasionally he comes very close to a correct analysis of the relationship: "As the diversity is supposed due only to external comparison, anything taken *per se* is expected and understood always to be identical with itself, so that the second law need not interfere with the first."[112]

Thus charity demands that we ignore the wrongheaded attempt

to show a conflict among the three laws. Moreover, it would be quite undialectical of Hegel to insist on, or to try to make much of, the alleged conflict by formulating the laws in the truncated version: Everything is identical; everything is diverse; everything is opposite. These formulations would be one-sided, in the precise sense that in each of the three relationships underlying the three laws, Hegel would be focusing on only one term of the relationship, so as to attribute a mere property to it. In other words, the three laws express universal relations, not universal properties; trying to make a property out of a relation is no difficult task for abstract understanding: "*a* is the father of *b*" becomes "*a* is the father of someone," and this in turn "*a* is a father"; similarly, "*a* is opposite to *b*" becomes "*a* is an opposite." But to do this is precisely what dialectic warns us against. Finally, there is no need for Hegel to show a conflict among the three laws, which would not lead him anywhere. It is enough for him to point out that the law of identity is one-sided.

But so far I have only discussed this law's content. Hegel also argues that attempted justifications of it are also one-sided. For example, it is sometimes said that the law of identity is presupposed in all experience. Now, all experience is concrete, and Hegel does not deny that "abstraction might succeed in extracting by analysis the Law of Identity from the concrete itself" (JS41). His concern is to point out that such a process of abstraction "would not have left experience as it is, but would have changed it; for experience contained Identity in unity with Variety [or Diversity] namely Identity never separated from Variety" (JS41).

Finally, there is one-sidedness in applications or instantiations of the law. These are expressions such as: "A tree is a tree," "A plant is a plant," "God is God." Such utterances are not exactly false but are odd, boring, and tedious. Now, "if we consider more closely this tedious effect of such truths, we find that the beginning 'A plant is _____' sets out to say something, to produce a further determination. But only a repetition is made" (JS41). Thus, instead of having two terms, we have only one. We may then speak of linguistic one-sidedness as having produced such sentences.

Thus Hegel's analysis of the law of identity is mixed: He seems to misapply his own concept of the dialectic when he tries to make it conflict with the laws of diversity and of opposition, but he properly applies it when he points out its one-sidedness. On the other hand, he is clearer about something he calls Leibniz's law.[113] This in an allegedly deeper version of both the principle of the identity of indiscernibles and the "law of diversity." It states that "no two things are completely like each other" (M422), or that there is at least one "determinate difference" between any two things, or "that things are different from one another through unlikeness" (M422–23). Hegel admits this law is not analytic, when he says, "This proposition that unlikeness must be predicated of all things, merely stands in need of proof" (M423). But that is not his main point. He is primarily concerned with arguing that, whether true or false, Leibniz's law is one-sided, since it implies that no two things are completely *unlike* each other. In other words, whoever is prepared to admit that all things are unlike, should also admit that all things are alike as well. Hegel's argument is, I believe, correct: "Two things are not perfectly alike: so they are at once alike and unlike; alike, simply because they are things, or just two, without further qualification – for each is a thing and a one, no less than the other – but they are unlike *ex hypothesi*" (M423). Of course, one might object that the properties they must share – that they are things and that they are unities – are trivial, but Hegel could reply that their unlikeness may be equally small or insignificant.

Despite this greater clarity, here, too, Hegel proceeds to an undialectical attempt to truncate the relationships of likeness and unlikeness, by eliminating one of the two things being compared. In fact, he goes on to conclude that "we are therefore presented with this determination, that both moments, likeness and unlikeness, are different *in one and the same thing*" (M423, my italics). This conclusion does not follow if the emphasized phrase is equated to the *two* things being compared. But it may refer to the reflective process or activity of comparing, as Hegel himself reluctantly suggests when he says, "It is this reflection that, in *one and the same activity*, distinguishes the two sides of likeness and unlikeness, hence contains both in one activity" (M423). But then there is no (logical) contradiction, and we do not *need* to fall into that attitude derided by Hegel as "the usual tenderness for things, whose only care is that they do not contradict themselves" (M423). We do not need it, because his own dialectical principle of avoiding one-sidedness suffices.

When we come to those laws of thought that are closer to what would nowadays be recognized as logical principles, the discussion gets more interesting but also more difficult. One underlying problem is that unlike his approach with the previous laws, where Hegel tried to stretch their differences into oppositions, here he does the opposite of *this* and almost confuses four different things under the label of the "law of contradiction." The easiest to disentangle is his own law of contradiction, which is related to the metaphilosophical principle of contradiction and resolution mentioned earlier, and which asserts that everything is self-contradictory (M439). This is Hegel's own addition to the first series of laws, those of identity, of diversity, and of opposition, about which I shall say no more for the moment. But there are three others, best called the law of negation of the negation (M416), the law of the excluded middle (M438), and the law of noncontradiction (M438–39).

The negation of the negation is examined primarily in the context of the examination of the law of identity. It is introduced as the negative expression of the law of identity, labeled "law of contradiction," stated in a way reminiscent of the law of noncontradiction, but *analyzed* as negation of the negation. All of this occurs when Hegel says that "the other expression of the law of identity: *A cannot at the same time be A and not-A,* has a negative form; it is called the *law of contradiction.* . . . In this proposition, therefore, identity is expressed – as negation of the negation" (M416). What Hegel seems to have in mind, if not in his mouth, is the thesis that A = not-(not-A). He expresses his puzzlement at how negation, which is a form of difference, should find its way into the law of identity. But his main point is itself a paragon of puzzlement for us, namely, that "from this it is evident that the law of identity itself, and still more the law of contradiction, is not merely of *analytic* but of *synthetic* nature" (M416). I believe the notion of one-sidedness provides the way to decipher this conclusion. Hegel is saying that the negative expression of the law of identity as usually understood (A cannot be not-A, or $A \neq$ not-A) is analytic, but one-sided; it has another interpretation, another side, which is a synthetic one, presumably: A = not-(not-A).

The immediate reason given by Hegel for this conclusion is that this law "contains in its expression not merely empty, simple equality-with-self, and not merely the other of this in general, but what is more, *absolute inequality, contradiction per se*" (M416). What to make of this is unclear, but another, more relevant argument in the *Encyclopedia* is that "contradiction, when cancelled [*aufgehobene*], does not leave abstract identity; for that is itself only one side of the contrariety [*Gegensatzes*]."[114] So to think that to negate not-A yields A is one-sided.

Hegel seems to be questioning the universal validity of the principle of double negation. His critique of it is dialectical in pointing out its limitations and the one-sidedness of the abstract interpretation of it as analytic.

The law of the excluded middle is examined by Hegel in the context of the law of opposition, which he claims to be its deeper meaning (M438). At times he seems to equate it with the law of noncontradiction, as when he says that "the Maxim [*Satz*] of Excluded Middle is the maxim of the definite understanding, which would fain avoid contradiction."[115] One of its formulations is that "*something is either A or not-A; there is no third*" (M438). But he claims that "it has also been expressed, Of two opposite predicates the one only can be assigned to anything, and there is no third possible."[116] Hegel points out its limitations as follows: Consider such opposite predicates as sweet and nonsweet, green and nongreen, and square and nonsquare, and take "spirit" as the thing to be predicated upon. We get that spirit is sweet or not sweet, green or not green, and square or not square. But neither of the predicates in each pair is really applicable to the thing chosen. Spirit is neither sweet nor not sweet; it is "indifferent" to the predicate in question. This is the "third" alternative that the law of excluded middle one-sidedly neglects.[117]

An authentic discussion of the law of noncontradiction occurs in the same context, where it is clearly formulated in the proposition "that there is nothing which is at once A and not-A" (M438), namely in modern notation, $-(\quad x)(Ax \& - Ax)$. Typically, however, and confusingly, Hegel labels this the law of *contradiction* and it is one of the laws from which "the law of the excluded middle is also distinguished" (M438). In view of the ensuing arguments, this last "distinction" is apt to be misleading. Nevertheless, the argument is clear. The law of noncontradiction "implies that there *is* nothing that is *neither A nor not-A*" (M438), namely that $-(\quad x) - (Ax \text{ v} - Ax)$, which is correct. This in turn means that there is nothing "that is indifferent to the opposition" (M438), which is also right. But, continues Hegel, there is in fact such a something, namely, the predicate A. In this sense, "A is neither $+A$ nor $-A$ and is equally well $+A$ and $-A$" (M438–39).

If we ignore the "excluded middle" aspect of the argument, which raises no new issue, what Hegel apparently wants to show is a limitation of even the law of noncontradiction. When we claim there is nothing that is both A and not-A, we are correct only insofar as we (one-sidedly) take our universe of discourse to be the domain of individuals, and exclude second-order considerations.

We may conclude that Hegel's critique of the so-called laws of thought is a dialectical analysis of them. Although he occasionally misuses his own concept of the dialectic, most of the time he is practicing his dialectical theory. The avoidance of one-sidedness is the conceptual element of this theory implicit in the discussion. It is the same element that, as seen earlier, he explicitly articulates in metaphilosophical terms again in this chapter of the *Logic*.

In this chapter Hegel also analyzes the so-called determinations of reflections, namely, the categories of identity *(Identität)*, difference *(Unterschied)*, diversity or variety *(Verschiedenheit)*, opposition *(Gegensatz)*, contradiction *(Widerspruch)*, likeness *(Gleichheit)* and unlikeness *(Ungleichheit)*, and the positive *(das Positive)* and the negative *(das Negative)*. Therefore, this conceptual analysis is best regarded as a theoretical clarification of Hegel's concept of the dialectic, because we already saw that (besides philosophizing and the avoidance of one-sidedness) the three other notions of his definition of the concept are the unity of opposites, the positivity of the negative, and identity in difference or diversity within unity.

This Hegelian analysis may be approached in two ways. One can search in it for an abstract systematization of the determinations of reflections, and then equate this system with Hegel's theory of dialectic; a systematic theory like this would define each determination and examine their interrelations. Another approach would be to seek to clarify in each other's terms the three notions of unity of opposites, positivity of the negative, and identity in difference; this clarification would involve showing how each notion inheres in the Hegelian analysis, and how the unity of opposites and positivity of the negative may be seen as identity in difference, how the positivity of the negative and identity in difference may be seen as unity of opposites, and how identity in difference and unity of opposites may be seen as positivity of the negative. The first approach takes the point of view of the abstract understanding; the second, that of dialectic. Thus, it may seem that the latter is preferable.

I, however, shall follow *both* procedures in turn, for the following reason. It is certainly desirable to interpret Hegel as practicing his dialectic, even as he theorizes about it in his analysis of the determinations of reflections. But it is even more important that his theory and practice of the dialectic should correspond (which is not to say that they should be equated, but merely that they should be properly related after being distinguished), and it is not obvious that they will under the second interpretation, and that they will not under the first. Moreover, it is also desirable that I myself follow a dialectical approach in my own interpretation; but the present context is one where I try to articulate the systematization of dialectical notions in Hegel's analysis of the determinations of reflections, clearly the most likely place for it to be found. Hence, my neglect of the point of view of abstract understanding would be one-sided, and an exclusively dialectical approach would be itself undialectical. So let me turn to Hegel's systematization.

It is perhaps not surprising that the abstract systematization turns out to be *somewhat* inadequate, for *too great* a success in this direction might make Hegel's theory one-sided with respect to the distinction between understanding and dialectic. Some concrete evidence illustrates this inadequacy. First, since the concepts in question (identity, difference, etc.) are basic, the problem is how each could be defined in terms more comprehensible than the definiendum. In fact, we usually find in the definiens such technical terms as "determination," "reflection," "positedness," "essence," and "mediation." For example, the definition of "identity" in the *Encyclopedia* reads: "The Essence lights up *in itself* or is mere reflection: and therefore is only self-relation, not as immediate but as reflected. And that reflex relation is *self-Identity.* "[118] The *Logic* explains that "the positive is positedness as reflected into self-likeness. . . . The negative is positedness as reflected into unlikeness" (M424–25), a definition that prompted even McTaggart to say, "I must own myself entirely unable to understand what he means by this."[119]

Second, there is the possibility of clarifying the meanings of these concepts by interrelating them. Hegel is certainly deeply committed to this procedure. Too often, however, by the time he has finished interrelating pairs like identity and difference, likeness and unlikeness, positive and negative, opposition and contradiction, he seems to have succeeded pretty well in confusing the members of each pair. A typical example is identity and difference. To begin with he tells us that the kind of identity he is talking about is *"essential* identity" (M411), and that the kind of difference in question is "the *difference of essence"* (M417). Then, just as identity is a kind of "negativity" (M411), so is difference (M417); they are also both simple (M412, 417); and "each is a self-relation" (M418). Moreover, "difference is the whole and its own *moment,* just as identity equally is its whole and its moment" (M417). Finally, "both identity and difference . . . are reflections each of which is unity of self and its other" (M419). If this is so, how are they different? Unfortunately, the confusion is more widespread because the *same pattern* just documented is repeated for almost all the other pairs, and hence we find Hegel formulating such conclusions as "Likeness and unlikeness . . . vanish together in their likeness" (M421) and "The positive and negative are the same" (M434).

Nevertheless, from the point of view of abstract understanding, Hegel's account is not a complete failure. It may be reconstructed as follows. He is *distinguishing* two kinds of relations: internal relations that a thing can have to itself, and external ones between two different things. The three main internal relations are self-identity, self-difference, and self-contradiction; whereas the three main external relations are likeness, unlikeness, and opposition. The two groups may also be *related* insofar as likeness is external identity; that is, there is a likeness when there is identity of a property belonging to two different things; unlikeness is external difference insofar as an unlikeness results from the existence of two different properties, each belonging to one thing but not the other; opposition is external contradiction inasmuch as two things are opposed if, and only if, they have contradictory properties. Although the relation between self-identity and self-difference and between likeness and unlikeness is perhaps irreducible, the distinction between self-difference and self-contradiction and between unlikeness and opposition may be bridged: This is done by conceiving opposition as *essential* difference and unlikeness as "indifferent" difference, and similarily self-contradiction is merely the carrying to an extreme of self-difference. In this framework the primitive notions are then identity and difference, internal and external, and essential and unessential (indifferent). In their terms one distinguishes and interrelates the other notions. One can also show that identity and difference presuppose each other, and so do the concepts of internal and external, and essential and unessential.

Is such a theory of dialectic following a dialectical approach? It is, in the sense of the element of Hegel's concept of the dialectic that we have termed the notion of identity in difference or diversity within unity. In fact, this notion has been understood as a principle of differentiation and unification, such as expressed in the first of the four metaphilosophical principles formulated in this chapter of the *Logic* and discussed above. But this raises the question whether this principle, which is also one of the main substantive elements that Hegel finds in the history of the dialectic, should now be reinterpreted in the light of the present theory of dialectic. Or, conversely, is the systematization just given, though admittedly dialectical in the sense specified, really a theory of *dialectic?* One might reply that if this Hegelian analysis of the determinations of reflections is not a theory of dialectic, then nothing in Hegel is such a theory. Another reply would be that nothing crucial depends on whether Hegel's system of the determinations of reflections is a theory of *dialectic*; if it is not, then it is still a theory of those determinations, hence a piece of philosophical practice, which is dialectical for the reason given. In other words, although this Hegelian theory of dialectic has a form corresponding to his *concept* of the dialectic that we have been analyzing in this investigation, it may not have a content corresponding to it. Such considerations provide additional motivation for undertaking the other type of interpretation mentioned earlier, to which we now turn.

The unity of opposites is examined explicitly when Hegel analyzes the concept of opposition, and implicitly insofar as he views as instances of opposition the pairs identity and difference, diversity and opposition, likeness and unlikeness, and positive and negative. The analysis of opposition reveals that an opposition is an essential difference where each opposite is defined in terms of the other, but at the same time is "a self-subsistent, independent unity-with-self" (M426). This sounds self-contradictory, and Hegel can at least be given credit for recognizing this when he says that "opposites, therefore, contain contradiction in so far as they are, in the same respect, negatively related to one another or *sublate each other* and are *indifferent* to one another" (M441). Thus, the "contradiction" is not in Hegel's mind but in the process of opposition, and it is what gets resolved through change. In this analysis, it is not clear what the unity of the opposites is: whether it is the resolution of the contradiction, or the mutual interdefinition of the opposite terms.

The implicit analysis is not too helpful either. In fact, the unity of identity and difference turns out to be a moment of each: "Both identity and difference, as has just been demonstrated, are reflections, each of which is unity of itself and its other; each is the whole" (M419). The unity of diversity and opposition seems to lie in the concept of difference: "Difference as such contains its two sides as *moments*; in diversity they fall *indifferently* apart, in opposition as such they are . . . mutually indifferent and mutually exclusive" (M431). The unity of likeness and unlikeness is like that of identity and difference just quoted: "Likeness is not like itself; and unlikeness, as unlike not itself but something else unlike it, is itself likeness. The like and the unlike are therefore *unlike themselves*. Consequently each is this reflection: likeness, that it is itself and unlikeness, and unlikeness, that it is itself and likeness" (M421). In these three cases, the unity of opposites seems to lie in the interrelationships of the opposite concepts. What Hegel says about the unity of positive and negative, however, reproduces the earlier ambiguity, because he now refers to the process of resolution when he says that "the resolved contradiction is therefore ground, essence as unity of the positive and negative" (M435).

Thus, let us recognize the ambiguity and conclude that Hegel's dialectical notion of unity of opposites has two different meanings here: the resolution of contradictions in opposite things, and the mutual interdependence of opposite concepts. In a way, this difference is not surprising, for the first meaning comes from the content of Hegel's theorizing, and the second comes from its form; it also corresponds to the distinction between objective and subjective dialectic. What is surprising, and problematic, is that the two meanings do not correspond to each other. Hence, the dialectic of "the real" is not reflected in the dialectic of "the ideal," and the onto-phenomenological interpretation is further disconfirmed.

What about the positivity of the negative? This notion is being analyzed explicitly when Hegel examines positive and negative numbers in algebra (M427–31), and when he discusses his own law of contradiction, that all change involves contradiction (M439–43). It is also analyzed implicitly throughout his chapter, since the positive and negative are the conceptual pair underlying the discussions of opposition and of contradiction and are frequently treated as almost alternative terms for identity and difference, respectively.

I earlier interpreted the positivity of the negative as meaning the necessity of the negative. This interpretation is confirmed when Hegel, referring to it (as well as to the converse phenomenon of the negativity of the positive), explicitly acknowledges that "this transition also, in fact, remains mere confusion when there is no awareness of the necessity of the transformation" (M436). Moreover, a clear point is added when he argues that negative qualities in mathematics have a reality of their own, just as much as positive ones; they are not nothing; here, positivity means reality. And this brings us to Hegel's own law of contradiction.

In fact, the connection seems so close that this controversial law might better be termed the "law or principle of the positivity of the negative," as implicitly suggested by Hegel himself in the introduction to the *Logic*. Here contradiction simply means real conflict, as shown when at a certain point he turns into an ordinary-language philosopher, noting that "common experience itself enunciates it when it says that at least *there is* a *host* of contradictory things, contradictory arrangements, whose contradiction exists not merely in an external reflection but in themselves" (M440). The negative is contradiction itself, since Hegel says that "contradiction is not to be taken merely as an abnormality which only occurs here and there, but is rather the negative as determined in the sphere of essence" (M440). And positivity means functionality in the process of change, as seen when Hegel objects to ordinary thinking on the grounds that "in considering contradiction, it stops short at the one-sided *resolution* of it into *nothing*, and fails to recognize the positive side of contradiction where it becomes *absolute* activity and absolute ground" (M442). Putting the three elements together, we may express the principle of the positivity of the negative with Hegel's concluding words:

> In general, our consideration of the nature of contradiction has shown that it is not, so to speak, a blemish, an imperfection or a defect in something if a contradiction can be pointed out in it. On the contrary, every determination, every concrete thing, every Notion, is essentially a unity of . . . contradictory moments . . . its resolved contradiction . . . its negative unity. (M442–43)

If this is the content of Hegel's explicit examination of the positivity of the negative, its form is simply that of an attempt to establish the principle. There is no significant sense in which the discussion exemplifies the dialectical notion about which it is theorizing.

Turning now to his implicit discussion (M424–38), we find that Hegel is primarily concerned with establishing the following points: First, "the positive" and "the negative" are general terms used to refer to any pair of opposites, and conversely any opposition may be conceived as involving a negative pole and a positive one. Second, there is a symmetry between the two in that it is basically arbitrary which one is regarded as positive and which as negative. From this point of view, one may question whether these ideas are being applied to his discussion of the opposition between identity and difference, diversity and opposition, and likeness and unlikeness. There is little doubt that he associates identity and likeness mostly with the positive, difference and unlikeness with the negative, and *both* diversity and opposition with the negative as well; I am not sure these associations could be reversed.

Thus, from the point of view of the positivity of the negative, Hegel's discussion of the determinations of reflection does make a contribution to his dialectical theory, insofar as its content is the elaboration of the "law" that only contradiction yields change. The discussion, however, does not exemplify a dialectical approach, insofar as its form does not conform to the practice of the positivity of the negative. Of course, this is not to deny the dialectical features mentioned earlier, from the point of view of other conceptual elements of the dialectic.

As regards identity and difference, it is obvious that they are not only the first pair of determinations of reflections treated by Hegel but also the most fundamental. In fact, diversity, opposition, and contradiction are, to begin with, "determinations" of difference. These two concepts are thus discussed both explicitly and implicitly throughout his chapter. To begin to make theoretical (i.e., dialectic-theoretical) sense out of their discussion, we must construe identity in the sense of (the activity of) identification, and difference as (the procedure of) differentiation. This is required because the above meanings are the dialectically relevant ones, as shown by my whole inquiry so far, notably by the first principle of philosophical methodology mentioned at the beginning of my analysis of this section of the *Logic*. It is also suggested by specific textual evidence, such as Hegel's talk of *Das Unterscheiden*[120] in subsection A.2, between Remark 1 and Remark 2, of the present chapter in the *Logic*. And it is generally supported by Hegel's whole discussion therein, as we shall now argue.

The actual thesis in Hegel's explicit analysis of identity and difference is that both identification and differentiation are aspects of a single procedure, which may be viewed now as one and now as the other; in his own language this reads: "Difference is the whole and its own *moment*, just as identity equally is its whole and its moment" (M417). The supreme importance of this connection is emphasized by him in no uncertain terms, and this importance is both "logical," and ontological; in fact, he immediately adds that "this is to be considered as the essential nature of reflection and as the *specific, original ground of all activity and self-movement*" (M417). In general, Hegel's argument seems to be that in order to identify anything, it has to be distinguished from other things, and that in order to make a distinction between two or more things, then one has to have *some* notion of the identity of these things. One "side" of the argument shows the sense in which the procedure of identifying is present in that of distinguishing: "Differentiation is the positing of Not-being as the Not-being of Other. But the Not-being of Other is cancellation of Other, and therefore of differentiation

itself. Thus differentiation is here found to be a self-relating negativity" (JS39); this in turn means that differentiation is "Difference
not from an Other, but from its own self: it is not itself, but its
Other. But that which is different from Difference is Identity. Difference is therefore both itself and Identity" (JS44). The other side
of the argument shows how differentiation is present in identification:

Identity is the reflection-into-self that is identity only as internal repulsion,
and is this repulsion as reflection-into-self, repulsion which immediately
takes itself back into itself. Thus it is identity as difference that is identical
with itself. But difference is only identical with itself in so far as it is not
identity but absolute non-identity. But non-identity is absolute in so far
as it contains nothing of its other but only itself, that is, in so far as it is
absolute identity with itself.

Identity, therefore, is *in its own self* absolute non-identity. But it is also
the *determination* of identity as against non-identity. (M413)

Here Hegel is obviously using and applying his own dialectical
principle in his own discussion. His practice is thus dialectical in
the same sense. It is also obvious that his procedure amounts to
avoiding one-sidedness with respect to the two categories being
analyzed.

Seen this way, the concepts of likeness and unlikeness become
instruments for the procedure of comparing, as Hegel himself
admits when he tells us that "external reflection relates what is diverse to likeness and unlikeness. This relation, which is a *comparing*,
passes to and fro between likeness and unlikeness" (M420).
Through them, comparing is seen as a type of identification-
differentiation. Hegel's distinction between diversity and opposition, in terms of inessential difference versus essential difference,
identifies each as a difference while it distinguishes them; moreover,
the differentiation of two opposite terms is the identification of an
opposition. Finally, the unity of opposites, which Hegel introduces
in his analysis of contradiction, is an instance of identity in difference; in fact, "difference as such is already *implicitly* contradiction;
for it is the *unity* of sides which are, only in so far as they are *not
one* – and it is the *separation* of sides which are, only as separated
in the same relation" (M431).

Thus the notion of identity in difference, unlike those of synthesis
of opposites and positivity of the negative, is not only theorized
about in Hegel's analysis of the determinations of reflections, but
also practiced. In this regard it is like the notion of the avoidance
of one-sidedness, which, as noted earlier, was both explicitly ad-

vocated through the formulation of various principles of philosophic methodology, and implicitly used in his analysis of the laws of thought. This confirms my earlier judgment that, although all four of these notions are part of the meaning Hegel attaches to the concept of the dialectic, identity in difference and avoidance of one-sidedness are more fundamental. My investigation also suggests that these two notions are themselves two aspects of the same thought process, although it is beyond its scope to elaborate this connection.

HEGEL'S AND GRAMSCI'S DIALECTIC

I have attempted to establish what meaning Hegel attaches to the concept of dialectic, by examining the main interpretations given by Hegelian scholars, the principal definitions and explicit explanations he provides, and his implicit use of the concept in some discussions of crucial and classic importance. The main result has been that Hegel conceives the dialectic as the distinctive characteristic of philosophical method and as intimately connected with the notions of the unity of opposites, the principle of the positivity of the negative, the concept of one-sidedness, and the categories of identity and difference. Besides having great textual support, such a metaphilosophical type of interpretation has the unique advantage of being able to do justice both to what Hegel says about the dialectic and to how he uses the concept, thus establishing a correspondence between his dialectical theory and his dialectical practice.

I began by classifying interpretations into four types, designed to help one understand and criticize the secondary literature, and to pave the way for the interpretation I believe to be correct: The *triadic view* sees the dialectic as the synthesis of thesis and antithesis; for the *systemic-immanent* account the dialectic is the process whereby higher categories of thought and forms of consciousness emerge from lower ones; the *onto-phenomenological* interpretation regards the dialectic as an ontological process automatically reflected in the mind of the appropriately situated philosopher; and the *metaphilosophical* approach construes the dialectic as a philosophical method. All but the last type were criticized for lacking a foundation in Hegel's integrated theory and practice of dialectic: The triadic dialectic can be found neither in his theory nor in his practice; the systemic-immanent dialectic may inhere in his practice but not in his theory; and the onto-phenomenological may be found in his theory but

228

not in his practice. These interpretations, however, were appreciated, respectively, for the insight of connecting the concept of the dialectic with the notions of synthesis, totality, and negativity. The metaphilosophical view was traced to the works of Croce, Gadamer, and Mure, which were also shown to make the concepts of identity and difference central to the dialectic.

My direct examination of Hegel's dialectic involved analyzing the introduction and the chapter on the determinations of reflection in the *Science of Logic*, the preface to the *Phenomenology*, the account of the history of the dialectic interspersed in the three volumes of the *Lectures on the History of Philosophy*, and, from the *Encyclopedia*, the accounts of the dialectic (pars. 79–83) and of the determinations of reflection (pars. 115–20). What is common to these texts is that they are all *explicitly* dialectical in content, in that they give pedagogical definitions, elucidatory explanations, historical applications, metaphilosophical applications and connections, or analysis of definitional elements of the concept of dialectic. My examination also revealed the considerable extent to which these discussions by Hegel are dialectical in form or approach, and occasionally I criticized this form or approach for going against or disregarding his own concept of dialectic.

The purpose of this historical interpretation of Hegel's concept of the dialectic was twofold. One aim was to provide an evaluation of the concepts of the dialectic that I extracted from Gramsci in the preceding chapter; thus, my interpretation of Hegel constitutes a vindication of the essential correctness of Gramsci's thesis that the dialectic is a way of thinking that avoids one-sidedness and searches for distinctions-relations. Second, I wanted to provide a theoretical elucidation of the relation between theory and practice within the domain of dialectical thinking, a problem arising from Chapter 6 but having more general import insofar as frequently the *concept* of the dialectic is in the *mind* of those who least use the *word*, is *in practice* fruitfully exploited by those who are its greatest foes *in theory*, and is mistreated by its self-styled advocates; the result has been a series of instructive examples of various forms that the theory-practice distinction-relation may take.

A by-product of my analysis is the partial substantiation of Gramsci's thesis about the dialectic and classical European culture. That is, the view that the dialectic is the approach used by Hegel in philosophy, by Ricardo in economics, and by the French Jacobins in politics. Only the part about Hegel has been confirmed in the present chapter. Indeed, I am inclined to think that the other parts need modification, so as to say that the same dialectical approach is best exemplified by Karl Marx in economics, and by Gramsci himself in politics. So modified, the thesis about Marx is obviously beyond the scope of the present inquiry, but the point about Gramsci has already received support from the arguments and interpretation in this chapter and the two that precede it.

Chapter 8

Gramsci and the evaluation of Marxism

It is now time to find out whether my various inquiries possess more unity than that deriving from the hermeneutical program I announced in the introduction. They are indeed systematizations and interpretations of four central themes of Gramsci's Prison Notebooks, augmented by evaluations of three of these four Gramscian themes; and the evaluations are grounded, respectively, on critical analyses of Croce's philosophy, of Bukharin's sociology, and of Hegel's dialectic. My investigation would acquire additional significance, however, if it could be related to other problems of current or perennial interest. Because the subject of Marxism recurs in the Notebooks, it seems a promising one to serve as focus for the integration I am seeking. It turns out that this topic will enable me to formulate an overarching interpretation and an overarching evaluation of Gramsci's thought, and that these are relevant to a background problem to which I now turn.

THE PROBLEM OF THE EVALUATION OF MARXISM

There is little need to belabor the social, political, and cultural importance of Marxism. Adapting an aphorism applicable in many contexts, one might say that Marxism is far too important to be left to Marxists. Therefore, the understanding and evaluation of Marxism may be regarded as a central problem of our time, and hence a crucial topic for social philosophy.

A central fact of the *phenomenon* of Marxism is that it began as a science and has now become a religion. The scientific origins of Marxism are evident in Marx's claim that "one basis for life and another for science is *a priori* a lie"[1] and in Engels's talk about the transition of socialism from utopian to scientific. The religious metamorphosis[2] of Marxism may be seen, for example, in the

Spanish Communists' criticism of the Soviet Communist Party as a new Catholic church;[3] in the commitment and even fanaticism with which Marxist terrorists in developed countries, and Marxist revolutionaries in the Third World, pursue their beliefs; and in the near "excommunication" of the Italian Communist Party by Russian Communists because the former criticized the latter over the Polish martial-law controversy.[4]

This apparently simple fact is, in reality, very complex. For example, it cannot be treated as merely conveying information about Marxism but must be taken as making a claim about the *concept* of science and the *concept* of religion. But once we realize this, questions immediately arise: What is science? What is religion? What if science defines merely the pretension of Marxism, which is allegedly bad, or pseudo, science?[5] And what if the religious dimension of Marxism constitutes a denied or unpalatable feature for so-called Marxists themselves? Are religion and science essentially different anyway? What if, as some would hold,[6] science is itself a religion? And if religion is essentially a world view tied with a corresponding ethic,[7] and if science is the *philosophia activa* (à la Bacon), would they not both be syntheses of theory and practice? And if so, would not that make Marxism not only *both* a science *and* a religion but also the philosophical justification of both? Moreover, what is the *evaluative* import of those categorizations? Do not some take the religious possibilities of Marxism to be one of its *valuable* features?[8]

Deep-seated and wide-ranging as the religious and the scientific aspects of Marxism are, they are somewhat overshadowed by its ominous geopolitical presence. After all, it is the political dimension of Marxism that gives it its world-historical and sociocultural significance today. Here, too, there is irony. For Marxism had something of an apolitical birth. Its founders were originally convinced that politics is an epiphenomenon, a belief they expressed with classic eloquence when they wrote that "the executive of the modern state is but a committee for managing the common affairs of the whole bourgeoisie."[9]

But how is one to understand the political practice of Marxists, when they have contributed so little to its theory? When, indeed, they hardly recognize the autonomy and legitimacy of the field of political theory. At any rate, was Marx really advocating the transcending of politics, or was he merely proposing a new way of doing politics? If the latter is the case, was this primarily a new political *program*, or was it a new *concept* of politics? And if it was a new concept, why should it be regarded as a concept of *politics* rather than of something else? What connection would the new notion have with the old or with the ordinary one, so as to entitle us to say we are still dealing with things "political"? And what about the relationships among politics, science, and religion? If the latter two are the above-mentioned syntheses of theory and practice, is politics also a kind of such synthesis? What kind?

I believe a good way to gain an understanding and come to an evaluation of Marxism in general, and to explore solutions to these questions about its scientific, religious, and political status, is through an examination of Antonio Gramsci's Prison Notebooks.[10]

This work, in fact, has already become a modern classic of social philosophy and political theory, and it has earned Gramsci high praise and respect from the most diverse quarters. For example, British historian James Joll calls him a "true intellectual hero of our time"[11] because, besides being "the greatest Marxist writer of the twentieth century, paradoxically, [Gramsci] is also one of the greatest examples of the independence of the human spirit from its material limitations."[12] French philosopher Louis Althusser regards him as the only thinker "who has *really* attempted to follow up the explorations of Marx and Engels."[13] The *New York Review of Books* has stated that Gramsci is "a political theorist, perhaps the only major Marxist thinker who can be so described."[14] And the *Times Literary Supplement* (London) has referred to him as "a cultured and open-minded Marxist, his main theses are ours today – workers' self-management, the role of education and the media, the nature of cultural revolutions."[15]

MARXISM AND METHOD IN GRAMSCI'S CRITICISM

In regard to the problem of the evaluation of Marxism, the views from the Prison Notebooks that have been analyzed here seem to constitute a fruitful conceptual framework and methodological orientation for discussing questions about the status of Marxism as a religion, as a science, and as politics. Gramsci's specific, substantive answers are not always acceptable, although their occasional untenability does not invalidate the soundness of his underlying concepts and approach.

Let us review these arguments. One of the most common criticisms of Marxism is that when all is said and done, it is a vulgar new version of religion and a philosophically outdated kind of theology. As such, it has its popular oversimplifications, myths, and rituals on the one hand, and its transcendent metaphysics on the other. The substance of these items is, of course, different from those of previous religions and theologies, but their form and function are the same. Thus, so the criticism goes, it is a vulgar oversimplification to say that behind every event there are economic motives that made it happen; it is a myth that there exists a class (the proletariat) whose conditions are getting more and more miserable; it is a ritual to conduct a politically motivated strike; and the classless society and kingdom of freedom are transcendent entities like the God of the older theologies.

One of the first thinkers to criticize Marxism in this way was Benedetto Croce.[16] In the Prison Notebooks, Gramsci answers that it is inconsistent for Croce to defend, as he did, the legitimacy of popular, watered-down versions of Catholicism for mass consumption, and yet to regard "vulgar" Marxism as illegitimate. On the contrary, given Croce's own definition of religion as a world view tied to a corresponding ethic, then "vulgar" Marxism becomes a legitimate form of religion. In fact, it is a form especially appropriate and appealing for modern industrial workers. In short, Gramsci defends so-called vulgar Marxism as anything but vulgar, as, rather, a "religious" phenomenon.[17]

Gramsci's thesis is, then, that popular Marxism is a new religion, and as such it has all the philosophical legitimacy that religions have. The main concept underlying his argument is the Crocean concept of religion; this concept is, of course, different from the Marxist view that "religion is the opium of the people."[18] So the logic of Gramsci's defense is to draw some pro-Marxist, anti-Crocean conclusions by starting with other anti-Marxist, pro-Crocean premises. What this means is that Gramsci's defense of Marxism is, from another point of view, a criticism of it, and conversely that his criticism of Croce is in part a defense of him.

The subtlety of this hermeneutical method requires that more be said about its character. Since it so happens, as I have argued, that this is an adaption of Croce's own style and method of criticism, I undertook a comprehensive examination of Croce's voluminous writings on philosophy, history, and literature, from the point of view of critical methodology. Moreover, since in his critique Gramsci, although aware that he is *specifically* indebted to Croce, does not seem to be aware of his *methodological* dependence, this is another reason for elaborating the critical dimension of Croce's work. Finally, because of the greater weight given by Gramsci to his conclusions (vis-à-vis his assumptions and his methods), and because this was reflected in my own analysis, the resulting anti-Crocean, pro-Marxist impression had to be balanced by a more positive treatment of Croce. Such a generally favorable analysis of Croce's work was not, however, totally favorable since it turned out that his theoretical reflections on criticism are not as plausible as his actual criticism.

One of the most common claims by Marxists is that Marxism is a science, specifically, a sociology or social science, insofar as it applies the method of physics and natural science to human affairs and social phenomena. Marxist sociology thus is, or tries to be, determinist, predictive, and generalizing; it searches for causes of phenomena and for the laws of motion of society, and it makes predictions about future historical events.

Parts of the Prison Notebooks criticize this enterprise by arguing that it presupposes an untenable philosophy of science – known as scientism, according to which to be scientific is to use the method of physics in one's own field.[19] For Gramsci, the correct concept of science is such that scientific inquiry is simply serious inquiry, which in general prescribes such things as[20] judiciousness in transposing a method successful in one field into another, modesty in using empirical generalizations, soundness of inference, methodological self-confidence, understanding of the concepts one is using, awareness of previous contributions, caution in drawing conclusions, and depth and fairness in one's criticism. In short, Gramsci's criticism is that Marxist sociology is pseudoscientific because it pretends to be scientific but succeeds in being merely scientistic, and thus is violating most canons of genuine scientific method.

This criticism seems valid in that it is grounded on a sound concept of science, and such a concept does entail that scientism is wrong. Its accuracy and relevance depend, however, on whether Marxist sociology is, in fact, an instance of scientism. The example used by Gramsci is certainly a classic example of Marxist sociology, namely, Nikolai Bukharin's *Historical Materialism: A System of Sociology*. Therefore, I had to determine whether Gramsci's interpretation of Bukharin is accurate and fair. My examination of this matter revealed that although Bukharin is scientistic in his theory of science expounded in the more philosophical and self-reflective chapters of his work, his actual sociological theorizing (i.e., his practice of science) has a dialectical rather than a scientistic character. Because of this lack of correspondence between Bukharin's theory and practice of science, one cannot transfer objections applicable for the first case to the second. In fact, Gramsci is misusing in his critical practice his own notion of the synthesis of theory and practice.

In other words, Gramsci argues that Bukharin's sociology is unscientific because it is an instance of scientism and scientism is unscientific. The major premise here is both correct and correctly defended by Gramsci. However, the minor premise is in one sense true and in one sense false. It is true if taken to mean that Bukharin's sociology is presented by him as scientism in his philosophical reflections; but it is false when understood to mean that Bukharin's sociology in its actual details is scientistic. Gramsci's conflation of these two meanings not only invalidates his criticism of Bukharin's actual sociological theorizing but signifies an improper method of criticism. Such an impropriety could probably be conceptualized as undialectical and as "unscientific" in Gramsci's own sense, and because it is rather common,[21] its exposure can be highly instructive.

Regarding the notion of politics, Gramsci attempts to forge a more or less "Marxist" concept partly from a creative and constructive interpretation of Machiavelli's politics and partly from an original analysis and application of the concept of dialectic. His interpretation of Machiavelli is somewhat dialectical in its procedure, and his interpretation of the concept of dialectic is somewhat political in content.

In fact, the remarks on Machiavelli in the Prison Notebooks contain both a historical argument about Machiavelli and a conceptual clarification of the notion of the autonomy of politics. The former consists of rather plausible answers by Gramsci to the anti-Machiavellian criticism that Machiavelli was a ruthless advocate of the end's justifying the means, that his words were inconsistent with his deeds (because he supposedly preached authoritarianism and deception but acted democratically and openly), that he was unrealistically out of touch with what was feasible in his time, and that his military proposals were unprogressively flawed. And in his elaboration of an autonomous concept of politics, Gramsci examines the relationships and differences between aesthetic activity and political art, sociology and the science of politics, politics and morality, and politics and economics; and he discusses various types of politics in terms of the polarities of great versus small politics, force versus consent, and individualism versus party spirit. The connection between the historical defense and the analytical construction is that, for Gramsci, the concept of politics articulated in his analysis is the one found *in nuce* in Machiavelli; moreover, our analysis showed Gramsci to be a judicious practitioner of the art of criticism, or hermeneutics, in a way formally analogous to the way Gramsci's interpretation exhibits Machiavelli as a judicious practitioner of the art of politics. It is in this sense that one is entitled to say that Gramsci's interpretation of Machiavelli is dialectical.

This led me to examine Gramsci's explicit remarks on the dialectic, a concept that for him is intimately connected with that of politics. In fact, Gramsci holds that the dialectic is the methodological, as distinct from substantive, heritage of classical German philosophy, classical British economics, and classical French Jacobin politics. Unlike the first, which culminated with Hegel, and the second, which culminated with Marx, the third has not been properly understood and conceptualized, and Gramsci may be seen as attempting to do in politics what Hegel did in philosophy and Marx did in economics. This is why some of Gramsci's most interesting discussions of the dialectic examine its connection with the nature of political revolution, reformism, and bureaucratic administration. For example, he argues that the notion of permanent revolution is a valid and dialectical concept when construed as a historiographical principle for understanding past events, but it is *not always* dialectical if regarded as a political program, especially when labor unions and mass-based political parties are allowed. He argues that something analogous holds for the concept of evolutionary reformism: It is always of *potential* applicability in trying to understand history, but it is sometimes invalid and undialectical, specifically when used in practical politics to domesticate the opposition by absorbing it into the ranks of one's own faction and eliminating it as a separate political force.[22] Perhaps the clearest indication that Gramsci's view of the dialectic amounts to a "political" interpretation of the concept is his definition of the type of bureaucratic administration that he likes best and that he calls "democratic centralism"; its essential point is the "critical search for what is equal in the apparent diversity, and distinct and even opposite in the apparent uniformity,"[23] and this is equivalent to the essential meaning he attaches to the concept of dialectic.

Gramsci's interpretation led me to undertake a more elaborate examination of the nature of the dialectic, by going to its most authoritative source – Hegel. This was required partly in order to evaluate Gramsci's concept of the dialectic, by seeing whether what he calls "dialectic" is indeed so. Partly such an examination was needed in order to give more depth and content to the Gramscian definition just given, which is obviously reminiscent of Hegel's dialectic. In part, the investigation is also an attempt to deal with certain difficulties besetting Gramsci's interpretation of Machiavelli and of the dialectic. Gramsci himself raises the question that the concept of politics he elaborates in his Machiavellian analyses is perhaps a purely theoretical construct of no practical relevance; that is to say, it is not clear how the theory and the practice of such "Machiavellian" politics are to be related. The other difficulty arises in Gramsci's discussion of the dialectic, since in various places he seems to attach to it a formalist, triadic meaning as the process of synthesis of thesis and antithesis, which is inconsistently different from his primary definition mentioned above, in terms of unification and differentiation.

My analysis of Hegel's concept of the dialectic strengthened this primary Gramscian definition; revealed the great significance of another complementary meaning Gramsci also attaches to the dialectic, namely, a way of thinking that avoids one-sidedness; and illustrated various questions about the interrelation of dialectical theory and dialectical practice. The examination began with a classification and a criticism (constructive as well as destructive) of the most common interpretations of Hegel's dialectic, and proceeded to reconstructions of the dialectical structure and content of relevant texts from the introduction and the chapter "Determinations of Reflection" in the *Science of Logic,* the preface to the *Phenomenology of Spirit,* and the interpretation of precursors in the *Lectures on the History of Philosophy,* as well as from the *Encyclopedia.*

THE SYNTHESIS OF THEORY AND PRACTICE

Finally, let us analyze more carefully the synthesis of theory and practice, a central theme in the whole preceding inquiry, and one that will enable us to formulate a central criticism of Gramsci. We have seen that the dialectic of theory and practice in the Notebooks suffers from four difficulties. First, Gramsci's critique of Croce arrives at anti-Crocean conclusions by using Crocean basic principles and critical methods; an analysis of Croce's writings substantiates this thesis by illustrating Croce's main ideas and critical methodology, and by exploring the interplay between his actual criticism and his theory of criticism. Second, Gramsci's critique of Bukharin dismisses his sociological analysis as positivist on the basis of evidence that his explicit philosophy of science is positivist; an analysis of Bukharin's work faults this by showing that the epistemology implicit in his sociology is not positivism but a sound dialectical methodology. Third, Gramsci's analysis of Machiavelli arrives at a notion of politics that appears useful, but only for the theoretical understanding of past politics and not for practical orientation in political struggle. And fourth, Gramsci's analysis of the dialectic conceives it in two different ways – as a mechanical process (the law of clash between thesis and antithesis) when he defines explicitly its meaning and as a mental process (a way of thinking that avoids one-sidedness) when he uses the notion in the context of other discussions; an analysis of the relevant texts in the Hegelian corpus strengthens this second Gramscian conception of the dialectic by showing it to be the only interpretation of the concept that Hegel both explicitly articulated and implicitly used in his writings.

The first of Gramsci's failures is merely one of self-awareness, for we have the self-image and the pretension of an anti-Croce, accompanied by very real Crocean commitments. The theory-practice distinction here takes the form of a distinction between the conclusions of an inferential process, on the one hand, and its premises and the character of its procedure, on the other. Because Gramsci's ("anti-Crocean") conclusions do plausibly follow, and because his Crocean premises are also plausible and the method is fruitful, the conclusions are anti-Crocean only in the sense that they were not reached or were denied by Croce, but that he *should* have reached and not denied them. Consequently, in such a situation it seems that practice should take precedence over theory, and that the way to synthesize practice and theory is to make the latter conform to the former. In short, self-images and pretensions should adjust themselves to the reality of the situation, at least until and unless this reality changes or is changed. Note that there is an analogous failing with which one can charge Croce in this context – the combination of his self-image as an anti-Marxist with a commitment to ideas that could be regarded as Marxist.

The second failing in terms of the distinction between self-image and actual behavior is that although Gramsci pretends to be anti-positivist (and almost always succeeds in so being), in his critical examination of Bukharin's system of sociology, he practices a method of criticism that could, not unfairly, be described as positivist. For Gramsci uncritically assumes that just because Bukharin explicitly expresses a positivist view of science in the early, epistemologically oriented chapters of his work, he is in fact conforming to that view when engaged in the sociological analysis of concrete problems, as if Bukharin were a machine whose behavior was determined by its programming principles. This betrays a kind of mechanism on Gramsci's part, which is uncharacteristic of him but typical of positivists and scientists. Obviously, on this occasion the discrepancy should have been corrected in a way opposite to that of the previous failure, for now the proper thing would be for Gramsci to modify his criticism of Bukharin, not his antipositivist image.

In this case, however, the discrepancy between Gramsci's self-image and his critical practice is relatively minor, since the crucial point is his failure to recognize the discrepancy between Bukharin's epistemological self-image and his concrete sociological discussions, and to undertake the construction of the epistemological theory to which Bukharin's sociological practice would correspond. In fact, Gramsci's conclusion to the effect that Bukharin's sociological analysis is positivist, *does not follow* from the evidence he gives, namely, that Bukharin's epistemological reflections are positivist. Although the premise in this inference is indeed true, the conclusion would have to be supported by evidence about the structure and content of Bukharin's actual sociological discussion; and, as we have seen, when this is done, the warranted conclusion is that Bukharin's sociology is not positivist but sophisticated, insightful, and even dialectically sound.

The difference between these two instances of Gramsci's failure may perhaps be described as follows: The situation of Croce is that, *up to a certain point*, Croce's thinking is Marxian but his self-image is anti-Marxian; this discrepancy is recognized by Gramsci, indeed, that is one aspect of his criticism. He fails, however, to recognize one further consequence, namely, that although his own self-image is anti-Crocean, his actual thinking is Crocean. Thus, in his critique of Croce, Gramsci's merit is that he perceives the discrepancy between Croce's theory and practice, while Gramsci's weakness lies in failing to recognize the discrepancy in his own theory and practice. On the other hand, in the case of Bukharin, Gramsci fails to recognize not only the discrepancy in his own theory and practice but also the one in Bukharin's, for Gramsci does not see that whereas Bukharin's epistemological self-image is positivist, his sociology is not; nor does Gramsci see that his own procedure in criticizing Bukharin is somewhat positivistic, and thus counter to his generally antipositivist attitude. There is merit in Gramsci's critique of Bukharin, but its merit lies elsewhere, namely, in the elaboration of an antipositivist conception of science. It is relevant to recall that a main element of the latter is Gramsci's emphasis on the synthesis of intellectual activity and practical experimentation.

Similarly, it should be recalled that the concept of religion that Gramsci adapts from Croce speaks of the synthesis of a world view and an ethic, grounded on faith.

In Gramsci's critique of Machiavelli, the difficulty is in the synthesis of theory and practice of neither Gramsci nor Machiavelli but in the notion of politics toward which Gramsci is groping. In fact, a central point of Gramsci's interpretation of Machiavelli's politics is to defend Machiavelli from the common objection that although he preached authoritarianism and deception in his advice to princes, he acted democratically and openly in publishing his book, and that although he theorized about a unified Italian state, such a union was impossible in practice at the time. Similarly, no problem arises with Gramsci's critical procedure, which is judicious or dialectical in the same sense that Machiavelli's political approach is. But the concept of judicious or dialectical politics that Gramsci judiciously or dialectically extracts from this Machiavellian politics may be questioned as being useful only for interpreting the past, and not for changing the present. Because Gramsci himself raises this objection against such a concept, it would be unfair to turn it into a criticism of him, unless the objection is groundless.

There are two sorts of considerations here. One is that Gramsci may be *confusing* theory and practice in making the objection. For it would seem that *by definition* a concept of politics is an instrument for understanding the world. Although it is quite proper to be concerned also with the formulation of political programs, or guidelines for political practice, it does not seem right to expect that such guidelines be derivable from a view of what is the meaning of "politics." In other words, a concept of politics is a theoretical instrument, and that it is not a practical instrument is no shortcoming.

In his objection Gramsci may also be saying something else. Rather than criticizing the dialectical concept of politics, Gramsci may be objecting to opportunistic shortsightedness. But in this case a difficulty emerges: How can it be that the examination of past political history always reveals that the outcome has been a synthesis of opposites, and yet in our own political practice we should try to bring about not what has always happened (the mediation of opposites) but, rather, what we know did not happen, namely, the extreme program proposed by a specific political force? To say this seems to involve proposing a divorce, an undialectical separation, of theory and practice.

Thus, Gramsci's objection either is not distinguishing theory and practice or is not relating them. Given the concept of the dialectic elaborated in our examination of Hegel, it is precisely this procedure that represents a violation of dialectical thinking. But when Gramsci's objection calls antidialectical the judicious mediation of oppositions, he is conceiving the dialectic as the historical process whereby a thesis clashes with an antithesis and results in a synthesis. This discrepancy means that Gramsci in fact fails to practice dialectical thinking, although he pretends to be dialectical. This is a failure between the practice and the theory of the dialectic, which leads to a final criticism.

In fact, my analysis of Gramsci's notes on the dialectic revealed the existence of the two different concepts just discussed. The one to which Gramsci pays lip service is always the same: The dialectic is conceived as the historical process of synthesis of thesis and antithesis. But implicit in his discussion of other problems, he uses the notion according to which the dialectic is a way of thinking that avoids one-sidedness by searching for differences underlying uniformities and for uniformities underlying differences. This second concept may therefore be said to be the one that he practices, whereas the former is the one he theorizes about. The discrepancy remains despite my criticizing his theory on the basis of his practice, which was taken as primary, and which was then also justified by an account of Hegel's concept of the dialectic.

From the present viewpoint, then, Gramsci failed to notice the discrepancy between his anti-Crocean pronouncements and his Crocean procedure; he failed to appreciate the significance of the discrepancy between the positivist epistemology and dialectical sociology of Bukharin; he postulated a dubious discrepancy between his notion of Machiavellian politics and his idea of political struggle; and he attached two different meanings to the dialectic. The interplay of theory and practice is as recurrent a theme as Gramsci's mishandling of it. In this sense, we can speak of Gramsci's failure to synthesize theory and practice.

Conclusion: Dialectical methodology and textual criticism

The present investigation has given new depth to the question of the historical roots of Gramsci's thought. For we have seen that the influence of Croce can be demonstrated not only in the context of Gramsci's explicit attempt to come to terms with Croce's philosophy but also when Gramsci is trying to learn from other sources. Thus, on the one hand, the explicit "anti-Croce" turns out to a large extent to be the logical and methodological exercise of exploring the internal coherence of the corpus of Croce's doctrines and techniques, in particular his theories of religion, of philosophy, of history, and of politics; his style and method of criticism; and his liquidationist dismissal of Marxism. On the other hand, in the critique of Bukharin, although Gramsci makes a significant advance beyond Croce by formulating a sound conception of the nature of science, he does so not only while under the influence of Crocean antipositivism and antisociologism in general but also while applying the Crocean conception of philosophy and doctrine of the nature of prediction. Moreover, in the critique of Machiavelli, although it would be improper to deny Gramsci's originality vis-à-vis Croce, it is clear he is elaborating the Crocean historical interpretation of Machiavelli as the Marx of Italian unification, and the Crocean intuition that the study of Machiavelli can lead to an analytical understanding of the nature of political activity. Finally, although the details of Gramsci's analysis of Marxian-Hegelian dialectic are extremely complicated, two relevant points are to be made: One is that Gramsci is adapting from Croce the alleged law that there is no dialectic of distincts but only a dialectic of opposites, even though new meaning is being given to this principle; the other is that since the correspondence between Gramsci's primary concept of the dialectic and Hegel's is established by interpreting the latter along the metaphilosophical lines suggested by Croce, we have here a deeper example of Croce's influence on Gramsci.

DIALECTICAL METHODOLOGY: HISTORICAL EXAMPLES

These intellectual ties between Gramsci and Croce give one type of historical import to the present work, for they may be taken to strengthen the reality of what has been called the tradition of Italian Marxism.[1] It should be obvious, however, that my emphasis has been on the tradition of dialectical thought and the methodology of the dialectic. In fact, a deep-structural conceptual unity underlies the diverse topics I examined from several of Gramsci's Notebooks. The concept of the dialectic is implicit in the notebooks on Croce, Bukharin, and Machiavelli, and explicit in the scattered notes discussing its nature. And we saw that the primary meaning Gramsci attaches to the dialectic is a methodological one: "the critical search for what is equal in the apparent diversity, and distinct and even opposite in the apparent uniformity."[2]

Moreover, it was evident throughout this investigation that the substantive content of Gramsci's thinking is Marxism, in that he is normally concerned with various Marxist or Marxian topics, themes, problems, and questions. It was stressed in the preceding chapter that all these discussions could be integrated, at the interpretative level, from the viewpoint of the evaluation of Marxism and, at the critical level, in terms of a failure of the synthesis of theory and practice. Let us now ask how Gramsci's approach to this problem may be characterized. The fact that he is sometimes defensive and sometimes critical vis-à-vis Marxism, and the fact that several aspects of the phenomenon are distinguished without being divorced from each other, suggests that here we have a dialectic of Marxist criticism.

In addition to this overarching example of dialectical methodology, we have had others more limited in scope. The account of Croce's critical philosophy (Chapter 2) did not contain any explicit discussion of the dialectic, but it is obvious that my interpretation can be seen as an account of Croce's dialectic of criticism, for the following reasons. First, his attempt at a general theory of critical understanding says that to understand something critically is to distinguish it from the rest and to relate it to the rest, and this is simply what later chapters (6 and 7) claim is the meaning of dialectical analysis. Second, in much of his actual criticism, Croce practiced distinguishing and interrelating the realms of the historical, the political, the philosophical, and the aesthetic. Finally, to the extent that his theory of criticism and his critical practice did not correspond, there would be a failure of dialectical accomplishment in the domain of criticism.

A more explicit example of the dialectic was provided by Bukharin's sociology. I argued at length, *pace* Gramsci, that it is dialectical insofar as it consists of attempts at judicious syntheses of such opposites as the individual and society, society and nature, structure and superstructure, and evolution and revolution.

Gramsci's interpretation of Machiavelli's politics was the next illustration of the dialectic. In fact, we saw that Gramsci's historical account consists of a plea for the avoidance of one-sidedness in anti-Machiavellian criticism, involving the charges of ruthlessness, democratic duplicity, political utopianism, and military incompetence.

In contrast to this example of Gramscian dialectic of historical interpretation, the concept of politics he extracts from Machiavelli provided an illustration of the dialectic of politics. This involved the distinction and interrelation among politics and art, sociology, morality, and economics, and between great and small politics, force and consent, and individualism and party spirit. We then saw that there was a difficulty about whether such a dialectic of politics is viable, and the following chapter (6) may be considered an exploration of this difficulty.

Our analysis of Hegel's concept of the dialectic was a case study of dialectical methodology in the fields of metaphilosophy and history of philosophy. This was made explicit in my analysis, and there is no need to elaborate further here.

Thus, if from a narrower historical point of view this investigation adds new meaning to the tradition of Italian Marxism, from a broader and more methodological point of view it contributes to the elaboration of what may be called the history and the theory of dialectic. The methodological concept of the dialectic mentioned above is elaborated in terms of concrete historical examples: Croce's dialectic of (general) criticism, Bukharin's dialectic of social science, Gramsci's historical interpretation of Machiavelli, Machiavelli's dialectic of politics, Hegel's dialectic of metaphilosophy and history of philosophy, and Gramsci's dialectic of Marxist criticism.

THE HERMENEUTICS OF NEGATIVE EVALUATION

The existence of these Gramscian theses, concepts, methods, and occasional errors has hitherto been hidden from readers, owing to the lack (until 1975) of a complete edition of the Prison Notebooks, as well as to the notorious hermeneutical difficulties stemming from their fragmented *literary* structure.[3] These problems can, however, be overcome if we ourselves abide by sufficiently rigorous hermeneutical requirements. This is the justification of what may otherwise appear as an excessively pedantic style of exposition on my part. The answer to such a criticism is simply that there is no royal road to knowledge, and that in the present case anything less would be royalty.

I attempted to compensate for the hermeneutical single-mindedness of most of my exposition in a number of ways. For one thing, I began with topically easier and hermeneutically less exacting analysis in the earlier chapters, and I hope the progression will facilitate readability. For another, I deliberately adopted a freer and more easygoing style in my discussion of Croce, partly out of respect for, and sympathy with, his skill and brilliance as a writer, but partly also because the vast scope of my exposition would have made detailed textual references unfeasible; nevertheless, I have included a few detailed textual analyses even there.

Third, I should like to call attention to what might be called the dialectic of attitudes expressed in the chapter sequence. Thus, I have alternated chapters that are primarily analytical and expository of Gramsci's views (1, 3, and the pair 5–6) with chapters that are primarily evaluative of Gramsci through the analysis and exposition of the relevant views of others (Croce, Bukharin, and Hegel). Moreover, within *my* analytical subsequence there is a spectrum of *Gramscian* attitudes: first that of favorable and positive defense, then that of an unfavorable and negative criticism, and then that of more or less neutral and constructive interpretations. Finally, in *my* evaluative subsequence of chapters, there is a multiplicity of valuational attitudes: My discussion of the basic features of Croce's critical methodology *strengthens* Gramsci's "religious" argument of the previous chapter; my examination of Bukharin's sociology *weakens* (or destroys) Gramsci's earlier critique; whereas my analysis of Hegel's dialectic confirms certain parts of Gramsci's two dialectical and political interpretations and disconfirms others.

I hope that besides avoiding monotony, this has avoided both confusion and disjointedness, and that it will create a dialectical interplay: for *and* against Marxism,[4] for *and* against Gramsci, for *and* against religion, for *and* against science, for *and* against the concept of politics, for *and* against the synthesis of theory and practice, for *and* against hermeneutics, for *and* against the dialectic itself.

The hermeneutical theme is especially important. I should clarify the point that hermeneutics is here taken in the dictionary sense, as the art or science of *textual* interpretation, rather than in one of the increasingly influential technical senses deriving from various schools of, or approaches to, philosophy.[5] Now, I believe that one of the most important hermeneutical requirements is what may be called the principle of the asymmetry of negative and positive evaluation; this prescribes that the textual evidence needed to justify a negative, unfavorable evaluation must be of a high quality, strength, and rigor, whereas for a positive evaluation less exacting standards are sufficient.[6]

This principle may be seen as implicitly applied and illustrated in three cases already mentioned. One is Gramsci's negative critique of Croce,[7] charging him with inconsistency and with misapplication of his own principles and methods to the particular phenomenon of "vulgar Marxism"; the extensive evidence from Croce[8] is thus an essential element of the substantiation of this charge. Another is Gramsci's unfavorable critique of Bukharin,[9] charging that he is pseudoscientific; the extensive documentation from Bukharin's work[10] has, therefore, the function of *testing* Gramsci's criticism. The third instance concerns Gramsci's objections[11] to certain forms of political moderatism and of political reformism as undialectical; my lengthy analysis of Hegel's concept of the dialectic[12] is needed to determine whether this negative criticism is justified.

There is also a more general and more direct way in which this hermeneutical principle is implicitly elaborated in my whole investigation. This occurs insofar as I am myself engaged in criticizing Gramsci. In fact, although it is not altogether fair to regard him as merely or primarily a Marxist, it is certainly proper to take him as an outstanding example of a Marxist thinker for anyone who wants to come to terms with Marxism by trying to gain and to provide a critical understanding of the phenomenon; thus my study of Gramsci is an exercise in Marxist criticism. From this viewpoint, my book contains three interrelated criticisms of Gramsci.

First, he did not realize the depth and extent of his Croceanism, since his critique of Croce uses not only Crocean assumptions but Croce's style and method of criticism; to substantiate this charge I give overwhelming evidence about the content and structure of both Gramsci's critique and Croce's critical methodology. Second, Gramsci did not realize the extent and depth of his methodological positivism and scientism, since in his destructive critique of Bukharin's sociology he is unable to extend into his own critical practice the sound concept of science that he held against Bukharin; again, this charge must be more than merely stated, and enough evidence must be given about the details of both Gramsci's critique and Bukharin's work to make the charge stick. Third, Gramsci's project of developing a concept of dialectical politics is a failure, since the notion turns out to be either political but undialectical or dialectical but unpolitical, meaning that if it has practical political import, then it is not avoiding one-sidedness, and if it is judiciously balanced in every way, then it is a mere instrument for interpreting past events; here one needs to show exactly what concept he constructs out of Machiavelli's politics, exactly what Gramsci understands by the dialectic, and exactly what the dialectic is. Each criticism involves, in a way, a failure properly to synthesize theory and practice: the *self-image* as an anti-Crocean with the *actual* thought as a Crocean; the self-image as a "scientist," in the antipositivist and antiscientistic sense of "serious inquiry," with an actual critical procedure that is "positivist" in practice;[13] and the self-image of being first and foremost a practitioner of the "art and science of politics" with the actual accomplishment of a notion of dialectical politics that cannot be both political art and dialectical science.

In short, there are six concrete applications and illustrations of the hermeneutical principle about the justification of negative evaluations. Three involve critiques advanced *by* Gramsci, and three others are my criticism *of* him. They may all be interrelated by construing the first triad *as part* of the second, and by summarizing the latter in terms of a thesis criticizing the synthesis of theory and practice in Gramsci's Prison Notebooks. This thesis would then constitute the central substantive result of my whole investigation, while the application of the above-mentioned hermeneutical principle would define its general procedure.

Could such a method of textual criticism be regarded as dialectical? To be sure, since the dialectic was not an idea with which my investigation began but, rather, one that emerged gradually, my dialectic of textual criticism may be expected to be merely implicit. Moreover, it should be noted that the absence of a dialectical approach would not by itself invalidate my procedure, although its presence would add another methodological coherence to the investigation. I believe the issue would depend on whether the proper distinctions and interrelations had been made. Some relevant terms would be: the primary text (e.g., Gramsci) and other relevant texts (e.g., Croce, Bukharin, and Hegel), the interpretation and the evaluation of the primary text, the favorable and the unfavorable evaluation of the primary text, and the element of theory and the element of practice within a text. It is clear my analysis is highly sensitive to distinguishing and interrelating these items. To that extent, I may then say, it contains the prospects for a genuine dialectical approach in the field of textual criticism.

Appendix: Concordance of critical edition and English translations

All of my quotations from Gramsci's writings were taken from the original Italian and translated into English by me. This was a natural procedure to follow, given that my aim was to develop my own interpretation of his thought, and given that no complete translation of his works (or even of the Notebooks) exists in English. There exist, however, two useful English translations of large portions of the Notebooks: *Selections from the Prison Notebooks* and *Selections from Cultural Writings*. Therefore, to facilitate the consultation of Gramsci's text for readers with no access to the original Italian, I have compiled the following table, which gives the location in the critical edition (*Quaderni del carcere*) of all passages from the Notebooks translated in these two volumes. I have listed the pages of the critical edition first, so that when the readers want to consult the passages from which my quotations are taken, they can easily look up the number and get the corresponding page for the English. Note that the frequent gaps in the pagination from the critical edition indicate that many passages are not included in the available translations. Some pages of these translations have no Italian counterpart because they contain commentary by the translators and editors. Note also that the correspondence is precise only to the extent of indicating which Gramsci note in the original corresponds to which page(s) in translation; for notes of less than one page, this makes no difference; however, for longer notes this entails further work by the reader to find the exact passage. Finally, page numbers preceded by "PN" refer to the first, and those preceded by "CW" to the second, of the two volumes of translations.

Quaderni	Translations	Quaderni	Translations
56–57	PN259–60	293	CW273
90–91	CW316–17	294–95	CW326–27
95–96	CW327–28	311–12	PN275–76
103–10	CW390–99	319–21	PN223–26
120–22	PN231–33	323–27	PN272–75
122–23	PN229–31	328–32	PN196–200
284–86	CW260–62	332–33	CW389–90
288–89	CW262–64	334–35	CW345–46

Appendix

Appendix

Appendix

Quaderni	Translations	Quaderni	Translations
1721–22	CW404–5	1987–89	CW246–47
1723–24	CW132–33	1998–99	CW244
1724–25	CW129–31	2004–6	CW241–44
1726–28	CW125–27	2010–34	PN55–84
1728–30	PN240–41	2035–46	PN90–102
1732–35	PN151–55	2046–48	PN102–4
1736–37	CW405–6	2048–54	PN84–90
1737–40	CW203–6	2107–10	CW199–201
1740–42	CW406–8	2110–12	CW353–55
1742–43	PN254–56	2112	CW293–94
1744	PN256–57	2113	CW264–65
1746	CW408	2113–20	CW206–12
1750–51	PN155–57	2120–23	CW359–62
1751	PN269	2123–24	CW364–65
1752–55	PN144–47	2124–25	CW365–67
1759–61	PN157–58	2126–27	CW367–69
1765–66	PN243–45	2128–29	CW369–70
1766–69	PN108–11	2129–33	CW370–74
1771–72	CW266–67	2133–35	CW374–75
1772–74	PN111–13	2139–40	PN279–80
1774–75	PN106–8	2140–47	PN280–87
1775–76	PN269–70	2147–50	PN294–97
1777–79	CW117–19	2150–52	PN287–89
1780	PN364–65	2152–53	PN306–7
1781–82	PN113–14	2153–58	PN289–94
1784–85	PN361	2158–59	PN307–8
1792–93	CW296–97	2160	PN297–98
1793–94	CW108–10	2160–64	PN298–301
1801–802	CW236–37	2164–69	PN301–6
1810–11	PN170–71	2169–71	PN308–10
1820–22	CW99–102	2171–75	PN310–13
1822–24	PN104–6	2175–78	PN313–16
1825–27	PN416–18	2178–80	PN316–18
1827	PN114	2185–86	CW91–93
1840–44	PN382–86	2186	CW146
1844–46	PN414–15	2187–90	CW93–98
1854–64	PN388–99	2191–92	CW133–34
1879–82	CW355–59	2192–93	CW98
1884–85	PN415–16	2193–95	CW122–23
1889–93	CW380–85	2195–98	CW212–16
1907	CW217	2198–2202	CW301–6
1908–10	CW217–20	2202	CW306
1912–14	CW220–22	2203	CW321–22
1914–15	CW247–49	2203–5	CW318–20
1917–18	CW313–14	2205	CW310–11
1920	CW314 [vii]	2206–8	CW335–37
1925–26	PN372–73	2209	CW99
1926<23>	PN461–62	2210	CW320
1926<24>	CW314 [viii]	2210–11	CW323–24
1933–34	CW375–77	2211–12	CW317
1939–40	PN148–50	2212–13	CW324–26
1944–45	CW272–73	2214–15	CW322–23
1947–48	PN266–67	2216<29>	CW328–29
1979–80	CW245	2216<30>	CW329

Appendix

Notes

1   P. Anderson, "The Antinomies of Antonio Gramsci." I do not, however, share other judgments of Anderson's; for a direct criticism of
some, see my "Gramsci's Crocean Marxism," pp. 19–20; for an indirect
criticism, see Chapter 3 of the present volume.

2   A. Gramsci, *Quaderni del carcere.*

3   E. J. Hobsbawm, "The Great Gramsci," p.39. This thesis had long
before been advanced by E. Garin, for example, when he says that
"there is no serious person who can doubt his [Gramsci's] constant
'scuffle' with Croce, as well as his having consciously immersed himself
completely in the most flourishing Italian cultural tradition" ("Gramsci
nella cultura italiana," p. 417); see also Garin's "La formazione di
Gramsci e Croce" and "Politica e cultura in Gramsci: Il problema degli
intellettuali." Some of the most enlightening analyses of the relationship between Gramsci and Croce, with regard to their historical views
and historiographical approaches, may be found in G. Galasso, *Croce,
Gramsci e altri storici.* Of some use is also G. Lentini, *Croce and Gramsci.*

4   See Chapters 1 and 2 of the present volume, my "Gramsci's Crocean
Marxism," my "Review of Gentile's *Filosofia di Marx*," and my "Croce
and Marxism: A Bibliographical Prolegomenon."

5   Gramsci, *Quaderni*, vol.3, pp. 1840–41. The four volumes are continuously paginated, and so references to the volume are unnecessary.
All translated quotations are my own, unless otherwise noted.

6   The importance of a methodological approach to the Prison Notebooks
has been noted by no less an authority than V. Gerratana, the editor
of the critical edition, when he says that their essential legacy is the
"theoretical construction of a complex critical methodology to attack
actively the processes going on in the contemporary world" ("Prefazione" to *Quaderni del carcere*, p. xxxiv). The distinction between
method and result has also been underscored in one of the more orig-

inal and well-grounded interpretations of recent years (L. Razeto Migliaro and P. Misuraca, *Sociologia e marxismo nella critica di Gramsci*, esp. pp. 13–14 and 127–28).

7   Gramsci, *Quaderni*, pp. 1841–42.

8   See Chapter 2. The "critical" interpretation of Croce's work may be regarded as the elaboration of a Gramscian theme, namely, the interpretation of Croce's philosophy of history and politics as an attempt to develop a critical alternative to Marxism, suggested by Gramsci in Notebook 10 and discussed in Chapter 1 of the present volume. Hence the "critical" interpretation of Gramsci acquires a firmer and more internal character because it is thus seen as based on the philologically indisputable preoccupation with Croce, and on Gramsci's own view of the Crocean leitmotif.

9   A. Gramsci, *Lettere dal carcere*, p. 390.

10 Gramsci, *Quaderni*, p. 2301. V. Gerratana deserves the credit for having called attention to this passage and to the critical nature of Gramsci's thinking ("La ricerca e il metodo," pp. 11–13).

11 See my "Labyrinth of Gramscian Studies and Femia's Contribution."

12 Cf. H. Portelli, *Gramsci et la question religieuse*; E. Masutti, *Perché Gramsci ateo?*; C. Vasale, *Politica e religione in Antonio Gramsci*; T. La Rocca, *Gramsci e la religione*; R. Vinco, *Una fede senza futuro?*; and my "Marxism, Science, and Religion in Gramsci: Recent Trends in Italian Scholarship."

13 Gramsci, *Lettere dal carcere*, p. 466.

14 Gramsci, *Quaderni*, pp. 1384–85.

15 See Chapter 1 below.

16 B. Croce, "Antonio Gramsci, *Lettere dal carcere*" (review), p. 86.

17 B. Croce, "Antonio Gramsci, *Il materialismo storico e la filosofia di Benedetto Croce*" (review); and *idem*, "Un gioco che ormai dura troppo."

18 P. Togliatti, *Antonio Gramsci*, p. 7.

19 *Ibid.*, p. 138.

20 *Ibid.*

21 *Ibid.*, pp. 218–19.

22 See, for example, J. Femia, *Gramsci's Political Thought*, esp. pp. 218–35; L. Razeto Migliaro and P. Misuraca, *Sociologia e marxismo nella critica di Gramsci*, esp. pp. 80–126; L. Salamini, *The Sociology of Political Praxis*, pp. 71–153; and A. Pizzorno, "Sul metodo di Gramsci: Dalla storiografia alla scienza politica."

23 Gramsci, *Lettere dal carcere*, p. 38.

24 K. R. Popper, *The Open Society and Its Enemies*; L. Kolakowski, *Main Currents of Marxism*; and S. Hook, *Marxism and Beyond*.

25 This is the impression I get from such works as L. Paggi, *Antonio Gramsci e il moderno principe*, vol. 1; *idem*, *Le strategie del potere in Gramsci*; M. L. Salvadori, *Gramsci e il problema storico della democrazia*; F. De Felice, *Serrati, Bordiga, Gramsci e il problema della rivoluzione in Italia. 1919–1920*; S. Suppa, *Il primo Gramsci: Gli scritti politici giovanili (1914–1918)*;

idem, Consiglio e stato in *Gramsci e Lenin;* G. Somai, *Gramsci a Vienna;* and F. Pierini, *Gramsci e la storiologia della rivoluzione (1914–1920).*

26 The severity of the problem may be seen from the fact that it is not escaped even by such an outstanding work as W. L. Adamson, *Hegemony and Revolution,* perhaps the best general account of Gramsci's career as a whole in either English or Italian; for my appreciation and criticism of Adamson's book, see my "Croce as Seen in a Recent Work on Gramsci" and my *Gramsci critico e la critica,* chap. 7.

27 See, for example, the authoritative judgment expressed in A. Asor Rosa, *Storia d'Italia,* p. 1553; the cogent justification in J. Femia, *Gramsci's Political Thought,* pp. 1–22, and in *idem,* "An Historicist Critique of 'Revisionist' Methods for Studying the History of Ideas"; the important results obtained in A. R. Buzzi, *La Théorie Politique d'Antonio Gramsci,* in H. Portelli, *Gramsci et le bloc historique,* in *idem, Gramsci et la question religieuse,* and in G. Francioni, *L'officina gramsciana;* the self-awareness displayed in A. Lepre, *Gramsci secondo Gramsci,* pp. 25–26; and the focus on Gramsci's thought in a very recent issue of *Critica marxista* (1987, vol. 25, no. 6), containing articles by N. Badaloni, G. Francioni, M. Montanari, and M. Telò. An apparently opposite proposal has been recently made in G. Eley, "Reading Gramsci in English: Observations on the Reception of Antonio Gramsci in the English-speaking World 1957–82," which concludes that "the philosophers have had their say. The historians should now take the stage" (p. 470). My answer to this is implicitly given above. Moreover, although one may admit that Eley's review is valuable as far as it goes, I should point out that its scope is limited to the English-speaking situation and to the Marxist orientation. I should add that there is a sense, probably not intended by Eley, in which his judgment could be endorsed. In fact, there exists a fifth approach to Gramsci, which is philosophical in the sense that it takes Gramscian passages as a pretext for engaging in a form of philosophical theorizing that has its own logic independently of Gramsci (see, for example, G. Nardone, *Il pensiero di Gramsci;* N. Badaloni, *Il marxismo di Gramsci;* G. Prestipino, *Da Gramsci a Marx;* and, on a less philosophical but equally theoretical plane, J. Hoffman, *The Gramscian Challenge*). In contrast to this approach, my own analytical and conceptual approach could be described as historical, insofar as it is centrally concerned with the analysis of Gramsci's own concepts and rigorously based on his texts.

1. GRAMSCI'S CROCEAN CRITIQUE OF CROCE'S PHILOSOPHY

1 A similar thesis was first elaborated by G. Morpurgo-Tagliabue in his article "Gramsci tra Croce e Marx." This old article has been unjustly neglected, not being listed, for example, in E. Fubini's bibliographies: "Bibliografia gramsciana" and "Bibliografia gramsciana 1968–1977." Yet Morpurgo-Tagliabue's insights can be helpful even today.

2 The claim about obsession can be found in A. Gramsci, *Quaderni del carcere*, p. 1240; but Gramsci is aware of the exaggeration in the light of his realization that "one must not look for a general philosophical problem in Croce" (*ibid.*, p. 1303), and his realization of the importance of Croce's work in aesthetics and literary criticism (*ibid.*, p. 1303). It should be noted that Gramsci's view of Croce's philosophy as an intended anti-Marxism, when properly qualified constitutes an important, original, and partially correct interpretation. This aspect of Gramsci's critique of Croce may be easily missed, one reason for developing the account of Croce given in Chapter 2 below.

3 See the preface to the 1906 edition, in B. Croce, *Materialismo storico ed economia marxistica*, p. xii.

4 B. Croce, *Cultura e vita morale*, pp. 150–59.

5 Croce, *Materialismo storico*, p. xii.

6 *Ibid.*, p. xi.

7 *Ibid.*, p. 102; the translation here and in all subsequent quotations from Italian works is my own.

8 *Ibid.*, pp. 102–3.

9 *Ibid.*, pp. 139–40.

10 B. Croce, preface to the 1917 edition, in *Materialismo storico*, p. xiv.

11 In "La rivoluzione control il *Capitale*," now in A. Gramsci, *Scritti giovanili 1914–1918*, pp. 149–53, and in A. Gramsci, *La città futura 1917–1918*, pp. 513–16, and translated in A. Gramsci, *History, Philosophy and Culture in the Young Gramsci*, pp. 123–26. As for Gramsci's self-image, in the Notebooks, referring to the year 1917, he says, "I was tendentially rather Crocean" (*Quaderni*, p. 1233).

12 See, for example, *Quaderni*, pp. 1215 and 1254.

13 *Quaderni*, p. 1232.

14 See G. Gentile, "Il marxismo di Benedetto Croce," reprinted in G. Gentile, *La filosofia di Marx*, pp. 295–99. See also my review of *La filosofia di Marx* in *The Thomist*. I should add that the diversity between Gentile's thought and Gramsci's cannot be undermined by the similar-sounding conclusions to which they arrive in their respective criticisms of Croce's alleged theoreticism or contemplativism. An elaboration of their similarity may be found in C. Riechers, *Antonio Gramsci*, and in A. Del Noce, *Il suicidio della rivoluzione*. Despite the high quality of Del Noce's effort, against such recent attempts N. Matteucci's earlier objection remains valid: "From a historical-critical point of view, it would not be proper to speak of an actualistic origination or suggestion apropos the problem of the identity of philosophy and politics, unless one wants to play games with oversimplified and empty concepts: Gentile's identity of ideology and philosophy, besides being purely verbal and abstract, and besides representing a 'degradation of traditional philosophy compared to the heights reached by Croce' [*Quaderni*, p. 1355], when it is translated into historicist language would lead to dissolving the superstructure into the structure, that is, it appears as a form of

economism; whereas, in Gramsci's thought, the unity of theory and practice (and thus of the superstructure and the structure) 'is not a mechanical factual datum but an historical becoming,' a 'critical act,' and 'a dialectical unity inherent in a social group' [*Quaderni*, p. 1385; *Quaderni*, p. 1780; and A. Gramsci, *Il materialismo storico e la filosofia di Benedetto Croce*, p. 200]" (N. Matteucci, *Antonio Gramsci e la filosofia della prassi*, p. 56).

15 A. Gramsci, *Quaderni*, pp. 1207–38. Subsequent references to the continuously paginated four volumes of this book ("Q") will be in parenthesis in the text, as done here.

16 The other thirty-nine sections are all from pt. II, specifically pars. 6–9, 12, 15, 19–21, 23–25, 27, 28, 30, 32, 35, 37.II, 38.II, 39, 40, 41.VII, 41.XIII, 43–46, 48, 50–55, 57, 58, 59.II, 60, and 61.

17 Pt. I, pars. 2 and 8; pt. II, pars. 1, 2, 3, 5, 11, 16, 26, 29.II, 31.I, 31.II, 33, 34, 36, 37.I, 38.I, 41.I, 41.VI, 41.VIII, 41.IX, 41.XI, 41.XII, 41.XV, 42, 59.III, and 59.IV. Here we have a good example of how the critical edition of the Prison Notebooks lifts Gramscian studies onto a qualitatively new plane. In fact, when scholars have examined Gramsci's critique of Croce, their emphasis has usually been on the Gramscian criticism of Croce's so-called idealism, that is to say, on metaphysical issues. The philological fact about Notebook 10 just mentioned suggests that the emphasis should be elsewhere, namely, on Croce's critique of Marxism. Even before the critical edition appeared, the more thoughtful scholars had a correct intuition on the matter, and even when they gave the metaphysical account, they confessed the desirability of focusing on Gramsci's critique of Croce's critique; see, for example, N. Matteucci, *Antonio Gramsci e la filosofia della prassi*, pp. 45–46. Matteucci also saw the need (*ibid.*, p. 45) for a systematic list of all of Croce's writings on Marxism, which has now been provided by my "Croce and Marxism: A Bibliographical Prolegomenon."

18 Pt. I pars. 1, 3, 5, 6, 7, 9, 10, 12, and 13; and pt. II, pars. 5, 14, 22, 29.I, 41.V, 41.X, 41.XIV, 41.XVI, 56, and 59.I.

19 Pt. I, pars. 1 and 4; and pt. II, pars. 10, 14, 17, 18, 41.II, 41.III, 41.IV, 41.X, 49, 59.IV, and zero. The last item is my notation for the introductory section of pt. II; cf. *Quaderni*, p. 1239.

20 This classification yields five sections belonging to more than one group, namely par. 1, of pt. I, and pars. 5, 14, 41.X, and 59.IV of pt. II.

21 B. Croce, *Storia della storiografia italiana nel secolo decimonono*, vol. 2, pp. 136–37.

22 *Ibid.*, pp. 125–26.

23 B. Croce, *Etica e politica*, p. 225.

24 At the 1930 World Congress of Philosophy in Oxford, reacting with comments on a paper delivered by a former Soviet minister of education, Lunacǎrskij, dealing with "bourgeois aesthetics." Cf. *La Nuova*

Italia 1, no. 10 (October 20, 1930):431–32; cf. also Gramsci, *Quaderni*, pp. 2745–46 and 2748.

25 Par. 41.I of pt. II.

26 Pt. I, pars. 1 and 8; and pt. II, pars. 11, 16, 26, 31.II, 34, 41.II, 41.IV.

27 Q1291, Q1301, and pars. 31.II and 34 of pt. II.

28 Q1291, Q1301, and pars. 11, 16, and 26 of pt. II.

29 Q1291–92.

30 Q1292, and par. 41.II of pt. II.

31 Q1292–93 and Q1294–96.

32 Q1293–94.

33 Q1298–99 and par. 8 of pt. I.

34 Q1299–1300.

35 Q1300.

36 Par. 1 of pt. I.

37 Pt. I, par. 1 (Q1213); and pt. II, par. 41.IV (Q1304–5).

38 Cf. B. Croce, *Materialismo storico*, pp. 9–15 and 74–85.

39 *Ibid.*, p. 108.

40 Here Gramsci is quoting from B. Croce, *Storia dell'età barocca in Italia*, p. 89.

41 B. Croce, *Storia d'Europa nel secolo decimonono*, p. 20.

42 *Ibid.*, p. 26.

43 *Ibid.*

44 B. Croce, "Marxismo e filosofia," in *Conversazioni critiche*, vol. 1, pp. 296–306. This is a review-essay occasioned by Emil Hammacher's *Das philosophisch-oekonomische System des Marxismus*. This objection continues to be heard and to be used specifically against Gramsci, as may be seen from F. Capucci, *Antonio Gramsci: Il materialismo storico e la filosofia di Benedetto Croce*, esp. pp. 119–28.

45 See, for example, B. Croce, *Logica come scienza del concetto puro*, pp. 184–95 (pt. 2, chap. 4), and pp. 283–90 (pt. 3, chap. 7); *idem, Teoria e storia della storiografia*, pp. 140–53; *idem, Filosofia e storiografia*, pp. 38–42 (pt. 1, chap. 4), and pp. 342–49 (pt. 8); *idem, Ultimi saggi*, pp. 395–400; and *idem, Il carattere della filosofia moderna*, pp. 1–23.

46 B. Croce, *Teoria e storia della storiografia*, pp. 1–17. Immediately after the passage just quoted (Q1242), Gramsci seems to contradict himself by apparently denying that Croce held this view: "But Croce cannot arrive all the way to this necessary conclusion, precisely because it leads to the identification of history and politics and hence of ideology and philosophy" (Q1242). This is indeed puzzling, especially in view of Gramsci's realization, expressed elsewhere (*Lettere dal carcere*, p. 157), that the book where the contemporariness of history is explicitly elaborated – the *Theory and History of Historiography* – "contains, not only a synthesis of the entire Crocean philosophical system, but a real, true revision of the system."

47 B. Croce, "Il filosofo," in *Ultimi saggi*, pp. 395–400.

48 B. Croce, *Storia d'Europa nel secolo decomonono; idem, Storia d'Italia dal 1871 al 1915.*

49 See B. Croce, "La concezione liberale come concezione della vita" and "Liberismo e liberalismo," in *Etica e politica*, pp. 225–34; see also B. Croce, *Storia come pensiero e come azione*, translated into English as *History as the Story of Liberty.*

50 B. Croce, "Elementi di politica" (especially the section on "Storia economico-politica e storia etico-politica"), in *Etica e politica*, pp. 225–34; *idem, La storia come pensiero e come azione.* The importance of the notion of ethico-political history in Croce's philosophy has received additional confirmation recently in the work of a somewhat orthodox interpreter and commentator, G. Sasso *(Benedetto Croce: La ricerca della dialettica).* This extremely detailed and comprehensive work of more than a thousand pages divides Croce's development into three periods, the middle one being the years 1909–38, during which he articulated a philosophy centered around the concept of ethico-political history.

51 See also Chapter 6.

52 For a fuller discussion and an evaluation of the complexities underlying this objection, see my "Croce as Seen in a Recent Work on Gramsci" and my *Gramsci critico e la critica,* chap. 7.

53 This is an ingenious interpretation by Gramsci, but I think that here he is misled by Croce's phrase and forgets that Croce means "ethico-political" to be synonymous with "moral." He avoids the latter term in order to prevent confusion with a moralistic approach, which he opposes. See B. Croce, *Etica e politica,* pp. 225–34.

54 A collection of all specific references supporting my point here would be too tedious, unmanageably long, and unnecessary because obvious even to a casual reader of Croce. See, for example, B. Croce, *La storia come pensiero e come azione,* pp. 133–35; *idem, Materialismo storico,* pp. 76–77; *idem, La poesia di Dante,* pp. 49–51; *idem, L'Italia dal 1914 al 1918,* pp. 292–96. A fuller elaboration of this point is given in Chapter 2.

55 B. Croce, *Materialismo storico,* pp. 9–15 and 74–75.

56 A. Gramsci, *Quaderni,* Notebook 10, pt. II, pars. 33, 41.V, 41.XII, 56, and 59.I.

57 At the end of and soon after World War II, Croce did become practically involved with the so-called Italian Liberal Party, but that period is obviously outside Gramsci's temporal frame of reference. For further discussions of Croce's noninvolvement, see W. L. Adamson, *Hegemony and Revolution,* and my critique of this important work in my "Croce as Seen in a Recent Work on Gramsci" and my *Gramsci critico e la critica,* chap. 7; see also E. Jacobitti, *Revolutionary Humanism and Historicism in Modern Italy.*

58 This tradition is in turn part of the larger one of Italian Marxism, as has been cogently argued by P. Piccone, *Italian Marxism.* Whether, however, one should speak of Marxism as I do here and as Piccone

does, or of "revolutionary humanism and historicism," as E. Jacobitti does *(Revolutionary Humanism and Historicism in Modern Italy)*, may be disputed. Such a dispute can easily degenerate into a verbal disagreement, but a helpful distinction to keep in mind is the one between method and substance in Marxism in general, and in Gramsci in particular. For a discussion of this issue, see my "Labyrinth of Gramscian Studies and Femia's Contribution" and my *Gramsci critico e la critica*, chap. 6.

2. CROCE AND THE THEORY AND PRACTICE OF CRITICISM

1 As clarified below, in the section on "Historicism," it makes sense to "criticize" historical events by first seeing them as the result of the actions of historical agents. I am certainly not attributing a moralistic attitude to Croce. But the evaluation of historical actions is not necessarily improper, as long as one distinguishes the practical-economic evaluation of the appropriateness of means and ends, from the moral evaluation of ends, and as long as one also distinguishes evaluation from explanation. Cf. B. Croce, "Azione, successo, giudizio," in *Ultimi saggi*, and N. Matteucci, *Antonio Gramsci e la filosofia della prassi*, pp. 90–103.

2 Cf. B. Croce, "Il manifesto degli intellettuali italiani antifascisti," in *Filosofia, poesia, storia*, pp. 1056–60; and *idem*, "Contro il dettato di pace," *ibid.*, pp. 1066–72.

3 B. Croce, *Ciò che è vivo e ciò che è morto della filosofia di Hegel*, now available in *Saggio sullo Hegel*, pt. 1, pp. 1–142, and translated by D. Ainslie in 1915 as *What Is Living and What Is Dead of the Philosophy of Hegel*. The other book is *Indagini su Hegel e schiarimenti filosofici*.

4 *La filosofia di G. B. Vico*, trans. R. G. Collingwood as *The Philosophy of Giambattista Vico*, 1913; and *Materialismo storico ed economia marxistica* (1900), trans. C. M. Meredith as *Historical Materialism and the Economics of Karl Marx*, 1914.

5 *Saggi sulla letteratura italiana del Seicento* (1911); and *Nuovi saggi sulla letteratura italiana del Seicento* (1931).

6 *La letteratura della nuova Italia*, vols. 1–4 (1914–15); vol. 5 (1939); vol. 6 (1940).

7 *Conversazioni critiche*, vols. 1–2 (1918); vols. 3–4 (1932); vol. 5 (1939).

8 *Goethe* (1919); trans. D. Ainslie, 1923.

9 *Ariosto, Shakespeare e Corneille* (1920), trans. D. Ainslie, 1920.

10 *La poesia di Dante* (1920), trans. D. Ainslie, *The Poetry of Dante*, 1922.

11 *Poesia antica e moderna* (1941).

12 *Poeti e scrittori del pieno e tardo Rinascimento*, vols. 1–2 (1945,); vol. 3 (1952).

13 *La letteratura italiana del Settecento* (1949).

14 *Storia della storiografia italiana nel secolo decimonono* (1921).

15 *Storia dell'età barocca in Italia* (1929).
16 *Poesia popolare e poesia d'arte* (1933).
17 *Letture di poeti e riflessioni sulla teoria e la critica della poesia* (1950).
18 *L'Italia dal 1914 al 1918: Pagine sulla guerra* (1919).
19 *Scritti e discorsi politici* (1963).
20 There are, respectively: *La rivoluzione napoletana del 1799* (1897), *La Spagna nella vita italiana durante la Rinascenza* (1917); *Storie e leggende napoletane* (1919); *Una famiglia di patrioti ed altri saggi storici e critici* (1919); *Storia del regno di Napoli* (1925), trans. F. Frenaye, *History of the Kingdom of Naples*, 1970; *Uomini e cose della vecchia Italia* (1927); *Storia d'Italia dal 1871 al 1915* (1928), trans. C. M. Ady, *A History of Italy*, 1929; *Storia d'Europa nel secolo decimonono* (1932), trans. H. Furst, *History of Europe in the Nineteenth Century*, 1963; *Varietà di storia letteraria e civile*, vol. 1 (1935), vol. 2 (1950); *Vite di avventure, di fede e di passione* (1936); *Aneddoti di varia letteratura* (1953).
21 *Estetica come scienza dell'espressione e linguistica generale* (1902), trans. D. Anslie, *Aesthetic as Science of Expression and General Linguistics*, 1909; *Logica come scienza del concetto puro* (1909), trans. D. Ainslie, *Logic as the Science of Pure Concept*, 1917; and *Filosofia della pratica* (1909), trans. D. Ainslie, *Philosophy of the Practical*, 1915.
22 *La storia come pensiero e come azione* (1938), trans. S. Sprigge, *History as the Story of Liberty*, 1941; *La poesia* (1936), trans. G. Gullace, *Poetry and Literature: Introduction to Its Criticism and History*, 1981; and *Il carattere della filosofia moderna* (1941).
23 *Problemi di estetica* (1910); *Nuovi saggi di estetica* (1920); *Etica e politica* (1931), trans. S. Castiglione, *Politics and Morals*, 1945; *Ultimi saggi* (1935); *Discorsi di varia filosofia* (1945), trans. E. F. Carritt, *My Philosophy*, 1949; and *Filosofia e storiografia* (1949).
24 This theory of critical understanding can be extracted from Croce's *Logic*, by construing its *concetto puro*, which literally means "pure concept," as meaning "critical understanding."
25 *Estetica*, pp. 4–5, my translation; cf. *Aesthetic*, trans. D. Ainslie, p. 2.
26 Croce, *Materialismo storico ed economic marxistica*, p. 162.
27 Croce, *Etica e politica*, p. 344.
28 *Ibid.*, p. 345; my last two sentences paraphrase Croce's.
29 Croce, *Materialismo storico*, p. 104; cf. also Chapter 5 of the present work.
30 *Aesthetic*, pp. 242–43.
31 *Saggio sullo Hegel*, p. 36.
32 *Materialismo storico*, p. 104.
33 *Aesthetic*, p. 242.
34 *Saggio sullo Hegel*, p. 3; cf. also Chapter 7 of the present work.
35 Or, more obscurely, "philosophy of spirit" (*filosofia dello spirito*).
36 *Aesthetic*, pt. 2, "History," pp. 169–534.

37 *Saggio sullo Hegel,* pp. 16–17.
38 *Conversazioni critiche,* vol. 5, p. 265.
39 This is the third part of the appendix; cf. *Teoria e storia della storiografia,* (1917), pp. 140–53.
40 *Ultimi saggi,* p. 388.
41 See, for example, D. F. Pears, *The Nature of Metaphysics.*
42 See, for example, K. R. Popper, *Conjectures and Refutations,* pp. 66–96; J. W. N. Watkins, "Influential and Confirmable Metaphysics"; and J. Agassi, "The Nature of Scientific Problems and Their Roots in Metaphysics," in *The Critical Approach to Science and Philosophy,* ed. M. Bunge, pp. 189–211.
43 *Ultimi saggi,* pp. 388–89.
44 *Storia come pensiero e come azione,* p. 128.
45 *Filosofia e storiografia,* pp. 41–42.
46 *Theory and History of Historiography,* pt. 2; and *Storia della storiografia italiana nel secolo decimonono.*
47 *Logica,* pp. 121–31.
48 *Filosofia, Poesia, Storia,* pp. 57–65; and *Philosophy, Poetry, History,* pp. 62–71.
49 *Logica,* pp. 126–26; the translation is my own.
50 *Ibid.,* p. 127.
51 *Ibid.,* pp. 127–28.
52 Croce, *Conversazioni critiche,* vol. 3, pp. 215–26.
53 *Macbeth,* 4:216.
54 Croce, *Ariosto, Shakespeare e Corneille,* trans. D. Ainslie, pp. 311–12.
55 *The Sonnets, Triumphs, and Other Poems of Petrarch,* p. 14. The original Italian, which is quoted by Croce (*Conversazioni critiche,* vol. 3, pp. 215–16), reads as follows:

> Movesi il vecchierel canuto e bianco
> dal dolce loco ov'ha sua età fornita,
> a da la famigliuola sbigottita
> che vede il caro padre venir manco;
>   indi, traendo poi l'antiquo fianco
> per l'estreme giornate di sua vita,
> quanto piú pò col buon voler s'aita,
> rotto dagli anni e dal cammino stanco;
>   e viene a Roma, seguendo 'l desio,
> per mirar la sembianza di Colui
> c'ancor lassú nel ciel vedere spera.
>   Cosí, lasso! talor vo cercand'io,
> donna, quant'è possibile, in altrui
> la disïata vostra forma vera.

56 Croce, *Conversazioni critiche,* vol. 3, pp. 215–16; quoted from *Giornale storico della letteratura italiana,* vol. 87, pp. 347–49.

57 *Ibid.*, pp. 216–17.
58 *Ibid.*, p. 221.
59 *Ibid.*, p. 225.
60 *Ibid.*, p. 223.
61 Croce, *Problemi di estetica*, pp. 172–76. Cf. the discussion in A. Gramsci, *Quaderni del carcere*, pp. 2341–42.
62 *Problemi di estetica*, p. 172; quoted from H. Steinthal, *Grammatik, Logik und Psychologie, ihre Principien und ihr Verhältniss zu einander*, p. 220.
63 *Problemi di estetica*, p. 173.
64 See, for example, B. Mates, *Elementary Logic*, pp. 20–22.
65 August Strindberg, *Plays*, trans. E. Sprigge, pp. 561–62.
66 Croce, "Conati pseudo-idealistici contro la logica," in *Conversazioni critiche*, vol. 5, p. 264.
67 Galileo Galilei, *Dialogue Concerning the Two Chief World Systems*, trans. S. Drake, p. 152. For more examples and a fuller discussion, see my *Galileo and the Art of Reasoning*, pp. 46–66.
68 Galilei, *Dialogue*, p. 127.
69 *Ibid.*, pp. 37–38.
70 *Ibid.*, p. 69.
71 This is not to deny the interest or importance of works like M. E. Moss, *Benedetto Croce Reconsidered*, and D. D. Roberts, *Benedetto Croce and the Uses of Historicism;* it is merely to say that their discussion would take us too far from the present focus.
72 This thesis corresponds to the interpretation of the *Aesthetic* given in Edmund Jacobitti, *Revolutionary Humanism and Historicism in Modern Italy*, and to the contrast between the *Aethetic* and *La poesia* discussed in Giovanni Gullace's "Introduction" to Benedetto Croce, *Poetry and Literature.*
73 A good example of this type of judicious adaptation is a brief discussion by Marcello Pera ("E uno scienziato, però ha stile"), in which he transfers Croce's notion of a historical "cycle" from the domain of art and poetry to that of science, in order to elucidate the reality of scientific progress while allowing that it may not be completely cumulative; cf. also M. Pera and J. Pitt, ed., *I modi del progresso;* and J. C. Pitt and M. Pera, ed., *Rational Changes in Science.*

3. GRAMSCI'S METHODOLOGICAL CRITICISM OF BUKHARIN'S SOCIOLOGY

1 A. Zanardo, "Il 'Manuale' di Bucharin visto dai comunisti tedeschi e da Gramsci."
2 L. Paggi, "Gramsci's General Theory of Marxism," p. 27. This article is a translation of L. Paggi, "La teoria generale del marxismo in Gramsci."
3 R. Paris, "Gramsci e la crisi teorica del 1923," p. 29.
4 L. Colletti, "Marxismo," pp. 11–13.

5 L. Paggi, *Le strategie del potere in Gramsci*, chap. 8, esp. p. 364.
6 See, for example, L. Razeto Migliaro and P. Misuraca, *Sociologia e marxismo nella critica di Gramsci*, esp. pp. 75–126. Another extensive examination of the Gramsci-Bukharin connection is in C. Buci-Glucksmann, *Gramsci et l' état*, but I am unsure what to make of it. Nevertheless, I hestitate to dismiss it (as so many others have done), given the author's obvious intelligence and the fact that in Chapter 6 I found her essay "Sui problemi della transizione" useful.
7 S. F. Cohen, "Marxist Theory and Bolshevik Policy," p. 40.
8 M. Lewin, *Political Undercurrents in Soviet Economic Debates*, p. xii. Lewin was writing these words in the 1970s about the 1960s, but they apply even more to the late 1980s, after the coming to power of Gorbachev in the Soviet Union and the essential rehabilitation of Bukharin at the beginning of 1988.
9 Quoted in D. Hoffman, "Bukharin's Theory of Equlibrium," p. 128, from V. I. Lenin, "Testament," *New Leader* (New York, 1962), p. 567.
10 S. F. Cohen, *Bukharin and the Bolshevik Revolution*, p. 19.
11 *Ibid.*, p. 393, n. 56.
12 *Ibid.*, p. 20.
13 *Ibid.*, p. 25.
14 *Ibid.*, p. 393, n. 56.
15 Lewin, *Political Undercurrents*, p. 5.
16 See Cohen, *Bukharin*, pp. 28, 42, and 396, n. 101; Lewin, *Political Undercurrents*, pp. 5–6; and Hoffman, "Bukharin's Theory of Equilibrium," p. 126.
17 Cohen, *Bukharin*, p. 83.
18 *Ibid.*, p. 97.
19 *Ibid.*, p. 96.
20 *Ibid.*
21 *The Great Purge Trial*, ed. Robert C. Tucker and S. C. Cohen, pp. xl–xlviii.
22 Cf. A. Zanardo, "Il 'Manuale' di Bucharin visto dai comunisti tedeschi e da Gramsci," p. 231. The English translation was published in New York by International Publishers, and a year later in London by Allen & Unwin.
23 *Archiv für Geschichte des Sozialismus und der Arbeiterwegung*, pp. 216–24. This was translated and published under the title "Technology and Social Relations," in *New Left Review*, pp. 27–34.
24 Antonio Gramsci, *Quaderni del carcere*, pp. 1396–1450; also found in his *Il materialismo storico e la filosofia di Benedetto Croce*, pp. 119–68; and in *Selections from the Prison Notebooks*, ed. and trans. Q. Hoare and G. Nowell Smith, pp. 419–72.
25 Ann Arbor, Michigan: University of Michigan Press, 1969.
26 D. Hoffman, "Bukharin's Theory of Equilibrium."
27 Cohen, *Bukharin*, chap. 4: *idem*, "Marxist Theory and Bolshevik Policy."

28 Introduction to R. Michels, *Political Parties*, p. 27, n. 22.
29 Introduction to N. Bukharin, *Historical Materialism: A System of Sociology*, p. 7A.
30 Paggi, "Gramsci's General Theory of Marxism," pp. 40–41.
31 Such a classification is exhaustive of the various paragraphs of the critique, as numbered by the editor of *Quaderni del carcere*. The correspondence is generally as follows: pedagogical criticism, pars. 13, 17, 20, 22.III, and 22.IV; philosophical criticism, pars. 14, 22.IV, 31, and 32; methodological, 15, 18, 19, 21, 22.II, 25, 26, 30, and 35; Marxist-rhetorical, 16, 22.I, 27, 29, 33, 62, and 63.
32 *Quaderni del carcere*, p. 1396. Quotations from this book are my own translations.
33 From here on, reference to the *Quaderni del carcere* will be made in parenthesis in the text, with the title abbreviated to "Q."
34 It is not literally true that, as Gramsci says, Bukharin's book "lacks any treatment of the dialectic. The dialectic is presupposed, very superficially, not expounded" (Q1424), since Bukharin's chapter 3 explains a number of principles of what he calls "dialectic materialism," namely, the interrelationship of all things, the developmental nature of all things, the working out of contradictions as the driving force of development, and the need for qualitative revolutionary changes even when resulting from gradual ones. I suppose Gramsci means that this has nothing to do with the dialectic as he understands it, but that is another matter. See also Chapter 6 below.
35 This strikes me as analogous to Albert Einstein's self-styled "opportunism" (in his "Replies," in *Albert Einstein, Philosopher-Scientist*, ed. P. A. Schilpp, p. 684), to Karl Marx's talk of "the proper logic of the proper object" (*Critique of Hegel's Philosophy of Right*, ed. J. O'Malley, p. 92), and to what I have called Galileo Galilei's "judgment" (in my *Galileo and the Art of Reasoning*, pp. 145–64. See also my "Concept of Judgment and Huygen's Theory of Gravity," pp. 185–218; my "Sztompka's Philosophy of Social Science," pp. 357–71; and Piotr Sztompka, *Sociological Dilemmas: Toward a Dialectic Paradigm*.
36 *Logica*, pt. 2, chap. 5, pp. 200–201.
37 N. Bukharin, *Historical Materialism* pp. 14–15.
38 Cf. Q1402, and B. Croce, *Materialismo storico ed economia marxistica*.
39 *Historical Materialism*, p. 15.
40 See, for example, A. Kaplan, *The Conduct of Inquiry: Methodology for Behavioral Science*, pp. 94–103; and M. Scriven, "Explanations, Predictions, and Laws," in *Minnesota Studies in the Philosophy of Science*, vol. 3, ed. Herbert Feigl and G. Maxwell, pp. 170–230.
41 *Historical Materialism*, pp. 27–28.
42 *Ibid.*, p. 29, italics mine.
43 *Ibid.*
44 *Ibid.*

45 Cf. *Historical Materialism*, pp. 194–95.

46 *Ibid.*, p. 122.

47 *Ibid.*, pp. 161–69.

48 *Ibid.*, p. 169.

49 Cf. Q2637 and *Historical Materialism*, p. 75.

50 *Historical Materialism*, pp. 9–15.

51 Gramsci does not explicitly mention Bukharin's book on Q1406–11. But this is a revised version of a text that does, namely, Q1043–44.

52 "From Spaventa to Gramsci," p. 35; see also his "Gramsci's Marxism: Beyond Lenin and Togliatti," his "Labriola and the Roots of Eurocommunism," and his *Italian Marxism*.

53 I could not help but be impressed by this passage because I have myself argued in support of a similar conception of science, on the basis of an original analysis of Galileo's work. See my *Galileo and the Art of Reasoning*, esp. chaps. 5 and 6.

54 One author who has suggested a similar thesis is P. Rossi, "Antonio Gramsci sulla scienza moderna," whose eloquent conclusion is difficult to excel (p. 57): "Gramsci was not concerned primarily or for long with questions connected with science, technology, and their history. But there is no doubt that on these topics also, he expressed significant ideas. And above all there is no doubt that he wanted to make the proletariat not only the heir of classical German philosophy, but also the heir of the scientific revolution."

55 B. Croce, *Logica*, pt 2, chap. 4; *idem, Il carattere della filosofia moderna*, chap. 1; and *idem, Philosophy, Poetry, History*, pt. 1, chap. 6. This doctrine was the one selected for inclusion in M. White, *The Age of Analysis*, pp. 43–52.

56 See, for example, Q1402–3, and Chapter 1 above.

57 As noted in the Introduction, the general importance of Gramsci's concern with religion has been a well-kept secret, but it is no longer in question, with books by Portelli, Masutti, La Rocca, Vasale, and Vinco. However, since, Gramsci sees the politics in religion, and the religion in politics, this means that socialist revolution is only one of his concerns, and that a reconstruction of even his *political* thought cannot limit itself to his theories of hegemony and of the party.

58 See Chapter 1 above.

59 See Chapter 1.

60 Valuable comparisons between Gramsci and Marx may be found in W. L. Adamson, *Hegemony and Revolution*, and in T. Nemeth, *Gramsci's Philosophy*.

4. BUKHARIN AND THE THEORY AND PRACTICE OF SCIENCE

1 The following account of these controversies is adapted from D. Joravsky, *Soviet Marxism and Natural Science, 1917–1932*, pp. 46–61 and

93–106; from S. F. Cohen, *Bukharin and the Bolshevik Revolution*, pp. 107–22; and from *idem*, "Marxist Theory and Bolshevik Policy: The Case of Bukharin's *Historical Materialism*."

2   Joravsky, *Soviet Marxism and Natural Science*, p. 51.

3   *Soviet Marxism*, p. 48; Cohen, *Bukharin*, p. 109.

4   *Soviet Marxism*, pp. 47–50.

5   *Bukharin*, p. 110.

6   *Ibid.*, p. 122.

7   *Ibid.*, p. 107.

8   *Ibid.*, p. 108.

9   *Ibid.*, p. 110.

10   *Ibid.*, p. 109.

11   *Ibid.*, p. 121.

12   *Quaderni del carcere*, pp. 1396–1401, 1411–16, 1418–20, and 1424–26.

13   *Ibid.*, pp. 1401–3, 1424–26, 1445–47.

14   *Ibid.*, pp. 1406–11, 1434–38, 1487–91.

15   Almost everything on pp. 1396–1430 of the *Quaderni*, other than the passages just quoted, but esp. pp. 1403–6.

16   For example, *Quaderni*, pp. 1420–22.

17   For example, *ibid.*, pp. 1422, 1439–42.

18   See, for example, *ibid.*, pp. 1448–49.

19   *Ibid.*, p. 1434.

20   *Ibid.*, pp. 1404–5.

21   *Ibid.*, pp. 1420–22.

22   *Ibid.*, p. 1406; cf. Bukharin's *Historical Materialism*, pp. 27–30.

23   *Quaderni del carcere*, pp. 1417–18, 1450, 1442–45, respectively.

24   *Ibid.*, pp. 1416–17.

25   *Archiv für Geschichte des Sozialismus und der Arbeiterwegung*, pp. 216–24; and "Technology and Social Relations," pp. 27–34.

26   "Technology and Social Relations," p. 34.

27   *Ibid.*

28   *Ibid.*, p. 27.

29   *Ibid.*

30   *Ibid.*, p. 28.

31   *Ibid.*

32   *Ibid.*

33   *Ibid.*, p. 29, italics in the original.

34   *Ibid.*, p. 33.

35   *Ibid.*, pp. 29–32.

36   See my *History of Science as Explanation*, pp. 223–28.

37   See my *Galileo and the Art of Reasoning*, pp. 157–64.

38   Lukács, "Technology and Social Relations," pp. 29–30; cf. Bukharin, *Historical Materialism*, pp. 120–21.

39   Lukács, "Technology and Social Relations," p. 30.

40 *Ibid.*, p. 31.
41 *Ibid.*, p. 29.
42 *Ibid.*, p. 30.
43 *Ibid.*, p. 32.
44 *Ibid.*
45 *Ibid.*, p. 33.
46 *Ibid.*, p. 29.
47 *Ibid.*, p. 32.
48 *Ibid.*, p. 32.
49 *Ibid.*
50 Quoted by Lukács, "Technology," pp. 32–33.
51 Quoted by Lukács, *ibid.*, p. 33.
52 *Ibid.*, p. 33; italics in the original.
53 Hereafter in this chapter, page reference to Bukharin's *Historical Materialism* will be made in parenthesis in the text, as here.
54 See Chapter 3, section on "Bukharin and Marxism."
55 See Chapter 3.
56 For those acquainted with Karl Popper's terminology, which may cause confusion to those who are not, we might say that the same description applies to Bukharin as Popper applies to Marx, namely, that although he is a "methodological individualist," he opposes "psychologism." Popper's "anti-psychologism" would correspond to what I am here calling "methodological sociologism," whereas his "methodological individualism" would correspond to what I am calling "ontological" or "metaphysical" individualism. See K. Popper, *The Open Society and Its Enemies*, pp. 87–99.
57 Cf. Chapters 6 and 7 of the present volume.
58 Quoted in D. Hoffman, "Bukharin's Theory of Equilibrium," p. 128, from Lenin's "Testament," *New Leader*, p. 567.
59 Cohen, *Bukharin*, p. 109.
60 For some related arguments, see my *Galileo and the Art of Reasoning*, pp. 332–41 and 421–24.
61 Quoted from Bukharin by Cohen as the epigraph of chap. 4 of his *Bukharin*.

5. GRAMSCI'S DIALECTICAL INTERPRETATION OF MACHIAVELLI'S POLITICS

1 A. Gramsci, *Lettere dal carcere*, p. 390.
2 We may also add that this step has some initial plausibility in view of the widespread equation, or at least association, among (1) Marx's politics, (2) Marxist politics, (3) Leninism, (4) opportunistic ruthlessness, (5) Machiavellianism, and (6) Machiavelli's politics. Examples of explicit association of 3, 4, and 5 may be found in C. Vigna, "Gramsci e l'egemonia," p. 60, and S. Hook, *Marxism and Beyond*, p. 81.

3 A. Gramsci, *Quaderni del carcere.*
4 A. Gramsci, *Note sul Machiavelli, sulla politica e sullo stato moderno,* pp. 11–12.
5 A. Gramsci, *Selections from the Prison Notebooks,* pp. 136–37.
6 G. Sasso, "Antonio Gramsci, interprete di Machiavelli," p. 92.
7 The second and third objections may be found in F. Alderisio, "Ripresa machiavelliana. Considerazioni critiche sulle idee di A. Gramsci, di B. Croce e di L. Russo intorno a Machiavelli," p. 213, n. 11.
8 As before, parenthetical references in the text are to Gramsci's *Quaderni.*
9 These are: Notebook No. 3, par. 128; Not. 8, pars. 52, 62, 69, 79, 141, 244; Not. 9, pars. 19, 21, 25, 27, 40, 62, 64, 68, 69, 70, 88, 133, 136, and 142; Not. 13, pars. 6, 7, 11, 12, 15, 18, 19, 22, 23, 24, and 26–40; Not. 14, pars. 53 and 68; Not. 15, pars. 2, 6, 7, 8, 11, 15, 17, 25, 47, 48, and 50; Not. 17, pars. 7, 37, 39, 41, 50, and 51.
10 These are: Not. 2, par. 36; Not. 4, par. 29; Not. 5, par. 115; Not. 6, par. 66; and Not. 18, par. 2.
11 These are: Not. 1, pars. 10 and 150; Not. 2, pars. 31 and 41; Not. 3, par. 47; Not. 4, pars. 4, 8, 10, 38, and 56; Not. 5, pars. 20, 25, 55, and 127; Not. 6, pars. 50, 52, 79, 85, 86, 110, and 130; Not. 8, pars. 21, 37, 43, 44, 48, 58, 61, 78, 84, 86, 114, 132, 162, and 163; Not. 9, par. 40; Not. 10, pars. 41.X and 61; Not. 13, pars. 1–5, 8–10, 12–14, 16, 17, 20, 21, 23, and 25; Not. 14, pars. 32, 33, and 51; Not. 15, pars. 4, 10, 16, and 72; Not. 17, par. 27; Not. 18, pars. 1–3.
12 A similar distinction between the historical and the conceptual aspects of Gramsci's interest in Machiavelli has been asserted also by L. Paggi, "Machiavelli and Gramsci," now in *Le strategie del potere in Gramsci,* p. 387. However, he motivates the distinction on the basis of a single Gramscian remark, and in the course of his lengthy discussion he does not, in fact, give a clear account of the two aspects; this is not to deny that his historical account is otherwise valuable and often insightful. See my *Gramsci critico e la critica,* chap. 8.
13 Not. 1, par. 10; Not. 2, pars. 31 and 41; Not. 4, pars. 8 and 10; Not. 6, pars. 85, 86, and 110; Not. 8, pars. 21, 43, 48, 78, 84, 114, and 162; Not. 13, pars. 1, 3, 5, 13, 16, 20, 21, 25, 32, 33; Not. 17, par. 27; and Not. 18, par. 3.
14 Not. 4, pars. 38 and 56; Not. 5, par. 127; Not. 6, pars. 79 and 130; Not. 8, pars. 37, 48, 56, 61, 86, 132, and 163; Not. 9, par. 40; Not. 10, par. 41.X; Not. 13, pars. 2, 5, 8, 10, 14, 17, and 23; Not. 14, par. 51; Not. 15, pars. 4, 10, 16, and 72.
15 Not. 1, par. 150; Not. 2, par. 31; Not. 3, par. 47; Not. 4, par. 4; Not. 5, pars. 20, 25, and 55; Not. 6, pars. 50 and 52; Not. 8, pars. 44 and 58; Not. 10, par. 61; Not. 13, pars. 4, 9, and 12; Not. 18, par. 1.
16 This is my reconstruction of the following notes: Not. 1, par. 10; Not. 2, par. 41; Not. 4, par. 10; Not. 8, pars. 21 and 114; Not. 13, pars. 1, 13, and 21; Not. 17, par. 27; and Not. 18, par. 3.

17 Cf. Not. 4, par. 8; Not. 13, pars. 20 and 25; and Not. 14, par. 33;
18 Cf. Not. 6, pars. 85, 86, and 110; Not. 8, pars. 43 and 84; and Not. 13, pars. 5 and 16.
19 See also A. Gramsci, Letter to Tania of May 14, 1932, in *Lettere dal carcere*, p. 589.
20 Not. 1, par. 10; Not. 8, pars. 78 and 162; and Not. 13, par. 13.
21 Cf. Not. 4, par. 56; Not. 8, par. 61; Not. 10, par. 41.X; and Not. 13, par. 10.
22 Gramsci's qualm is whether it is perhaps a contradiction in terms to speak of the *dialectic* of distincts, insofar as "dialectic" should refer to the process of opposition or contradiction. This semantical problem could perhaps be bypassed by speaking of the principle of the distincts. Or, alternatively, one can face the question head on and argue, as Milton Fisk has recently done, that the concept of contradiction itself needs to be generalized precisely to allow for differences or distinctions, in addition to oppositions and contrarieties; see his "Dialectic and Ontology," pp. 120–21 and 125–29. See also Chapter 6 below.
23 See Chapter 3 above.
24 K. Marx, *Critique of Hegel's Philosophy of Right*, p. 92.
25 R. Kilminster, *Praxis and Method: A Sociological Dialogue with Lukács, Gramsci and the Early Frankfurt School*, pp. 109–23 and 230–69.
26 Not. 8, par. 48; Not. 13, par. 5; and Not. 15, par. 72. Cf. the analysis just given of Machiavelli's politics versus Guicciardini's diplomacy in Not. 6, par. 86 and 110, and in Not. 13, par. 16.
27 For a more general discussion of the question, see my *Galileo and the Art of Reasoning*, chap. 15; for some other applications, see my "Methodological Criticism and Critical Methodology: An Analysis of Popper's Critique of Marxian Social Science."
28 B. Croce, *Etica e politica*, p. 205.
29 B. Croce, *Materialismo storico ed economia marxistica*, p. 104; cf. Gramsci, *Quaderni del carcere*, p. 1315.
30 Note that it cannot be mere coincidence that Gramsci entitled this special Notebook No. 13 "Noterelle sulla politica del Machiavelli," which is obviously reminiscent of Croce's "Noterelle per la storia della filosofia della politica," included in Croce's *Etica e politica*. The explicit recognition of this similarity of titles is perhaps the most interesting point in F. Sanguineti, *Gramsci e Machiavelli*, discussed on page 67, although the author adds that one must admit the difference in problem-situation between Gramsci and Croce, otherwise one is forced to dismiss the Gramscian view of Machiavelli as obsolete.
    It is also worth noting that, together with Croce's essays on Marx (in *Materialismo storico ed economia marxistica*), his "Noterelle per la storia della filosofia della politica" are copiously marked and annotated, more so than any of the books Gramsci read in prison, which usually he did not mark at all. I have been able to establish this by directly con-

sulting these books, which are now kept in the so-called Fondo Gramsci at the Istituto Gramsci in Rome.

31 See, for example, A. Showstack Sassoon, *Gramsci's Politics*, esp. p. 12.

32 Cf. Chapters 6 and 7 below.

33 For present purposes, this connection between judiciousness and judgment may be taken as a nominal definition, designed to suggest that there are similarities between Gramsci's procedure here and some of what goes on in those practical, fine, and deliberational arts where judgment is paradigmatic.

34 In stressing this antimechanism of dialectic, I am aware of ignoring the dynamic, developmental element of the concept. I would want to argue that such dynamicism is primaily a substantive feature of the entities most commonly dealt with in a dialectical approach, whereas for the moment I am dealing with the nature of dialectic as an approach.

35 See Chapters 6 and 7 below. I believe that such an enlargement of the concept also accords with the generalization of the concept of contradiction suggested in M. Fisk, "Dialectic and Ontology"; his critique of atomistic ontology and his emphasis on complex entities are the metaphysical counterparts of the judgmental and dialectical methodology here being attributed to Gramsci.

36 Gramsci is referring to, among other things, Marx's critique of Proudhon, in *The Poverty of Philosophy*, pp. 103–26 (chap. 2, "The Metaphysics of Political Economy," par. 1, "On Method"). For an appreciation of this problem, see N. Bobbio, "Nota sulla dialettica in Gramsci," pp. 82–84. The importance of this particular problem and, more generally, of the problem of dialectical politics may also be seen from a recent analysis of the post–World War II political situation in Italy by a leader of the Italian Socialist Party; Giuseppe Tamburrano, author of an earlier important work on Gramsci (*Antonio Gramsci. La vita, il pensiero, l'azione*), recently analyzed and criticized the fact that the general rule practiced by almost everyone in Italy is "si collude e non si collide" ("collusion rather than collision"), that is to say, "the image of the great politician in Italy is not that of someone who has a clear idea and puts it into practice, but that of someone who succeeds in confusing clear ideas, to cut options in half, in short to mediate the contradictions in order to come to a provisional and compromise solution" (*Perchè solo in Italia no*, pp. 124–25).

6. GRAMSCI'S POLITICAL TRANSLATION OF HEGELIAN-MARXIAN DIALECTIC

1 Gramsci, *Lettere dal carcere*, p. 390.

2 N. Bobbio, "Nota sulla dialettica in Gramsci," p. 73.

3 *Ibid.*

4 In that growth industry which is the interpretation and criticism of Gramsci, explicit studies of the dialectic are so few that they can be

profitably reviewed here. E. Fubini's 1967 bibliography of Gramsci studies from 1922 to 1967 (in *Gramsci e la cultura contemporanea*, vol. 2, pp. 477–544) lists about 1,100 entries. Her 1977 bibliography (in *Politica e storia in Gramsci*, vol. 2, pp. 649–733) lists about 1,500 entries. Of these 2,600 publications, only 4, to be discussed later in this note deal *explicitly* with the dialectic. *Implicitly*, of course, almost every publication on Gramsci deals with the concept. The neglect extends to book-length works published after 1977. For example, W. L. Adamson's otherwise excellent *Hegemony and Revolution: Antonio Gramsci's Political and Cultural Theory* does not even include "dialectic" in its index and discusses it only indirectly on pp. 9–10 and 130–39. The explicit studies are: N. Bobbio, "Nota sulla dialettica in Gramsci"; N. Vaccaro, "La dialettica quantità-qualità in Gramsci"; F. De Angelis, "Gramsci and Croce: The Living, the Dead, Marxism, and the Dialectic"; and P. Cristofolini, "Sulla dialettica di Gramsci e la storia filosofica delle 'facoltà.'" These are the most significant studies for our specific purpose here, that is, as an introduction to the conceptual problem of the dialectic in Gramsci. For the general purpose of merely becoming acquainted with Gramsci's concept, the most explicit discussion in English is perhaps that found in J. Joll, *Antonio Gramsci*, pp. 109–11; this, as Joll indicates in a footnote, is merely a summary of Bobbio's analysis. For the purpose of learning some of the general and specific uses of the concept of the dialectic by Gramsci, the topic is discussed in passing in A. Davidson's *Antonio Gramsci*; A. S. Sassoon's *Gramsci's Politics*; T. Nemeth's *Gramsci's Philosophy*; W. L. Adamson's *Hegemony and Revolution*; L. Salamini' *Sociology of Political Praxis*; and J. Femia's *Gramsci's Political Thought*. Despite the great differences among these works, they all share a neglect of the dialectic, and so it should be repeated that their discussions of the dialectic, however useful, are relatively indirect and implicit.

The first explicit analysis is still the best; it is "Nota sulla dialettica in Gramsci," by Bobbio. He reaches three conclusions, dealing respectively with the importance, meaning, and function of the concept. It is not hard for him to establish that for Gramsci, the dialectic has fundamental importance, and that this importance is by no means limited to philosophy but extends to history, politics, and economics; the reason is that, just as these activities are distinguished *conceptually* but not *separated* from each other by the philosophical science of the dialectic, the latter "cannot be separated, as theory of method, from the application of the method to problems of historical, economic, and political interpretation" (p. 75), and hence theory and application of the dialectic are merely conceptually distinct.

Bobbio's second thesis is that Gramsci means three different things by the term "dialectic" (and its derivatives). One meaning refers to the reciprocal interaction between two entities of a relationship or connection, and between two parts of a whole unity; examples of dialectically constituted pairs, that is, pairs whose elements reciprocally act on each other, are: man and nature, the intellectuals and the masses, theory and practice, and structure and superstructure. Gramsci's second meaning refers to the triad of "thesis-antithesis-synthesis," and in these contexts he speaks of a dialectical process, movement, development, or becoming. Third, "dialectic" refers to the transition from quantity to quality or quality to quantity. Bobbio notes in passing that these three meanings correspond, respectively, to Engels's three dialectical laws of the unity of opposites, the negation of the negation, and quantity-quality conversion, and that the second law is the most important and most typically Hegelian one.

Regarding the function of the dialectic, Bobbio gives two examples to show how central the concept is. Gramsci's philosophy of praxis may be seen with some plausibility the way he himself saw it, namely, as a dialectical synthesis of materialism and idealism; in particular, he criticizes Bukharin's work for being mechanist and undialectical, and Croce's for being pseudodialectical, that is, for pretending to be dialectical but not actually being so, since Croce took seriously the concept but not the actual process of dialectical becoming. Bobbio also discusses how Gramsci justifies his revolutionism by criticizing the tradition of Proudhon, Quinet, Cuoco, Gioberti, and Croce himself; what is wrong with their history and politics, according to Gramsci, is that their moderate approach mutilates the dialectic by trying to prevent the actual process of thesis-antithesis-synthesis from taking place, that is, by arbitrarily proposing an intellectualistically invented synthesis without letting the contradiction between the thesis and antithesis work itself out.

Bobbio does not have much to say on the dialectic of quantity and quality, although he does mention it. But another early study of Gramsci's dialectic, by Nicola Vaccaro, deals with precisely that topic.

Vaccaro tries to make the dialectic of quantity and quality all pervasive. He claims that "in the category of quantity we see contained the concepts of structure, necessity, economic life, while in that of quality those of superstructure, freedom, mind" (" La dialettica quantità-qualità in Gramsci," p. 328), as well as practice and theory, and nature and man, respectively. Then he finds this dialectic within each term of these pairs; for example, referring to material conditions, he says that "here precisely the quantity-quality dialectic inserts itself insofar as the historical homogeneity of the base or structure is not a mechanical but a contradictory homogeneity" (p. 330); and referring to the fact that measurement can be extended to the sphere of human activities, he says that "precisely this measurability brings the quantity-quality dialectic inside the very superstructure" (p. 331). Vaccaro's dialectic of quantity and quality seems to extend even to the process of thesis-antithesis-synthesis, when he says that "historical becoming is given by the development of the contradictions between man and matter" (p. 325), and when he speaks of "historical becoming as a process which develops not in a vulgarly evolutionary manner, but by means of the transition from quantity to quality" (p. 327). If Vaccaro had, like Bobbio, distinguished several meanings of the dialectic, and if he was now trying to interrelate them or even reduce them to one, all of this might make some sense. But the only meaning he recognizes is that of "the dialectical connection between two terms, that is, their reciprocal relation and action" (p. 328). Hence, his account lacks coherence; or, if we do not want to prejudge the matter, at least the apparent inconsistency between his study and Bobbio's yields the problem of whether there are really several meanings of "dialectic" in Gramsci, and whether they are reducible to one. Moreover, since Bobbio thinks that the concept of thesis-antithesis-synthesis is the most important, another problem is determining which concept such primacy belongs to.

Two more recent works are significant because they suggest a fourth different meaning of dialectic, or at least a fourth feature of the ultimately one and only concept of dialectic. In the course of criticizing Gramsci's sharp distinction between the works of Marx and those of Engels as undialectical, Frank De Angelis objects that "a dialectical analysis always connects the identity with the difference. The concrete totality is concrete to the extent that it is a unity of diverse elements" ("Gramsci and Croce," p. 44). Similarly, while praising a recent important book on Gramsci, Paolo Cristofolini claims that this book is "working within Gramsci's Marxism ("Sulla dialettica di Gramsci," p. 68), and that to do so amounts to "a dialecticization, in the sense of a decomposition and recomposition, of a series of concepts" (p. 69) of great importance.

Without discussing the *accuracy* of this criticism and this praise, we may say that their *relevance* to Gramsci presupposes that such a view of the dialectic is part of his concept. But neither of these authors makes any attempt to justify such relevance with textual evidence. It happens that it is possible to find appreciation in Gramsci for the substantive content of the idea referred to by these authors. For example, we find him saying that "the most delicate, misunderstood, and yet essential skill of the critic of ideas and of the historian of developments is to find the real identity under the apparent differentiation and contradiction, and to find the substantial diversity under the apparent identity" (*Quaderni*, p. 2268). But this raises a problem, since Gramsci is not labeling such a principle with the term "dialectical." The problem is that we need to determine whether such an approach belongs to Gramsci's concept of the dialectic or to his concept of something else.

Besides these problems internal to the secondary literature, there are others. First, at the time these studies were made, scholars were hampered by not having a critical edition of Gramsci's Prison Notebooks, which is available today, and thus what was available to them was incomplete, as Bobbio for one explicitly recognized. Another difficulty is that the accounts are merely expository (with respect to the dialectic) and it would be desirable to have some evaluation of Gramsci's views. Third, the approaches lack a dialectical character, so to speak; that is, they do not present the problems Gramsci was discussing, and thus we are deprived of a deeper insight into his views, which can be understood better when seen as overcoming problems.

Finally, I should mention three studies not included in Fubini's bibliographies. L. Sichirollo's otherwise useful history (*La dialettica*, 1973) concludes with a section on Gramsci but discusses primarily Gramsci's views on history, the historical bloc, and ideology, rather than on the dialectic as such. A. Petterlini's "La dialettica in Gramsci" (1979) is more relevant, and he even speaks of the ambiguity of Gramsci's concept, but this ambiguity has little in common with the one documented here. And F. Fergnani's interpretation of Gramsci's views on the dialectic of nature (*La filosofia della prassi nei "Quaderni del carcere,"* pp. 83–84) is similar to the one developed in this chapter, but he fails to see that for Gramsci the dialectic has other meanings than one I discuss in the section on "Dialectic and Reformism," which I call the "triadic law of development" or "law of the dialectical clash."

5   These are best denoted by referring to the critical edition (Gramsci, *Quaderni del carcere*, ed. Gerratana) by notebook, and by paragraph number, placing the latter in pointed brackets as this edition does. Moreover, when a given note has two different versions – an earlier one, which the critical edition calls type "A" text, and a later one, which it calls type "C" text – I write the numbers for the "A" text in parenthesis after the "C" text. For example, 13<27>(9<133>) denotes Notebook 13, paragraph 27, for which there is an earlier version in Notebook 9, paragraph 133. The thirty-one notes here are: 4<57>, 6<30>, 8<20>, 8<36>, 9<26>, 10–I<6>(8<225.4,6>), 10–II<41.XIV>(8<25,27,39>), 10–II<41.XVI>, 13<18>, 13<23>(9<40>), 13<27>(9<133>), 15<6>, 15<11>, 15<15>, 15<17>, 15<25>, 15<36>, 15<60>, 15<62>, 16<16>(9<97>), 17<37>, 19<53>(3<125>).

6   11<22.IV>(7<29>).

7   11<22>(7<20>), 11<30>(4<25>), 11<34>(4<43,47>), 11<37>(4<41>), and 11<62>(4<40,45>).

8   11<15>(8<197>), 11<26>, and 11<32>(4<32>).

9   3<56>, 6<128>, 11<67>(4<33>), 13<36.2>(9<68>), 13<38>(1<48,49>), 14<48>, and 15<13>.

10   11<6>(8<178,221>), 11<16>, 11<33>(4<39>), 11<41>(8<183>), and 11<44>(4<18,21>).

11 1<44>, 7<16>, 10–I<12>, 13<7>(8<52>), 13<17>(4<38>), 13<18>, 14<35>, and 14<68>.

12 10–II<1>, 10–II<41.I>(7<1>), 10–II<41.X>(4<56>), 10–II<59.III,IV>, and 13<10>(8<61>).

13 8<182>, 10–II<6.I>, 10–II<41.I>, 10–II<48.II>, and 11<12>.

14 10–II<1>, 11<62>, and 16<9>.

15 6<30>, 11<16>, 11<62>(4<45>), 13<40>(1<87>), and 24<3>(1<43>).

16 Gramsci, *Quaderni*, p. 1247; as here, subsequent page references to this book appear in parentheses in the text.

17 Gramsci, *Lettere dal carcere*, p. 629. For a recognition of this connection between dialectic and immanence, but a different interpretation of immanence, see G. Perrotti, "Gramsci, Ricardo e la filosofia della prassi," esp. pp. 127–47.

18 Cf. also Notebook 4, paragraph <45>, Q471.

19 Notebook 10–II, paragraph <9>; and *Lettere*, pp. 628–30. Gramsci also discusses (10–II<8> and 11<52>) the dialectical significance of Ricardo's concept of necessity and method of the "given that," but since these are said to pertain to the dialectic of quantity and quality, their importance is secondary. My analysis may be contrasted to G. Perrotti, "Gramsci, Ricardo e la filosofia della prassi"; while regarding these notions as constitutive of Ricardo's "immanence," he emphasizes the element of regularity and relative stability, which he then equates with Gramsci's conception of science. Despite Perrotti's attempt to interpret such "immanentistic" regularity and stability in a nonmetaphysical, nonnaturalistic fashion, the account sounds too positivistic to be a plausible interpretation of Gramsci.

20 See, for example, Q1478.

21 Q1265.

22 Notebook 10–II<33>, <36>.

23 K. Marx, *Capital*, vol. 3, chap. 13.

24 B. Croce, *Materialismo storico ed economia marxistica*.

25 K. Marx, *Capital*, vol. 1, chap. 12.

26 Q53, 54, 2032, and 2034. Cf. K. Marx and F. Engels, "Address to the Central Committee of the Communist League," in R. C. Tucker, ed., *The Marx-Engels Reader*, pp. 501–11.

27 Q1361; cf. Q1566, 1642, 2017, and 2034.

28 E.g., Q331, 423, 1468, 1471, and 2028.

29 Chapter 4, par. 4, "Critical Gloss No. 3." Cf. K. Marx and F. Engels, *The Holy Family: Or Critique of Critical Critique*, p. 55.

30 Q2024.

31 A similar analysis of Gramsci's notion of dialectic has also been given by A. Orsucci, "Del materialismo 'crudo.'" The context of his discussion is different, and he is not as explicit as I am here, but his paper can be read with great profit by the interested reader.

32 Q1283, 1279. A helpful discussion of this problem may be found in N. Matteucci, *Antonio Gramsci e la filosofia della prassi,* pp. 98–103. His way out is analogous to mine, although the context of his discussion is the relationship between Gramsci's account of the Risorgimento and his political commitment. Especially enlightening is Matteucci's reference to Croce's similar formulation of the problem, and his contrast between the Gramscian approach and the sectarian, classist approach advocated by Marxists who subscribe to Zdanovism.

33 11<16>(8<171>, <206>, <211>), 11<22.IV>(7<29>), 11<33>(4<39>), and 11<44>(4<18>,<21>).

34 Q1461–65.

35 Q1462. Cf. F. Engels, *Anti-Dühring,* pp. 19 and 31.

36 I am aware that some passages may *seem* to indicate that the dialectic is the "antithesis" of formal logic, a claim made, for example, by Bobbio ("Nota sulla dialettica in Gramsci," p. 76). I would question this interpretation as follows: When Gramsci says that "the lack of historical sense in perceiving the different aspects of a process of historical development [is] a viewpoint that is antidialectical, dogmatic, imprisoned in the abstract schemes of formal logic" (Q1408, cf. Bobbio, "Nota," p. 76), this does indeed show that he conceives of the dialectic as opposed to dogmatism and one-sidedness, a conception that has also been supported with other evidence in this chapter; concerning formal logic, however, the opposition is not between it and the dialectic but between the dialectic and *being imprisoned in the abstract schemes* of logic, which is a different thing, and which in fact presupposes that the "imprisonment" is not a necessity. Similarly, it is true that in his critique of Bukharin, Gramsci states that "dialectical thinking goes against vulgar common sense, which is dogmatic, eager for imperious certainties, and has formal logic as its expression" (Q1425; cf. Bobbio, "Nota," p. 76); but he goes on to clarify his meaning by comparing the relationship between logic and dialectic to that between elementary and relativistic or quantum physics. Although Gramsci does not elaborate and seems unaware of the problematic character of this latter relationship, if one pays close attention to scientific practice and avoids philosophical artificialities and externalistic impositions à la Popper, Feyerabend, and Kuhn, this relationship is best interpreted as one being an approximation to the other, or as the two dealing with different domains of reality.

37 Q1464, 1425–26.

38 Q1463.

39 Q1464.

40 Q1374–95.

41 Cf. Notebook 1<43>, Q33–34. The fact that this idea appears at the very beginning as well as toward the end (Notebook 24<3>, Q2268) of the Notebooks is evidence of Gramsci's deep commitment to it. The

only other author who has called attention to this passage is Pasquale Misuraca, "Politica, economia, diritto, sociologia come scienze dello Stato," p. 69.

42 Q1410, 1425, 1461. Gramsci is thinking primarily of Nikolai I. Bukharin, whose *Historical Materialism: A System of Sociology* contains a chapter entitled "Dialectic Materialism" and is, of course, the subject of an extended critique in the Notebooks (see Chapter 3 in the present volume). He also has in mind G. Plekhanov, whose *Fundamental Problems of Marxism* is mentioned by Gramsci on Q1461.

43 Q1410.

44 Q1442.

45 Q1449.

46 Georg Lukács, *History and Class Consciousness*, p. 24, n. 6. However, in the 1967 preface, Lukács seems to have taken back this dichotomy (pp. xvi–xvii).

47 Q451, 466, and 1446–47. Cf. Notebooks 4<40>, 8<197>, 10–II<9>, 11<14>(8<186>), 11<15>, 11<26>, 11<30>(4<25>), 11<32>(4<32>), and 11<62>.

48 Q1248, 1443, and 1455–57.

49 Cf. Q1054, 1059, 1248, 1403, and 1432.

50 Q1403–5. Cf. Chapter 4 in the present volume.

51 Cf. 3<56>, 6<128>, 11<67>(4<33>), 13<36.2>(9<68>), 13<38>(1<48>,<49>), 14<38.2>, 14<48>, and 15<13>.

52 See, for example, A. S. Sassoon, *Gramsci's Politics*, pp. 162–72.

53 Q1633 and 1139.

54 Q796 (6<128>), Q1650–51, and Q1707.

55 Most of the time Gramsci calls the objectionable type "organic centralism." But the phrase "bureaucratic centralism," which he sometimes employs, has more common usage, as a contrast with "democratic centralism"; this semantic convention is one reason for my choice in the text. Another reason is that, as Gramsci points out, "organic centralism" is a misnomer since "an organic nature can only belong to democractic centralism . . . it is 'organic' because it takes change into account, which is the organic manner in which historical reality reveals itself" (Q1634). Moreover, referring to the undesirable form, Gramsci says that "the more exact name would be that of bureaucratic centralism" (Q1634). Thus, there is no *conceptual* confusion in Gramsci; rather, the proper contrast is between bureaucratic and democratic centralism.

56 Q1642 and 1650. That is, in 13<38>(Q1650), Gramsci states that "the tie between organic [bureaucratic] centralism and Maurras is evident," and in 13<37>(Q1642) he gives an account of Maurras's role in French national life, declaring among other things that "Maurras is often exalted as a great statesman and as a very great *Realpolitiker*; in reality he is only an upside-down Jacobin."

57 Q1633.

58 Cf. the passage on Q2268 quoted earlier, in the section on "Logic and Dialectic."

59 A clear discussion of this distinction may be found in C. Buci-Glucksmann, "Sui problemi politici della transizione: classe operaia e rivoluzione passiva," esp. pp. 110–111.

60 This important insight is owed to Buci-Glucksmann, "Sui problemi politici della transizione," esp. pp. 112 and 124. Cf. 15<59>,<62>.

61 See, for example, Q1220.

62 Q1566 (13<7>) and Q1582 (13<17>).

63 6<138>, 7<16>, 10–I<12>, 13<7>(8<52>), 13<17>(4<38>), 13<18>, 13<27>(9<133>), 14<35>, 14<68>, and 19<24>(1<44>).

64 Q1235 and Q1566.

65 This correspondence is also suggested by A. Orsucci, "Del materialismo 'crudo.'" Again, his essay contains interesting and useful comments but does not contain a detailed elaboration of exactly what "dialectic" and "hegemony" are, on the basis of which they are to be identified.

66 In this interpretation I am heavily indebted to V. Gerratana, "Gramsci come pensatore revoluzionario," esp. pp. 92–99. He discusses the significance of Gramsci's dialectical modification of the Marxian text, which has an inferential connective relating the two principles.

67 This interpretation is also owed to Gerratana, "Gramsci come pensatore rivoluzionario," p. 96.

68 6<138>, 7<16>, 13<18> (Q1596), 14<68>, 19<24> (Q2032, Q2034).

69 4<57>, 8<20>, 8<36>, 9<26>, 10–I<6>(8<225.4,6>), 10–II<41.XIV>(8<25>, 8<27>, 8<39>), 10–II<41.XVI>, 13<18>:Q1591–92, 13<23>:Q1611–13 (9<40>), 13<27> (9<133>), 15<6>, 15<11>, 15<15>, 15<17>, 15<25>, 15<36>, 15<59.I>, 15<60>, 15<62>, 16<16>(9<97>), 17<37>, and 19<53>:Q2074–75(3<125>).

70 As his thinking developed, Gramsci suggested applying the concept to such historical developments as Fordism in American industry and fascism, and his interpreters have often argued plausibly that his notes also justify treating Stalinism as a passive revolution. Gramsci devoted one notebook (no. 22) explicitly to "Americanism and Fordism" (Q2137–81). On fascism, a useful study is W. L. Adamson's "Gramsci's Interpretation of Fascism." On Stalinism, see Buci-Glucksmann, "Sui problemi politici della transizione."

71 Q1767.

72 8<36> and 15<11>.

73 The notion of the "enlargement of the state" is insightfully elaborated in Buci-Glucksmann, "Sui problemi," esp. pp. 109–11, as part of her analysis of Gramsci's concept of passive revolution.

74 As stated in note 92, I owe this analogy between passive revolution

and bureaucratic centralism to Buci-Glucksmann's "Sui problemi," although her emphasis is *not* on the dialectic. Cf. 15<59> and 15<62>.

75 The tendential character of the concept is made clear by Buci-Glucksmann, "Sui problemi."

76 Q1766–67.

77 10–I<6>(8<225.4,6>), 10–II<41.XIV>(8<25>,<27>,<39>), 10–II<41.XVI>, 15<11>, 15<36>, 15<60> and 15<62>.

78 "Nota sulla dialettica in Gramsci."

79 I think Gerratana is correct in judging that although "to define Gramsci as a revolutionary thinker has the character of a simple self-evident truth if the term 'revolutionary' is used with the prevailing common meaning" ("Gramsci come pensatore rivoluzionario," p. 69), we can also make the following "essentially tautological judgment: if revolutionary is what extremism theorizes as such, Gramsci certainly is not that" (*ibid.*).

80 Q1221 and 1825.

81 13<23>:Q1611–13.

82 Q1612.

83 The term "anti-passive-revolution," as well as a conceptual analysis and a discussion of its significance, is owed to Buci-Glucksmann, "Sui problemi politici della transizione."

84 10–II<1>:Q1240, 10–II<41.I>:Q1300(7<1>:Q854), 10–II<41.X>:Q1316(4<56>:Q503), 10–II<59.IV>:Q1355, 11<12>:Q1386, 11<44>:Q1462–63, and 13<10>(8<61>).

85 For the views being summarized here, see B. Croce, *Logica*, esp. pt. 1, sec. 1, chaps. 5 and 6; and *idem, Ciò che è vivo e ciò che è morto della filosofia di Hegel*, esp. chaps. 1–4. Cf. Chapter 2 in the present volume.

86 Croce, *Saggio sullo Hegel*, p. 65.

87 See also Q854, 503, and 1240.

88 E.g., 8<182>.

89 E.g., Q1386.

90 Q977, 1316, and 1569.

91 Cf. also Q978 and 1861.

92 To my knowledge, no scholar has even shown awareness of the problematic meaning of Gramsci's phrase, let alone tried to give a coherent interpretation. This applies to E. Agazzi's "Filosofia della prassi e filosofia dello spirito," a study that as recently as 1977 was described, with some justice, as "perhaps the most pertinent to understand and to evaluate the relationship between Gramsci and Croceanism," by Marino Biondi (*Guida bibliografica a Gramsci*, p. 25). Agazzi does, of course, report and summarize Gramsci's critique (pp. 99–100), but his more obscure remarks are not included. Bobbio ("Nota sulla dialettica") avoids the phrase altogether. Adamson (*Hegemony and Revolution*), who, of course, is *not* primarily concerned with this topic, says on p.

127 that "for Gramsci . . . not only did his [Croce's] 'dialectic of distincts' suppress entirely the moment of antithesis, but it was conceived
as a 'pure conceptual dialectic,' " but on p. 181 he says that for Croce
"distincts are therefore not to be grasped dialectically," without resolving the apparent discrepancy. Quintin Hoare and Geoffrey Nowell
Smith explain what Croce's "distincts" are, but not what the dialectic
might be in Gramsci's talk of the "dialectic of distincts" ("Introduction"
to Antonio Gramsci, *Selections from the Prison Notebooks*, p. xxiii). I might
add that my own analysis has ignored the possible meaning and validity of Gramsci's charge of *ignoratio elenchi*, when in an earlier note
he wrote: "Problem of the dialectic in Croce and his postulation of a
'dialectic of distincts': is it not a contradiction in terms, a 'ignorantia
[*sic*] elenchi'?" (4<56>:Q503). I feel justified in my omission, since
Gramsci did not repeat the charge when he subsequently rewrote the
note (10–II<41.X>:Q1315–17).

93 My argument here is similar to Alexander Kojève's view that Hegel's
own thinking is not dialectical, indeed, that "Hegel does not need a
dialectical method because the truth which he embodies is the end
result of the real or active dialectic of world history which his thought
is satisfied to reproduce through his discourse" (quoted in Ch. Perelman, "Dialectic and Dialogue," in *The New Rhetoric and the Humanities*,
p. 78, from A. Kojève, *Introduction à la lecture de Hegel*, p. 462). See
also Chapter 7 of the present volume.

7. HEGEL AND THE THEORY AND PRACTICE OF DIALECTIC

1 Perhaps I should mention a fifth approach, which simply and literally
equates "Hegel's dialectic" with "Hegel's philosophy"; from this
viewpoint an interpretation of Hegel's dialectic is an account of his
whole philosophy. This interpretation has even less textual support
than the triadic view – which is to say, none. It may be taken as
trying to make the sound point that Hegel's concept of the dialectic
is *related* to everything else in his philosophy, but that is another
story, and anyway this relation cannot be understood if one *begins*
with a *confusion*. Moreover, it should be clear that the concern of the
present inquiry is a *specific* one within Hegelian philosophy, and that
I do not intend to get involved in all the controversies surrounding
it.

2 J. E. McTaggart, *Studies in the Hegelian Dialectic*; W. T. Stace, *The Philosophy of Hegel*, pp. 92–115; and G. R. G. Mure, *A Study of Hegel's
Logic*, e.g., pp. 350–51.

3 K. Marx, *The Poverty of Philosophy*, chap. 2, par. 1; for Gramsci, see
Chapter 6 of the present volume.

4 J. N. Findlay, *Hegel: A Re-Examination*, pp. 58–82 and 346–66; and *idem, Language, Mind, and Value*, pp. 217–31.

5 B. Croce, *Ciò che è vivo e ciò che è morto della filosofia di Hegel*, chaps. 5 and 9.

6 McTaggart, *Hegelian Dialectic*, pp. 230–55; and *idem, A Commentary on Hegel's Logic.*

7 W. Kaufmann, *Hegel: Reinterpretation, Texts, and Commentary*, pp. 167–75.

8 Findlay, *Hegel*, p. 353.

9 For the importance of this element of Hegelian dialectic, see, for example, R. Franchini, *Le origini della dialettica.*

10 J. Hyppolite, *Genesis and Structure of Hegel's Phenomenology of Spirit*, pp. 3–26.

11 J. N. Findlay, "The Contemporary Relevance of Hegel," in *Language, Mind, and Value*, pp. 217–31.

12 C. Taylor, *Hegel*, pp. 127–37 and 216–31.

13 *Ibid.*, pp. 133–34.

14 *Ibid.*, p. 229.

15 "The Contemporary Relevance of Hegel," pp. 219–22.

16 *Genesis and Structure of Hegel's Phenomenology of Spirit*, pp. 19, 24.

17 *Ibid.*, p. 23.

18 "Contemporary Relevance of Hegel," p. 219.

19 G. W. F. Hegel, *Phenomenology of Spirit*, p. 55.

20 *Ibid.*, p. 11.

21 N. Hartmann, "Aristoteles und Hegel," *Kleinere Schriften*, vol. 3, pp. 214–52. Another interpreter who has elaborated a comparison of Hegel and Aristotle is G. R. G. Mure, who, in *An Introduction to Hegel*, deals with Aristotle for the first half of the book; the work is interesting in many ways, but I am not sure how Mure's interpretation of the dialectic relates to the ones being discussed here. See also R. Franchini, *Origini della dialettica*, esp. chaps. 4 and 12.

22 Aristotle, *On Sophistical Refutations*, 165b1–5; cf. Ch. Perelman, "The Dialectical Method and the Part Played by the Interlocutor in Dialogue," in *The Idea of Justice and the Problem of Argument*, pp. 164–65.

23 Hartmann, *Kleinere Schriften*, vol. 3, p. 223, as quoted in Franchini, *Origini*, p. 62.

24 N. Hartmann, *Die Philosophie des deutschen Idealismus*, vol. 2: *Hegel*, p. 155, as quoted in Hyppolite, *Genesis and Structure*, pp. 18–19.

25 N. Hartmann, "Hegel und das Problem der Realdialektik," in *Kleinere Schriften*, vol. 2, p. 345, as quoted in Ch. Perelman, "Dialectic and Dialogue," in *The New Rhetoric and the Humanities*, p. 79. Cf. Franchini, *Origini*, pp. 62, 315. For a more theoretical discussion of this distinction and its relation to dialectic, see L. Colletti, "Marxism and the Dialectic: Contradiction and Contrariety," and cf. Franchini, chap. 9 on Kant.

26 A. Kojève, *Introduction to the Reading of Hegel: Lectures on the Phenom-enology of Spirit*, e.g., pp. 170–71, 181, 185–86, 190, 192.
27 *Ibid.*, p. 212, n. 15, and pp. 216–18.
28 *Ibid.*, p. 185.
29 *Ibid.*, p. 190.
30 *Ibid.*
31 *Ibid.*, p. 176.
32 *Ibid.*, p. 259.
33 *Ibid.*, p. 183. Notice that I am quoting not merely Kojève's *assertion* that Hegel does not use the dialectical method, but also Kojève's *argument* that Hegel does not *because* he uses the phenomenological-descriptive method and *because* he presumably came at the end of philosophical history, thus being in the unique position of dispensing with an explicit, active dialectical approach. But note that this si-multaneously implies that for Kojève, as he himself points out, there is a *secondary, indirect* sense in which Hegel is using the dialectical approach, namely, insofar as *what* he is describing is dialectical (real-ity) and insofar as he correctly describes it. It is precisely Kojève's point that such a reflected dialectic is a far cry from a genuine dialectic approach. It should be added that Kojève does not mean thereby to criticize Hegel for proceeding undialectically.
34 Cf. *ibid.*, pp. 191–94.
35 See also the criticism in L. Colletti's "Hegel and the 'Theory of Reflection,'" in his *Marxism and Hegel*, pp. 52–67.
36 B. Croce, *Hegel*; G. R. G. Mure, *An Introduction to Hegel, A Study of Hegel's Logic*, and *Idealist Epilogue*; and H.-G. Gadamer, *Hegel's Di-alectic: Five Hermeneutical Studies*.
37 Croce, *Ciò che è vivo e ciò che è morto della filosofia di Hegel*, chap. 1.
38 B. Croce, *Saggio sullo Hegel*, pp. 24, 53–55. My page references are to this edition of Croce's original monograph, which is the only one in print today. Unless otherwise noted, the translations are mine.
39 See, for example, G. R. G. Mure, *A Study of Hegel's Logic*, p. 364; and J. Hyppolite, *Studies on Marx and Hegel*, p. 176.
40 Croce, *Saggio sullo Hegel*, p. 36.
41 *Ibid.*, p. 49.
42 Chap. 4.
43 G. R. G. Mure, *A Study of Hegel's Logic*, p. 364.
44 *Ibid.*, pp. 350–51.
45 G. R. G. Mure, *An Introduction to Hegel*, pp. 165, 170.
46 *Ibid.*, p. 115.
47 *Ibid.*
48 Mure, *Study of Hegel's Logic*, p. 342.
49 Mure, *Idealist Epilogue*, p. 114.
50 *Ibid.*, p. 152.
51 Mure, *Study of Hegel's Logic*, p. 342.

52 *Ibid.*, pp. 96–105.
53 H. G. Gadamer, *Hegel's Dialectic*, pp. 5–34.
54 *Ibid.*, p. 23.
55 *Ibid.*, pp. 82–92.
56 *Ibid.*, pp. 75–99.
57 *Ibid.*, pp. 86–91.
58 *Ibid.*, p. 90.
59 G. W. F. Hegel, *Science of Logic*, trans. A. V. Miller, p. 56. Cf. G. W. F. Hegel, *Sämtliche Werke*, vol. 4, p. 54.
60 *Science of Logic*, trans. Miller, p. 49.
61 *Ibid.*, p. 54.
62 *Ibid.*, p. 56.
63 *Ibid.*
64 *Ibid.*
65 Quoted and translated in A. Kojève, *Introduction to the Reading of Hegel*, p. 202, which is much to be preferred to the translation of the *Encyclopedia* in *The Logic of Hegel*, trans. W. Wallace. Cf. Hegel, *Sämtliche Werke*, vol. 8, p. 195.
66 Quoted in Kojève, *Hegel*, p. 203.
67 Quoted in *ibid.*, p. 198.
68 Quoted in *ibid.*, p. 195.
69 *Encyclopedia*, par. 79, explanatory note.
70 Quoted in Kojève, *Hegel*, p. 199.
71 *Logic of Hegel*, trans. Wallace, p. 154. Cf. Hegel, *Sämtliche Werke*, vol. 8, p. 197.
72 *Logic of Hegel*, trans. Wallace, p. 154. Cf. Hegel, *Sämtliche Werke*, vol. 8, p. 197.
73 G. W. F. Hegel, *Lectures on the History of Philosophy*, vol. 1, pp. 264–65.
74 Hegel, *History of Philosophy*, vol. 1, p. 278.
75 *Ibid.*, p. 261.
76 *Ibid.*, p. 266.
77 *Ibid.*
78 *Ibid.*, p. 277.
79 *Ibid.*, p. 278.
80 *Ibid.*, p. 278.
81 *Ibid.*
82 *Ibid.*, p. 279.
83 Hegel, *History of Philosophy*, vol. 2, p. 53.
84 *Ibid.*, p. 49.
85 *Ibid.*
86 *Ibid.*, p. 54.
87 *Ibid.*, p. 65.
88 *Ibid.*, p. 436.
89 Hegel, *History of Philosophy*, vol. 3, pp. 450–51.

90 *Ibid.*, p. 451.

91 *Ibid.*

92 Cf. W. Kaufmann, *Hegel*, p. 363.

93 Gadamer and Croce, of course, make essential use of the preface and put forth many insightful points about it.

94 As translated in Kaufmann, *Hegel*, p. 448. In what follows I use two translations of the preface, the one by Kaufmann, just cited, and the one by Miller (Hegel, *Phenomenology of Spirit*, pp. 1–45). In the rest of this section, I quote now from the one and now from the other translation, depending on which I have found clearer, more incisive, or more satisfactory for a given passage after comparison with the original in *Sämtliche Werke*, vol. 2. Moreover, because of the frequency of quotations, references will be made in parenthesis in the text, by prefixing the page number(s) with a "K" for Kaufmann's translation, and with an "M" for Miller's.

95 *Phenomenology of Spirit*, trans. Miller, p. 40. See notational conventions outlined in note 94.

96 Despite their importance, these passages have not received the scholarly attention they deserve. General works on Hegel at best give uninspired and uninspiring summaries (Taylor, *Hegel*, pp. 260–62; Findlay, *Hegel*, pp. 189–94; Stace, *The Philosophy of Hegel*, pp. 182–88). Special works on the *Logic* are not much better: for example, W. T. Harris claims that "reflection is the key to the Hegelian method" (*Hegel's Logic*, p. 328) but gives only three and one-half pages (pp. 329–32) to a discussion of the "determinations of reflections," which is the Hegelian term under which he subsumes the concepts of identity and difference; G. R. G. Mure (*A Study of Hegel's Logic*, pp. 96–105) is a little better, but not much. A notable exception is J. M. E. McTaggart, who supplies an enlightening analysis and criticism (*A Commentary on Hegel's Logic*, pp. 103–18). Such scholarly neglect may be taken as another reason why these Hegelian passages deserve careful study.

97 See, for example, R. Norman and S. Sayers, *Hegel, Marx and Dialectic: A Debate*, p. 1.

98 *Science of Logic*, vol. 1 ("The Objective Logic"), bk. 2 ("The Doctrine of Essence"), sec. 1 ("Essence as Reflection Within Itself"), chap. 2 ("The Essentialities or Determinations of Reflections"); and *Encyclopedia*, par. 112–22. I feel completely justified in isolating this chapter of the *Logic* from the rest of the book, in view of Croce's judgment in his book on Hegel (*What Is Living and What Is Dead of the Philosophy of Hegel*, pp. 117–19): "A concrete content, taken from the history of philosophy, and in great measure from the Philosophy of spirit, a violent and arbitrary arrangement, imposed by the false idea of an *a priori* deduction of errors: that is how the Hegelian *Logic* presents itself to me. The arrangement injures the content. But in saying this

and in condemning the undertaking of Hegel, as embodied in the *Logic*, I do not intend to condemn to death and to oblivion that richest of all the books which bear the title *Logic*; on the contrary, I mean to place it in conditions favourable to its life and to the continued exercise of its profound influence upon the mind. He who takes up the *Logic* of Hegel, with the intention of understanding its development and above all the reason of the commencement, will be obliged ere long to put down the book in despair of understanding it, or persuaded that he finds himself face to face with a mass of meaningless abstractions. But he who, like the dog of Rabelais, 'a philosophical beast,' instead of leaving the bone alone, takes a bite at it, now here and now there, chews it, breaks it up and sucks it, will eventually nourish himself with the substantial marrow. Hegel and his disciples after him, have persistently pointed to the door by which the *Logic* can be entered: pure *being*, from which we must gradually pass by the vestibules and up the stairs of *nothing*, of *becoming*, of *determinate* being, of *something*, of the *limit*, of *change*, of *being for self*, etc. etc.: in order to reach the sanctuary of the Goddess, or the Idea. But he who obstinately knocks at that gate and believes the false information, that such and no other must be the door and the stair, will vainly attempt to enter the palace. That door, which has been indicated as the only one, is a closed, indeed a sham door. Take the palace by assault from all sides; thus alone will you reach the interior, and penetrate to the very sanctuary. And it may be that you will see the countenance of the Goddess lit with a benevolent smile, beholding the 'saintly simplicity' of many of her devotees."

99 *A Commentary on Hegel's Logic*, p. 117.
100 *Encyclopedia*, par. 120, as translated by Wallace, *Logic of Hegel*, p. 224. Cf. Hegel, *Sämtliche Werke*, vol. 8, p. 281. Cf. the argument in the *Science of Logic*, trans. Miller, p. 435.
101 Kojève, *Hegel*, p. 176.
102 *Science of Logic*, trans. Miller, pp. 54–55. Cf. Kaufmann, *Hegel*, p. 197.
103 *Encyclopedia*, par. 115, *Zusatz*, as translated by Wallace, *Logic of Hegel*, p. 214; cf. Hegel, *Sämtliche Werke*, vol. 8, p. 269.
104 *Science of Logic*, trans. Miller, p. 412. Hereafter, page references (preceded by "M") to this book will be in parentheses in the text.
105 *Encyclopedia*, par. 118, *Zusatz*, as translated by Wallace, *Logic of Hegel*, p. 219; cf. Hegel, *Sämtliche Werke*, vol. 8, p. 275.
106 *Encyclopedia*, par. 119, as translated by Wallace, *Logic of Hegel*, p. 220; cf. *Sämtliche Werke*, vol. 8, p. 276.
107 *Encyclopedia*, par. 119, *Zusatz* 1, as translated by Wallace, *Logic of Hegel*, p. 222; cf. *Sämtliche Werke*, vol. 8, p. 279.
108 G. W. F. Hegel, *Science of Logic*, trans. W. H. Johnston and L. C. Struthers, vol. 2, p. 57. Hereafter, page references (preceded by "JS") to this book will be in parentheses in the text. Occasionally it is better

to quote from this translation of the *Science of Logic* than from Miller's; for example, Miller does not always make as clear a distinction between *Unterschied* and *Verschiedenheit* as Johnston and Struthers do, as may be seen by comparing JS39–43, M413–16, and *Sämtliche Werke*, vol. 4, pp. 510–15.

109 *Encyclopedia*, par. 115, explanatory note, as translated by Wallace, *Logic of Hegel*, p. 213; cf. *Sämtliche Werke*, vol. 8, p. 268.

110 *Ibid.*

111 *Encyclopedia*, par. 119, explanatory note, as translated by Wallace, *Logic of Hegel*, p. 220; cf. *Sämtliche Werke*, vol. 8, p. 276.

112 *Encyclopedia*, par. 117, explanatory note, as translated by Wallace, *Logic of Hegel*, pp. 216–17; cf. *Sämtliche Werke*, vol. 8, p. 272; Cf. also *Science of Logic*, trans. Miller, p. 422.

113 *Sämtliche Werke*, vol. 8, p. 272.

114 *Encyclopedia*, par. 119, *Zusatz* 2, as translated by Wallace, *Logic of Hegel*, p. 223; cf. *Sämtliche Werke*, vol. 8, p. 281.

115 *Encyclopedia*, par. 119, explanatory note, as translated by Wallace, *Logic of Hegel*, p. 220; cf. *Sämtliche Werke*, vol. 8, p. 276.

116 *Ibid.*

117 *Science of Logic*, trans. Miller, p. 438; *Encyclopedia*, par. 119, explanatory note.

118 Par. 115, as translated by Wallace, *Logic of Hegel*, p. 212; cf. *Sämtliche Werke*, vol. 8, p. 267.

119 McTaggart, *Commentary on Hegel's Logic*, p. 114.

120 *Sämtliche Werke*, vol. 4, p. 509.

8. GRAMSCI AND THE EVALUATION OF MARXISM

1 K. Marx, *Early Writings*, p. 355. Cf. *Economic and Philosophic Manuscripts*, third manuscript, section on "Private Property and Communism," subsection 4. I thank Gregory Blue of the University of Cambridge for providing me with the exact location of this quotation.

2 Some scholars would speak not only of metamorphosis but of origin here, too, arguing that the religious element is significant both in Marx's own biography and in the defining characteristics of the Marxist revolutionary. For Marx's biography see, for example, L. P. Wessell, Jr., *Karl Marx, Romantic Irony, and the Proletariat: The Mythopoetic Origins of Marxism*; for revolutionists, see L. Pellicani, *I rivoluzionari di professione*. Pellicani has also tried to apply his general thesis to the case of Gramsci in *Gramsci: An Alternative Communism?*, but his Gramscian interpretation has little historical basis, as I argue in my "Gramsci: An Alternative Communism?" and in my *Gramsci critico e la critica*, chap. 5

3 See, for example, S. Carrillo, *Eurocommunism and the State*.

4 When the Italian Communist Party began to criticize the Soviets about

the matter, the controversy was reported in the popular press with religious-sounding language; see, for example, "Soviet Publishes Scathing Attack on Italian Party," *New York Times,* January 25, 1982, and "Italian Communists Reply to Soviet Charges with a Fierce Attack," *New York Times,* January 26, 1982.

5 As K. R. Popper might say. See his *Open Society and Its Enemies,* vol. 2, and his *Poverty of Historicism.*

6 E.g., P. K. Feyerabend, *Against Method* and *Science in a Free Society.*

7 This is B. Croce's view. See Chapter 1 of the present volume.

8 Here I am thinking of the works of E. Bloch, e.g., *On Karl Marx.*

9 K. Marx and F. Engels, *The Communist Manifesto,* sec. 1.

10 Some scholars also regard Gramsci as being of immense value for the understanding and evaluation of what they would call the "philosophical" aspect of Marxism, which I would rather call the metaphysical aspect. I am referring to A. Del Noce's thesis that Gramscism is the second phase of a development of alternatives to Leninism – the first being Fascism – and that Gramscism, like the other phase, stems from Giovanni Gentile's *Filosofia di Marx* (see A. Del Noce's *Il suicidio della rivoluzione*). I do not think the philosophical-metaphysical aspect of Marxism is as important as its scientific, political, and philosophical-religious dimensions; in holding this opinion I feel I am in agreement both with Gramsci (who did *not* discuss the metaphysical problem with comparable explicitness) and with Croce (who elaborated such a view in his correspondence with Gentile). For the controversy between Croce and Gentile, see G. Gentile, *La filosofia di Marx,* pp. 171–266, and my review of this work in *The Thomist.*

11 J. Joll, *Antonio Gramsci,* p. 24.

12 *Ibid.,* p. 148.

13 L. Althusser, *For Marx,* p. 114.

14 E. J. Hobsbawm, "The Great Gramsci," p. 41.

15 M. Clark, "The Patron Saint of the Left."

16 See Chapter 1 of the present volume.

17 Gramsci's persistent interest in the phenomenon of religion has been demonstrated beyond any reasonable doubt by such books as H. Portelli, *Gramsci et la question religieuse;* E. Masutti, *Perché Gramsci ateo?;* C. Vasale, *Politica e religione in A. Gramsci;* T. La Rocca, *Gramsci e la religione;* and R. Vinco, *Una fede senza futuro?* It is interesting and revealing, however, that Gramsci's approach to religion is as a political problem, although his view of politics is such that he is led to examine religion in all of its aspects: doctrinal, ethical, social, psychological, etc.; see, for example, La Rocca, *Gramsci e la religione,* esp. pp. 25–27 and 65–68.

18 K. Marx, "Contribution to the Critique of Hegel's *Philosophy of Right:* Introduction," in *The Marx-Engels Reader,* R. C. Tucker, ed., p. 54. Of course, it is not clear that Marx's dictum is a definition of religion;

perhaps it is just a claim about it. In the latter case, Gramsci would probably agree that religion, as he conceives it, *sometimes* becomes the opium of the people, as, for example, Catholicism presumably became with the Counter-Reformation in Italy. That is, Gramsci is not in principle opposed to religion, but that does not mean he cannot be contingently critical of it. For an excellent discussion of this and other aspects of the problem, see Portelli, *Gramsci et la question religieuse,* esp. chap. 1, and Vinco, *Una fede senza futuro?,* chap. 2 and pp. 142–46.

19   Obviously Gramsci's antiscientism (or antipositivism) should not be equated with an antiscientific attitude, on pain of confusing actual science with the positivist image of science. For a clear account of Gramsci's views and a critique of such a confusion, see P. Rossi, "Antonio Gramsci sulla scienza moderna."

20   See Chapter 3 in the present volume.

21   I am referring to difficulties in K. Popper's general critique of Marx in *The Open Society and Its Enemies,* and in G. Lukács's critical review of Bukharin's *Historical Materialism* in *Archiv für Geschichte des Sozialismus und der Arbeiterbewegung.* For the details of such criticism, see, respectively, my "Methodological Criticism and Critical Methodology: An Analysis of Popper's Critique of Marxian Social Science" and Chapter 4 in the present volume.

22   On such occasions we would have instances of what Gramsci terms "passive revolution." See Chapter 6 in the present volume.

23   A. Gramsci, *Quaderni del carcere,* vol. 3, p. 1635.

CONCLUSION

1   For one of the best accounts, see P. Piccone, *Italian Marxism.*

2   A. Gramsci, *Quaderni del carcere,* vol. 3, p. 1635.

3   Note that I speak of literary structure, which reflects the prison conditions. Regarding Gramsci's *thought,* however, I agree with N. Bobbio that the Prison Notebooks are "sustained by a fundamental unity of inspiration" ("Gramsci e la concezione della società civile," p. 79).

4   I adapt this expression from R. L. Heilbroner, *Marxism: For and Against,* esp. p. 26.

5   I am thinking of the philosophies associated with such names as Dilthey, Heidegger, and Gadamer, and the related meanings in R. Rorty, *Philosophy and the Mirror of Nature,* pp. 343–44, and in H. L. Dreyfus, "Holism and Hermeneutics."

6   This is partly an analogue of the different jurisprudential rules about evidence in criminal and civil cases. It also has an analogue in logic and the theory of reasoning, where a valid argument has intrinsic value, whereas normally an invalid one has interest only if it is an accurate reconstruction of an original (see my *Galileo and the Art of*

Reasoning, pp. 338–41). There is something similar in historical inquiry, where the explanation of a human action needs less stringent documentation if it portrays the action in a favorable rather than an unfavorable light (see, e.g., L. Laudan, *Progress and Its Problems*, pp. 164–70). Finally, in the field of art criticism, E. H. Gombrich (*The Story of Art*, p. 5) has argued that "whereas I do not think there are wrong reasons for liking a statue or picture . . . there *are* wrong reasons for disliking a work of art."

Chapter 1 in the present volume.

Which I provide in Chapter 2.

Chapter 3.

Chapter 4.

In Chapters 5 and 6.

In Chapter 7.

Note that this lack of correspondence does *not* mean that Gramsci was unable to practice his own sound concept of science when he dealt with other matters; for example, many of Gramsci's reflections constitute serious and important contributions to sociology and to political science. See, for example, J. Femia, *Gramsci's Political Thought*, esp. pp. 218–35; L. Razeto Migliaro and P. Misuraca, *Sociologia e marxismo nella critica di Gramsci*, esp. pp. 80–126; L. Salamini, *The Sociology of Political Praxis*, pp. 71–153; and A. Pizzorno, "Sul metodo di Gramsci: dalla storiografia alla scienza politica."

Bibliography

Adamson, Walter L. "Gramsci's Interpretation of Fascism." *Journal of the History of Ideas* 41 (1980): 615–34.

Hegemony and Revolution: Antonio Gramsci's Political and Cultural Theory. Berkeley: University of California Press, 1980.

Agassi, Joseph. "The Nature of Scientific Problems and Their Roots in Metaphysics." In Mario Bunge, ed., *The Critical Approach to Science and Philosophy*, pp. 189–211. New York: Free Press, 1964.

Agazzi, Emilio. "Filosofia della prassi e filosofia dello spirito." In Alberto Caracciolo and Gianni Scalia, eds., *La città futura*, 2d ed, pp. 93–175.

Alderisio, Felice. "Ripresa machiavelliana. Considerazioni critiche sulle idee di A. Gramsci, di B. Croce e di L. Russo intorno a Machiavelli." *Annali dell'Istituto universitario di Magistero* (Salerno). Vol. 1 (1949–50), pp. 205–66.

Althusser, Louis. *For Marx.* Translated by B. Brewster. London: NLB, 1977.

Anderson, Perry. "The Antinomies of Antonio Gramsci." *New Left Review* 100 (Nov. 1976–Jan. 1977): 5–78.

Asor Rosa, Alberto. *Storia d' Italia.* Vol. 4: *Dall' Unità ad oggi*, tome 2: *La cultura.* Turin: Einaudi, 1975.

Badaloni, Nicola. "Egemonia e azione politica: una discussione critica." *Critica marxista* 25, no. 6 (1987): 5–17.

Il marxismo di Gramsci. Turin: Einaudi, 1975.

Bergami, Giancarlo. *Gramsci comunista critico. Il Politico e il pensatore.* Milan: Franco Angeli, 1981.

Biondi, Marino. *Guida bibliografica a Gramsci.* Cesena: Bettini, 1977.

Bloch, Ernst. *On Karl Marx.* Translated by J. Maxwell. New York: Herder & Herder, 1977.

Bobbio, Norberto. "Gramsci e la concezione della società civile." In P. Rossi, ed., *Gramsci e la cultura contemporanea*, vol. 1, pp. 75–100. Translated as "Gramsci and the Conception of Civil Society." In C. Mouffe, ed., *Gramsci and Marxist Theory*, pp. 21–47.

"Nota sulla dialettica in Gramsci." In Istituto Gramsci, ed., *Studi gramsciani*, pp. 73–86.

Bibliography

Boggs, Carl. *The Two Revolutions: Gramsci and the Dilemmas of Western Marxism.* Boston: South End Press, 1984.

Bonetti, Paolo. *Gramsci e la società liberaldemocratica.* Rome: Laterza, 1980.

Buci-Glucksmann, Christine. *Gramsci et l'Etat: Pour une théorie matérialiste de la philosophie.* Paris: Fayard, 1975.

"Sui problemi politici della transizione: classe operaia e rivoluzione passiva." In F. Ferri, ed., *Politica e storia in Gramsci,* vol. 1, pp. 99–125.

Bukharin, Nikolai I. *Historical Materialism: A System of Sociology.* Ann Arbor: University of Michigan Press, 1969.

Buzzi, A. R. *La Théorie politique d'Antonio Gramsci.* Louvain: Nauwelaerts, 1967.

Capucci, Flavio. *Antonio Gramsci: Il materialismo storico e la filosofia di Benedetto Croce.* L'Aquila: Japadre, 1978.

Caracciolo, Alberto, and G. Scalia, eds. *La città futura.* 2d ed. Milan: Feltrinelli, 1976.

Carrillo, Santiago. *Eurocommunism and the State.* Translated by N. Green and A. M. Elliot. Westport, Conn.: Lawrence Hill, 1978.

Clark, Martin. "The Patron Saint of the Left." *Times Literary Supplement* (London), 3842 (October 31, 1975), p. 1280.

Cohen, Stephen F. *Bukharin and the Bolshevik Revolution.* New York: Knopf, 1973.

"Marxist Theory and Bolshevik Policy: The Case of Bukharin's *Historical Materialism.*" *Political Science Quarterly* 85 (1970): 40–60.

Colletti, Lucio. *Marxism and Hegel.* London: Verso, 1979.

"Marxism and the Dialectic: Contradiction and Contrariety." *New Left Review,* no. 93. (Sept.-Oct. 1975): 3–29.

"Marxismo." *Enciclopedia del novecento,* vol. IV, pp. 1–18. Rome: Istituto della Enciclopedia Italiana, 1979.

Cristofolini, Paolo. "Sulla dialettica di Gramsci e la storia filosofica delle 'facoltà.'" *Aut aut* 15 (Jan.-Feb. 1976): 68–72.

Croce, Benedetto. *Aesthetic as Science of Expression and General Linguistics.* Translated by D. Ainslie. London: Macmillan, 1909. Rpt., New York: Noonday press, n.d.

Aneddoti di varia letteratura, 4 vols. 2d ed. Bari: Laterza, 1953.

"Antonio Gramsci, *Lettere dal carcere.*" *Quaderni della critica,* 3, no. 8 (1947): 86–88.

"Antonio Gramsci, *Il materialismo storico e la filosofia di Benedetto Croce.*" *Quaderni della critica* 4, no. 10 (1948): 78–79.

Ariosto, Shakespeare e Corneille (1920). 4th ed. Bari: Laterza, 1950. English translation by D. Ainslie. New York: Holt, 1920.

Il carattere della filosofia moderna (1941). 3d ed. Bari: Laterza, 1963.

Ciò che è vivo e ciò che è morto della filosofia di Hegel. Bari: Laterza, 1906.

Conversazioni critiche. Vols. 1–2 (1918), 3d ed., Bari: Laterza, 1942. Vols. 3–4 (1932), 2d ed., Bari: Laterza, 1951. Vol. 5 (1939), 2d ed., Bari: Laterza, 1951.

Cultura e vita morale. 3d ed. Bari: Laterza, 1955.
Discorsi di varia filosofia (1945). 2d ed. Bari: Laterza, 1959.
Estetica come scienza dell'espressione e linguistica generale (1902). 9th ed. Bari: Laterza, 1950.
Etica e politica (1931). Economical edition. Bari: Laterza, 1967.
European Literature in the Nineteenth Century. Translated by D. Ainslie, 1924. New York: Haskell House, 1967.
Una famiglia di patrioti ed altri saggi storici e critici (1919). 3d ed. Bari: Laterza, 1949.
Filosofia, poesia, storia. Milan: Riccardo Ricciardi, 1952.
Filosofia della practica (1909). 6th ed. Bari: Laterza, 1950.
La filosofia di G. B. Vico (1911). Economical edition. Bari: Laterza, 1967.
Filosofia e storiografia (1949). 2d ed. Bari: Laterza 1969.
"Un gioco che ormai dura troppo." *Quaderni della critica* 6, nos. 17–18 (1950): 231–32.
Goethe (1919). 4th in 2 vol. Bari: Laterza, 1946. English translation by D. Ainslie. London: Methuen, 1923.
Historical Materialism and the Economics of Karl Marx. Translated by C. M. Meredith, 1914. Rpt., New York: Russell & Russell, 1966.
History as the Story of Liberty. Translated by S. Sprigge. Chicago: Regnery, 1970.
History of Europe in the Nineteenth Century. Translated by H. Furst. New York: Harcourt Brace & World, 1963.
A History of Italy. Translated by C. M. Ady. Oxford: Clarendon Press, 1929.
History of the Kingdom of Naples. Translated by F. Frenaye. Chicago: University of Chicago Press, 1970.
Indagini su Hegel e schiarimenti filosofici (1952). 2d ed. Bari: Laterza, 1967.
L'Italia dal 1914 al 1918: Pagine sulla guerra (1919). 4th ed. Bari: Laterza, 1965.
La letteratura della nuova Italia. Vols. 1–4 (1914–15), 5th ed., Bari: Laterza, 1947–49. Vol. 5 (1939), 3d ed., Bari: Laterza, 1950. Vol. 6 (1940), 3d ed., Bari: Laterza, 1950.
La letteratura italiana del Settecento. Bari: Laterza, 1949.
Letture di poeti e riflessioni sulla teoria e la critica della poesia. Bari: Laterza, 1950.
Logic as the Science of Pure Concept. Translated by D. Ainslie. London: Macmillan, 1917.
Logica come scienza del concetto puro (1909). Economical edition. Bari: Laterza, 1967.
Materialismo storico ed economia marxistica (1900). Economical edition. Bari: Laterza, 1968.
My Philosophy. Translated by E. F. Carritt. London: Macmillan, 1949.
Nuovi saggi di estetica (1920). 3d ed. Bari: Laterza, 1948.

Bibliography

Nuovi saggi sulla letteratura italiana del Seicento (1931). 2d ed. Bari: Laterza, 1949.

Philosophy, Poetry, History. Translated by C. Sprigge. Oxford University Press, 1966.

The Philosophy of Giambattista Vico. Translated by R. G. Collingwood, 1913. Rpt., New York: Russell & Russell, 1964.

Philosophy of the Practical. Translated by D. Ainslie. London: Macmillan, 1915. Rpt., New York: Biblo & Tannen, 1967.

La poesia (1936). 5th ed. Bari: Laterza, 1953.

Poesia antica e moderna (1941). 2d ed., Bari: Laterza, 1943.

La poesia di Dante (1920). 11th ed. Bari: Laterza, 1966.

Poesia e non poesia (1923). 8th ed. Bari: Laterza, 1974.

Poesia popolare e poesia d'arte (1933). 2d ed. Bari: Laterza, 1946.

Poeti e scrittori del pieno e tardo Rinascimento. Vols. 1–2, Bari: Laterza, 1945. Vol. 3, Bari: Laterza, 1952.

Poetry and Literature: Introduction to Its Criticism and History. Translated by G. Gullace. Carbondale: Southern Illinois University Press, 1981.

The Poetry of Dante. Translated by D. Ainslie. London: Allen & Unwin, 1922.

Politics and Morals. Translated by S. Castiglione. New York: Philosophical Library, 1945.

Problemi di estetica (1910). 4th ed. Bari: Laterza, 1949.

La rivoluzione napoletana del 1799 (1897). 5th ed. Bari: Laterza, 1948.

Saggi sulla letteratura italiana del Seicento (1911). 3d ed. Bari: Laterza, 1948.

Saggio sullo Hegel (1913). 5th ed. Bari: Laterza, 1967.

Scritti e discorsi politici. 2 vols. Bari: Laterza, 1963.

La Spagna nella vita italiana durante la Rinascenza (1917). 4th ed. Bari: Laterza, 1949.

La storia come pensiero e come azione (1938). Economical edition. Bari: Laterza, 1966.

Storia del regno di Napoli (1925). 3d ed. Bari: Laterza, 1944.

Storia della storiografia italiana nel secolo decimonono (1921). 2 vols. 5th ed. Bari: Laterza, 1964.

Storia dell'età barocca in Italia (1919). 2d ed. Bari: Laterza, 1946.

Storia d'Europa nel secolo decimonono (1932). Economical edition. Bari: Laterza, 1965.

Storia d'Italia dal 1871 al 1915 (1928). Economical edition. Bari: Laterza, 1967.

Storie e leggende napoletane (1919). 4th ed. Bari: Laterza, 1948.

Teoria e storia della storiografia (1917). 9th ed. Bari: Laterza, 1966.

Theory and History of Historiography. Translated by D. Ainslie. London: George G. Harrap, 1921.

Ultimi saggi (1935). 3d ed. Bari: Laterza, 1963.

Uomini e cose della vecchia Italia (1927). 2 vols. 2d ed. Bari: Laterza, 1943.

Bibliography

Varietà di storia letteraria e civile. Vol. 1 (1935), 2d ed., Bari: Laterza, 1949. Vol. 2, Bari: Laterza, 1950.

Vite di avventure, di fede e di passione (1936). 2d ed. Bari: Laterza, 1947.

What Is Living and What Is Dead of the Philosophy of Hegel. Translated by D. Ainslie, 1915. Rpt., New York: Russell & Russell, 1969. Rpt., Lanham, MD: University Press of America, 1985.

Davidson, Alistair. *Antonio Gramsci: Towards an Intellectual Biography.* London: Merlin Press, 1977.

De Angelis, Frank. "Gramsci and Croce: The Living, the Dead, Marxism, and the Dialectic." *Revolutionary World* 10 (1974): 43–55.

De Felice, Franco. *Serrati, Bordiga, Gramsci e il problema della rivoluzione in Italia. 1919–1920.* Bari: De Donato, 1971.

Del Noce, Augusto. *Il suicidio della rivoluzione.* Milan: Rusconi, 1978.

Dialettica e filosofia della prassi. Milan: Franco Angeli Editore, 1979.

Dreyfus, Hubert L. "Holism and Hermeneutics." *Review of Metaphysics* 34 (1980–81): 3–23.

Dubla, Ferdinando. *Gramsci e la fabbrica.* Manduria: Lacaita Editore, 1986.

Einstein, Albert. "Replies." In Paul A. Schlipp, ed., *Albert Einstein, Philosopher-Scientist.* Evanston, Ill.: Library of Living Philosophers, 1951.

Eley, Geoff. "Reading Gramsci in English: Observations on the Reception of Antonio Gramsci in the English-speaking World 1957–82." *European History Quarterly* 14 (1984): 441–78.

Engels, Friedrich. *Anti-Dühring.* New York: International Publishers, 1939.

Fagone, Virgilio. *Il marxismo tra democrazia e totalitarismo.* Rome: Edizioni La Civiltà Cattolica, 1983.

Femia, Joseph V. *Gramsci's Political Thought: Hegemony, Consciousness, and the Revolutionary Process.* Oxford: Clarendon Press, 1981.

"An Historicist Critique of 'Revisionist' Methods for Studying the History of Ideas." *History and Theory* 20 (1981): 113–34.

Fergnani, Franco. *La filosofia della prassi nei "Quaderni del carcere."* Unicopli, n.p. [1976].

Ferri, Franco, ed. *Politica e storia in Gramsci.* 2 vols. Rome: Editori Riuniti–Istituto Gramsci, 1977.

Feyerabend, Paul K. *Against Method.* Atlantic Highlands, N.J.: Humanities, 1975.

Science in a Free Society. London: NLB, 1978.

Findlay, John. *Hegel: A Re-examination.* New York: Humanities, 1964.

Language, Mind, and Value. London: Allen & Unwin, 1963.

Finocchiaro, Maurice A. "The Concept of Judgment and Huygens' Theory of Gravity." *Epistemologia* 3 (1980): 185–218.

"Croce and Marxism: A Bibliographical Prolegomenon." *Rivista di studi crociani* 17 (1980): 157–63.

"Croce as Seen in a Recent Work on Gramsci." *Rivista di studi crociani* 21 (1984): 139–54.

Galileo and the Art of Reasoning: Rhetorical Foundations of Logic and Scientific Method. Boston: D. Reidel, 1980.

"Gramsci: An Alternative Communism?" *Studies in Soviet Thought* 27 (1984): 123–46.

Gramsci critico e la critica. Rome: Armando Editore, 1988.

"Gramsci's Crocean Marxism." *Telos* 41 (Fall 1979): 17–32.

History of Science as Explanation. Detroit: Wayne State University Press, 1973.

"The Labyrinth of Gramscian Studies and Femia's Contribution." *Inquiry* 27 (1984): 291–310.

"Marxism, Science, and Religion in Gramsci: Recent Trends in Italian Scholarship." *The Philosophical Forum* 17 (1985–86): 127–55.

"Methodological Criticism and Critical Methodology: An Analysis of Popper's Critique of Marxian Social Science." *Zeitschrift für allgemeine Wissenschaftstheorie* 10 (1979): 363–74.

"Review of Gentile's *Filosofia di Marx.*" *The Thomist* 39 (1975): 423–26.

"Sztompka's Philosophy of Social Science." *Inquiry* 23 (1980): 357–71.

Fisk, Milton. "Dialectic and Ontology." In John Mepham and D-H. Ruben, eds., *Issues in Marxist Philosophy*, Vol. 1: *Dialectic and Method*, pp. 117–43. Atlantic Highlands, N.J.: Humanities, 1979.

Franchini, Raffaello. *Le origini della dialettica.* 2d ed. Naples: Giannini, 1965.

Francioni, Gianni. "Gramsci tra Croce e Bucharin: sulla struttura dei *Quaderni 10 e 11.*" *Critica marxista* 25, no. 6 (1987): 19–45.

L'officina gramsciana. Ipotesi sulla struttura dei "Quaderni del carcere." Naples: Bibliopolis, 1984.

Fubini, Elsa. "Bibliografia gramsciana." In P. Rossi, ed., *Gramsci e la cultura contemporanea*, vol. 2, pp. 477–544.

"Bibliografia gramsciana 1968–1977." In F. Ferri, ed., *Politica e storia in Gramsci*, vol. 2, pp. 649–733.

Gadamer, Hans-Georg. *Hegel's Dialectic: Five Hermeneutical Studies.* Translated by P. C. Smith. New Haven, Conn: Yale University Press, 1976.

Galasso, Giuseppe. *Croce, Gramsci e altri storici.* 2d ed. Milan: Il Saggiatore, 1978.

Galilei, Galileo. *Dialogue Concerning the Two Chief World Systems.* 2d ed. Translated by S. Drake. Berkeley: University of California Press, 1967.

Garin, Eugenio. "La formazione di Gramsci e Croce." In *Prassi rivoluzionaria e storicismo in Gramsci*, Quaderno no. 3 of *Critica marxista* (1967), pp. 119–33. Rome: Editori Riuniti, 1967.

"Gramsci nella cultura italiana." In Istituto Gramsci, ed., *Studi gramsciani*, pp. 395–418.

"Politica e cultura in Gramsci: Il problema degli intellettuali." In P. Rossi, ed., *Gramsci e la cultura contemporanea*, vol. 1, pp. 37–74.

Gentile, Giovanni. *La filosofia di Marx* (1899). 5th ed. Florence: Sansoni, 1974.

Bibliography

"Il marxismo di Benedetto Croce." *Il Resto del Carlino* (Bologna), May 14, 1918.

Gerratana, Valentino. "Gramsci come pensatore rivoluzionario." In F. Ferri, ed., *Politica e storia in Gramsci*, vol. 2, pp. 69–101.

"Prefazione." To Antonio Gramsci, *Quaderni del carcere*, pp. xi–xlii.

"La ricerca e il metodo." *Rinascita* 32, no. 30 (1975): 11–13.

Gombrich, E. H. *The Story of Art*. 13th ed. Englewood Cliffs, N.J.: Prentice-Hall, 1983.

Gramsci, Antonio. *La città futura 1917–1918*. Edited by S. Caprioglio. Turin: Einaudi, 1982.

La costruzione del partito comunista 1923–1926. Turin: Einaudi, 1971.

Cronache torinesi 1913–1917. Edited by S. Caprioglio. Turin: Einaudi, 1980.

History, Philosophy, and Culture in the Young Gramsci. Translated by P. Cavalcanti and P. Piccone. St. Louis: Telos Press, 1975.

Gli intellettuali e l'organizzazione della cultura. Turin: Einaudi, 1949.

Letteratura e vita nazionale. Turin: Einaudi, 1950.

Lettere dal carcere. Edited by S. Caprioglio and E. Fubini. Turin: Einaudi, 1965.

Letters from Prison. Edited and translated by L. Lawner. New York: Harper, 1973.

Il materialismo storico e la filosofia di Benedetto Croce. Turin: Einaudi, 1948.

Il nostro Marx 1918–1919. Edited by S. Caprioglio. Turin: Einaudi, 1984.

Note sul Machiavelli, sulla politica e sullo Stato moderno. Turin: Einaudi, 1949.

Nuove lettere. Edited by Antonio A. Santucci. Rome: Riuniti, 1986.

L'Ordine Nuovo 1919–1920. Turin: Einaudi, 1954.

L'Ordine Nuovo 1919–1920. Edited by V. Gerratana and A. A. Santucci. Turin: Einaudi, 1987.

Passato e presente. Turin: Einaudi, 1951.

Quaderni del carcere. 4 vols. Critical edition edited by V. Gerratana under the auspices of the Gramsci Institute. Turin: Einaudi, 1975.

Quaderno 13. Noterelle sulla politica del Machiavelli. Edited by C. Donzelli. Turin: Einaudi, 1981.

Quaderno 19. Risorgimento italiano. Edited by C. Vivanti. Turin: Einaudi, 1977.

Quaderno 22. Americanismo e fordismo. Edited by F. De Felice. Turin: Einaudi, 1978.

Il Risorgimento. Turin: Einaudi, 1949.

"La rivoluzione contro il *Capitale*." *L'Avanti* (Milan), November 24, 1917.

Scritti giovanili 1914–1918. Turin: Einaudi, 1958.

Selections from Cultural Writings. Edited by D. Forgacs and G. Nowell-Smith. Translated by W. Boelhower. Cambridge, Mass.: Harvard University Press, 1985.

Selections from Political Writings, 1910–1920. Edited and translated by Q. Hoare and J. Mathews. New York: International Publishers, 1977.

Bibliography

Selections from Political Writings, 1921–1926. Edited and translated by Q. Hoare. New York: International Publishers, 1978.

Selections from the Prison Notebooks. Edited and translated by Q. Hoare and G. Nowell Smith. New York: International Publishers, 1971.

Socialismo e fascismo. L'Ordine Nuovo 1921–1922. Turin: Einaudi, 1966.

Sotto la mole 1916–1920. Turin: Einaudi, 1960.

Gullace, Giovanni. "Introduction" to B. Croce, *Poetry and Literature*, pp. xiii-lxxiv.

Hammacher, Emil. *Das philosophisch-oekonomische System des Marxismus*. Leipzig, 1909.

Harris, William T. *Hegel's Logic* (1890). Rpt., New York: Kraus Reprint, 1970.

Hartmann, Nicolai. *Kleinere Schriften*. Vol. 2. Berlin, 1957.

Kleinere Schriften. Vol. 3. Berlin, 1958.

Die Philosophie des deutchen Idealismus. Vol. 2: *Hegel*. Berlin, 1929.

Hegel, Georg W. F. *Lectures on the History of Philosophy*. 3 vols. Translated by E. S. Haldane and F. H. Simson. London: Routledge & Kegan Paul, 1892.

The Logic of Hegel. Translated by William Wallace. 2d ed. Oxford University Press, 1892.

Phenomenology of Spirit. Translated by A. V. Miller. Oxford: Clarendon Press, 1977.

Sämtliche Werke. Jubilee Edition in 20 volumes. Stuttgart: Fromman, 1927–30 and 1965.

Science of Logic. 2 vols. Translated by W. H. Johnson and L. S. Struthers. London: Geroge Allen & Unwin, 1929.

Science of Logic. Translated by A. V. Miller. London: George Allen & Unwin, 1969.

Heilbroner, Robert L. *Marxism: For and Against*. New York: Norton, 1980.

Hoare, Quintin, and Geoffrey Nowell Smith. "Introduction" to Antonio Gramsci, *Selections from the Prison Notebooks*, pp. xvii–xcvi.

Hobsbawm, E. J. "The Great Gramsci." *New York Review of Books* 21, no. 5, April 4, 1974, pp. 39–44.

Hoffman, David. "Bukharin's Theory of Equilibrium." *Telos* no. 14 (Winter 1972): 126–36.

Hoffman, John. *The Gramscian Challenge: Coercion and Consent in Marxist Political Theory*. Oxford: Basil Blackwell, 1984.

Hook, Sidney. *Marxism and Beyond*. Totowa, N.J.: Rowman & Littlefield, 1983.

Hyppolite, Jean. *Genesis and Structure of Hegel's Phenomenology of Spirit*. Translated by S. Cherniak and J. Heckman. Evanston: Northwestern University Press, 1974. First French edition published in 1946.

Studies on Marx and Hegel. Translated by G. O'Neill. New York: Basic, 1969.

Istituto Gramsci, ed. *Studi gramsciani*. Rome: Editori Riuniti, 1958.

Bibliography

Jacobitti, Edmund E. *Revolutionary Humanism and Historicism in Modern Italy.* New Haven, Conn.: Yale University Press, 1981.

Jocteau, Gian Carlo. *Leggere Gramsci.* Milan: Feltrinelli, 1975.

Joll, James *Antonio Gramsci.* New York: Penguin, 1977.

Joravsky, David. *Soviet Marxism and Natural Science, 1917–1932.* New York: Columbia University Press, 1961.

Kaplan, Abraham. *The Conduct of Inquiry: Methodology for Behavioral Science.* San Francisco: Chandler, 1964.

Kaufmann, Walter. *Hegel: Reinterpretation, Texts, and Commentary.* New York: Doubleday, 1965.

Kilminster, Richard. *Praxis and Method: A Sociological Dialogue with Lukács, Gramsci and the Early Frankfurt School.* Boston: Routledge, 1979.

Kiros, Teodros. *Toward the Construction of a Theory of Political Action: Antonio Gramsci.* Lanham, Md.: University Press of America, 1985.

Kojève, Alexandre. *Introduction à la lecture de Hegel.* 2d ed. Paris, 1968.

Introduction to the Reading of Hegel: Lectures on the Phenomenology of Spirit. Translated by J. H. Nichols, Jr. Edited by A. Bloom. Ithaca, N.Y.: Cornell University Press, 1980. First French edition published in 1947.

Kolakowski, Leszek. *Main Currents of Marxism: Origins, Growth, and Dissolution.* 3 vols. Translated by P. S. Falla. Oxford University Press, 1978.

La Rocca, Tommaso. *Gramsci e la religione.* Brescia: Queriniana, 1981.

Laudan, Larry. *Progress and Its Problems.* Berkeley: University of California Press, 1977.

Lentini, Giacinto. *Croce e Gramsci.* Palermo-Rome: Edizioni Mori, 1967.

Lepre, Aurelio. *Gramsci secondo Gramsci.* Naples: Liguori, 1978.

Lewin, Moshe. *Political Undercurrents in Soviet Economic Debates.* Princeton, N.J.: Princeton University Press, 1974.

Lipset, Seymour M. "Intoduction" to *Political Parties,* by Robert Michels, pp. 15–39. New York: Free Press, 1962.

Lukács, Georg. *History and Class Consciousness.* Translated by R. Livingstone. Cambridge, Mass.: MIT Press, 1971.

"Technology and Social Relations," *New Left Review* 39 (1966): 27–34. Translation of his review of Bukharin's *Historical Materialism* from *Archiv für Geschichte des Sozialismus und der Arbeiterwegung* 11 (1923): 216–24.

McTaggart, John E. *A Commentary on Hegel's Logic* (1910). Rpt., New York: Russell & Russell, 1964.

Studies in the Hegelian Dialectic (1896). Rpt., New York: Russell & Russell, 1964.

Marx, Karl. *Critique of Hegel's Philosophy of Right.* Edited by J. O'Malley. Cambridge University Press, 1970.

Early Writings. Translated by R. Livingstone and G. Benton. Harmondsworth: Penguin, 1975.

The Poverty of Philosophy. New York: International Publishers, 1963.

Marx, Karl, and Friedrich Engels. *The Holy Family; or Critique of Critical Critique.* Translated by R. Dixon. Moscow: Foreign Languages Publishing House, 1956.

Masutti, E. *Perché Gramsci ateo?* Udine: Grillo, 1975.

Mates, Benson. *Elementary Logic.* 2d ed. Oxford University Press, 1972.

Matteucci, Nicola. *Antonio Gramsci e la filosofia della prassi* (1951). 2d ed. Milan: Giuffrè, 1977.

Melchiorre, Virgilio, Carmelo Vigna, and Gabriele De Rosa, eds. *Antonio Gramsci: Il pensiero teorico e politico, la "questione leninista."* 2 vols. Rome: Città Nuova Editrice, 1979.

Meyer, Alfred G. "Introduction" to *Historical Materialism: A System of Sociology* by N. I. Bukharin.

Michels, Robert. *Political Parties.* New York: Free Press, 1962.

Misuraca, Pasquale. "Politica, economia, diritto, sociologia come scienze dello Stato." *Critica marxista* 18, no. 5 (1980): 65–87.

Montanari, Marcello. "Razionalità e tragicità del moderno in Gramsci e Weber." *Critica marxista* 25, no. 6 (1987): 47–71.

Morpurgo-Tagliabue, Guido. "Gramsci tra Croce e Marx." *Il ponte* 4, no. 5 (May 1948):429–38.

Moss, M. E. *Benedetto Croce Reconsidered: Truth and Error in Theories of Art, Literature and History.* Hanover, N.H.: University Press of New England, 1987.

Mouffe, Chantal, ed. *Gramsci and Marxist Theory.* Boston: Routledge, 1979.

Mure, Geoffrey R. G. *Idealist Epilogue.* Oxford: Clarendon Press, 1978.

An Introduction to Hegel. Oxford: Clarendon Press, 1940.

A Study of Hegel's Logic. Oxford: Clarendon Press, 1950.

Nardone, Giorgio. *Il pensiero di Gramsci.* Bari: De Donato, 1971.

Nemeth, Thomas. *Gramsci's Philosophy: A Critical Study.* Atlantic Highlands, N.J.: Humanities, 1980.

Norman, Richard, and S. Sayers. *Hegel, Marx and Dialectic: A Debate.* Sussex: Harvester Press, 1980.

Orsucci, Andrea. "Del materialismo 'crudo.' Gnoseologia e divisione sociale del lavoro nel Gramsci dei 'Quaderni.'" In *Dialettica e filosofia della prassi,* pp. 191–219.

Paggi, Leonardo. *Antonio Gramsci e il moderno principe.* Rome: Riuniti, 1970.

"Gramsci's General Theory of Marxism." *Telos* 33 (Fall 1977): 27–70. (Reprinted in C. Mouffe, ed., *Gramsci and Marxist Theory,* pp. 113–67.)

Le strategie del potere in Gramsci. Rome: Riuniti, 1984.

"La teoria generale del marxismo in Gramsci." In *Annali Feltrinelli XV* (1973), pp. 1319–70. Milan: Feltrinelli, 1974.

Panichi, Nicola. *Antonio Gramsci, storia della filosofia e filosofia.* Urbino: Università degli Studi di Urbino, 1985.

Paris, Robert. "Gramsci e la crisi teorica del 1923." In P. Rossi, ed., *Gramsci e la cultura contemporanea,* vol. 2, pp. 29–44.

Bibliography

Pears, D. F. *The Nature of Metaphysics*. New York: Macmillan, 1957.

Pellicani, Luciano. *Gramsci: An Alternative Communism?* Stanford, Calif.: Hoover Institution Press, 1981.

Gramsci e la questione comunista. Florence: Vallecchi, 1976.

I rivoluzionari di professione. Florence: Vallecchi, 1975.

Pera, Marcello. "E uno scienziato, però ha stile." *Il Corriere della Sera* (Milan), February 12, 1985, p. 3.

Pera, Marcello, and Joseph Pitt, eds. *I modi del progresso. Teorie ed episodi della razionalità scientifica*. Milan: Il Saggiatore, 1985.

Perelman, Chaim. *The Idea of Justice and the Problem of Argument*. London: Routledge, 1963.

The New Rhetoric and the Humanities. Boston: D. Reidel, 1979.

Perrotti, Gabriele. "Gramsci, Ricardo e la filosofia della prassi." *Lavoro critico* 9 (January-March 1977): 109–56.

Petrarch. *The Sonnets, Triumphs, and Other Poems of Petrarch*. Translated by various hands. George Bell & Sons, 1904.

Petterlini, Arnaldo. "La dialettica in Gramsci." In Melchiorre, Vigna, and De Rosa, eds., *Antonio Gramsci: Il pensiero teorico e politico, la "questione leninista,"* vol. 1, pp. 90–102.

Piccone, Paul. "From Spaventa to Gramsci." *Telos* 31 (Spring 1977): 35–65.

"Gramsci's Marxism: Beyond Lenin and Togliatti." *Theory and Society* 3 (1976): 485–512.

Italian Marxism. Berkeley: University of California Press, 1983.

"Labriola and the Roots of Eurocommunism." *Berkeley Journal of Sociology* 32 (1977–78): 3–44.

Pierini, Franco. *Gramsci e la storiologia della rivoluzione (1914–1920)*. Rome: Edizioni Paoline, 1978.

Pitt, Joseph C., and Marcello Pera, eds. *Rational Changes in Science: Essays on Scientific Reasoning*. Dordrecht: Reidel, 1987.

Pizzorno, A. "Sul metodo di Gramsci: dalla storiografia alla scienza politica." In P. Rossi, ed. *Gramsci e la cultura contemporanea*, vol. 2, pp. 109–26.

Popper, Karl. R. *Conjectures and Refutations*. New York: Harper, 1963.

The Open Society and Its Enemies. Vol. 2 (1945). 5th ed. Princeton, N.J.: Princeton University Press, 1966.

The Poverty of Historicism. London: Routledge, 1957.

Portelli, Hugues. *Gramsci et la question religieuse*. Paris: Anthropos, 1974.

Gramsci et le bloc historique. Paris: Presses Universitaires de France, 1972.

Prestipino, Giuseppe. *Da Gramsci a Marx*. Rome: Riuniti, 1979.

Razeto Migliaro, Luis, and Pasquale Misuraca. *Sociologia e marxismo nella critica di Gramsci*. Bari: De Donato, 1978.

Riechers, Christian. *Antonio Gramsci: Marxismus in Italien*. Frankfurt: Europaische Verlagsanstalt, 1970.

Roberts, David D. *Benedetto Croce and the Uses of Historicism*. Berkeley: University of California Press, 1987.

Bibliography

Rorty, Richard. *Philosophy and the Mirror of Nature.* Princeton, N.J.: Princeton University Press, 1979.

Rossi, Paolo. "Antonio Gramsci sulla scienza moderna." *Critica marxista* 14, no. 2 (March-April 1976): 41–60.

Rossi, Pietro, ed. *Gramsci e la cultura contemporanea.* 2 vols. Rome: Editori Riuniti–Istituto Gramsci, 1969.

Salamini, Leonardo. *The Sociology of Political Praxis: An Introduction to Gramsci's Theory.* Boston: Routledge, 1981.

Salvadori, Massimo L. *Gramsci e il problema storico della democrazia.* 2d ed. Turin: Einaudi, 1977.

Sanguineti, Federico. *Gramsci e Machiavelli.* Bari: Laterza, 1982.

Sartori, Giovanni. *Stato e politica nel pensiero di Benedetto Croce: Una radiografia critica delle strutture essenziali della dottrina politica crociana.* Naples: Morano, 1966.

Sasso, Gennaro. "Antonio Gramsci, interprete di Machiavelli." *Lo spettatore italiano* 3, no. 4 (April 1950): 91–93.

Benedetto Croce: La ricerca della dialettica. Naples: Morano, 1975.

Sassoon, Anne Showstack. *Gramsci's Politics.* New York: St. Martin's, 1980.

Sassoon, Anne Showstack, ed. *Approaches to Gramsci.* London: Writers & Readers, 1982.

Sbarberi, Franco. *Gramsci: Un socialismo armonico.* Milan: Franco Angeli, 1986.

Schilpp, Paul A., ed. *Albert Einstein, Philosopher-Scientist.* Evanston, Ill.: Library of Living Philosophers, 1951.

Scriven, Michael. "Explanations, Predictions, and Laws." Herbert Feigl and G. Maxwell, eds., *Minnesota Studies in the Philosophy of Science,* vol. 3, pp. 170–230. Minneapolis: University of Minnesota Press, 1962.

Sichirollo, Livio. *La dialettica.* Milan: ISEDI, Istituto Editoriale Internazionale, 1973.

Simon, Roger. *Gramsci's Political Thought: An Introduction.* London: Lawrence & Wishart, 1982.

Somai, Giovanni. *Gramsci a Vienna: Ricerche e documenti 1922–1924.* Urbino: Argalia, 1979.

Spriano, Paolo. *Gramsci in carcere e il partito.* Rome: Riuniti, 1977.

Stace, W. T. *The Philosophy of Hegel.* New York: Dover, n.d.

Steinthal, H. *Grammatik, Logik und Psychologie, ihre Principien und ihr Verhältniss zu einander.* Berlin: Dümmler, 1855.

Strindberg, August. *Plays.* Translated by E. Sprigge. Chicago: Aldine, 1955.

Suppa, Silvio. *Consiglio e stato in Gramsci e Lenin.* Bari: Dedalo, 1979.

Il primo Gramsci: Gli scritti politici giovanili (1914–1918). Jovene, 1977.

Sztompka, Piotr. *Sociological Dilemmas: Toward a Dialectic Paradigm.* New York: Academic Press, 1979.

Tamburrano, Giuseppe. *Antonio Gramsci. La vita, il pensiero, l'azione.* Manduria: Lacaita, 1963. 2d ed. *Antonio Gramsci. Una biografia critica,* Milan: Sugarco, 1977.

Bibliography

Perchè solo in Italia no. Bari: Laterza, 1983.

Taylor, Charles. *Hegel.* Cambridge University Press, 1974.

Telò Mario. "Gramsci, il nuovo capitalismo e il problema della modernizzazione." *Critica marxista* 25, no. 6 (1987): 73–102.

Texier, Jacques. "Gramsci, Théoricien des Superstructures." *La pensée* 139 (1969): 35–60.

Togliatti, Palmiro. *Antonio Gramsci.* Rome: Riuniti, 1972.

Tucker, Robert C., ed. *The Marx-Engels Reader.* 2d ed. New York: Norton, 1978.

Tucker, Robert C., and S. F. Cohen, eds. *The Great Purge Trial.* New York: Grosset & Dunlap, 1965.

Vaccaro, Nicola. "La dialettica quantità-qualità in Gramsci." In Istituto Gramsci, ed., *Studi gramsciani,* pp. 323–35.

Vasale, Claudio. *Politica e religione in A. Gramsci: L'ateodicea della secolarizzazione.* Rome: Edizioni di storia e letteratura, 1979.

Vigna, Carmelo. "Gramsci e l'egemonia. Una interpretazione metapolitica." In Melchiorre et al., eds., *Antonio Gramsci: Il pensiero teorico e politico, la "questione leninista,"* vol. 1, pp. 11–69.

Vinco, Roberto. *Una fede senza futuro? Religione e mondo cattolico in Gramsci.* Verona: Mazziana, 1983.

Watkins, J. W. N. "Influential and Confirmable Metaphysics." *Mind* 67 (1958): 344–65.

Wessell, Leonard, P., Jr. *Karl Marx, Romantic Irony, and the Proletariat: The Mythopoetic Origins of Marxism.* Baton Rouge: Louisiana State University Press, 1979.

White, Morton, ed. *The Age of Analysis.* New York: Mentor Books, 1955.

Zanardo, Aldo. "Il 'Manuale' di Bucharin visto dai comunisti tedeschi e da Gramsci." In Istituto Gramsci, ed., *Studi gramsciani,* pp. 337–68; and in *Società* 14 (1958): 230–62.

Index

abstract definitional sentences, 49–50
abstract formalism, 200
abstraction, determined, 151–52
Action Party, 167, 173
action versus thought, 5–6; *see also* synthesis, of theory and practice
Adamson, Walter L., 256n26, 260n57, 267n60, 273, 280n70, 281n92
aesthetics: illustration of Croce's, 54; and literary criticism, 9; versus logic and grammar, 57–64
Agazzi, Emilio, 281n92
allegorical interpretation of poetry, 52
Althusser, Louis, 233
Anderson, Perry, 254n1
antihistoricism, 82
antinomies, Kant's, 196
antisociologism, 135–36
antiteleologism, 104
Aquinas, Saint Thomas, 30, 46
Aristotle, 46, 62–63, 83, 186, 191
art, political versus aesthetic, 134–35
artillery, 132
Augustine, Saint, 30, 46
avoidance of one-sidedness, *see* one-sidedness, avoidance of
Azzalini, M., 134

Bacon, Francis, 232
Badaloni, Nicola, 256n27
Blue, Gregory, 288n1
Bobbio, Norberto, 148, 171, 272n36, 273–75, 278n36, 281n92, 290n3
Bodin, Jean, 126–27
Bolshevik Revolution, 70
Bolshevism, 68
Bonaparte, Napoleon, 164
British classical economics, 149, 151–52

Buci-Glucksmann, Christine, 265n6, 280n59, n60, n70, n73, 281n74, n75, n83
Bukharin, Nikolai, 2, 5, 7, 68–122 passim, 123, 147, 148, 149, 159, 231, 235–36, 238–40, 243, 244, 246, 247, 248; and antihistoricism, 82; and antiteleologism, 104; as Crocean, 98–99; and dialectic, 72–75, 105, 115–22, 147, 235, 244–45, 266n34; and mechanism, 96–97, 104–6; as reactionary, 86–87; and revolution, 11–14; and technologism and positivism, 102–4; *see also* historical materialism; Lukács, Georg; Marxism
Burckhardt, Jacob, 31
bureaucracy, 162
bureaucratic centralism, 162–63, 168

Capital, 119
Carducci, Giosuè, 20
Catholicism, 3
Catholic modernism, 13, 16–17
causal explanation, 79–80
Cavour, Camillo Benso, Count of, 146, 167, 169, 171, 174
centralism, 149, 279n55; bureaucratic, 162–63, 168; democratic, 162–63, 237
centralization and dialectic, 162–63
change: and dialectic, 272n34; versus permanence, 205
Christ, Jesus, 29, 52
city-country alliance, 132
class in itself versus class for itself, 115
class relations versus work relations, 109
class struggle, 114–15
Cohen, Stephen C., 69, 95, 116, 121

Index

Guicciardini, Francesco, 129–31
Gullace, Giovanni, 264n72

Hartmann, Nicolai, 185–86
Hegel, Georg W. F., 21, 24, 29, 30, 31,
    33, 46, 105, 134, 149, 150, 152, 154,
    171–72, 177, 178, 181–231 passim,
    237, 239, 242, 243, 246, 247, 248;
    and conflict of philosophies, 151;
    confusions of, 201; and Croce, 11,
    40–44, 65, 182–83, 188–91, 286n98;
    and history of philosophy, 30; and
    Jacobinism, 154–55; and philoso-
    phy stood on its head, 18
and dialectic, 237–38; definition of,
    192–94; and determinations of re-
    flection, 211–28; history of, 194–
    97; and laws of thought, 214–20;
    and metaphilosophical interpreta-
    tion, 182, 188–92; and necessity of
    contradiction, 192–93; negative
    versus positive, 192–94; onto-phe-
    nomenological interpretation of,
    182, 185–88, 211–12, 228–29; and
    philosophy, 197–211, 245; positivi-
    ty of negative, 192–93; practice of,
    207–10; and systemic-immanent
    interpretation, 182–85, 187; and
    triadic interpretation, 182–83, 187;
    and unity of opposites, 192–93
    works of: *Encyclopedia*, 193, 208, 211,
    229, 238; *Lectures on the History of
    Philosophy*, 185, 194–97, 208, 229,
    238; *Phenomenology of Spirit*, 183,
    185, 192, 197–211, 214, 229, 238;
    Science of Logic, 183, 185, 191, 192,
    193, 208, 211–29, 238
hegemony, 139, 165, 168
Heraclitus, 194, 195, 196
hermeneutics, 245–48
hieroglyphics in Gramsci's Notebooks,
    1, 5
historical materialism, 12, 83–85; and
    Bukharin, 69–71, 75; and Croce, 9,
    77–78; *see also* Marx, Karl; Marx-
    ism
historical method, 6
historical understanding, 48
historicism, 47–50, 172; and conception
    of philosophy, 19, 48–50, 89; and
    Croce, 30; in Gramsci, 87; and rel-
    ativism, 88
history: as contemporary, 19; as criti-
    cism, 32; ethico-political, 23; ver-
    sus historiography, 48; and philos-
    ophy, 19, 48–50, 75–76, 89, 98–99;

philosophy of, 10, 12, 21; and pol-
    itics, 19; versus theory, 118
Hoare, Quintin, 282n92
Hobsbawm, E. J., 1, 254n3
Homo oeconomicus, 151–52
Hook, Sidney, 6, 269n2
Hume, David, 29
Hyppolite, Jean, 183–85

idealism, 73, 88, 159–60; and Bukharin,
    75, 114; versus materialism, 105,
    158
identity: category of, 220–28; and di-
    alectic, 196; and difference, 191,
    207, 222, 226–28; in difference,
    190, 194, 199–200; and identifica-
    tion-distinction, 157–58; and iden-
    tification versus differentiation,
    226–27; of indiscernibles, 216–17;
    law of, 215–16
ideology: and Bukharin, 86, 88; and
    Croce, 25
images in poetry, 53–56
immanence and dialectic, 150
indiscernibles, identity of, 216–27
individualism: and party politics, 139–
    40; in society and in sociology, 85;
    versus socialism, 119
individualization, 48–50
individual judgment, 48–50
instruments: in science, 83–84; versus
    workers, 107–8
intellectualism, 170–71
intellectuals: dialectic of, and masses,
    178; function of, 86–87
intentions in poetry, 55–56
interpretation, textual, 246–48
irrationalism, 172
"is" versus "ought," 130
Italian communism, 2, 4; party of, 232
Italian Communist Party, 232

Jacobinism, 24, 152–54, 163, 166, 167,
    173, 229, 237; and Croce, 21; in
    Machiavelli, 127
Jacobitti, Edmund, 260nn57–58, 264n72
Jesus Christ, 29, 52
Johnston, W. H., 287n108
Joll, James, 233, 273
Joravsky, David, 95
journalism, 156–57
judgment, 143, 175; definitional, 48–50;
    individual, 48–50; and judicious-
    ness, 272n33
judiciousness, 117–22, 143, 272n33
justification of interpretations, 141

Index

Kant, Immanuel, 20, 29, 30, 46, 194–97; and antinomies, 196; and teleology, 85, 100
Kaufmann, Walter, 183, 286n94
Koestler, Arthur, 70
Kojève, Alexandre, 185–87, 212, 282n93, 284n33
Kolakowski, Leszek, 6

Labriola, Antonio, 9, 89
La Rocca, Tommaso, 267n57, 289n17
Lateran Treaty, 17
law of contradiction, 217–19, 224–26
law of diversity, 215–16
law of excluded middle, 218–19
law of identity, 215–16
law of negation of negation, 218–19
law of noncontradiction, 218–19
law of opposition, 215–16
law of tendency, 78, 152
laws of thought, 214–20
lay approach to Gramsci, 4
Leibniz's law, 216–17
Lenin, V. I., 23, 68–70, 101, 120
Leonardo da Vinci, 30
Lewin, Moshe, 69
Lewis, Sinclair, 155
liberalism, 21, 22, 26, 170
libertinism, 22
likeness and unlikeness, 217, 220–28
Lipset, Seymour Martin, 70
liquidationist criticism of Marxism, 10
literary criticism, 9, 30, 50–56
logic: and aesthetics, 57–64; and dialectic, 155–58; formal, 73–74, 78–80, 155–58; versus grammar, 57–59; and laws of thought, 214–20; and literary criticism, 50–56; and poetry, 50–56, 61; principles of, 217–19
Lorentz force law, 80
Lukács, Georg, 70, 96, 115, 122, 159–60; criticism of Bukharin by, 100–4
Luther, Martin, 13, 15

Macbeth, 51
Macduff, 51
Macgregor, translator of Petrarch, 51
Machiavelli, Niccolò, 2, 3, 5, 7, 68, 123–28 passim, 154, 159, 236–38, 241, 243, 244, 248; and anti-Machiavellian criticism, 126–33; Croce on, 123–25, 141–42; and democracy, 127–29; and dialectic of politics, 141–46, 245; and Gramsci's notes, 125–26; 245; and Machiavellianism, 128; and Marxism,

41, 123–25, 129; *The Prince* by, 3, 126; relevance of, 126–27; versus seventeenth-century moralists, 14
McTaggart, John E., 182, 211, 221
Marx, Karl, 8, 29, 31, 46, 47, 83, 106, 134, 150, 165, 166, 178, 233, 237, 243; *Capital* by, 152; *Communist Manifesto* by, 82, 112; and "critique" of political economy, 151, 164; Croce on, 40–44, 65, *see also* Croce, Benedetto, *and* Crocean Marxism; and dialectic, 149–55, 182, 230; eleventh thesis of, on Feuerbach, 18–19; as founder of philosophy of praxis, 89; *The Holy Family* by, 154; as Machiavelli of proletariat, 41, 141–42; and permanent revolution in 1848–50, 152; on rise of manufacturing, 102; on science and life, 231; on social change, 164; *see also* historical materialism; Marxism
Marxism, 1, 6, 8–27 passim, 68–93 passim, 147, 231–43 passim, 246, 247; and Bukharin, 69–71, 101, *see also* Bukharin, Nikolai; crisis of, 9; and Croce, 3, 8–27, 29, *see also* Croce, Benedetto; and dialectic, 149–55; French Revolution, 149; in Gramsci's Notebooks, 244; and historical economism, 14; Italian, 244, 245; and Machiavelli, 41, 123–25, 129; and metaphysics, 12; as politics, 123, 232–33, 236–37; problem of evaluation of, 6, 231–33; and religion, 3, 11–17, 231–32; and science, 71, 76–88, 232–33, 235–36; vulgar, 10, 17, 111, 234, 247; Western, 68; *see also* historical materialism; Marx, Karl; orthodoxy in Marxism
Marxism-Leninism, 68
Masonic criticism of religion, 13, 14
masses and intellectuals, dialectic of, 178
Masutti, E., 267n57, 289n17
materialism: dialectical, 158–59; historical, *see* historical materialism; versus idealism, 105, 158; metaphysical, 158–59
material versus mental progress, 113–14
mathematics versus philosophy, 204–5
matter: concept of, 84–85, 158–59, and mind, 120; and spirit, 18

Index

Matteucci, Nicola, 257n14, 258n17, 261n1, 278n32
Mazzini, Giuseppe, 128, 167, 173
mechanism, 155, 161; in Bukharin, 104–6; and Croce, 24; and Deborinism, 94–96; and dialectic, 143, 146
mediation, 149, 170
Mehring, Franz, 101
mentalism, 49
mention and use, 59
mercantilism, 131–32
Merleau-Ponty, Maurice, 70
metaphilosophy, 197–211; Croce's, 15, 18; and exposition in philosophy, 198; in Hegel's *Logic*, 212–14; and metaphilosophical interpretation of Hegel's dialectic, 228, 229; and multiplicity of philosophical systems, 199–200; and philosophical demonstration, 198; and philosophical truth, 198; *see also* philosophy
metaphysics: and Croce's conception of philosophy, 45–46; and Marxism, 12; and metaphysical materialism, 158–59; versus methodology, 45–46, 119; and philosophy, 45–46, 75–76; *see also* philosophy
method: of philology and criticism, 136, 146; in philosophy, 205–6; versus result in philosophy, 205; versus substantive thesis, 1, 23
methodology: and Croce's view of philosophy, 44–47; versus metaphysics, 45–46, 119; and methodological criticism, 101; philosophic, 212–14; versus philosophy, 44–47, *see also* metaphysics; philosophy
Meyer, Alfred G., 71
military forces, 137–38
Miller, A. V., 286n94, 287n108
mind: and matter, 120, *see also* matter; philosophy of, in Croce, 65–66
Misuraca, Pasquale, 255n6, 265n6, 278n41, 291n13
moderation, 147, 149; and Croce, 21; and Moderate Party, 167; and moderate tradition in Italy, 170; and moderatism, 247
modernism, Catholic, 13, 16–17
morality versus politics, 136–37
Morpurgo-Tagliabue, Guido, 256n1
Moss, M. E., 264n71
Mure, Geoffrey R. G., 188, 190–91, 229
Mussolini, Benito, 30

Napoleon Bonaparte, 164
Nardone, Giorgio, 256n27
nationalism, 22
naturalistic approach, 160–61
natural sciences: versus philosophy, 213; versus social sciences, 79–80, 102–4
nature: concept of, 160–61; dialectic of, 149, 159–61; versus man, 160–61; and society, 107–8
negation, 218–19
negative and positive, category of, 220–28
Nemeth, Thomas, 267n60, 273
New Economic Policy, 69, 95
Newton, Isaac, 67
Nietzsche, Friedrich W., 29
noncontradiction, law of, 218–19
Nowell Smith, Geoffrey, 282n92

obedience in politics, 140
one-sidedness, 181, 183, 199–200; avoidance of, 157–58, 180, 192, 205, 207, 242, 248; and dialectic, 26, 143, *see also* dialectic; and Hegel's dialectic, 193–94; of Kant's dialectic, 196–97; of law of identity, 215–16; of law of negation of negation, 218–19; of laws of thought, 214–20; of principle of identity of indiscernibles, 216–17
onto-phenomenological interpretation of Hegel's dialectic, 182, 185–88, 211–12, 228–29
opportunism, 146
opposition: category of, 220–28; law of, 215–16; and synthesis of opposites, 120–21, 188–89; and unity of opposites, 199–200, 207, 223–24
Orsucci, Andrea, 177n31, 280n65
orthodoxy in Marxism, 86–88, 90–91
"ought" versus "is," 130

Paggi, Leonardo, 270n12
Paris Commune, 164
party politics, 139–40
passive revolution, 146, 149, 163, 166–76
patriotism, 22
pedagogy, philosophical versus scientific, 74–75
Pellicani, Luciano, 288n2
Pera, Marcello, 264n73
permanence versus change, 205
permanent revolution, 23, 164, 165, 169

310

Index

Perrotti, Gabriele, 277n17, n19
Petrarch, 50–56
Petterlini, Arnaldo, 276n4
philology, method of, 136, 146
philosophy: versus abstractions, 200, 212–13; conceptual nature of, 200; Croce's definition of, 18, 44–47; and dialectic, 188, 197–211; good versus bad, for Hegel, 212; historicity of, 19, 48–50, 89; of history, 10, 12, 21; identity of history and, 48–50, 75–76, 98–99; and integral journalism, 156–57; versus mathematics, 204–5; versus methodology, 44–47; of mind in Croce, 65–66; versus natural science, 213; necessity of negative, 202–3; and philosophical theory and scientific practice in Bukharin, 115–22; and philosophical methodology, 212–14; pluralism in, 200; popular versus technical, 72–75; of praxis, 3, 12, 68, 88–93, 124–25, 133–34, 159, 177; self-referential nature of, 203; as self-reflective, 201; as "spiritual," 202; and subject-predicate sentences, 206–7; as systematic, 202; truth versus falsity, 204; as undogmatic, 204; *see also* metaphilosophy; metaphysics; methodology
physics: classical versus modern, 73; as model science, 76–78
physiocratic economics, 132
Piccone, Paul, 260n58, 290n1
Pius X, Pope, 16
Plato, 30, 46, 191, 194–96
Plekhanov, Georgi, 101
pluralism in philosophy, 200
poetry: allegorical interpretation of, 52; critical explanation of, 53–54; images in, 53–56; intentions in, 55–56; of logic, 60–64
politics: art and science of, 134–36; autonomy of, 123, 236–37; and Croce, 24; and dialectic, 126, 133–34, 147, 237; versus diplomacy, 130–31; versus economics, 137–38; great versus small, 138–39; and history, 19; and Machiavelli, 123–25; Machiavellian and Marxian, 123; versus morality, 136–37; nature of, 124–25, 133–34; obedience in, 140; party, 127, 139–40, 142, 162; and political forces, 137–38; and political-military forces, 138;

and political science, 25, 135–36; primacy of, 134; pure, 126–27
Popper, Karl, 6
Portelli, Hugues, 3, 267n57, 289n17, 290n18
positive and negative, category of, 220–28
positivism, 290n19; in Bukharin, 102–3; in Gramsci, 239–40, 247; and science, 76–78, 90–91; and scientism, 235–36
positivity of negative, 209–10, 224–26
practical origin of errors, 15–16
practice, conceptions of, 116; *see also* synthesis, of theory and practice
praxis, philosophy of, 3, 12, 68, 88–93, 124–25, 133–34, 159, 177
prediction, nature of, 77, 104
prince, 127
Proclus, 194, 196
productive forces versus productive relations, 11–12
"Prometheus" (Goethe), 82
Protestant Reformation, 15, 20
Proudhon, Pierre-Joseph, 149
Proudhonism, 146
Ptolemy, Claudius, 62
Pythagoras, 30

quantity and quality, dialectic of, 149, 274

Ranke, Leopold von, 31
Rap Brown, H., 34
rational reconstruction, 39
Razeto Migliaro, Luis, 225n6, 265n6, 291n13
reality of external world, 72–74
reasoning, art and science of, 155–58
reciprocity, 33
reflections, determinations of, 214, 220–28, 238
Reformation, 15, 20
reformism, 166–76, 237, 247
regulation, 79–80
relating: and distinction-relation, 38, 174, 180, 242; and distinguishing, 36–38; and internal versus external relations, 222
relativism, 43–44
religion, 3, 92; Croce's definition of, 14, 17–18; versus Croce's philosophy, 3; and Marxism, 3, 11–17, 231–32; Masonic criticism of, 13, 14; and science, 232
Renaissance, 20

311

Index

representative government, 127
revolution, 163–66, 237; Bolshevik, 70; in Bukharin, 11–14; democratic, 163, 168, 173; and dialectic, 163–166; French, 149, 152–54, 163–66; 168; passive, 146, 149, 163, 166–76; permanent, 23, 164, 165, 169; phases of, 112; Russian, 10
Ricardo, David, 150, 151, 154, 229
Riechers, Christian, 257n14
Risorgimento, 21, 166, 167, 169, 175
Roberts, David D., 264n71
Robespiere, Maximilien, 20
Rossi, Paolo, 267n54, 290n19
Rousseau, Jean-Jacques, 128
rulers versus ruled, 135, 139–40
rules, particular versus universal, 136–137
Ruskin, John, 29
Russian Revolution, 10
ruthlessness, 126–127

Sagredo, 62–64
Salamini, Leonardo, 273, 291n13
Salviati, 62–64
Sanguineti, Federico, 271n30
Sasso, Gennaro, 260n50
Sasson, Anne Showstack, 273
Savonarola, Girolamo, 130–31
science: concept of, 80–81; Crocean philosophy of, 66–67; empiricist conception of, 76–78; experimental, 89–90, 160; fairness in, 82–83; and formal logic, 78–80; and Gramsci studies, 4–5; instruments in, 83–84; and Marxism, see Marxism, and science; natural versus social, 79–80, 102–4; of politics, 25, 135–36; and positivism, 76–78, 90–91; and religion, 232; and scientific method, 161; and scientific progress, 83–84; as "serious" inquiry, 74, 76–78, 80–82, 135, 235; and synthesis of theory and practice, 89–90
scientism, 235–36, 290n19; see also positivism
sectarianism, 140
secularism, 19
self-confidence, methodological, 81
separating versus distinguishing, 37–38
"serious" approach, 74, 76–78, 80–82, 135, 235
Shakespeare, William, 51, 54, 67

Sichirollo, Livio, 276n4
Simplicio, 62–63
social growth, 113–14
socialism, 9
social sciences versus natural sciences, 79–80, 102–4
society: versus individual, 106; and nature, 107–8
sociology: epistemological status of, 135–36; and science of politics, 135–36; and sociological laws, 78; and sociologism, 106–7, 119
Socrates, 29, 46, 184
Sorel, Georges, 9
Spaventa, Bertrando, 89
speculation: concept of, 156; and dialectic, 193, 195–96; and speculative language in Croce, 19, 22
spirit and matter, 18
Spirit in Croce's philosophy, 123–25, 133, 177
Spirito, Ugo, 174
Stalin, Joseph, 69 70, 95
Stamler, Rudolf, 13, 79–80, 100
state spirit, 140
static versus dynamic approach, 120
Steinthal, H., 57–58
straw-man principle, 82–84
Strindberg, August, 59–60
structure versus superstructure, 12–13, 16, 109–11, 124–25, 133–34, 137, 138, 177
Struthers, L. C., 287n108
subject-predicate sentences, 198–99
superstructure, see structure versus superstructure
surplus labor, 152
synthesis
    and dialectic, 183 188
    of opposites, 120–21, 188–89; see also dialectic; opposition; unity, of opposites
    of theory and practice, 116–22, 145–46, 172–73, 175, 188–89; in Bukharin, 115–22, 147, 235–36; conception of, 97–98; in Croce, 64–67, 235; and Gramsci, 98–100, 238–42; 248; in Hegel, 208–10; see also dialectic
    of thesis and antithesis, 150, 170, 180, 181, 182, 188–89, 238, 242; see also dialectic; opposition; triadic interpretation of Hegel's dialectic
systemic-immanent interpretation of Hegel's dialectic, 211, 228–29

Index